Ready-to-Use Multicultural Activities for Primary Children

Saundrah Clark Grevious

Illustrated by Carrie Oesmann

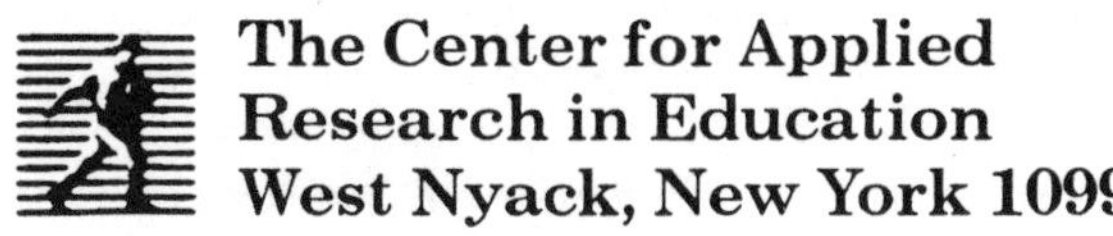

The Center for Applied Research in Education
West Nyack, New York 10995

10 9 8 7 6 5 4 3

Library of Congress Cataloging-in-Publication Data

Grevious, Saundrah Clark.
Ready-to-use multicultural activities for primary children / Saundrah Clark Grevious ; illustrated by Carrie Oesmann.
p. cm.
Includes bibliographical references.
ISBN 0-87628-849-2
1. Education, Primary—United States—Activity programs.
2. Intercultural education—United States—Activity programs.
I. Title.
LB1537.G74 1993
372.5—dc20 93-16912
CIP

C8492-5
ISBN 0-87628-849-2

The Center for Applied Research in Education, Professional Publishing
West Nyack, New York 10995
Simon & Schuster, A Paramount Communications Company

Printed in the United States of America

DEDICATION
For Shannon Gayle and Sharon Corinne

My Freedom to Be....To Become

My freedom to be...To become
Is closely tied to the number of times you,
My mother, my father, my teacher, my friend...
Give me books, maps, charts and let me sing.
Tell me, show me, teach me, let me discover.

That I and my ancestors,
We are as fine as you,
My teacher, my friend, my fellow human being.
Give me time, love, opportunity and let me wonder,
My co-inhabitor of this earth.

Take my hand, if only for a moment, my neighbor.
Lead me towards the sunlight, fill my empty pages.
For life is a book waiting to be written.
Teach me to question, search for answers,
Meet new people, create new ideas, and grow in wisdom.

Through you, my teacher, my friend, my father, my mother,
I will learn to be...to become
More than I thought I could be.
Give me truth, trust, safety and let me dream.
Then, I'll win and because of you...I'll be free.

Saundrah Clark Grevious

ACKNOWLEDGMENTS

To my family and friends, I extend my deepest appreciation for your love, support, and patience. You've bolstered my spirits and given me the encouragement I've needed to complete "The Project."

I am especially indebted to Winfield Huppuch and Deborah Kurtz for their belief in the concept of the book and their positive feedback on the earliest proposal.

To my editor, Susan Kolwicz, your knowledge, insight, and professionalism are all-encompassing. My task was made easier by your enthusiasm and tireless attention to detail. I am deeply grateful. My heartfelt thanks to Dana Newmann, as well, for her meticulous review of the manuscript.

I extend much gratitude to my brother, Preston Clark. Like a tiger, you cleared the path for me to get started. To my sister, Frances Clark, you've helped me to focus on the techniques most crucial to successfully relating these concepts to primary children. I am indebted to you for your consultations on all of the lessons.

My sincere thanks to all of you, in the interest of the children of the globe...citizens of the 21st century.

ABOUT THE AUTHOR

Saundrah Clark Grevious received her Bachelor of Arts degree from Chicago Teachers College and her Master of Education degree from the Harvard University Graduate School of Education. She has done post-graduate work at the University of California at Berkeley. She is certified in grades K–12 and has taught on all of these grade levels. In addition, Mrs. Grevious has directed a Headstart program, worked as a Consultant in Curriculum and Instruction for the New Jersey State Department of Education, and is a Teacher Consultant for the Bay Area Writing Project. Most of her teaching experiences have been in culturally diverse environments in cities such as Chicago, Baltimore, Boston, Fairbanks, Minneapolis, and Oakland.

Mrs. Grevious has written many educational materials including, *Teaching Children and Adults to Understand Human and Race Relations* and *All-Write: A Quality Control Writing Competency Program*. She conducts inservice programs in an effort to raise the awareness of educators to the power that they have to change the world for the better. Saundrah Clark Grevious presently teaches in the Piscataway Township Public Schools in Piscataway, New Jersey.

About This Resource

The average school-aged child in America goes to school with children from many different places in the world. Too often, these children know little, if anything, of one another's backgrounds and cultures. Learning to understand and respect those who are different can be a wonderful experience for young children, especially when they can see themselves in the lessons. **READY-TO-USE MULTICULTURAL ACTIVITIES FOR PRIMARY CHILDREN** is a book designed to prepare our future citizens for life in a culturally diverse society, beginning with their own families, schoolmates, and people in their neighborhoods.

Since the early years are the most impressionable, the concepts and activities in this book are prepared with the young child in mind. Unfortunately, it is during these formative years that children often learn negative behaviors and develop biases—the destructive "we-they" attitudes that cause so much conflict in society today. Throughout this resource there are many opportunities for children to develop good feelings about themselves and their cultural heritage. There are 67 detailed lessons and over 150 reproducible activities to help children extend respect and concern for all regardless of their color, race, physical characteristics, religion, or ethnic origin.

On the whole, the activities speak for themselves. They are easy to use without the teacher having to constantly refer to the directions. It is important, however, for the teacher to read the entire book before beginning instruction in order to get an overview of the author's purpose and a sense of cohesiveness for the lessons to be taught. To maximize student comprehension, the recurring themes of human commonalities, diversity, and interdependence are woven throughout the lessons. It is suggested that the teacher introduce challenging and difficult vocabulary prior to teaching each activity.

READY-TO-USE MULTICULTURAL ACTIVITIES FOR PRIMARY CHILDREN is a book written for the busy teacher who must meet the needs of diverse groups of young children. These activities not only help reduce or eliminate the need for separate exercises in multicultural education, they also provide year-round strategies for integrating these concepts into existing content area lessons. Many foreign language experiences are included in order to help children understand and respect aspects of cultures which are different from their own. In addition, there is an emphasis on the universal concept of human dignity through lessons on self-esteem, mutual respect, similarities and differences, interdependence, and multicultural contributions. Celebrations like Black History Month, Diwali, and other cultural traditions, which focus on the pride and aspirations of various ethnic groups are also covered in this book. The intent of the book is to integrate and equalize the participation of European, African, Asian, Hispanic, and Native American people into the history and ongoing development of our society.

Special Features of This Resource Include:
• Step-by-Step Teacher Directions and Materials Needed List for Each Lesson • A Chart for Year-Round Content Area Integration of Multicultural Activities • Foreign Language Lessons and Lists • Sign Language • Genealogy and Immigration • Origin of Family and Personal Names • Literature Connections—annotated suggestions for further reading • Concepts in Age, Gender, and Disabilities • Historical and Contemporary Multicultural Perspectives • Multicultural Art, Games, Puzzles, and Music • English as a Second Language Concepts • Higher-Level Thinking Skills • Learning Styles—auditory, visual, and kinesthetic • Cooperative Learning Strategies • Whole Language Concepts • Performance Objectives • Detailed Lesson Plan Guide • Emphasis on Vocabulary • Appendix of Resource Materials • A Glossary

In short, these ready-to-use multicultural activities are easy-to-use, fun, and educationally sound, as they prepare young children for life in a culturally diverse society!

Saundrah Clark Grevious

MULTICULTURAL CURRICULUM INTEGRATION CHART

Many activities in **Ready-to-Use Multicultural Activities for Primary Children** can be used year round in several content areas of the curriculum. Each activity is coded according to Section and lesson number. Letters are used to identify multiple sheets within ONE lesson. SAMPLE CODE: 1-3A—MY BIRTHDAY CAKE. The entire code is listed on the Table of Contents which can serve as both a means of locating lessons and as a checklist.

Activities	Section 1		Section 2		Section 3	
1. LANGUAGE	1-1	1-13	2-1	2-14	3-1	3-12
ARTS	1-2	1-14	2-2	2-15	3-2	3-13
•Reading	1-3	1-15	2-3	2-16	3-3	3-14
•Writing	1-4	1-16	2-4	2-17	3-4	3-15
•Listening	1-5	1-17	2-5	2-18	3-5	3-16
•Speaking	1-6	1-18	2-6	2-19	3-6	3-17
	1-7	1-19	2-7	2-20	3-7	3-18
	1-8	1-20	2-8	2-21	3-8	3-19
	1-9	1-21	2-10	2-22	3-9	3-20
	1-10	1-22	2-11	2-23	3-10	
	1-11	1-23	2-12	2-24	3-11	
	1-12		2-13	2-25		
2. CREATIVE	1-11	1-22	2-4	2-13	3-5	3-14
WRITING	1-12	1-23	2-5	2-14	3-9	3-19
	1-14		2-10	2-15	3-13	3-20

(THESE ARE SAMPLES ONLY—EVERY ACTIVITY OFFERS OPPORTUNITIES FOR CREATIVE WRITING)

Activities	Section 1		Section 2		Section 3	
3. SOCIAL STUDIES	1-1	1-13	2-1	2-14	3-1	3-11
	1-2	1-14	2-2	2-15	3-2	3-12
	1-3	1-15	2-3	2-16	3-3	3-13
	1-4	1-16	2-4	2-17	3-4	3-14
	1-5	1-17	2-5	2-18	3-5	3-15
	1-6	1-18	2-6	2-19	3-6	3-16
	1-7	1-19	2-7	2-20	3-7	3-17
	1-8	1-20	2-8	2-21	3-8	3-18
	1-9	1-21	2-10	2-23	3-9	3-19
	1-10	1-22	2-11	2-24	3-10	3-20
	1-12	1-23	2-13	2-25		
4. SCIENCE	1-1	1-12	2-1	2-13	3-1	3-13
	1-4	1-13	2-5	2-16	3-3	3-14
	1-5	1-14	2-6	2-20	3-4	3-15
	1-6	1-15	2-8	2-23	3-5	3-16
	1-7	1-16	2-10		3-7	3-17
	1-8	1-19			3-8	3-18
	1-9	1-20			3-9	3-19
	1-10	1-21			3-10	3-20
	1-11				3-11	
5. HEALTH	1-1	1-16	2-1	2-17	3-1	3-14
	1-2	1-17	2-5	2-18	3-2	3-15
	1-4	1-19	2-8	2-19	3-4	3-18
	1-7	1-20	2-11	2-20	3-5	3-19
	1-10	1-21	2-13	2-21	3-8	3-20
	1-14		2-15	2-23		
			2-16			
6. MATH	1-1	1-17	2-3	2-16	3-2	3-14
	1-2	1-18	2-8	2-17	3-3	3-15
	1-3	1-19	2-10	2-18	3-4	3-16
	1-9	1-21	2-11	2-20	3-5	3-20
	1-10	1-23	2-15	2-24	3-7	
	1-13					
7. FOREIGN LANGUAGE	1-1	1-11	2-5	2-14	3-12	3-17
	1-2	1-15	2-6	2-15	3-13	3-19
	1-8	1-16	2-8	2-17	3-14	3-20
	1-9	1-17	2-10	2-18	3-15	

Activities	Section 1		Section 2		Section 3	
	1-10	1-19	2-11	2-23		
			2-12	2-24		
			2-13	2-25		
8. PHYSICAL EDUCATION	1-4	1-20	2-3	2-19	3-15	
	1-7	1-21	2-7	2-20	3-20	
	1-19	1-23	2-17			
9. ART	1-2	1-14	2-1	2-16	3-1	3-13
	1-3	1-15	2-5	2-17	3-2	3-14
	1-5	1-16	2-7	2-18	3-3	3-15
	1-7	1-17	2-8	2-19	3-4	3-16
	1-8	1-18	2-9	2-21	3-7	3-17
	1-10	1-19	2-11	2-22	3-8	3-19
	1-11	1-22	2-12	2-23	3-9	3-20
	1-13	1-23	2-13	2-24	3-11	
			2-14	2-25	3-12	
			2-15			
10. MUSIC	1-7	1-13	2-5	2-14	3-1	3-14
	1-8	1-14	2-7	2-17	3-7	3-17
	1-11	1-19	2-13			
	1-12	1-20				
11. CHARACTER DEVELOP-MENT	1-5	1-17	2-1	2-14	3-2	3-14
	1-6	1-18	2-2	2-15	3-5	3-15
	1-7	1-19	2-3	2-16	3-6	3-16
	1-8	1-20	2-4	2-17	3-8	3-17
	1-9	1-21	2-5	2-18	3-10	3-18
	1-12	1-22	2-6	2-19	3-11	3-19
	1-15	1-23	2-7	2-20	3-12	3-20
	1-16		2-8	2-21	3-13	
			2-11	2-23		
			2-13	2-24		

(ALL ACTIVITIES PROVIDE CHARACTER DEVELOPMENT OPPORTUNITIES)

NOTE: These Multicultural Activities Can Be Used All Year Long in Several Ways:

- To Motivate Students for In-Depth Study of Content Area Subjects
- To Instruct Students in Core Subjects

- To Provide Enrichment for Subject Areas
- To Culminate Content Area Units of Study

Most Activities Cover Several Content Area Requirements.

REMEMBER! A Year-Round Implementation of Multicultural Concepts into the Ongoing Curriculum Is Suggested.

A LESSON PLAN GUIDE FOR MULTICULTURAL ACTIVITIES

A Whole Language Approach*

SECTION TITLE________________________________ CODE/TITLE__________

ACTIVITY TITLE____

CONTENT AREA FOCUS____

PERFORMANCE
OBJECTIVES ____

(See Teacher's Directions)_______________________________________

MATERIALS____

____

PROCEDURES ____

____

____

____

EVALUATION____

____

____

RECURRING WHOLE LANGUAGE ELEMENTS:

1. LISTENING– Students will listen attentively as the teacher introduces and presents background information on the subject to be discussed and states the objective. Teacher will read selections from the LITERATURE CONNECTION.
2. SPEAKING– Students will use prior knowledge as the teacher gives them the opportunity to relate their experiences and tell what they know about the subject.
3. READING– Teacher will introduce vocabulary pertaining to the lesson, hold discussions and give each student a copy of the activity sheet. Then students will read silently and perform the dictates of the activity.
4. WRITING– Students will practice the spelling of several words chosen by the teacher from the various activities. Students will use these words in skill-based and creative writing assignments on multicultural themes.
5. CHARACTER– DEVELOPMENT Students will write a brief statement explaining what they have learned from the lesson and tell how it will affect their attitudes and behavior.

*Whole language elements will be adapted to fit content areas. Opportunities for students to work and exchange ideas in cooperative groups increases the impact of the whole language approach.

Table of Contents

SECTION 2 MUTUAL RESPECT

SECTION 3 MULTICULTURAL CONTRIBUTIONS

APPENDIX 307–332

GLOSSARY 333–334

BIBLIOGRAPHY 335

INDEX 336

Section 1
SELF-ESTEEM

INTRODUCTION

Section 1 presents a variety of reproducible activities to help children develop a positive image of themselves at home, at school, and in the community. The following provides a list of materials needed and step-by-step directions for using each activity, along with answer keys where appropriate. Each activity is keyed to the Table of Contents by number and title.

Several activities address building up the self-confidence of the student who has physical disabilities. Moreover, those who are not disabled are exposed to positive experiences which will help them to appreciate the fact that those who are physically challenged are just as worthy and warranting of respect as other human beings.

Diversity in the form of race, gender, nationality, culture, ethnicity, and language are inherent in a series of activities which are designed to approach the building of the self-concept of young children from the vantage point of the whole child. The overall objective is to build a base of commonalities to which children of many races and cultures can relate and which they may internalize as they grow and develop.

To introduce the activities in this section, show the children pictures of diverse groups of people and discuss the fact that they are all individual members of the human race. (See *Life* Magazine, The Family of Man, The Family of Children and/or *National Geographic* for such pictures.) Explore the term individual as related to special. Explain that individuals can be identified from others by special features or qualities. Emphasize, however, that in spite of the different races, religions, colors, nationalities, languages, and so on, human beings are alike in many ways.

During field testing of activities, children discovered that they were, indeed, different and complimented each other on their individual variations. However, daily they exclaimed that they were more alike than different. This feedback prompted the following CLASS MOTTO which can be used at any time for reinforcing self-concepts, while simultaneously building a strong foundation for mutual respect based on an understanding of human commonalities.

WE MAY BE DIFFERENT ON THE OUTSIDE,
BUT WE'RE JUST ALIKE ON THE INSIDE.
OUR HEARTS OF LOVE BEAT WITHIN,
WE'RE BROTHERS AND SISTERS BENEATH THE SKIN.

Discuss the meanings of the more difficult concepts in the CLASS MOTTO for younger children. For example, explain the connotation of the human heart as a SYMBOL of deep inner feelings that people have for each other. Also, explain the term "beneath the skin" as a reference to the fact that people of every race have the same physical make-up, except for the outer covering, the skin. The use of information on NAMES and how diverse groups of people choose names for their babies will deepen student comprehension of commonalities among various cultures.

The overall purpose of this section is that of bolstering the self-image of all children, despite their physical attributes, socio-economic, educational, religious, cultural, national, racial, ethnic, or familial backgrounds. Students are captive within the walls of the school and it is the responsibility of adult care-givers and educators to make each child's educational experience rewarding and pain-free. Therefore, notes of caution for teacher sensitivity and awareness to the needs of children who might require special attention, are interjected at various points in the teacher directions.

Although there are many features which make this book unique in its treatment of the relationships among the various racial and cultural groups in society, the LITERATURE CONNECTION suggestions for readings verify the fact that human beings have much in common and that they are, have been, and always will be unavoidably intertwined. That all human beings are interdependent and a part of each other emerges as the reverberating theme when children work on the activities together. Frequent opportunities for children to respond to the literature through discussions, drawings, etc., should be provided.

DIRECTIONS FOR SECTION ONE ACTIVITIES

Activity 1-1 ABOUT MYSELF

Help children to each recognize special things about themselves and note that they are people of diverse backgrounds and experiences. Yet, look for ways to weave in common threads of human qualities which transcend racial and ethnic differences. For example, despite outward appearances, all human beings have hearts and brains. Point out the significance of being able to identify individuals, nevertheless, through such things as fingerprints, voices, personality, and the like. Have students repeat the MOTTO for reinforcement of the need for similarities and differences among human beings. (Be certain that each child understands the words of the motto, including "hearts of love...within" and "beneath the skin").

Materials Needed:

- Copy of activity sheet 1-1, *About Myself*
- Fingerpaints
- Crayons
- Tape measure
- Hand mirror
- Stamp pad
- Pictures of diverse groups of people
- Magnifying glass

Directions:

1. Give each child a copy of activity sheet 1-1, then ask children to examine lines in their hands and fingers for differences. Have them dip their fingers into the paints or onto a stamp pad. Have them make fingerprints on paper and then compare their prints. Emphasize individuality within the context of this common human trait by having students examine the swirls and lines with a magnifying glass. Note that because no two people have the same patterns of prints, police can often readily identify missing persons.

2. Arrange a visit to the school nurse to get each child's height and weight. Ask the nurse to show the students how to record individual size, height and weight on the activity sheet. Discuss children's individual differences in size. Teacher sensitivity to the needs of children who are exceptional in size, i.e., the tallest, heaviest, thinnest, and so on is crucial. Emphasize the beauty of variation in size, etc. (physical differences).

3. Ask students what language they speak at home. Have children demonstrate languages other than English by asking bilingual students to identify things in the classroom in their home language. For example, book is "libro" in Spanish. Print the names of the different languages represented by children in the classroom on the board and have each child print the language spoken in his/her home in the appropriate box on the worksheet. Say, "Buenos Dias" or "Annyong Ha Se Yo." Explain that people all over the world say "hello" or "good morning." These foreign language words say "good morning" in Spanish and Korean.

4. Pass a hand-mirror around and ask the children to each closely observe their face (eyes, nose, mouth). Discuss with children the fact that each child has different features...different coloring, different hair, eye color, and so on. Have them close their eyes and feel the configuration of their own features. Then have each child draw a picture of his/her face on the activity sheet. Encourage all of them to feel proud of the results of their self-portraits.

5. Compliment all students, individually and collectively, on a variety of personal qualities or class accomplishments. "I am so proud of you for...." Encourage the children to compliment each other, as well. For example, "James...I like your drawing because...."

6. Tell the children to think of some good things about themselves and complete the last sentence on the worksheet. This activity can be shared with members of the class, family members and friends by comparing and contrasting the sentences.

LITERATURE CONNECTION: *Pepito's Story* by Eugene Fern. This is a story of two children who help each other discover that things which make people different also make them special. Yarrow Press, New York, © 1990. Illustrated.

Activity 1-2A **MY SPECIAL DAY**

Activity 1-2A **MY SPECIAL SOMEONE—Alternative***

Activity 1-2B **MY BABY PICTURE**

Activity 1-2C **NAME THE BABIES**

Have children recall how their families and friends become excited when a baby is about to be born. An effort is made to give the new child a special name. Talk about the origin of names and use this as a means of further demonstrating the commonalities among people of diverse cultural, ethnic and racial backgrounds. (See Family Name Origins in the Appendix.) Describe celebrations which take place at the birth of a new baby into a family. Some families give parties, many take photographs and have christenings when the baby is born.

*Teacher sensitivity to the needs of children who are adopted or are living with grandparents, foster, single parents, and other unique familial situations is crucial. Create positive feelings in these children and concern and understanding on the part of their peers. Use the *My Special Someone-Alternative* activity 1-2A for children from special familial settings.

Materials Needed:

- Copy of activity sheet 1-2A, *My Special Day*
- Copy of activity sheet 1-2A, *My Special Someone-Alternative** if necessary
- Copy of activity sheet 1-2B, *My Baby Picture*
- Copy of activity sheet 1-2C, *Name the Babies*
- Pencil or felt-tip pen
- Baby photo and paste (optional)
- Picture of babies in a hospital nursery
- A chart with each child's name
- A box with various names from different nationalities written on slips of paper
- Information on the origin of names (See Appendix and/or books on names)
- Pictures of older people (grandparents)
- Puzzles of different types (toys, crossword, word search, and so on)

Directions:

1. Show students examples of different kinds of puzzles, including crossword, wooden and cardboard pictures, word search, and the like. Demonstrate techniques for solving some or all of them, especially the word search. Allow children to do one puzzle with you. Give each child a copy of activity sheet 1-2A, *My Special Day,* and ask children to locate, in the word search, the names of all the people who were happy when they were born. *Answers*: MOTHER, FATHER, BROTHER, SISTER, AUNT, COUSIN, UNCLE, NANA (GRANDMOTHER), PA (GRANDFATHER), FRIENDS, THE DOCTOR. (Teacher sensitivity and awareness of the needs of children from single parent, adoptive, foster care or other special familial situations might warrant the use of the alternative activity, 1-2A, *My Special Someone*.)

2. Discuss how most people have pictures made of newborn babies and ask children to bring in a baby picture. Show pictures of grandparents and ask what names they call their grandmothers and grandfathers. Write PA and NANA on the board as examples of special names people might call their grandparents. Give each

child a copy of activity 1-2B, *My Baby Picture.* Have each child paste or draw a picture of himself/herself in the space provided on the activity sheet. (Caution students and parents not to bring or send any photo of which there is no copy.) Provide opportunities for children to share and display their completed worksheets.

3. Explore the origin of names by asking students if they know who named them, and/or whether they have received the name of a close family member, friend, or a famous person. Make class charts recording students' names, the reasons for them, and, if possible, their meanings. (Use information from the Appendix and/or from books on family name origins to impress upon children the importance of names.) Elicit from children the fact that human beings of different racial and cultural backgrounds can share the same first and last names.

4. Students will enjoy pulling a name out of the box and reading how babies are named in some cultures. For example, in Ghana, some parents name their boys and girls for the days of the week. Have students locate various reasons for the names children receive.

5. Pass a box with names from different nationalities on slips of paper, or on 3 × 5 cards. Ask children to choose names to give to the newborns in the activity, 1-2C, *Name the Babies.* Give students an opportunity to share information about the origin of their names. It could be fun for each child to give one "newborn" his or her name and/or names from other cultures. Encourage children to see the physiological and social commonalities among human beings by discussing their answers to the multiple choice questions.

> **LITERATURE CONNECTION**: *Tikki Tikki Tembo* by Arlene Mosel. Here is a story of how Chinese children came to have short names. Viking Press, New York © 1968. Illustrator, Blair Lent.
>
> *Everett Anderson's Nine Month Long* by Lucille Clifton. Discover what happens when a new baby comes to share in the family's love. Henry Holt, New York, © 1988. Illustrated.

Activity 1-3A MY BIRTHDAY CAKE

Activity 1-3B CELEBRATING BIRTHDAYS WITH OTHERS

Children will enjoy coloring their own birthday cake in this activity. Sharing the ways people celebrate birthdays in various families, as well as in different cultures, can occur before and during the activity. Make a bulletin board or calendar with the names and birthdates of all students in the class. The self-esteem of students can be enhanced by adding the names of and doing research on famous historical and contemporary contributors who share the same birthdays/birthmonths of the children. Help children identify with contributors in terms of race, gender, ethnicity, language, and culture. A real cake can be brought in and decorated by the children. Plan a FAMILY AND FRIENDS birthday calendar for students to take home as an extension of appreciating the commonalities among diverse families.

Materials Needed:

- Copy of activity sheet 1-3A, *My Birthday Cake*
- Copy of activity sheet 1-3B, *Celebrating Birthdays with Others*
- Lists of birthdays of famous people
- Books, magazines, news articles, and so on of contemporary and historical contributors
- World Book Encyclopedia-Childcraft Vol. 9
- A recording of the Happy Birthday song
- A real cake (plain)
- Pictures of and small squeeze containers of different flavors of frosting
- Ingredients for frosting: powdered sugar, butter, cream, vanilla, cocoa, food coloring and so on. Other decorations (optional)
- Monthly Birthday Chart/Calendar
- Candles, cardboard or real—do not light
- Crayons or markers of different colors

Directions:

1. Discuss favorite flavors of frosting such as lemon, chocolate, or vanilla. Also, show pictures of other types of decorations for birthday cakes. Make frosting from powdered sugar and butter. Because of food allergies avoid nuts, peanuts, and the like. Give children opportunities to decorate the cake by taking turns. Discuss birthdates and use the newly frosted cake to celebrate birthdays of students. Talk about the fun connected with birthday celebrations, parties, games, and food. Give each child a copy of activity sheet 1-3A, *My Birthday Cake.*

2. When children have finished coloring their cakes on the previous worksheet, have them notice that each one is decorated in a special, unique way. Compliment students on their ability to make individual decisions. Also, recall the special ways families and friends have of celebrating this yearly event. For example, in some cultures people have days for celebrating their NAMES on their birthdays. Others gather to protect the birthday person from bad spirits. This is how birthday parties began. The idea of baking cakes and using candles began in Greece. Greeks worshipped their goddess of the moon, Artemis (AHR tuh mihs),

by bringing round cakes (like the full moon) to her temple each month. To make the cake glow like the moon they used lighted candles. (Volume 9-Childcraft-World Book Encyclopedia-1981)

3. Make and display a calendar reflecting the shared birthdates of classmates, family, friends and famous people. Celebrate these common birthdays by playing a recording of and/or singing the birthday song. Give each child a copy of the activity 1-3B, *Celebrating Birthdays with Others*. Students will write the names on each shape. Have them include at least ONE famous person for each month. Use books, encyclopedias, lists and the like to locate the birthdates of contemporary and historical contributors from various cultural, ethnic, and racial backgrounds.

> **LITERATURE CONNECTION**: *Who Paddled Backward With Trout?* by Norman Howard. In this Asian-American story, children who do not like the names their parents give them can change them. Little, Brown & Co., Boston, © 1987. Illustrated by Ed Young.
>
> *Hello Amigos!*, by Tricia Brown. A nonfiction sampling of Hispanic culture is offered at Frankie Valdez's birthday party. Henry Holt, New York, © 1986. Photographs by Fran Oritz.

Activity 1-4A I CAN TAKE CARE OF MYSELF

Activity 1-4B THE HUMAN BODY IS FANTASTIC

Personal care and grooming skills are promoted in this activity to help students develop an understanding of the concepts of dependence, independence, and decision-making. Also, students will develop higher self-esteem and assume a greater sense of responsibility concerning the care of their own bodies through a brief look at the systems of the human body. As a result of discussions about what it takes to stay healthy, children will develop an aversion to harmful drugs, tobacco, and alcohol. For young children, a careful overview of unusual and challenging words depicting the Skeletal, Respiratory, Digestive, Nervous, and other systems, is essential. If the teacher chooses to go into depth on the systems of the body, explanations and diagrams are important to student comprehension. Moreover, a greater understanding of these common human traits elevates the self-esteem of all. The CLASS MOTTO can be recited here. OPTIONAL: A scientific discussion on the development of the human body from conception to birth.

Materials Needed:

- Copy of activity sheet 1-4A, *I Can Take Care of Myself*
- Copy of activity sheet 1-4B, *The Human Body Is Fantastic*

- Pencils or markers/chalk/crayons/paints
- Pictures of and some information about the human body—Encyclopedias, books
- Construction paper/paste/scissors
- Pictures of adults, children and babies of different colors, races, and cultures
- Pictures of items which babies need: bottles, diapers, carriages, and the like
- Culturally diverse infant needs and practices can be elicited from students and their families or researched. For example, in some cultures a cloth is soaked in milk for the baby to suck, instead of a milk bottle. A wooden box on wheels pulled by a goat is used instead of a carriage in other cultures. Baby boys wear dresses and many babies don't wear diapers or any other clothing outdoors in some cultures.

Directions:

1. Write the word *dependence* on the chalkboard. Ask different children to tell how all babies need someone to care for them when they need to be fed, bathed, and diapered. Elicit information from students which indicates their understanding that babies are dependent.

2. Demonstrate the concept of *independence* by asking a student to lift a lightweight object. Compare the helplessness of babies to the increasing independence of growing boys and girls, as they learn to take care of their own needs. Use pictures of babies, toddlers, older children, adults, and items needed by babies to stimulate discussions on the topic of independence.

3. Ask children to make a list of their abilities to care for themselves and contrast it with one which illustrates the things that babies and toddlers can do. Then discuss their routines of preparing for school each day (bathing, brushing teeth, dressing). Give each child a copy of the activity sheet 1-4A, *I Can Take Care of Myself.* Compare the results.

4. Show pictures of the human body, including the skeletal system, cell structure, muscles, nervous system, skin, respiratory system, and organs. Building upon prior knowledge to aid comprehension is possible because children are already familiar with their bodies, from a practical if not a scientific standpoint. Therefore, it is important not to rush the explanations of the systems. You might spend a day's session on each system so that children do not become confused. Also, giving students time to absorb new information makes it possible to add to and build on what they already understand about the human body.

Elicit from children the obvious parts of the body: HEAD, NECK, EYES, ARMS, LEGS, BACK. Discuss the importance of exercise and healthful eating as a means of keeping in shape. In addition, elicit from children the importance of staying away from harmful chemical substance, tobacco, and alcohol, as a means of maintaining healthy bodies. Use information from encyclopedias to extend this study and to help each child appreciate the wonder of his/her own body and what it is capable of doing. Emphasize the fact that human beings of all races have the same physical make-up. Give each child a copy of activity sheet 1-4B, *The Human Body Is Fantastic.*

LITERATURE CONNECTION: *Three Strong Women* by Claus Stamm. A wrestler who thinks he is the best among all others learns humility. Viking Press, New York, © 1990. Illustrated by Jean Tseng & Mou Sten Tseng.

Activity 1-5A MY FAMILY TREE (cut-outs)

Activity 1-5B MY FAMILY TREE (paste on)

In this activity, children will identify themselves as social beings, beginning as members of a particular family. Define social beings from the standpoint of the gregarious nature of all human beings; people need to live with others. Lead children into an appreciation of and satisfaction with their family's racial heritage by evaluating admirable traits which have been exhibited by all groups represented in the class, school, and community. Give examples of how people of many races help each other during crisis situations (earthquakes, floods, etc.). Leave the children with a sense of the commonalities which bind them rather than with feelings of separation and antagonism. Have them recite the CLASS MOTTO and discuss what it means to each of them.

Materials Needed:

- Copy of activity sheets 1-5A, *My Family Tree* (cut-outs) and 1-5B, *My Family Tree* (paste-on)
- Pencils or markers
- Scissors
- Paste
- Crayons (optional)
- Pictures of multiracial groups of families engaged in various activities (swimming, sports, board games, eating, reading, talking, playing, working) (Sources: magazines, local newspapers, family albums, religious institutions, etc.)

Directions:

1. Ask children to name some of the people they are with every day. Discuss how they interact with family members daily in preparing meals, shopping, raking

leaves, worshipping, cleaning, and washing. Use pictures to stimulate ideas for discussion.

2. Discuss some special things about each child's family and compliment them on their ethnic and racial heritage. Ask students to share information about their special holidays, religions, and traditions. Discuss marriage, children, and family as universal traditions that all cultures have in common. Explain that this is how the human family is able to survive. Compliments can be given over a short period of time to individuals and small groups as a way to ensure sincerity.

3. Show pictures of families involved in various types of celebrations. For example, reunions, Christmas, Hanukkah, Kwanzaa, Diwali, Easter, Mother's Day, weddings, or any event in which family members are sharing time, fun, and food. Have children suggest other ways in which family and close friends celebrate. Discuss the words "generations" and "traditions," and who usually participates in family gatherings. Give each child copies of 1-5A and 1-5B, *My Family Tree,* to complete. Ask children to cut out the leaves and glue them on the tree.

> **LITERATURE CONNECTIONS**: *Kwanzaa* by A. P. Porter. A non-fiction account of the African-American holiday, its meanings and rituals. Carolrhoda Books, Minneapolis, Minnesota, © 1991. Illustrations by Janice Lee Porter.

Activity 1-6 CAN YOU FIND THEM?

Have children relate specific things that people do in their homes, schools, and communities. For example, in the home, mothers and fathers work and provide for their children. In schools, principals, librarians, and teachers provide services. In the community, the mayor, supermarket clerks, bus drivers, and construction workers provide people with goods and services. Ask each child to share what he/she might choose as a career and elicit suggestions as to what contributions he/she can make in this profession.

Materials Needed:

- Copy of activity sheet 1-6, *Can You Find Them?*
- Pencils or markers
- Pictures of men, women, boys and girls
- A wheel displaying male and female contributors from racial origins
- Chart paper
- Short Biographies of Contributors (See Appendix)

Directions:

1. Show pictures of people from many racial/ethnic backgrounds who have made contributions to the building of America. Encourage students to identify with both men and women contributors in the building of America. Then give children copies of activity 1-6, *Can You Find Them?*

2. Ask students if they can be contributors. Discuss ways in which they, as children, do help others. Develop a chart of classroom contributors. Ask if they can think of ways to contribute at home, at school or in their community. Ask how helping others makes them feel about themselves.

> **LITERATURE CONNECTION**: *A Letter to the King,* story and pictures by Leong Va, translated from the Norwegian by James Anderson. A girl wins her father's freedom by daring to write to the King in a society where males are preferred to females. Harper Collins, New York, © 1988.

Activity 1-7A HUMAN BEINGS ARE ALIKE AND DIFFERENT

Activity 1-7B WINNING THE RACE FOR ME

Use comparison/contrast methods to discuss the various religions, races, and cultures represented in the class. Show pictures of dolls from various ethnic origins. Have the children describe the differences and similarities among them. Ask students if real people have the same kinds of likenesses and differences. Explain that even though it's great to be similar in some ways, it would be unexciting if every person were just the same. Create an atmosphere of understanding, tolerance, and acceptance of diversity in race, religion, culture, and physical capabilities (as concerning the disabled). Children who are physically challenged demonstrate the extent to which they are independent in both physical and mental aspects and experience increasing levels of self-esteem, as a result of their participation in these activities. Plan to read the information on activity sheet 1-7B to your students.

Materials Needed:

- Copy of activity sheet 1-7A, *Human Beings Are Alike and Different*
- Copy of activity sheet 1-7B, *Winning the Race for Me*
- Pencils
- Article about a disabled runner (Appendix)

- Pictures of and/or devices used by people who are disabled, for example, braille, wheelchairs, and hearing aids
- Pictures of people from different races and/or dolls from various ethnic groups
- Picture of a microscopic section of human skin.

Directions:

1. Emphasize the commonalities in the human body regarding the largest organ, the skin. Discuss the fact that the human skin has its own built-in thermostat. There is a rare condition which does not permit the body to perspire, but in most cases, all human beings have the ability to sweat. This controls, regulates, and keeps the body temperature at 98.6 degrees. Have children observe and admire their own skin color and that of their classmates.

Discuss the chemical substance MELANIN as the reason for variations in skin color and explain how it protects the human skin from sunburn. People whose ancestors lived in hot climates such as Africa, the Virgin Islands, India, and Hawaii, have darker skin colors than those whose ancestors lived in colder places. Elicit from students the understanding of how much more interesting it is to see or have a wide variety of skin colors among human beings. What a dull world it would be if all people were the same shade and had the same hair and eye colors, too.

Show students a section of human skin. Prepare them for independent work on the activity sheet by introducing the scientific vocabulary for human skin. Show them the enlarged microscopic view of the skin. Write the words MELANIN, EPIDERMIS, GLANDS, DERMIS, BLOOD VESSEL, PORE, DEPOSITS, NERVE ENDINGS on chart paper or on the board. Ask students to repeat the words and copy them into their notebooks or on paper. Emphasize that all human beings have the SAME kind of skin. Explain the term MICROSCOPIC and discuss the enlarged view of a section of human skin. Elicit from children that the only DIFFERENCE is the color of the skin. Have children admire the various colors of skin among the members of the class. Explain why there are differences by recalling the term MELANIN. Give each student a copy of activity 1-7A, *Human Beings Are Alike and Different.*

2. Read excerpts from articles about physically challenged people who are creative and/or independent. Elicit from students the meaning of the word CONFIDENCE as believing in one's abilities to succeed. Note students who have had problems learning how to ride a bike, read, study, make good grades, and so on. Help to increase their self-esteem by emphasizing turning points. Compliment individual students on some of their successes.

Discuss the importance of trying to reach goals, feeling good about oneself, and developing a high level of self-confidence without making others feel bad.

Everyone benefits from learning that the disabled are human beings who are good and capable of making life better for themselves and others. Give each student a copy of activity 1-7B, *Winning the Race for Me.* The teacher or volunteer should read the information aloud to the students. Define the difficult vocabulary prior to reading the interview and emphasize the high level of confidence shown by the physically challenged soccer player. Elicit from children the fact that everyone, able-bodied people included, can learn from this confident soccer player who accepted and met his challenge.

> **LITERATURE CONNECTION**: *Knots in a Counting Rope* by Bill Martin, Jr. and John Archambault. A blind boy gains confidence and courage to face his disability, as he remembers his grandfather's stories. Henry Holt, New York, © 1990. Illustrated by Ted E. Rand.

Activity 1-8A THE FIVE SENSES

Activity 1-8B THAT ICE CREAM TASTES GOOD!

Explain how human beings depend upon the senses of taste, touch, smell, sight, and sound to help them understand the world around them. Also elicit ideas as to how people develop preferences and make individual decisions about how things look or taste. For example, why can something be seen as "pretty" by one person and "ugly" by another? Or how can something taste "good" to one person and "bad" to someone else? Students will have fun as they contemplate ice cream as a favorite dessert for people all over the world and that it, as with many other things, cannot be enjoyed without benefit of the senses. Discuss how, depending on the extent of the disability, people often are able to compensate for impaired senses by hearing aids, seeing-eye dogs, braille, and natural intelligence.

Materials Needed:

- Copy of activity sheet 1-8A, *The Five Senses*
- Copy of activity sheet 1-8B, *That Ice Cream Tastes Good!*
- Paper for crumbling
- Recordings of various sounds
- One or more of the following fragrances: cologne, spices, flowers, candy
- Box with various concealed objects
- Crayons or markers and pencil
- Information about deafness and blindness
- Helen Keller biography/encyclopedias

Directions:

1. Discuss the importance of the senses of sight and touch. Have students explore contents of a "Guess What I Am Box" which contains various shapes, textures, and surfaces. Children are to try and guess what each object is through their sense of touch. Discuss different answers. Let a child take each object out of the box, after everyone has had a turn. As children look at the items, emphasize how important the sense of sight is to human beings in determining the exact identity of (the) things (in the box).

2. Discuss the senses of smell and taste. Ask the children to name some of their favorite foods and tell why they like them. Note differences in choices. Allow children to smell different spices: cinnamon, sage, nutmeg, and so on. Discuss preferences in types of candy such as chocolate, peppermint, and caramel. Allow them to smell fresh flowers and/or colognes. Note differences in reactions to smells. Ask, "Again, why do we enjoy different scents?" Compare and contrast the functions of the senses of taste and smell and what this means to individuals.

3. Discuss the sense of sound. Secretly select one child to crumple a piece of paper behind his/her back at a given signal. Then ask children to be quiet, close their eyes, and listen to discern what is happening (signal to the child to crumple the paper). Allow time for children to describe what they heard. Explain that the structure of the human ear allows people to hear the same sounds. Have others make different sounds while their peers guess the source and objects used: SOUNDS—tap a pencil on a desk, or a spoon on a glass, whisper, close a door, clap hands, knock. Then see if students can discern the differences between loud and soft sounds. Play recordings of music, drama, and speech to demonstrate the extent of sounds which can be heard by the human ear.

4. Explain that there are many ways to help the deaf understand the sounds around them and to help those who are blind to read, write, and to be able to go where they need to go. Also, discuss the fact that the physically disabled are just as intelligent as those who have no disabilities. CAUTION: Teacher sensitivity towards those who may have brain damage or disorders is necessary. Read about Helen Keller who was both deaf and blind and how her eagerness to learn made it possible for her to help herself and others. Discuss the fact that even when some senses are missing or impaired, all people are important and can accomplish good things in their lives. Give each student activity 1-8A, *The Five Senses.*

5. Reemphasize the fact that human beings all over the world have and use the same five senses. Have children say them. Give each child a copy of activity 1-8B, *That Ice Cream Tastes Good!* Have them say ice cream in Swahili, one of the languages of East Africa. If students of other nationalities know the word, ice cream, in their language, ask them to teach it to the class.

LITERATURE CONNECTION: *The Balancing Girl* by Bernice Rabe, a story of a physically disabled child who delights her peers with her balancing skills. Dutton Children's Books, New York, © 1988. Illustrated.

Activity 1-9A FOREIGN LANGUAGE FUN

Activity 1-9B PARTNER TALK

Children will observe the ethnic, racial, and cultural diversity represented among their classmates by looking at languages. They will recite foreign words for familiar things and, thereby, learn some of the richness of language from various cultures. Furthermore, they will see that all human beings, no matter what their race or culture, use their voices to communicate. Methods of forming letters and words with fingers and hands to "talk" with those who are deaf will be shared as students practice sign language. Children who have auditory problems or who are legally blind will feel an important part of the efforts of others to understand and improve communication with them. Moreover, students who speak foreign languages will feel an important part of the efforts of others to verify their language. All students will benefit from increased efforts of diverse groups of human beings to find common needs and common reasons for sharing information.

Materials Needed:

- Copy of activity sheet 1-9A, *Foreign Language Fun*
- Copy of activity sheet 1-9B, *Partner Talk*
- Globe or world map with multiracial pictures
- Pictures of human vocal chords
- Pictures of different sign languages
- World Book Encyclopedia Vol. 17—Sign Language
- Pictures of devices needed by the auditorily and visually impaired
- Japanese, Chinese, Swahili, Russian, Korean, Polish, and Hungarian words
- Several foreign language dictionaries
- Information about Alexander G. Bell
- Foreign Language Lists (Appendix)
- Scotch tape
- Construction paper (multicolored)
- Markers and/or crayons
- Scissors
- Manual Alphabet/Sign Language Chart

Directions:

1. Show a map or globe and discuss the various races and cultures of human beings who live in the world. Ask children to identify themselves and members of

their families with one or more of these groups. Explain how important it is to learn a new language in order to better understand people of other cultures. Encourage bilingual students to explain a few words in their native language while reminding everyone of the importance of languages in helping people to talk to each other. Give examples of the many "English" words which have originated from Spanish, French, Italian, Yiddish, and so on.

2. Refer to the Foreign Language Lists in the Appendix to help students identify words for familiar items. Find words like book, paper, pencil, chalkboard, door, hallway, telephone, water, desk, and table. Check their Spanish (S) and German (G) words for: Cup (S) *una taza* (G) *die Tasse*; Water (S) *el agua* (G) *das wasser*; Sun (S) *el sol* (G) *die summer*; Tree (S) *el arbol* (G) *der Baum*; House (S) *la Casa* (G) *das Haus*; Door (S) *la puerta* (G) *die Tur*. Use the globe and map to point out various nations and discuss the national origin and languages represented in the classroom. Give each student a copy of activity 1-9A, *Foreign Language Fun*. Help students extend their appreciation of the common need that human beings have to communicate, by labeling items in the classroom in several different languages. Use construction paper, scotch tape, and markers to make and attach temporary labels.

3. Human beings can learn to understand each other in ways other than by using voices. Formulate the words, "Hello, how are you?" with your lips only. This will serve as an example of what the world of communication is like for those who are deaf. Discuss other ways that people talk to each other. List these on the board as discussion points under the heading ALL HUMAN BEINGS CAN UNDERSTAND EACH OTHER BY: a. Speaking, b. Listening, c. Writing, d. Sign Language, e. Translating, f. Braille, g. Other ______. Ask students to add other ways of communicating to the list, such as music, drama, and art.

4. Discuss Alexander Graham Bell, who invented the telephone and methods to help the deaf to communicate with other people. Read information about sign language to students. Explain that this is another form of communication which helps human beings to understand each other better. Ask students if any of them know sign language and if so, give them an opportunity to demonstrate. Give each student a copy of activity 1-9B, *Partner Talk* and the Manual Alphabet/Sign Language Chart. Compare the results. Extend this concept in varied communication techniques by giving students opportunities to find the words CLOCK and FLAG in languages other than English. (See Appendix, Foreign Language Lists.) Encourage students to teach family members and friends what they have learned.

LITERATURE CONNECTION: *Hand Talk: An A B C of Finger Spelling and Sign Language* by Remy Charlip and Mary Beth. Macmillan (Aladdin Books), New York, © 1986. Illustrated by George Acano.

Activity 1-10A FAVORITE FOODS

Activity 1-10B NAME THAT FOOD

Students will focus on cultural diversity as related to foods and simultaneously learn that food is a basic human necessity. Americans eat foods from various cultures on a daily basis: pizza, chili, rice, lasagna, cornbread, sauerkraut and hot dogs, and yogurt. The fact that food is necessary for the survival of human beings of all races, colors, religions, and languages will emerge as students taste and talk about different types of foods. Also, students will compare and contrast various flavors and ways that different ethnic groups prepare common foods, such as rice and other popular dishes. Elicit from students their ideas as to why different ethnic groups may enjoy diverse spices and seasonings such as hot peppers or sweet and sour sauces, and the like.

Materials Needed:

- Copy of activity sheet 1-10A, *Favorite Foods*
- Copy of activity sheet 1-10B, *Name That Food*
- Pencils
- Crayons
- Pictures of different kinds of foods
- Recipes of foods from different countries
- Samples of multiethnic foods for tasting
- Information from multiethnic parents and community members on the origin of foods from their cultures

Directions:

1. Ask children to describe how they feel when they are hungry. All human beings need food. In fact, people can purchase many different kinds of foods in this country. Explain how it is not as easy for people to buy food in some countries as it is in America.

Encourage children to talk about their preferences for cereals, breads, meats, desserts, snacks, and special family dishes. Have children tell their favorite meal, i.e., breakfast, lunch, or dinner, and explain the reason for this choice. Ask the role that the senses of smell, touch (texture/temperature), sight, and taste have in individual choices of foods. Check for food allergies, then give students opportunities to taste a variety of foods. (Discuss briefly what an allergy is and what causes it. Briefly describe symptoms.) Compare and contrast their reactions to each food. Give each child activity 1-10A, *Favorite Foods*.

2. Show pictures of many types of foods and point out the varieties of international foods eaten by Americans of all races and colors. For example, many Americans like Italian pizza. Ask students to name other ethnic foods which are commonly enjoyed by people of diverse racial and cultural backgrounds. Help them to locate descriptive language needed for specificity in stating reasons for liking or not liking a food. For example, "I don't like cottage cheese because the lumps stick in my throat," or "spinach is too slippery," or "I like the warm, cheesy pizza melting in my mouth." Give each child a copy of activity 1-10B, *Name That Food.* Extend these experiences through creative writing and/or art.

3. Many foods have been "Americanized" to the extent that people do not realize that, originally, these foods came from another country. Discuss some of the foods that students of various ethnic backgrounds all eat. Have students develop a list of familiar foods and their origins. Read some of the recipes in various cookbooks and have students compare and contrast the ingredients. Parents, teachers, and students can plan an international banquet. To avoid full-scale dinner preparations, plan to have guests only sample small portions of international dishes. Explain the term "Americanization" as the changing of a food from another country by using ingredients and spices available in America.

> **LITERATURE CONNECTION**: *Everybody Cooks Rice* by Norah Dooley. While searching for her brother who is late for dinner, a girl discovers that, no matter what their ethnic background, every family is having a rice dish for supper. Easy recipes for students are included. Carolrhoda Books, Minneapolis, Minnesota, ©1991. Illustrated by Peter J. Thornton.

Activity 1-11A MUSICAL INSTRUMENTS

Activity 1-11B MUSIC IS UNIVERSAL

Children use their senses of sight and hearing to develop a deeper understanding of their individuality in this activity. The importance of the human voice in speaking and singing will emerge as students react to and discuss music. Students will analyze music from various cultures through comparing and contrasting sound patterns, rhythm, and texture. Sensory imagery is artistically represented through music and simultaneously conveys the beauty of diversity and harmony. This concept should be transferable to the beauty of diversity and the need for harmony among the individual members of the class and, ultimately, among members of the larger society.

Materials Needed:

- Copy of activity sheet 1-11A, *Musical Instruments*
- Copy of activity sheet 1-11B, *Music Is Universal*
- Recordings of choir music
- Pictures of various musical instruments
- Sound recordings of birds, clapping, laughing, bells, drums, and violins
- Recording of orchestral music
- A partition/screen made from cardboard
- A picture of Stevie Wonder and a cassette recording of some of his music
- Pictures of musical instruments from different cultures
- Recordings of music from different cultures
- Pencils/markers/crayons
- Short sentences for voice demonstrations

Directions:

1. Ask four or five children, of different ethnic or racial origins, to stand behind a screen or partition. Give each child a short sentence to read. Have students who are listening identify the race or color of the readers. Chances are that they will not be able to match voices with the correct children. Explain the fact that the human voice cannot be identified by color but only by the quality of the sound made by the individual who is speaking.

Play records of choir music and discuss the variety in the voice sounds of soprano, tenor, bass, and alto. Emphasize that, like beautiful flowers, musicians come in many colors, sizes, shapes, and races. There can be soprano or tenors who are Asian, Hispanic, black or white. And all voices make various sounds when they speak, sing, or yell. Play orchestral music to demonstrate that like human voices, musical instruments can only be distinguished by sound (when eyes are closed). Give each student activity sheet 1-11A, *Musical Instruments*.

2. Play some of Stevie Wonder's music. Explain that he has compensated for his blindness by excelling in music. He sings, plays the harmonica, piano, and keyboards. In addition, he reads braille, writes his own lyrics, and composes his own songs. Explain how Stevie Wonder and others have the will and ability to overcome problems because they have self-confidence and they try very hard to succeed. Discuss problems that individual students have solved or goals they have accomplished.

3. Discuss the fact that bells, organs, pianos, violins, drums, guitars, harps, trumpets, and voices can be enjoyed by people of many races and religions. Define the term "universal" as pertaining to the whole world. Then elicit their ideas as to how music is a "universal language." Help children further explore "universal" as a word which means that race and color have nothing to do with understanding

and hearing music and that people all over the world have music with which they identify and which others can enjoy, as well.

Play a few recordings for the purpose of discussing students' individual preferences (with the understanding that different music pleases different people—again a matter of taste) and for comparing and contrasting the way the instruments look and sound. Give each child in the class an opportunity to develop his/her musical, singing, or composing talents by planning a multicultural concert. Talents can include: reciting poetry, singing a song, playing an instrument, or performing a skit. Invite parents and members of the community to the program. Give each student a copy of activity 1-11B, *Music Is Universal.*

LITERATURE CONNECTION: *Las Navidades: Popular Christmas Songs from Latin America,*selections and illustrations by Lulu Delacre. A collection of bilingual songs and traditions of Hispanic origin. Scholastic, New York, © 1990.

Dancing Tepees: Poems of American Indian Youth by Virginia Driving Hawk Sneve. The author, a Rosebud Sioux, has selected works reflecting the oral traditions of the North American Indians and the works of contemporary tribal poets. Holiday House, New York, © 1989. Illustrated by Stephen Grammell.

Activity 1-12A WHAT AM I?

Activity 1-12B MAKING YOUR OWN RIDDLES

In this activity, children will elevate their self-esteem by adding to their base of knowledge. Higher-level thinking skills will continue to be developed as students analyze and synthesize information about the world around them. Students will develop self-confidence in their ability to learn, retain, recall, and apply information by solving and writing riddles. This activity also provides opportunities for students to further increase their personal knowledge bank by doing research on multicultural contributors.

Materials Needed:

- Copy of activity sheet 1-12A, *What Am I?*
- Copy of activity sheet 1-12B, *Making Your Own Riddles*
- Hardcover book
- Riddles (oral)
- Pictures of or lists of items which can be used to write riddles
- Books of riddles

- Pencils
- Books, encyclopedias, and biographies
- Box of miscellaneous items, i.e., balls, buttons, and pictures of things like flowers, vacuum cleaners, trees, jewelry, and people
- Newsprint

Directions:

1. Explain that in riddles the objects or people often describe themselves and ask questions like "What Am I?" or "Who Am I?" Conceal a hardcover book, after asking the children to close their eyes. Describe parts of the book and allow the students to guess what you have. Say, "I have something which has pages, a spine, a cover, and letters "What am I?" Give more clues, if necessary. (Show the book and let the students provide the answer, "A book." Then show and rename the parts. Give them another riddle. Say, "Here is another riddle. I have branches, roots, and a trunk. What am I?" Answer, "A tree." Encourage children to create short riddles for the class (and YOU) to enjoy together. Give each student a copy of activity 1-12A, *What Am I?* Share results.

2. Share with children information and humorous riddles from books and/or other sources. Then write this riddle on the board, "I come in many colors, I can fly, I have a beak, feathers, two wings, I live in a nest, I lay eggs, and I sing. What am I?" After students have provided the answer, a bird, ask them to dramatize riddles they know. Then pass around a box of various items, such as buttons, fabric, feathers, glue, pencils, hats, paper, flowers, gloves, and the like. Or, make a list of these items on the chalkboard. Encourage all students to make up and share at least one riddle as a means of raising their self-confidence. Have them applaud individual efforts, as they apply the new knowledge of writing original riddles. Give each child a copy of activity 1-12B, *Making Your Own Riddles.* Or print the riddles on newsprint beforehand and use for display.

3. Explain "Who Am I?" riddles. For example, "Many people use my invention to call and talk with family and friends everyday. I came from a family who helped the deaf learn to speak. Who am I?" The answer, "Alexander Graham Bell, inventor of the telephone." Students can build a broader knowledge base by doing research on other contributors and creating more multicultural riddles. Plan time to go to the library to do class research and compile all original work into a class book of riddles. List ALL names as authors. Encourage individual creativity in the choice of subjects and wording which the students use in their riddles. Verify students' roles as contributors and increase their levels of self-esteem by recording their recitations, listening to audience responses, and by sharing their work with other classes, parents, and the community.

LITERATURE CONNECTION: *Chinese Mother Goose Rhymes* by Robert Wyndham. A book of more than 40 rhymes, riddles, lullabies, and games in Chinese and English. Putnam (Sandcastle Books), New York, © 1989. Illustrated.

Activity 1-13A WHERE DO THEY BELONG?

Activity 1-13B WHAT DO I NEED?

Classification, an important thinking skill, is reinforced in this activity. Also concepts regarding the multifaceted world of people, animals, and objects are presented. The ability to classify objects, organize experiences, and think about appropriate roles adds to each child's store of knowledge. How each child sees himself/herself within the home, school, and community is an important element of self-esteem. Encourage all children to get a good education so that they can achieve the highest possible goals. Discuss people of many racial backgrounds in a variety of admirable jobs.

Materials Needed:

- Copy of activity sheet 1-13A, *Where Do They Belong?*
- Copy of activity sheet 1-13B, *What Do I Need?*
- Pictures of animals, people, and things
- Multicultural groups of people at work
- Scissors
- Paste
- Pictures of living/nonliving things
- Chart paper labeled "Alive"/"Not Alive"
- Three-dimensional objects (books, cloth, letters, numbers, stuffed animals)
- Classification Chart (See Appendix)
- Labels with names of various occupations
- Boxes for items to be classified
- List and/or pictures of different types of jobs and some tools/equipment used in various trades and professions

Directions:

1. Show pictures of animate and inanimate objects. Ask children to define the words "alive" and "not alive." Have them volunteer items they can think of which fit into these two categories. Write a list of words on the board for students to classify beneath these headings:

ALIVE NOT ALIVE

Suggested words/objects for classification. Ask students to think of each item in its most natural state and/or habitat.

fox tree banana building fish dog worm water book flower letter house cookie box rabbit doctor pencil idea computer squirrel rain boy numbers parrot music furniture paper telephone

---

2. Give children opportunities to classify things like stuffed animals, artificial foods, books, cloth, numbers and letters, balls, chalk, combs, brushes, spices, flowers, computer disk, and paper. Have them place these in boxes which are labeled: FOOD, ANIMALS, PLANTS, SCHOOL, GROOMING. Give each child a copy of activity 1-13A, *Where Do They Belong?* Check all responses for accuracy.

3. Ask each child to share what he/she would like to be in the work world of the future. Encourage them to choose, orally or graphically, occupations such as a banker, lawyer, coach, engineer, teacher, conductor, pilot, reporter, bus driver, doctor, electrician, and so on. Compliment them on their choices and explain that, with an education, they can reach any position they want and, simultaneously, make contributions to their families and communities.

Ask students if they can describe something they know pertaining to the world of work. Ask them what things the following people have to know in order to do their jobs: teacher, scientist, salesperson, childcare worker, construction worker, and doctor. Ask if there are any jobs that only a woman can do, or only a man. Have them try to explain the reasoning behind their responses. EMPHASIZE how most jobs can be done by women or men.

Discuss the kinds of tools these and other workers use. Pass around lists and/or pictures of occupational "tools" which are mixed up (hammer, stethoscope, calculator, bus, ladder, and so on). Have students classify the "tools" and discuss which worker needs certain tools. Then have each child share the kind of occupational tool he/she will need in a future job. Give each student a copy of activity 1-13B, *What Do I Need?*

LITERATURE CONNECTION: *Hawaii Is a Rainbow* by Stephanie Feeney. Colorful photographs of the people, places, plants, and animals of Hawaii are organized according to the colors of the rainbow. University of Hawaii Press, Honolulu, Hawaii, © 1980. Illustrated by Jeff Reese.

Activity 1-14A WHO ARE THE PEOPLE IN YOUR NEIGHBORHOOD?

Activity 1-14B IT'S GREAT TO BE HUMAN!

Children will begin to recognize and enjoy the richness of their communities because of the various races, cultures and ethnic groups who live there. They will also examine the common physiological and sociological traits of the different kinds of people who make up the human family. Students will take a brief look at the geographical origin of the races, work cooperatively on a mural, and depict the commonalities among various ethnic groups in a neighborhood. As they draw people shopping, using the post office, taking the bus, or eating in restaurants, children will discern that there are many commonalities among the various racial and ethnic groups. Furthermore, individual and group pride will increase as, through the development of a mural, children of diverse backgrounds share things about their heritage. The validation of each child's ethnic, racial, and national origin will do much to increase his/her self-image.

Materials Needed:

- Copy of activity sheet 1-14A, *Who Are the People in Your Neighborhood?*
- Copy of activity sheet 1-14B, *It's Great to Be Human!*
- Crayons
- Pencils
- Paper/construction/brown wrapping for a mural
- Pictures of houses, apartment buildings
- Pictures of multiracial groups of people
- Pictures of families of different races
- Paints
- Scissors
- Brushes
- Building blocks
- Parents/volunteers/relatives from many places
- Map showing various continents
- Architectural magazines for reference
- Music

Directions:

1. Explain the words "neighborhood and community." Show pictures of multiracial groups of people. Give students an opportunity to "build" a neighborhood using blocks or draw pictures of a special part of their neighborhood and include themselves in the scenes. Discuss the completed work and display it in a special place, at their eye-level.

2. Mention the various compositions of families which might live in homes in these neighborhoods. Families differ in many ways for example; a family might have a mother, father, and children, or a single parent and children, foster parents, adopted children, grandparents, step-parents, extended families, or family friends. Point out that all families are good, unique, and special in some way. Encourage children of diverse racial, cultural, and ethnic backgrounds to see that their religions, languages, holidays, and foods are important.

Give children the activity 1-14A, *Who Are the People in Your Neighborhood?* Have students copy, learn, and share the poem about the human family. Teacher sensitivity to the needs of students from unique familial situations (i.e., divorced, same gender, common-law, temporary shelters) is necessary to prevent pain or feelings of rejection on the part of any child.

3. Play music so students can dance. Allow a few minutes for free, interpretative movement. Have children notice how individual their movements are when they dance. Ask students to differentiate between the things humans of all racial and ethnic groups can do, but animals and inanimate objects cannot do. It is important for students to see that humans are higher-level beings because of their physical make up and their ability to reason. Whereas animals are living, they cannot think, make decisions, and relate to others except by instinct.

Although some animals can be trained, they cannot listen to each other's deepest secrets, communicate in English, Spanish, Mandarin, Gujarati, Yiddish, or Arabic. Also, like plants, animals cannot go to the mall or to the supermarket to purchase items to wear or eat. Unlike people, plants, animals, and nonliving things cannot dance, cry, eat, and perform other human actions. Elicit from each child the extent to which he/she appreciates his/her individuality and humanity. Ask students to imagine how life would be for them as a toy or an animal. Give each student a copy of activity 1-14B, *It's Great to Be Human!*

4. Ask students to notice the form of the human body and the common physiological frames of different races of people. This realization can be the basis for their developing respect for one another. Recall the previous activity and compare the human intellect and abilities to those of animals. That humans of every race and color are more alike than they are different is reinforced. Have students recite the CLASS MOTTO. Follow with handshakes and smiles.

Now that children are thinking and working together in an environment of tolerance and respect, they can begin to think of taking care of the home of the people of the world. Explain that all races (all human beings) share ONE SPECIAL HOME, THE EARTH. Show the map or globe and elicit from students the fact that there are people of almost every race and culture in the world living in America. Define the words POLLUTION, RECYCLING, ENVIRONMENT, SMOG, and LITTER. Explain that these and other words are used in ecology campaigns to raise the awareness of everyone to the urgent need we have to protect the Earth.

Elicit from children the need for each person to have a sense of responsibility about caring for the Earth and bringing about peace.

Also, discuss specific things that groups and individual students can do to accomplish both of these goals. Explain how important it is to start by getting along with other people and taking care of their own homes, neighborhoods, and school. Ask children to volunteer to start two clubs, one for PEACEMAKERS, and the other for PROTECTING THE EARTH. (The names of the clubs [groups] can be changed. Teacher autonomy in making certain that groups are racially and culturally diverse is necessary.)

5. Show pictures of different kinds of buildings which are usually seen in urban, suburban, or farm areas. Have children work on a colorful mural which depicts the multicultural heritage of their communities. Extend students' understanding of classification by allowing them to choose a certain area to draw on the mural—LISTED CHOICES: HOUSES, PEOPLE, BUSINESSES, ANIMALS, CHURCHES, TEMPLES, MOSQUES, BANKS, PARKS, TRAINS, ROADS, CARS, SCHOOLS, SUPERMARKETS, HOSPITALS, TREES, and MALLS. Emphasize the diversity in the people, animals, and other things in the community. Encourage creativity by allowing each child's ideas and drawings to go on the mural. Find a suitable place to display the mural at the children's eye-level in the school or in the community.

LITERATURE CONNECTION: *All-of-a Kind Family* by Sydney Taylor. A story of the adventures of five daughters from a fun-loving Jewish family. Dell, New York, © 1980. Illustrated.

Activity 1-15A COSTUMES AND CUSTOMS

Activity 1-15B MULTICULTURAL CELEBRATIONS IN AMERICA

Children in all school environments will learn that America is a better place, because its inhabitants come from many different places in the world. In addition, each child will demonstrate how the different languages, traditions, customs, and values of his/her culture have contributed to the richness of the environment in which she/he lives. The wealth of various cultures comes into focus as information is shared among diverse groups during periods of interaction. In this activity, students will take a closer look at the multicultural flavor of America through learning about multiethnic costumes, customs, and holidays.

Materials Needed:

- Copy of activity sheet 1-15A, *Costumes and Customs*
- Copy of activity sheet 1-15B, *Multicultural Celebrations in America*
- Pictures of clothing worn by people who live in different parts of the world; *Examples*: Sari—India, Kilt—Scotland, Fez—Turkey, Beret—France, Duku—Ghana (See Appendix for more information)
- Information about festivals, holidays, and religions of different groups; *Examples:* African—American—Kwanzaa, Israel—Passover, India—Diwali, Chinese New Year
- Books about various holidays, costumes, festivals, and customs
- Optional: Information about the family background of students in the classroom
- Encyclopedia information regarding Native American, Hispanic, and other cultures

Directions:

1. Show some pictures of the native dress of various groups who live in America. (For example, Amish, Native Americans, East Indians, African-Americans, Arabs, Sikhs, Orthodox Jews, Continental Africans, Spanish, and Chinese.) Analyze the types of materials used and calculate the amount of time it might have taken to make certain items of clothing. For example, the Sari, a dress worn by women of East India, is wrapped around the body and tucked in various places. In comparison, the pleated kilt, worn by men, the Highlanders of Scotland, is obviously stitched and therefore takes more time to make. Invite parents and friends to visit the class and talk about their native dress. Encourage them to bring samples of ethnic attire. Plan a fashion show with costumes students may have at home. Ask for parental assistance in order to ensure authenticity.

2. Share information about the customs of different cultural groups who live in America. Ask if students have pictures of family celebrations like weddings, birthdays, religious holidays, reunions, and ceremonies. Read about Kwanzaa, Hanukkah, Christmas, Chado–The Way of Tea, Black History Month, Diwali, and other cultural/religious celebrations. Invite parents and other members of the community to talk about some of the beliefs and the values of their culture regarding raising children, marriage, women who work outside the home, music, family names, and education. Invite parents and/or members of the community to demonstrate aspects of their cultural heritage for the class.

Elicit from children that people from every race and ethnic group have certain ways of living. Use information about Native Americans to illustrate how human beings work to provide basic necessities. Explain that the daily life of Native Americans (during the time before Europeans came to America) centered around their search for food. Tribes who followed buffalo herds used the meat for their main food, the skin for clothing, bedding and tepees, and the horns and bones for tools and utensils.

All Native Americans (Indians) used the things of nature for their daily living. Sometimes tribes would fight each other for territory, food, and so on. When arguments were settled, they would have Peace Ceremonies with peace pipes made of stone, bone, and the like. Some Native Americans also used stone, bone, deer antlers for arrow points and knife blades and beaver teeth for knives. Animal skins were used for clothing, homes, and beds. Bark from trees was used to make canoes, and herbs and plants were used for medicine. Many customs and practices of Native Americans were used by Early Europeans. Give each student a copy of activity 1-15A, *Costumes and Customs*. Discuss the results.

3. Make a chart of the various holidays and celebrations which occur among the families represented in the classroom. Encourage the addition of specific details and discuss how knowledge of other cultures helps each person to become a better citizen, because he/she knows more about other human beings and other ways of thinking about life. (See page 30.)

Give each child a copy of activity sheet 1-15B, *Multicultural Celebrations in America.*

LITERATURE CONNECTION: *Molly's Pilgrim* by Barbara Cohen. A story about a Jewish immigrant who makes a doll for Thanksgiving. Bantam, New York, © 1990. Illustrated.

First Came the Indians by M. J. Wheeler. The diversity among representative groups is shown through an introduction to various Native American origins and customs. Macmillan Children's Group, New York, © 1983. Illustrated.

The Way of Tea by Rand Castile. The techniques of the Japanese tea ceremony and its place of importance in Japanese life, including its art, history, aesthetics, and philosophy. (Teacher reference). Weatherhill, New York & Tokyo, © 1971. Illustrated.

Activity 1-16A WHO LIVES HERE?

Activity 1-16B WE ALL LIVE HERE!

In this activity, children will investigate the basic human need for shelter and discuss the fact that families of all cultures need homes. All students, including those who speak a foreign language, will recognize the validity of the family in all ethnic groups. Furthermore, students will assess the relationship

MULTICULTURAL CELEBRATIONS IN AMERICA

CULTURE COUNTRY	*NAME OF HOLIDAY CELEBRATION*	*ORIGIN PURPOSE*	*DATE SEASON*
1. JAPAN	CHADO—THE WAY OF TEA	FOUNDER'S DAY	NEW YEAR
2. ISRAEL JEWISH	HANUKKAH	MIRACLE OF THE RETURN OF LIGHT TO THE TEMPLE	WINTER SOLSTICE
3. AFRICAN-AMERICAN	KWANZAA	FIRST FRUITS	WINTER SOLSTICE
4. INDIA	DIWALI	HINDU RELIGION	NEW YEAR (OCTOBER)
5. AMERICA	THANKSGIVING	HARVEST FESTIVAL	NOVEMBER
6*. ________	________	________	________

*ADD INFORMATION FOR STUDENTS OF CULTURES OTHER THAN THESE

between family shelter and the concept that the Earth is the home of people of every race, culture, and ethnic group in the world. People in neighborhoods live in different houses, whereas people of the Earth live on different continents. Opportunities are provided for observing and learning about similarities, differences, and the place for the individual within these contexts. Finally, students will understand that individuals should take responsibility for preserving the Earth and its resources.

Materials Needed:

- Copy of activity sheet 1-16A, *Who Lives Here?*
- Copy of activity sheet 1-16B, *We All Live Here!*

- Pencils
- Crayons
- Globe, map of the world or a beach ball
- The word for "house" in other languages
- Encyclopedias—Pictures of various kinds of houses
- Childcraft-Volume 3-1962, Stories of Children Everywhere (31 countries)
- Clay or play dough
- Building blocks
- Newspaper and paste for papier-mâché

Directions:

1. Show pictures of different kinds of homes that people live in. Identify tents, igloos, single-family homes, apartment buildings, huts, and the like. Discuss the various climates in which these types of homes exist. Find synonyms for the word house. Ask foreign language students to share words for house in their native tongue.

Discuss homelessness and the various ways that individuals can volunteer to help. Give each child a copy of activity 1-16A, *Who Lives Here?* Ask them to share the results. ANSWER: JIA usually means HOUSE and FAMILY in the Chinese language. Depending on the meaning to be conveyed, there are other words and characters. For example, Family– "Jia ting" and House– "Fangzi".

2. Write the words "globe" and "protect" on the board. Define "globe" as a model of the Earth and ask children to tell some of the things they see on the Earth, i.e., water, plants, animals, and people. Ask students what would happen to people if all the water dried up and if there were no plants. Discuss their expected responses that people would die if there were no water to drink or plants for food. Ask what can people do to take care of and protect water, plants, animals, the air, and other things human beings need to survive. Emphasize that the meaning of "protect" is the same as "take care of."

Pass a globe around for children to hug and hold. (Substitute a large ball and pretend that it is a globe, if necessary.) Explain that this replica of the Earth represents the home and life support system of all human beings. Use a space analogy to describe how important it is for all individuals to take care of themselves by taking care of their global home, the Earth. Ask students to predict what would happen to astronauts if they did not have their space suits or space ships. Likewise, if earthbound people do not have adequate supplies of oxygen, water, food, and other resources, they will not survive. Human beings live here but cannot survive much longer if we do not take care of the planet. Have each child write about what he/she can do to help save the Earth. Share their compositions with classmates, family, and the community. Possibly, they can send their ideas to local newspapers and environmental agencies.

Give students the materials to construct a variety of houses from building blocks, clay, papier-mâché, wire, and so on. Use clay or play dough to make family members to live in the houses. Place these homes in geographically correct places on a large flat world map. Give each child a copy of activity 1-16B, *We All Live Here!*

3. Extend students' enjoyment of the multicultural characteristics of America and the world. Read several stories about children from many lands from Childcraft, Volume 3, 1982 Edition. Discuss some of the countries in which the stories take place.

LITERATURE CONNECTION: *The Way to Start a Day* by Byrd Baylor. A story of how the sun greets the people of many different cultures every day. Macmillan (Aladdin Books), New York, © 1986. Illustrated by Peter Parnell.

The Green Kingdom, World Book Encyclopedia, Childcraft, Volume 6. Also, pages 275-293 describe, through prose and poetry, human's threats to plant and animal life on Earth and some ideas for solving the problems. Extensive vocabulary adds to the value of this section. Childcraft-The How and Why Library, © 1982. Beautifully illustrated.

Activity 1-17A FOODS FROM GHANA, WEST AFRICA

Activity 1-17B A GREAT RECIPE FROM ___________

Each child's uniqueness will be highlighted during this activity when discussion centers on various cultural events. The ability to relate to people of diverse cultures will be further developed as children examine their experiences, particularly regarding foods and how they have been adopted and adapted to fit the appetites of Americans. The "Americanization" of foreign foods provides a common base upon which to build positive relationships among people of different backgrounds. The amount of adaptations of the original foods can only be limited by the available spices, ingredients, and the creativity of the cook. Individuals from various cultures can prepare basic foods creatively. The observations of preparation and consumption of "new" foods can be a lot of fun. For example, what could someone from East India add to the basic pizza recipe to make it an "East Indian Pizza"? Give students from various cultures opportunities to create "new" kinds of pizza. Encourage individual students to evaluate the special things about foods and food preparation from their native lands.

Materials Needed:

- Copy of activity sheet 1-17A, *Foods from Ghana, West Africa*
- Copy of activity sheet 1-17B, *A Great Recipe from* ____________
- Recipe books from different countries
- Computers (optional)
- Pencils
- Crayons
- Pictures of different ethnic foods (use magazines and/or cookbooks)

Directions:

1. Discuss the various cultural groups represented in the class and see if anyone is from the country of Italy. Hold up a picture of pizza. Ask each child to tell what kind of pizza, if any, he/she likes. Explain that the origin of pizza, a food enjoyed by many Americans, is the country of Italy. Explain that many other popular foods are from other nations; hot dogs originated in Germany, egg rolls in China, chili in Mexico, and so on.

2. Families from Ghana, a country in West Africa, have contributed foods which many Americans eat. One of these is a dish called Joliof. The ingredients are: beef, chicken, onions, peppers, carrots, rice, tomatoes, and spices. Explain that for all cultures, it is how the food is prepared and the types of spices used which give dishes their ethnicity. For example, the people of Ghana eat yams (similar to sweet potatoes), plantains (similar to bananas), fish, and beef, among many other familiar foods. But, when yams and plantains are pounded together they form a dough which the people of Ghana call "fu fu." In many Hispanic families plantains are often fried and taste much like sweet potatoes. Explain that foods are often named for an activity. For example, a West African dish called "PALAVER SAUCE" is based on the activity of talking. The word "palaver" means a conference, especially with African tribes. It is from the Portuguese word "palavra" and also means talking or chattering. Ask the students how this recipe might have gotten its name and why they think it was called this. Give each child a copy of activity sheet 1-17A, *Foods from Ghana, West Africa*. Encourage students from Ghana or other countries and cultures to demonstrate and/or describe food preparation techniques. Have students compare and contrast their experiences.

3. Create an atmosphere where curiosity, respect, and wonder are valued, as children discover the special qualities of their ethnicity while still recognizing commonalities regarding food as a basic human need. Plan and develop a cooperative project for a multicultural recipe book. If computers are available, have the students process the recipes and duplicate them for an in-school publication. Each student will contribute at least one recipe. They can use multiethnic cookbooks

and/or ask parents and friends for recipes. Give each student activity 1-17B, *A Great Recipe from* _______________ (country). Compile results and plan for a distribution within the school. *NOTE*: In homogeneous settings this activity can be adapted to fit variations in foods from different areas of the country, family traditions, and the like.

> LITERATURE CONNECTION: *Corn Is Maize: The Gift of the Indians* by Aliki. A description of how corn was found by Native Americans thousands of years ago and how it is grown and used today. A Let's Read and Find Out Science Book. Harper Collins, New York, © 1976. Diagrams & Illustrations.

Activity 1-18A MY GIFT TO YOU

Activity 1-18B AN OPEN LETTER FROM ME TO YOU

Developing higher levels of self-esteem is closely connected to the ability to show appreciation to others. In this activity, students will have an opportunity to give a gift, a certificate, to someone who means a lot to them. A natural outgrowth of "giving" is that of enjoyment and a sense of personal satisfaction in making someone else happy. The human responses of joy in "giving" and "receiving" should further bond the diverse groups represented in the class. Moreover, in racially and ethnically homogeneous settings, diversity in family background, goals, experiences, and so on, can play a major role in teaching children to appreciate their differences.

Materials Needed:

- Copy of activity sheet 1-18A, *My Gift to You*
- Copy of activity sheet 1-18B, *An Open Letter from Me to You*
- Markers
- Names of special people to receive gifts (suggestions of recipients for students)
- Flowers
- 25-30 small trinkets for children to wrap and/or exchange—place in a box
- Construction paper
- Scissors, paste
- Crayons

Directions:

1. Have children choose a trinket from the box to present as a gift to a classmate. Have students exchange trinkets with each other. Define the word "appreciation" and ask the children to use it in telling how they feel about the gift they received. Also, ask children to express how it makes them feel inside to say "thank you" to someone. The ability to show appreciation builds self-esteem for both the giver and the receiver.

2. Describe a variety of free gifts which make others happy such as: handshakes, smiles, notes, drawings, songs, a box decorated with foil, comics, a pretty stone, seashell, original poems, or stories. Give children the opportunity to shake hands. Ask them to offer friendship in the form of at least five smiles each day. Give each child paper to make a special card, a flower, a puzzle, a maze, or a valentine for someone to whom they want to show appreciation. Ask children to tell what they think the word APPRECIATION means. When they understand that it means to be grateful or thankful, ask how they can show these feelings of gratitude. Explain that the word PRESENT means "to give" (verb). Some students will see the example of homographs (present—to give, and present—a gift [noun]).

Tell children that it makes others feel good to receive gifts and/or awards of appreciation and thanks. Have each child identify someone in his/her family or community to whom he/she wants to show appreciation. Give students activity 1-18A, *My Gift to You.* Suggest parents, nurse, custodian, secretary, teacher aides, bus drivers, principals, peers, or librarians as recipients. Make sure that each child decorates, signs, dates, and writes the reason for his/her appreciation on the Gift Certificate of Honor. (Some reasons might be, for example ... The school secretary—for making sure that I had lunch on the day I forgot my lunch money...The school bus driver—for finding my new tennis shoes on the bus and returning them to me...The school crossing guard—for stopping the cars when I needed to cross the busy streets...The custodian—for keeping the school warm and clean.)

3. Ask children to describe how it feels when someone they love goes away on a trip. If they express feelings of loneliness, have them compare this to the joy of that person's homecoming. Discuss the types of welcome that family and friends can give to a returning loved one. An unusual gift might be a public or open "letter" of welcome written on cards and placed on trees on the pathway home. Give students activity sheet 1-18B, *An Open Letter from Me to You.* (The unscrambled message reads: WELCOME BACK I'M GLAD TO HAVE YOU HOME—8 WORDS.)

Have them think of other unusual gifts which would bring joy to both the giver and the recipient. Define this as "Mutual" joy. Extend the impact of this activity by having students keep a running list of NICE people and reasons for honoring them. Have them make plans to give free gifts to different people, especially smiles, as often as possible.

LITERATURE CONNECTION: *What Mary Jo Shared* by Janice Udry. A story of a girl, her father and a special gift. A. Whitman & Co., Morton Grove, Illinois, © 1966. Illustrated by Eleanor Mill.

Activity 1-19A WHERE ARE YOU IN YOUR NEIGHBORHOOD?

Activity 1-19B WHO ARE YOU IN YOUR SCHOOL?

As children work on this activity, they will develop a deeper awareness of their own personal talents and abilities. Efforts should be made to build upon prior knowledge and experiences in the family, school, and community so that students can reflect on their relationships with others, as they try to become the best possible persons that they can be. Upon completing this activity, students should know more about their abilities and potential and, as a result, they should be able to function better in a multicultural environment.

Materials Needed:

- Copy of activity sheet 1-19A, *Where Are You in Your Neighborhood?*
- Copy of activity sheet 1-19B, *Who Are You in Your School?*
- Crayons or markers
- Pictures of a community and various kinds of people and activities
- Paints
- Tape
- Drawing paper
- Magazines, books, newspapers, or maps (various kinds of resource materials)
- Composition books/notebook paper
- Pencils/pen/markers
- Identification information (passports, driver's licenses, social security numbers, report cards, and so on)

Directions:

1. Show pictures of a community with multicultural groups of people involved in different kinds of activities. Ask children to notice the varieties of buildings, activities, and people. Ask each child to describe what he/she thinks goes on in parks, restaurants, libraries, and other neighborhood establishments. For example, people go to parks to play, have picnics, and so on. Also, ask what

languages they think the people would speak in these places. Elicit from students that they are members of the community. On the chalkboard make a list, suggested by the children, of some of the places which can be found in the neighborhood. For example, supermarket, laundromat, telephone company, post office, music store, bank, school, courtroom, hospital, television studio, playground, and the like. Give each child a copy of activity 1-19A, *Where Are You in Your Neighborhood?* Allow students opportunities to describe their pictures. Place them on display and/or have students take them home to share.

2. Explain the fact that schools are responsible for educating America's future citizens no matter what their racial or ethnic origin. Have each child identify things he/she likes about school. Also help them to see the relationship between gaining knowledge and making contributions to society when they get older. Define *literacy* and *illiteracy*. List some of the skills which people have to have in order for them to function independently in society: READING, MATH, WRITING, MAP READING, HEALTH, SPEAKING, and LISTENING skills. Elicit from children the fact that when individuals have these skills, they are happier and they can WORK, SHOP, TRAVEL, VOTE, and COMMUNICATE with many different people.

3. Extend this activity by giving students an opportunity to explore their community. Plan walks through the neighborhood and/or field trips to the post office, bank, supermarkets, real estate office, train and/or bus station. Encourage each child to think of what job he/she would like to do as an adult. Have each student write a "Thank You" note to the people in the places visited.

4. Discuss the importance of individual identification in a society of many people. Elicit from students the significance of knowing their names, addresses, telephone numbers, and social security numbers. Ask each child if he/she plans to drive a car. Explain the need for a driver's license. Ask if anyone plans to travel, or has traveled overseas. Have someone define the word "passport" and why it is needed for foreign travel. Show students school attendance records and report cards. Each student should discern that people need identification. Owning various forms of identification gives each child a place in school and in society; this contributes to the development of self-confidence. Bilingual students may wish to have both an English language ID and a foreign language ID. Give each child a copy of activity 1-19B, *Who Are You in Your School?* Make holders (wallets) for ID cards from cardboard or construction paper.

LITERATURE CONNECTION: *Aekyung's Dream* written and illustrated by Min Paek. Finding it difficult to learn English and adjust to school after being in America for six months, a Korean girl is unhappy until she finds a solution to her problem. Children's Book Press (Talman), San Francisco, © 1988.

Activity 1-20 WE HELPED BUILD AMERICA AND THE WORLD

Children will observe the self-sufficiency and uniqueness of disabled or physically challenged people in the larger society, the workplace and in the school. They will also investigate some of the contemporary and historical contributions of the disabled and note that many of them operate, as American citizens, from positions of strength. For example, some are politicians, others are experts in business, science, music, sports, and medicine. Students who are physically challenged will experience higher levels of acceptance and self-esteem. In addition, these students will exert greater effort as they emulate their predecessors and participate in activities which include them as totally equal members of a multicultural society. All students, disabled and able-bodied, can identify with these contributors.

Materials Needed:

- Copy of activity sheet 1-20, *We Helped Build America and the World*
- World Book Encyclopedia information about Franklin Roosevelt (historical)
- List of contributors who happen to be disabled (contemporary)
- Pictures of disabled people in action (Special Olympics)
- Pencils
- Crayons or markers
- Short biographies on contributors who are not handicapped (See the Appendix)

Directions:

1. Ask children if they have ever seen a disabled person who needs a wheelchair, a seeing-eye dog, a cane, crutches, or a specially equipped van. Some children and/or their family members might use some of these things. Discuss the fact that the loss of sight, hearing, speech, or limbs does not make that person less intelligent. Those who are disabled are as capable and can often do the same kind of work as able-bodied people. Ask students to name various types of jobs they imagine that physically challenged people may perform. Place this or a similar list on the chalkboard or on paper (note that in each case these are the same types of jobs that able-bodied people have).

Disabled citizens can: (Depending on the disability)

• talk on the phone • cook • drive cars/vans • sing • type • use computers • plant gardens • work in a supermarket • be a senator • be the President of the United States • make art • be an entertainer • rescue someone in trouble

• other ______________________ • other ______________________

2. Read about the Special Olympics and organize information about historical and contemporary figures, including a president, who were or are disabled. Explain that multiethnic groups can serve various functions in a community, if given the opportunity. Emphasize that it does not matter if a singer or a piano player is blind, or if a person who is a bank employee is in a wheelchair. Discuss the fact that one U.S. president, Franklin Roosevelt, was disabled (in a wheelchair) and continued to perform his job well. Ask students to think of many areas of services provided by the disabled. Give each child a copy of activity 1-20, *We Helped Build America and the World.* See Appendix for short biographies on each contributor.

LITERATURE CONNECTION: *Barbara Jordan: The Great Lady from Texas* by Naurice Roberts. A biography of the first black woman from the South to be elected to Congress. Although Barbara Jordan is confined to a wheelchair, she continues to serve her country. Children's Press, Chicago, Illinois, © 1984. Illustrated with photographs.

Activity 1-21A MAKING CHOICES FOR MY LIFE

Activity 1-21B MAKING CHOICES AT HOME

Activity 1-21C MAKING CHOICES AT SCHOOL

Activity 1-21D MAKING CHOICES IN THE COMMUNITY

This section provides children with a sense of who they are in their social roles in environments where they need to make individual decisions about their own lives. Also, the fact that these decision-making abilities transcend race, culture, and ethnicity will emerge as students discuss the effects of personal choices. Each child will develop a strategy for making choices which are essential and beneficial for survival and for mental and physical health. In this section, children will be exposed to several scenarios which present opportunities to choose positive, rather than negative courses of action. Take the necessary time to go through each scenario so that the children can internalize and benefit from the concepts.

Challenging vocabulary should be defined for students prior to giving them the worksheets. Each child's view of his/her role in a multicultural society will develop as he/she discusses human NEEDS and WANTS, RIGHT and WRONG, and the consequences and benefits of these choices in the settings of home, school, and community. As a result of participating in these exercises, each child's critical thinking, reasoning, and decision-making skills will develop.

Materials Needed:

- Copy of activity sheet 1-21A, *Making Choices for My Life*
- Copy of activity sheet 1-21B, *Making Choices at Home*
- Copy of activity sheet 1-21C, *Making Choices at School*
- Copy of activity sheet 1-21D, *Making Choices in the Community*
- Pictures of people of many races and ethnic backgrounds involved in many different kinds of activities, i.e., working, playing, singing, reading, watching television, and walking
- Charts with items—NEEDS and WANTS, RIGHT and WRONG
- List of BENEFITS and CONSEQUENCES which can result from positive and/or negative choices
- Scenarios of conflicts which might arise in different environments
- Pencils/markers/pens
- Crayons
- Drawing paper
- Encyclopedias, books, and maps

Directions:

1. Present the idea of individual decision making. Ask children to recall some of the things which members of their family and people in their neighborhoods do everyday. Make a comparison between things which must be done and those things which are done only because a person wants to do them. Discuss the importance of individuals making choices. Have them share their favorite television programs. Ask if they NEED to watch these shows or if they WANT to watch them. Discuss the word "survival" and determine that NEEDS have to do with the ability of people to continue to live. Display the chart of NEEDS and WANTS and ask the students to contribute items for each section such as ice cream under WANTS and shoes under NEEDS.

2. Present the idea of making personal choices which influence the quality of life. For example: The consequences of unwise choices could ruin life while wise choices should make life better. The consequences of lying could be punishment or failure.

The consequences of stealing could be jail, loss of independence, and a loss of respect. And the consequences of taking drugs would be ruined physical and mental health. Students will recognize the need to make wise choices in order to avoid trouble. In making individual choices that are wise, children will build their self-concepts and gain other specific benefits.

SCENARIO #1—Jan finds a pair of pretty glasses. She likes them and she can see out of them. They are not her glasses and she does not

NEED them. What should Jan do? What would the consequences and/or benefits be for her choices?

Discuss the choices of the students in light of NEEDS and WANTS and RIGHT and WRONG. Ask which choices make them feel better. With the children make up other scenarios which give students opportunities to consider individual decisions and help them to develop decision-making and good citizenship skills. Other possible topics: Stealing, Drugs, Alcohol, Smoking, Choosing Friends, Lying, Exercise, Chores, Homework, Television Time, or Secrets. Give each child a copy of activity 1-21A, *Making Choices for My Life.* Share the results.

LITERATURE CONNECTION: *Why Mosquitoes Buzz in People's Ears, a West African Tale* by Verna Aardema. A story of how the sun doesn't shine because a mosquito doesn't tell the truth. Dial Books/ Young, New York, © 1978. Illustrated.

3. Present the idea of decision making at home. Define the following words: WORK, PLAY, WORSHIP, and CELEBRATION. Discuss the pictures of families of many ethnic and racial backgrounds involved in these activities. Ask students to describe some of their favorite family experiences such as, going on vacations, watching parades, walking in the forest, eating meals, playing board or video games, doing chores, playing football.

Have each student assess his/her role within the home during family gatherings and tell what choices he/she makes. For example, setting the table, packing personal belongings, or watching a younger brother or sister.

SCENARIO #2—You have not done your chores and your friends want you to go to the mall later. Also, your favorite television program is coming on in five minutes. What choices will you make and how will this help your family?

Have the children think of and describe several other ways that they can increase positive contributions to their families. Talk about the mutual benefits of good relationships in the family. Ask children to identify things which might have negative effects, such as disobedience, selfishness, or laziness. Discuss how family members of all races, cultures and religions can work together to overcome these negatives. Elicit from children how each individual family member has certain things which he/she NEEDS and other things which he/she WANTS. Discuss the difference between what is needed for human survival and what is not necessary to live. Give students activity 1-21B, *Making Choices at Home.* Compare results.

LITERATURE CONNECTION: *A Chair for My Mother* by Vera B. Williams. Rosa, her mother, and grandmother move after their house burns down and begin saving for a chair. Greenwillow, New York, © 1982. Illustrated.

4. Present the idea of making choices at school. Ask students to demonstrate some of the knowledge they have already gained during their short school career. They might read a passage from a reader, recite poetry or multiplication tables, or report on a hobby or special interest project. Children can apply concepts they have learned to new situations (working problems on the chalkboard or asking peers questions about many subjects). Explain that people have to want to learn and be willing to work hard to get an education. Help students to make connections between getting an education, finding work later in life, and feeling good about oneself.

SCENARIO #3—Larry was the coolest boy in school. He never carried books and always had the latest news to tell his friends. He could read but he didn't like to, especially when his favorite teams were on television. Larry's report card grades were not too good, even though his teachers and his parents knew that he was a very smart young man. What should Larry do? What choices does he have? What would you do if you were Larry?

Encourage students to make up other scenarios about the choices students have to make in school. For example, choosing friends, getting into fights, working to earn good grades, joining athletic or social clubs, honoring school staff, or planning a multicultural program. Identify the types of decisions students should make in order to become successful in their efforts to get an education. Elicit from students the definition of the word "education" as meaning "to know." Discuss the meanings of SUCCESSFUL and UNSUCCESSFUL. Help each child to understand that he/she is capable of success in school. List some of the things that successful students do on the chalkboard: ASK QUESTIONS, DO HOMEWORK, PAY ATTENTION, STUDY, MAKE EXCELLENT GRADES, PUT FORTH EFFORT, ASK FOR HELP, etc. Encourage students to eliminate negative choices, i.e., no homework, poor grades, and so on. Give each child a copy of activity sheet 1-21C, *Making Choices at School.*

5. Present the idea of making decisions in communities. Many neighborhoods have billboards advertising beer and other alcoholic beverages. Some children have seen drug dealers and people of various racial and cultural origins who are homeless and living on the streets, in bus terminals or in cars. Some children know about these things from having lived them or having seen television programs that vividly describe them. Explain that while it is not always the fault of people who suffer, some of these sad circumstances are the result of unwise, unhealthy choices that people have made. Human beings of all races and cultures need to have

compassion for everyone who is homeless, unemployed, or hungry. Within a community there are people who need attention and there are not always enough volunteers to help the homeless, the elderly, the sick, and the disabled. Explain that many young people can be volunteers in their communities, with adult supervision, of course (at the children's library, a soup kitchen, cleaning up litter, or organizing items for recycling).

LITERATURE CONNECTION: *Mr. Sugar Comes to Town: La Vista del Senor Azucar,* adapted by Harriet Rohmer and Gomez Cruz. In pictures and words, young children are cautioned about the dangers of drug abuse. Children's Book Press, Emeryville, California, © 1989. Illustrated by Enrique Chagoya.

6. *SCENARIO #4*—My Neighborhood Could Be Better (To be developed by students)

Make up other scenarios to help the students with decision making in the neighborhood. If there is a dirty vacant lot, work with others to clean it. If the hallways in an apartment building are dirty, clean them. Discuss recycling, gardening, and volunteering as other examples of positive things which can happen when individuals make wise choices. Ask how volunteering can help people to feel good about themselves. Place the following additional suggestions on the chalkboard: VOLUNTEERING IN THE COMMUNITY (Help the homeless, sick, elderly, severely disabled, youth, and so on.) Caution students not to try to volunteer unless they have adult supervision (parents, teachers, or scout leaders).

Discuss other things that individuals can do to make sure that more positive things occur in their community, such as starting neighborhood patrols, contributing to charitable institutions, and producing multicultural festivals, or block parties. Discuss things that families, neighbors, and friends do at various times, such as playing, working, going shopping or to the library, gardening, recycling, volunteering to help others, worshipping, painting, exercising, singing, talking, watching television, driving, or going to the bank. Ask each child to make a decision regarding his/her role. List all responses to the question, "What role will you fill in your community?" Give each child a copy of activity 1-21D, *Making Choices in the Community*. Evaluate the results and compliment individual decision making.

LITERATURE CONNECTION: *Pet Show,* written and illustrated by Ezra Jack Keats. A little boy and all of his friends win prizes at the neighborhood pet show. Macmillan Children's Group, © 1987.

My Grandmother's Stories by Adele Geros. A collection of Jewish folktales. Alfred Knopf, New York, © 1990. Illustrated by Jael Jordon.

Activity 1-22A MY BEST TIMES

Activity 1-22B MY STORY

Activity 1-22C MY SPECIAL POEM

In this activity, children will be able to name several high points in their lives and experience increased levels of self-esteem as a result of contemplating these highlights. Students will collect data about themselves from parents, older siblings, relatives and family friends, as a way of getting a more complete picture of what and who they are. After observing himself/herself more closely, each child can make adjustments in behavior, decision making, and goal setting. The sharing of good things about themselves can be done verbally in small groups and by writing and illustrating compositions or stories. During this process, students will see that their lives are beautiful narratives which are unfolding as they grow physically and mentally. Finally, students will see that their self-esteem is closely related to their ability to respect others, as they use synonyms to write "good words" poems about themselves, friends, and family members.

Materials:

- Copy of activity sheet 1-22A, *My Best Times*
- Copy of activity sheet 1-22B, *My Story*
- Copy of activity sheet 1-22C, *My Special Poem*
- Biographies of contributors (historical and contemporary)
- Some picture books
- Story with a child as the main character
- Crayons
- Chart paper
- Drawing paper
- Pencils/markers
- Baby pictures and/or school pictures of each child
- Thesaurus

Directions:

1. Almost all children have experienced fun at birthday parties, at a children's museum, looking at family heirlooms, listening to music, talking to a friend, opening or giving a gift, singing a song, dancing, visiting relatives, playing with a pet, toy, or stuffed animal, or going on vacation. Have each child tell about his/her favorite times and to describe his/her feelings when involved in any of these nice experiences. Encourage students to give details such as parts of a conversation, listing people who were there, or some of the objects they have to help them recall the fun. Have them describe a friend, pictures, a scrapbook, a souvenir, a

diary/journal, or any other person or item involved in this great experience. Give each child a copy of activity 1-22A, *My Best Times*. Share the results.

2. Read a story that has a child as a main character. Discuss the students' favorite parts and in some portions substitute some of the children's names in place of the main character. Then have them compose a "class story" using positive information about each other. Many children may want to add pictures. Explain that every individual has his/her own story to tell and this is called an "autobiography." Define the word *interview*. Set up a mock interview session to give each child an opportunity to act out or practice questioning someone and recording/remembering the responses. Post basic questions on chart paper. Students can question a parent or relative to gain information about their early years. They can use this to help them to write an autobiography.

3. Allow time for students to exchange ideas for cooperative work in writing autobiographies. For example, have them choose partners and ask each other questions, such as Name, Address, Birthdate, Birthplace, Native Language, Number of Siblings, Favorite Things (words, food, color, movie, place, book, song, game), Best Friend, or Hero. Discuss some of the elements of the autobiography, including memories, experiences, and accomplishments. Help students to see how we got the word "autobiography" in the English language. Explain the parts of the word, AUTO—means "self" in Greek, BIO—means "life" in Greek, and GRAPH(y)—comes from the Latin word "graphic" and means "to write." Discuss how people from different cultures borrow words and elicit from children the fact that languages change and grow, as people use them to communicate their ideas, feelings, and concerns. Give children copies of activity 1-22B, *My Story*, to complete. Encourage them to illustrate portions of their stories on drawing paper. Provide opportunities for group reporting. Extend the results of the experiences of personal narratives or autobiographies by "publishing" them.

> **LITERATURE CONNECTION**: *Amazing Grace* by Mary Hoffman. Grace, an avid reader, becomes anything and anyone she wants to, by using her imagination, props, and so on. Over the protests of her classmates, she becomes Peter Pan, not because she is black and a girl, but because she is the best one for the role. Dial Books for Young Readers, New York, © 1991. Illustrated by Caroline Binch.

4. Give students opportunities to further develop higher levels of self-esteem. Have them make up a special name poem using only good words. Make sure that these words can be understood by others. You may use a thesaurus with the students to help them each find "good words" to identify themselves. Also, explain the term *synonym*. Give each student a copy of activity 1-22C, *My Special Poem*. Creatively display the poems by printing them on greeting cards, place mats, stationery, and so on. Have children formulate words poems for friends, family,

school staff, pastors, and give these as gifts, thus building self-esteem since this has much to do with one's ability to appreciate and respect others.

LITERATURE CONNECTION: *Honey I Love and Other Love Poems* by Eloise Greenfield. A collection of poems reflecting childhood experiences. Harper/Crowell, © 1978. Illustrated by Leo and Diane Dillon.

Activity 1-23A MY ROOTS

Activity 1-23B FAMILIES ARE DIFFERENT

Activity 1-23C FAMILY FAVORITES

Activity 1-23D FAMILY GRIOT

Although the intent of these activities is to increase positive self-concepts, undeniably each child must also see himself/herself as a member of a group. The family is the core group of society and children are nurtured in these close-knit groups as a prelude to venturing into the larger adult world. The purpose of this activity is to help children make a strong commitment to their families and to identify the common need of a family for children with diverse backgrounds. Teacher sensitivity to the problems of students who come from difficult family situations is crucial. For example, if a child is from a single parent family, lives in a shelter, is adopted, and/or lives with a grandparent, he/she should be encouraged to appreciate the adults who care for him/her. Teacher awareness of ways to help such children feel good about themselves is important. All children should understand that families are of different racial, cultural, and ethnic backgrounds and that they are all GOOD. Concepts include encouraging the child to look at his/her family roots, to discuss favorite family activities, and to identify a person who might be an expert on family history. It is suggested that the teacher read portions of Alex Haley's book *Roots* to encourage students to appreciate their roots.

Materials Needed:

- Copy of activity sheet 1-23A, *My Roots*
- Copy of activity sheet 1-23B, *Families Are Different*
- Copy of activity sheet 1-23C, *Family Favorites*
- Copy of activity sheet 1-23D, *Family Griot*
- Pictures of different kinds of families (various races, cultures, nationalities, compositions)
- A synopsis of *Roots* (Appendix)

- A copy of the book *Roots* by Alex Haley
- A genealogy chart
- Markers, crayons, pencils, pens
- Dictionaries, encyclopedias, maps

Directions:

1. Show children a genealogy chart and explain the purpose, that of tracing the descent of a person or a family from an ancestor. Explain the fact that their grandparents and great-grandparents are their "ancestors" and that this can extend back many years in time. Elicit from children that their parents or guardians who take care of them now are immediate ancestors. (Teacher should be aware of the need to help adopted children who might not know their parents, children from single parent homes who do not know or live with both parents, children whose grandparents are their "parents," etc.) Since everyone has roots, each child should be led into positive feelings regarding his/her background. (Use the word *relative* to explain ancestor.) Give each student a copy of activity sheet 1-23A, *My Roots*. Share and display them.

LITERATURE CONNECTION: *The Land I Lost: Adventures of a Boy in Vietnam* by Quang Nhuong Huynh. Fifteen true stories of the author's childhood. Harper Children's Books, New York, © 1990.

2. Point out pictures of different kinds of families. Elicit from children the fact that human beings function best in support groups called families. Have children focus on the various family sizes, colors, and races represented in the class and in the pictures. Compare these to the types of families which are in the school, the community, and in the larger society (world).

Discuss the fact that babies and young children need older people, usually parents, to care for them. Explain how the adults who care for children are sometimes both MOTHER and FATHER, sometimes just one parent or a grandparent. Encourage all children to have pride in their family types. Give each child a copy of activity sheet 1-23B, *Families Are Different*. Discuss the results.

LITERATURE CONNECTION: *A Russian Farewell* by Leonard Everett Fisher. A Jewish family decides to leave Russia because of anti-Jewish attitudes. Four Winds Press, New York, © 1980. Illustrated.

3. Encourage children to share things that their families have in common. Also, point out the comical and/or interesting interactions as the children speak about their experiences. (Caution students not to include private matters.) It might be fun to have parents come in and participate in the sharing sessions. Some children might have relatives who are good storytellers, others might have interesting hobbies or talents. Most children can think of certain words, songs, games, events, and activities that are enjoyed by their families. (Teacher sensitivity to the

needs of students from difficult familial settings is crucial.) Give each child activity 1-23C, *Family Favorites*. Analyze the results.

> **LITERATURE CONNECTION**: *Keep the Lights Burning, Abbie* by Peter and Connie Roop. A story of a girl who helps her father during a storm. Carolrhoda Books, Minneapolis, Minnesota, © 1985. Illustrated by Peter Hanson.

4. Read a portion of Alex Haley's story *Roots* to the class. Identify the source of his knowledge about Kunta Kinte, his African ancestor. Point out that his aunt and grandmother had heard the stories from their parents and carried the history of his ancestors in their heads, it was not written down. Each generation told the story over and over to the children. Introduce and define GRIOT. The Griot was the family member who memorized and recited the story of families in the African village where Haley's ancestor was born. Ask the children if there is someone in their family who knows about the history of their ancestors up to the present day. Have them identify this person as a "Griot" and plan to compile the information. If there is no family Griot, read the details about Alex Haley's Griot. (See "A Synopsis of *Roots*" in the Appendix.) Then have each student act as the "griot" in his/her own family setting. Give each child activity 1-23D, *Family Griots*. Share the results. Invite parents to participate by sharing their own "ROOTS" and "GRIOT" experiences.

> **LITERATURE CONNECTION**: Read portions of *Roots* by Alex Haley. A man's story of his search for his African ancestors. Doubleday, New York, © 1976.
>
> *The Hundred Penny Box* by Sharon Mathis. The story of a boy's relationship with his 100-year-old great-great aunt and the lessons he learns about his family's history. Viking Children's Books, New York, © 1975. Illustrated by Leo and Diane Dillon.

Name ______________________ Date ______________________

ABOUT MYSELF

Complete the items below:

1. Hi! My name is______________________________

2. I am like other people in many ways. But there are some special things about me. I'll show you.

See my fingerprint

This is my height and weight

____

____

My language is

____

I can draw my own picture

3. I like myself because______________________________

____

____

____

____

____

Name ______________________________ **Date** ______________________________

MY SPECIAL DAY

When you were born, you made those around you very happy. Your birth gave your family one of the greatest gifts...the gift of LOVE.

Find and *color* the names of the people who were happy when you were born.*

S	A	P	F	A	T	H	E	R
I	U	N	C	L	E	P	E	X
S	N	S	Q	G	J	H	S	W
T	T	B	R	O	T	H	E	R
E	F	Y	C	O	U	S	I	N
R	P	A	M	R	N	A	N	A
C	F	R	I	E	N	D	S	C
T	H	E	D	O	C	T	O	R

*Hint: Look for vertical, diagonal, and horizontal names.

Name ______________________________ Date ______________________________

MY SPECIAL SOMEONE

Someone takes care of you everyday. Think of the nice things this person does for you. In the space below, draw and color a picture of yourself and this special someone.

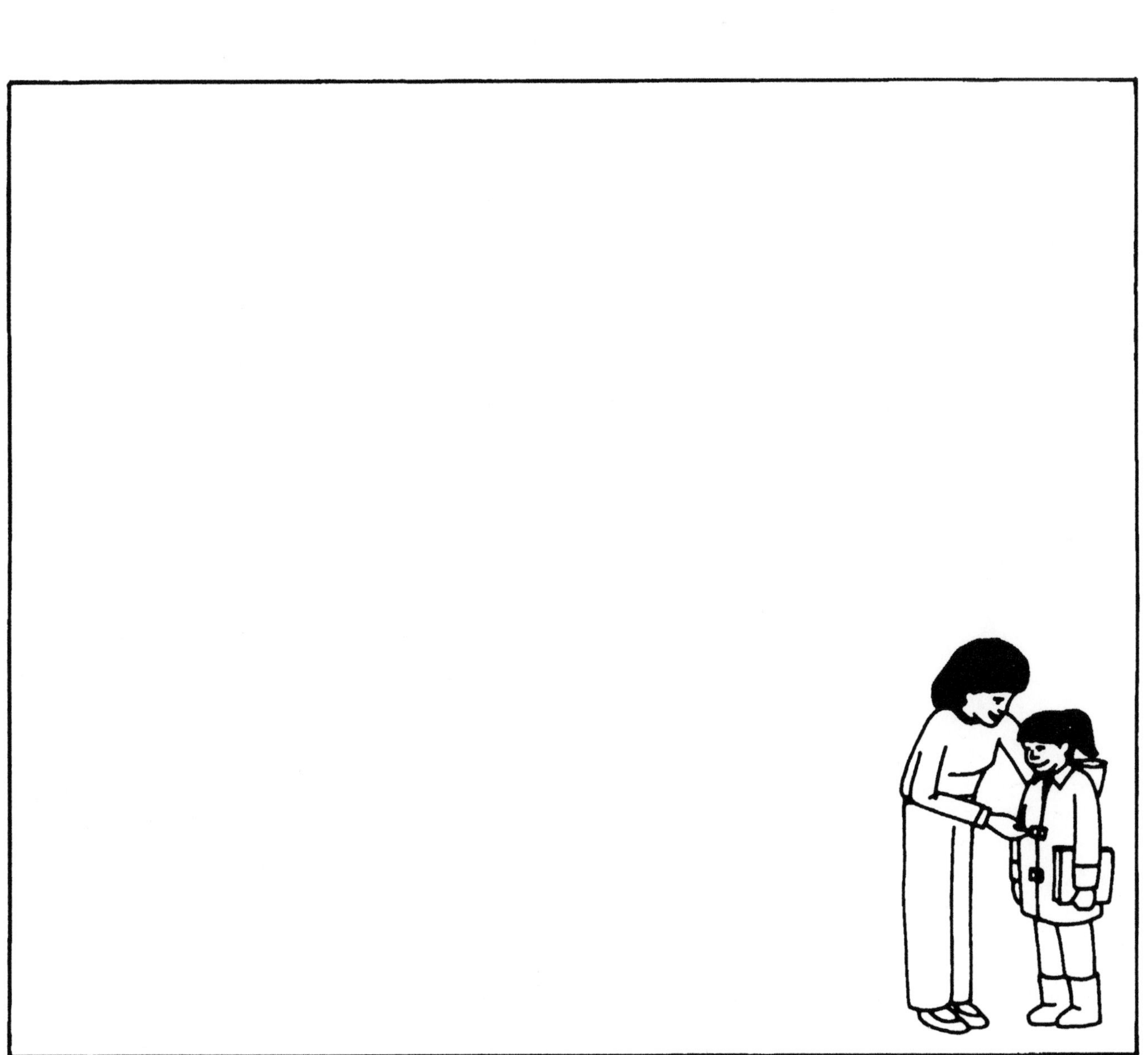

1-2B

Name ______________________ Date ______________________

MY BABY PICTURE

Paste a baby picture of yourself in the space below. Then write the correct information on the lines.

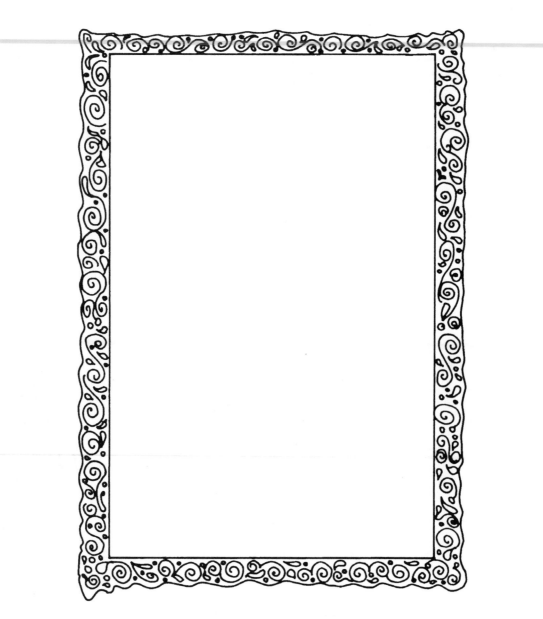

Birthdate______________________ Length______________________

Day of the week______________________ Time of Birth______________________

Weight______________________ Location______________________

Your grandmother's special name______________________

Your grandfather's special name______________________

Name ______________________________ Date ______________________________

NAME THE BABIES

Give each baby a name. Wouldn't it be nice to give one baby your name? Answer each question correctly. Circle ONE answer only.

________________ ________________ ________________ ________________
(NAME) (NAME) (NAME) (NAME)

1. Each baby will:

   a. speak English
   b. grow
   c. win the Olympics
   d. like music

2. How many fingers should each baby have on ONE hand?

   a. five
   b. two
   c. four
   d. three

3. How many babies are in the nursery?

   a. 9
   b. 2
   c. 4
   d. 7

4. Which babies are human beings?

   a. one
   b. two
   c. three
   d. all of them

5. All babies need love.

   a. true
   b. maybe
   c. no
   d. false

1-3A

Name ______________________________ Date ______________________________

MY BIRTHDAY CAKE

What is your favorite frosting? Some people like chocolate, others like vanilla. Some people like pudding or strawberry filling.

It's your birthday. Use your crayons or markers to decorate your cake with the kind of frosting and filling you like. If you want to, put candles on it. Then write your birthdate and age on the lines below the cake.

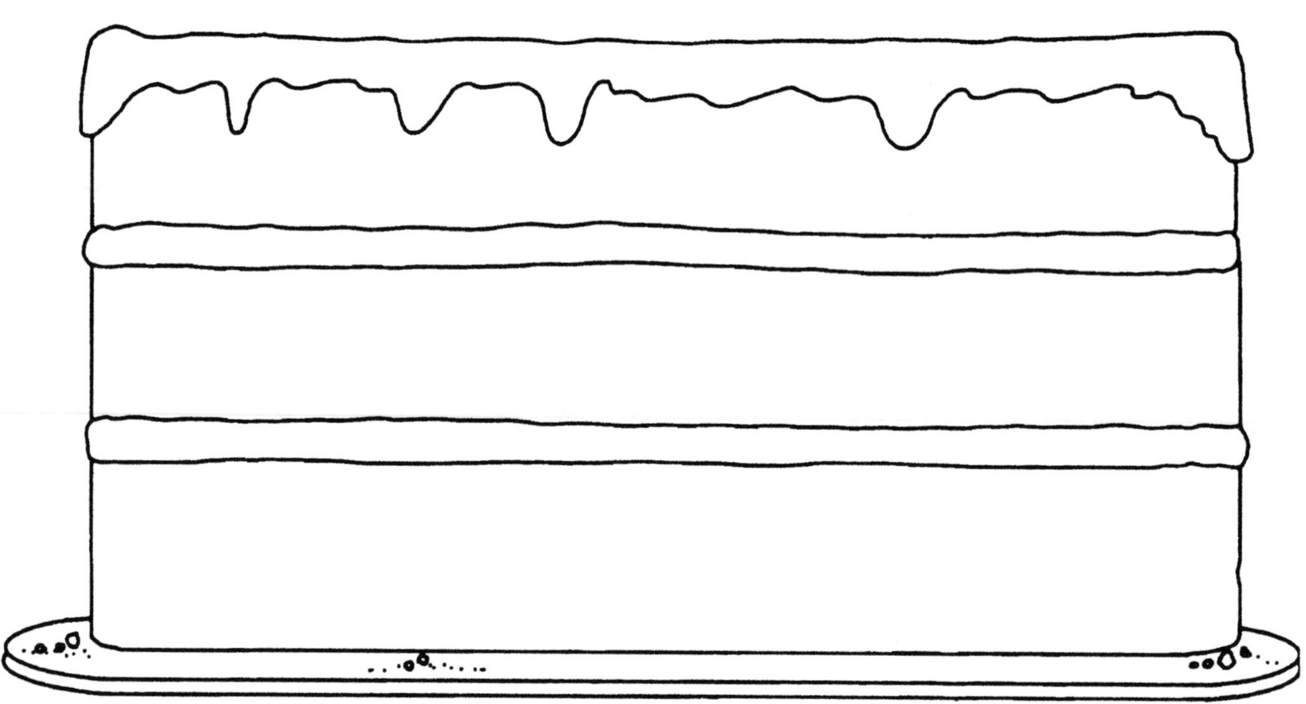

Each baby in every race of people was born on a certain day of the week during a certain month.

Month____________ Date____________ Year____________ Age____________

Name ______________________________ Date ______________________________

Directions: Write the names of classmates, family, friends, and famous people who also share the month of your birth.

CELEBRATING BIRTHDAYS WITH OTHERS

HAPPY BIRTHDAY TO YOU!

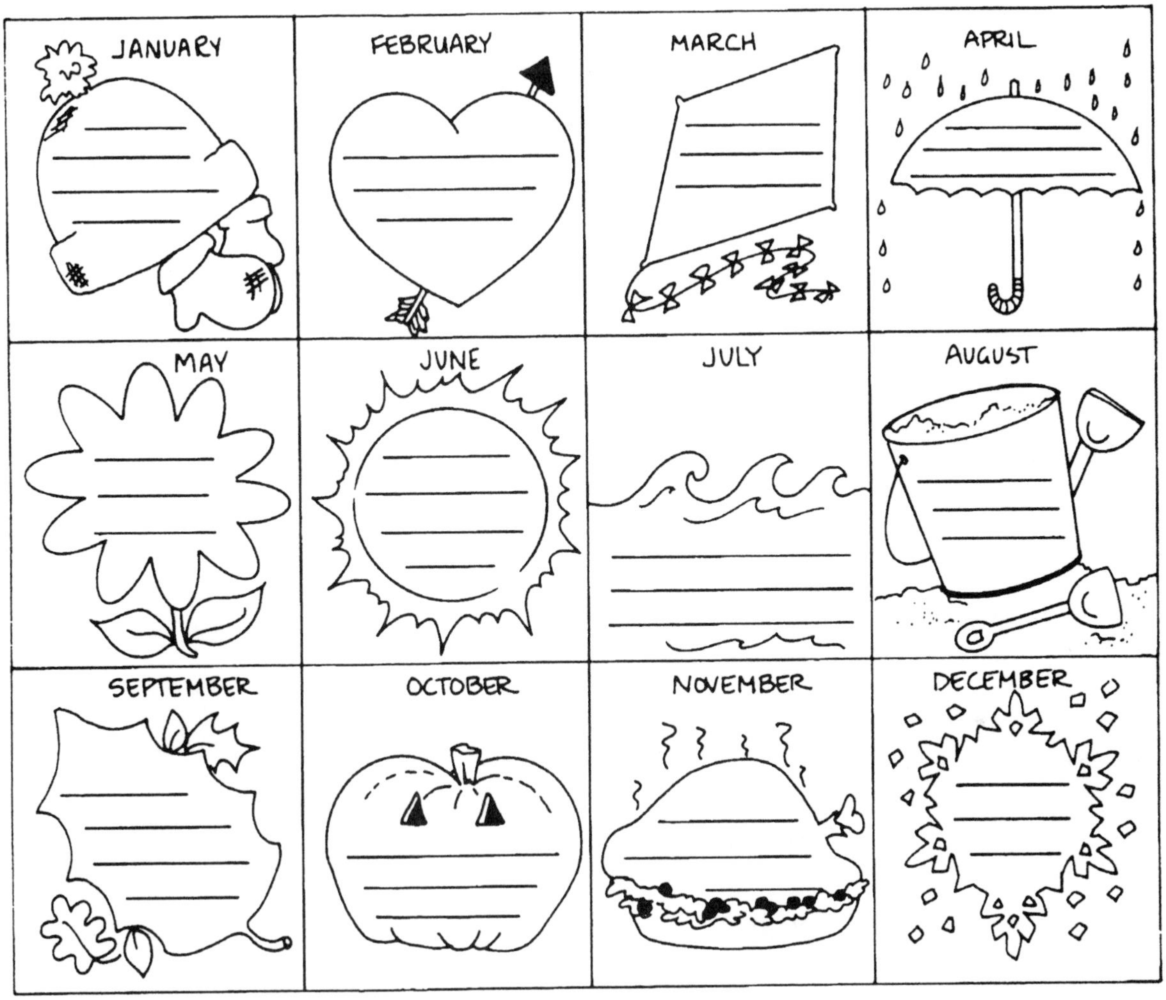

JANUARY
FEBRUARY
MARCH
APRIL
MAY
JUNE
JULY
AUGUST
SEPTEMBER
OCTOBER
NOVEMBER
DECEMBER

Bulletin board displays of birthdays in our classroom.

December
November
October
September
August
July
Herbert
Corinne
The Candles
January
February
March
April
May
June

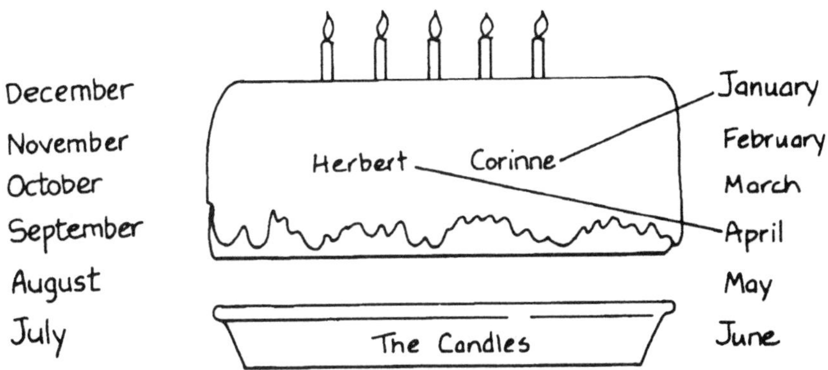

Removable candles for inserting on the cakes as each birthday is celebrated.

1-4A

Name ______________________ Date ______________________

I CAN TAKE CARE OF MYSELF

Read each item on the list. Then copy the words which show how you can take care of yourself.

NEEDS	THINGS I KNOW HOW TO DO NOW
1. Bathe myself	______________________
2. Brush my teeth	______________________
3. Comb and/or Brush my hair	______________________
4. Dress myself	______________________
5. Wash my own personal clothing	______________________
6. Clean my room	______________________
7. Feed myself	______________________
8. Exercise	______________________
9. Rest	______________________
10. Choose my own friends	______________________

Circle the word below that means that you can do things without someone else's help. *Draw a box* around the word that means that you need someone to help you.

INDEPENDENT DEPENDENT

Name ______________________________ Date ______________________________

THE HUMAN BODY IS FANTASTIC!

Identify as many parts of the human body as you can on the Word Search below. Use the list to help you find the words.

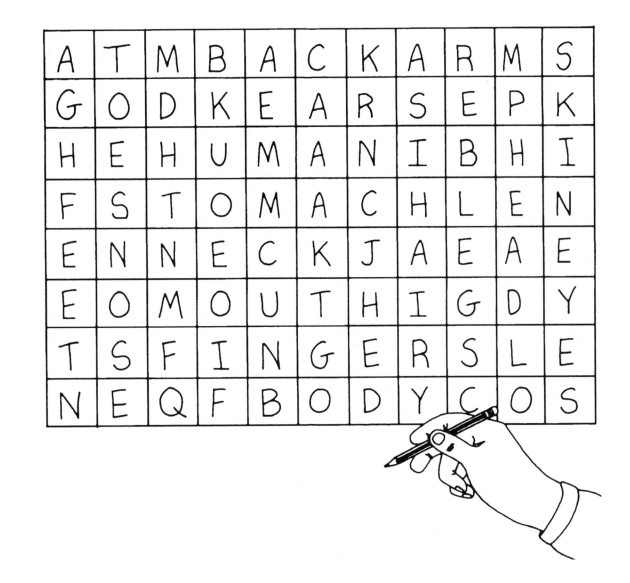

A	T	M	B	A	C	K	A	R	M	S
G	O	D	K	E	A	R	S	E	P	K
H	E	H	U	M	A	N	I	B	H	I
F	S	T	O	M	A	C	H	L	E	N
E	N	N	E	C	K	J	A	E	A	E
E	O	M	O	U	T	H	I	G	D	Y
T	S	F	I	N	G	E	R	S	L	E
N	E	Q	F	B	O	D	Y	C	O	S

HUMAN BODY WORD LIST

LEGS ARMS NECK HEAD EARS FEET SKIN TOES FINGERS

BACK STOMACH HAIR EYES NOSE MOUTH BODY HUMAN

Put a big X on the words below which name things that are bad for your body:

DRUGS FOOD SMOKING WATER ALCOHOL

Name ______________________ Date ______________________

MY FAMILY TREE

Decorate the family tree. Write the name of a family member on each leaf. Color, cut out, and paste each leaf onto a branch on the tree on the next page.

Name ______________________ Date ______________________

MY FAMILY TREE

Paste the leaves you cut out on the branches of the tree.

Name ______________________________ Date ______________________________

CAN YOU FIND THEM?

Color the triangle for each person who has helped build our country. These men and women are CONTRIBUTORS because they have helped others. Use the color RED to identify the MEN. Use the color BLUE to identify the WOMEN.

TRACE THE LETTERS BELOW. THEN READ THE SENTENCE.

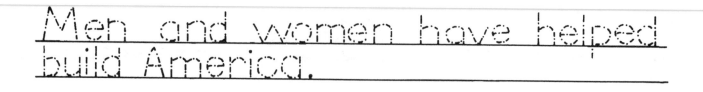

Men and women have helped build America.

Name ______________________________ Date ______________________________

HUMAN BEINGS ARE ALIKE AND DIFFERENT

People are the same in many ways. Examine the section of human skin below:

THE SKIN
All human skin has the same parts

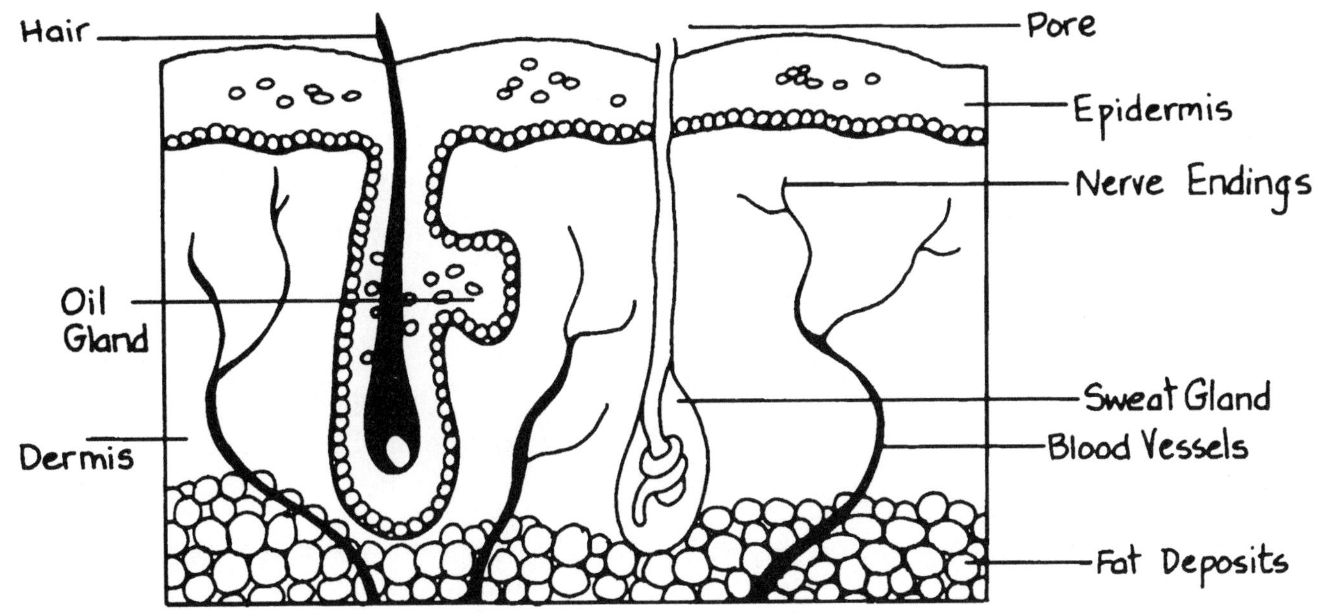

Color the word which gives human beings different skin colors.

MELANIN

Name ______________________ Date ______________________

WINNING THE RACE FOR ME

Jim is a great soccer player, even though he has no legs. He was born without legs. Read the interview and find out that Jim is not only an athlete, but he has confidence.

REPORTER: Jim, how did you manage to kick the winning goal into the net 3 seconds before the end of the game?

JIM: Well, it's like this. Our team members know this, that just because our bodies are not perfect, it doesn't mean that we can't try our best to win our games. So, we promised each other that we will play to win, to prove to ourselves that we can do it.

REPORTER: I understand that you and your team members are entering into the New York marathon race on Saturday. How do you plan to keep up with people who have real legs?

JIM: Well, these are real legs. A doctor had them made especially for me and I use them every day when I walk, ride my bike, and dance. Some of my friends are in wheelchairs, and they don't plan to lose. Neither do I.

REPORTER: Let me get this straight. You have artificial legs that you call "real." You walk, ride a bike, and dance. Now you and your friends are entering a race. What kind of people are you?

JIM: I'm glad you asked that. Maybe YOU don't think that we're real people, but we are. Don't you know that we have hearts that beat inside of us, just as you do? We have eyes, hands, arms, ears, and brains to think. We eat, cry, laugh, swim, read, and do lots of things that make us just like you and other people. We play basketball, soccer, and we're happy.

REPORTER: You're happy?

JIM: YES, because we are all fine. We have people who care about us. I have family, friends, and others to help me, when I need it. But for all who don't think I can run in the marathon, I'll be running on Saturday, and I'm winning this race for ME!

Do you think that Jim will win the race? Why or why not?

____

____

Name ______________________________ Date ______________________________

THE FIVE SENSES

Identify the senses that you and other human beings have by writing the correct words on each line above the pictures.

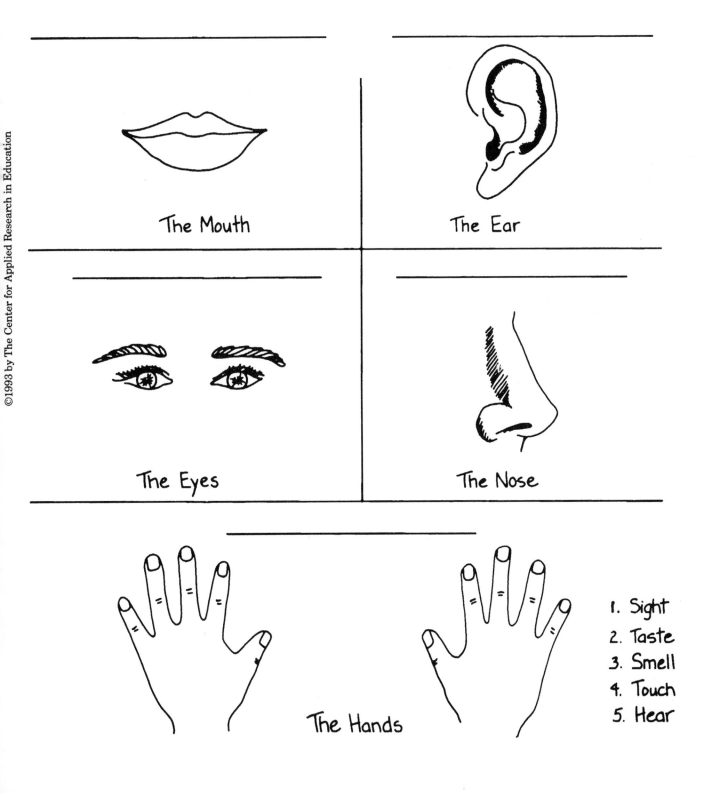

____

The Mouth

____

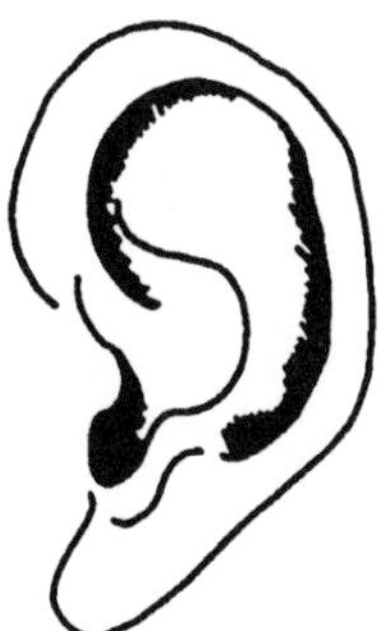

The Ear

____

The Eyes

____

The Nose

____

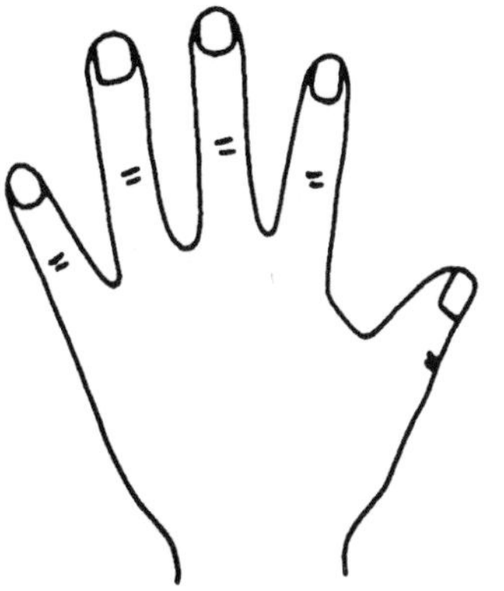

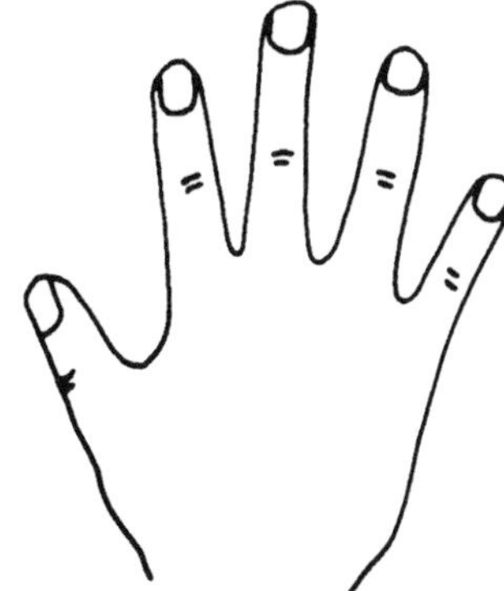

The Hands

1. Sight
2. Taste
3. Smell
4. Touch
5. Hear

1-8B

Name ______________________ Date ______________________

THAT ICE CREAM TASTES GOOD!

Do you like ice cream? What sense tells you that you're eating chocolate or vanilla ice cream? Do you know the five senses? Unscramble the words below, then color the ice cream cone vanilla, chocolate, strawberry, or whatever flavor you like best. How do you say "ICE CREAM" in another language?

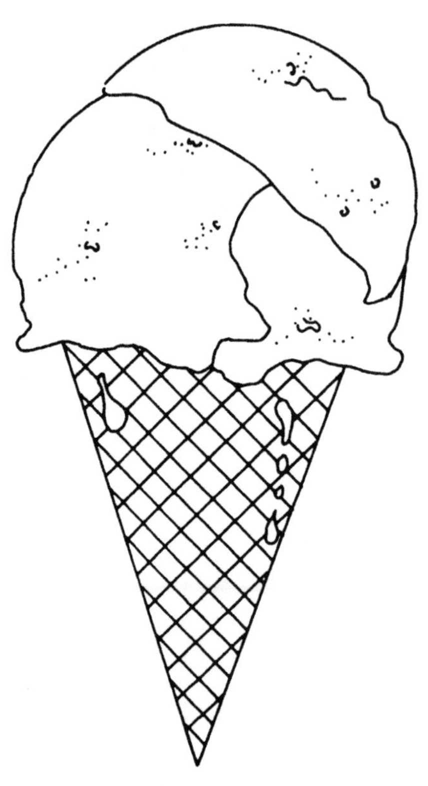

UNSCRAMBLE THE FIVE SENSES

1. LSEML______________________
2. ATSET______________________
3. THISG______________________
4. RAEH______________________
5. CHOTU______________________

AISKRIMU

(Swahili word for ice cream)

Name ________________________________ Date ________________________________

FOREIGN LANGUAGE FUN

Do you speak a foreign language? If so, teach it to someone else. Things people use and see every day can be labeled in many languages. Trace the dotted English letters for each item below. Then write the words in Spanish and German.

cup

foreign language

water

foreign language

sun

foreign language

tree

foreign language

house

foreign language

door

foreign language

Look around your classroom. Find things which you can label in YOUR language. Work with other students and write each item in as many languages as possible. (Use foreign dictionaries and the Foreign Language lists in the Appendix.)

Name ________________________________ Date ________________________________

PARTNER TALK

Learn to "talk" with your hands! Use the Manual Alphabet-Sign Language Chart on the next page to help you find the correct hand signals for the letters below. Then write the correct number on the lines above the letters for CLOCK and FLAG.

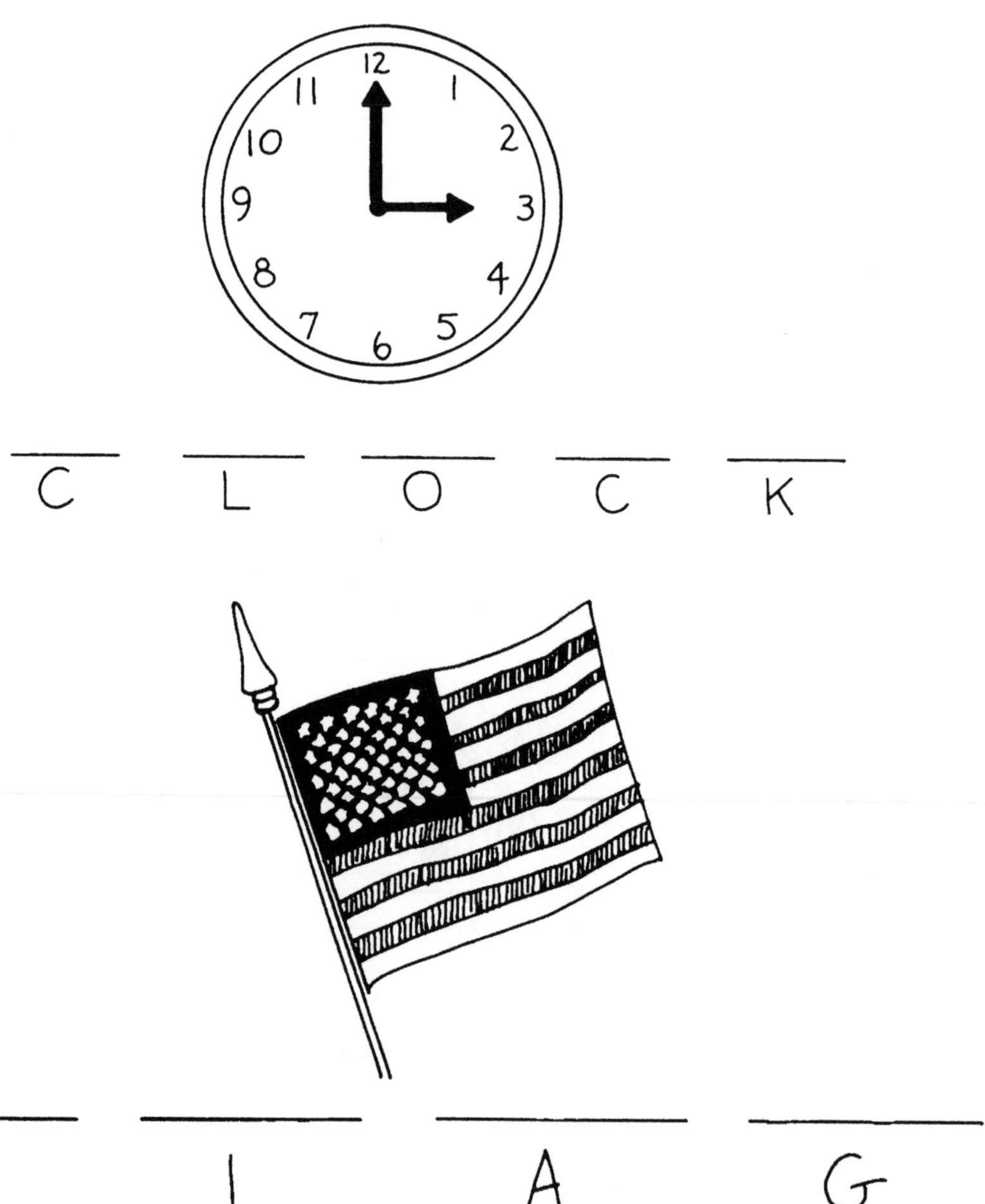

Now, on your own, use the Sign Language Chart to play the "I Spy" game with a partner. Find a number, picture, color, or object and spell it with the hand signals. Say, "I see (a) ____ ____ ____ ____ ." When your partner guesses correctly, it's his/her turn.

THE MANUAL ALPHABET—SIGN LANGUAGE

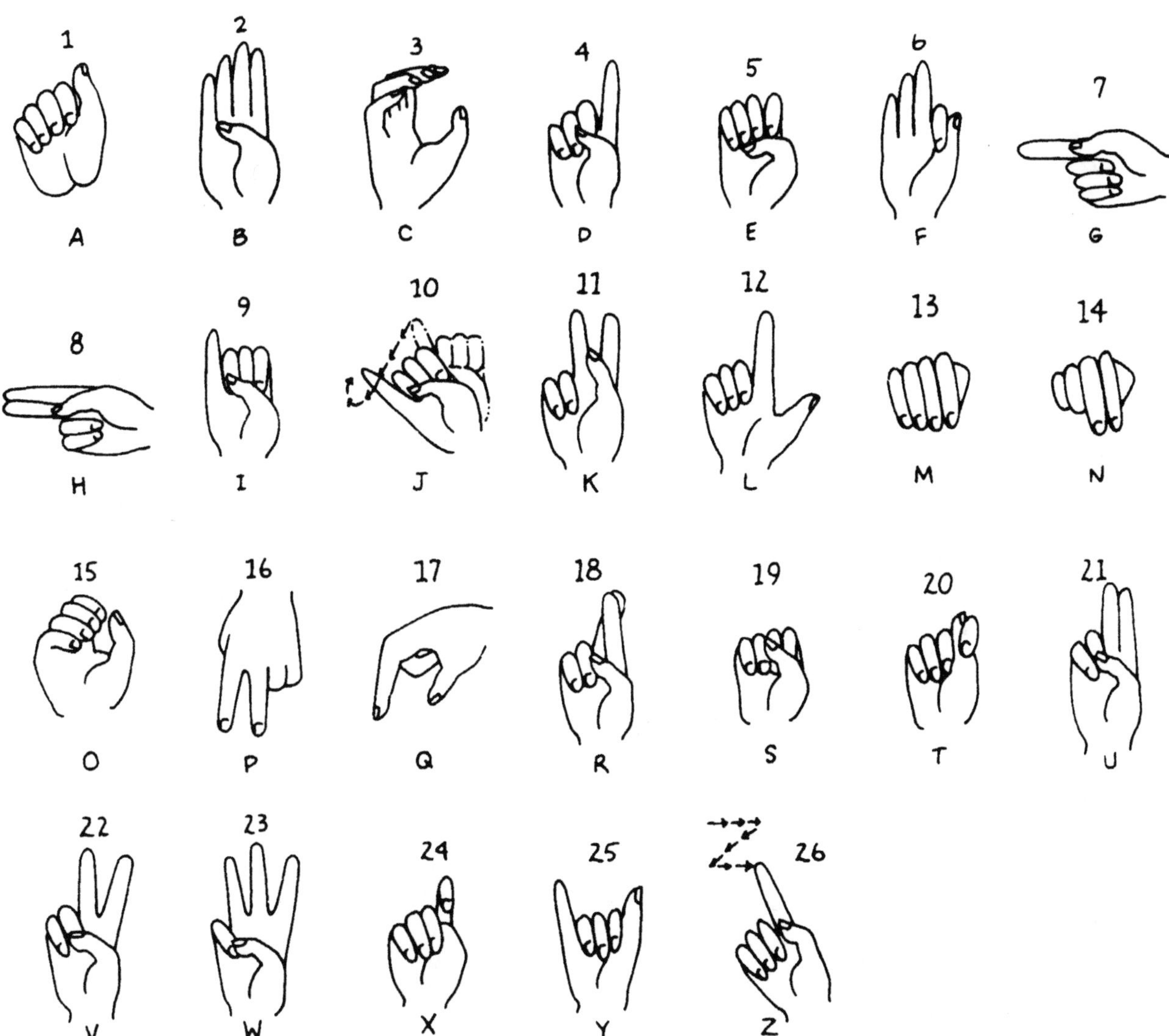

Name ______________________________ Date ______________________________

FAVORITE FOODS

Connect the dots in the box below. Then find the correct name for each food on the list and write its number on the line. Color the foods. Circle your favorite.

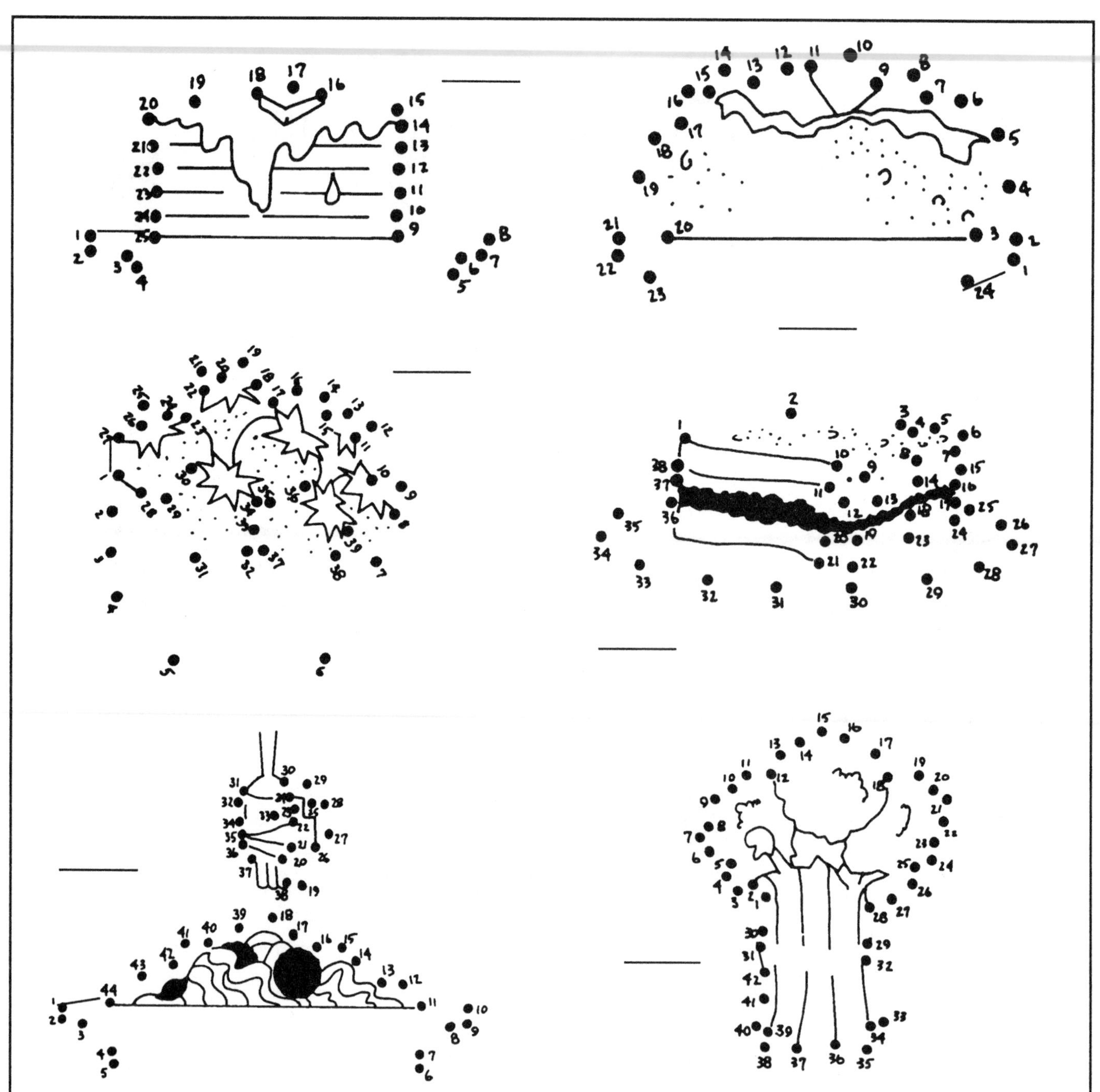

1. Spaghetti
2. Baked potato
3. Strawberries
4. Broccoli
5. Pancakes and syrup
6. Peanut butter and jelly sandwich

Name ______________________________ Date ______________________________

NAME THAT FOOD

Write the correct food beneath each picture. Use the list below.

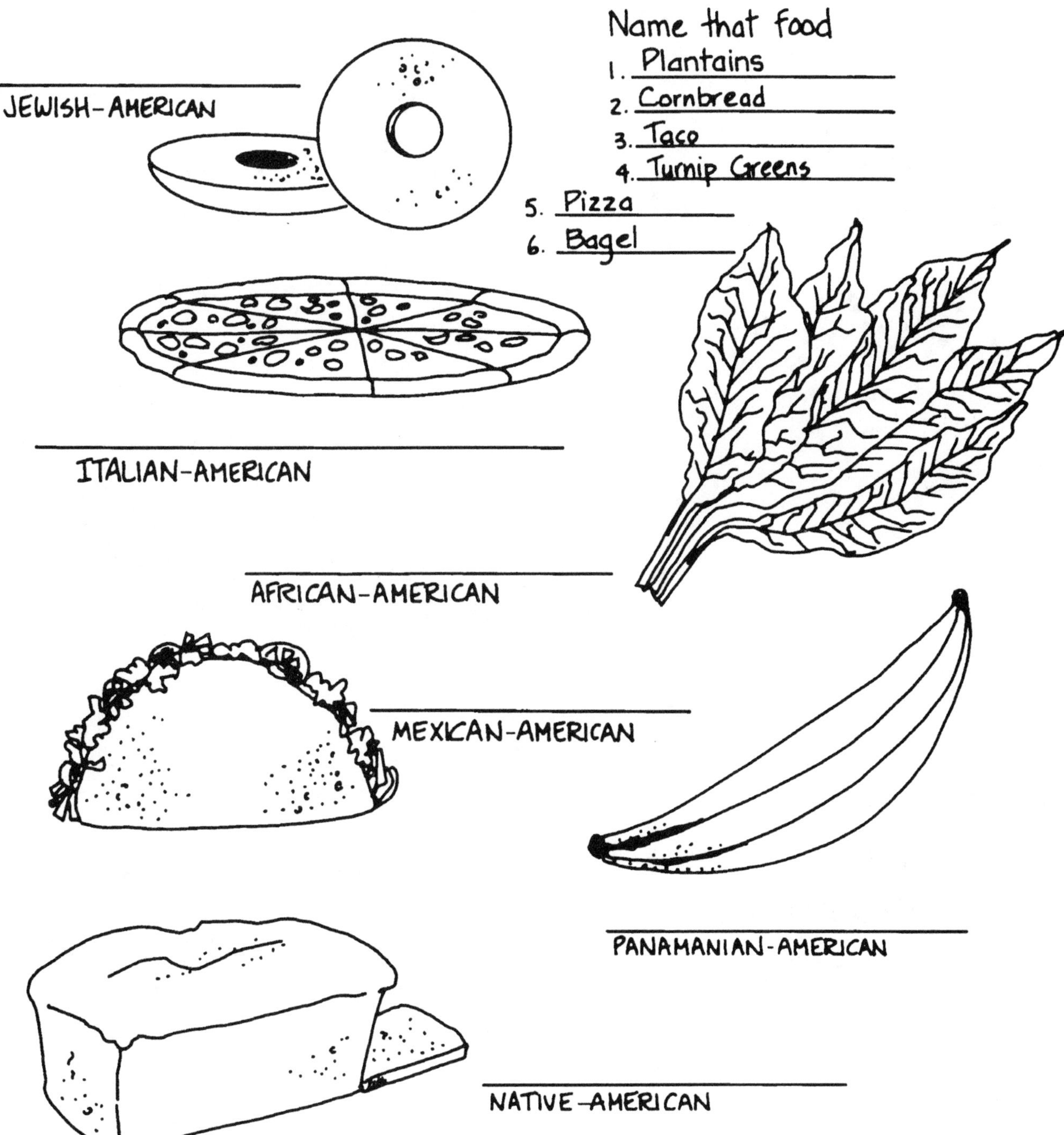

1-11A

Name ______________________________ Date ______________________________

MUSICAL INSTRUMENTS

Do you sing or play a musical instrument? All human voices and musical instruments have their own special sounds.

Trace the dots below to find different kinds of instruments. Color your pictures.

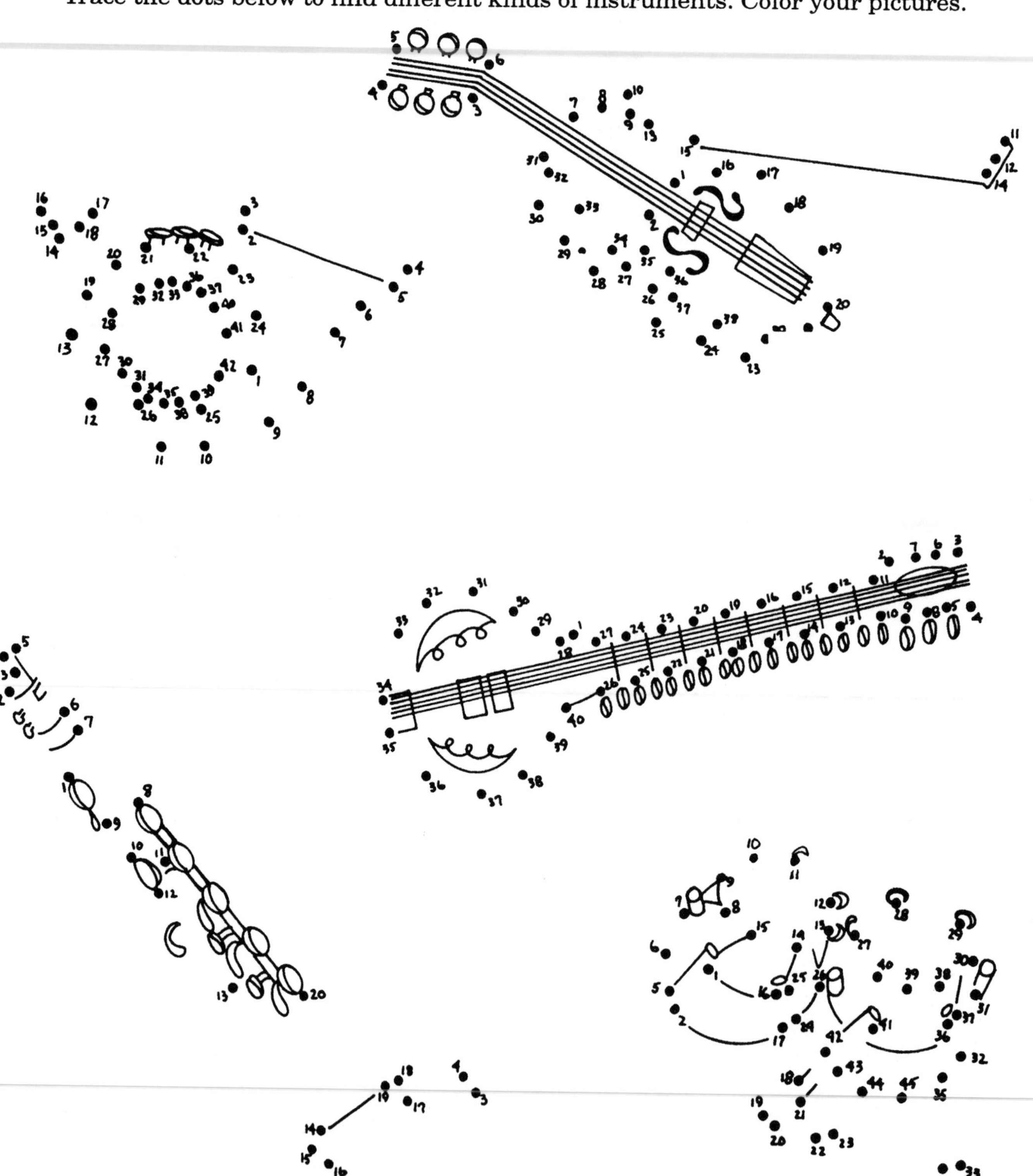

Name ______________________________ Date ______________________________

MUSIC IS UNIVERSAL

Listen to different kinds of music and record your individual reaction to what you've heard. Be certain to write details to support your responses to the music.

My reactions to____
(Name of Music)

____

____

____

____

____

____

____

____

____

____

Now, write something about your favorite kind of music or your favorite song below:

Song title:____

____

____

Song title:____

____

____

Name ________________________________ **Date** ________________________________

WHAT AM I?

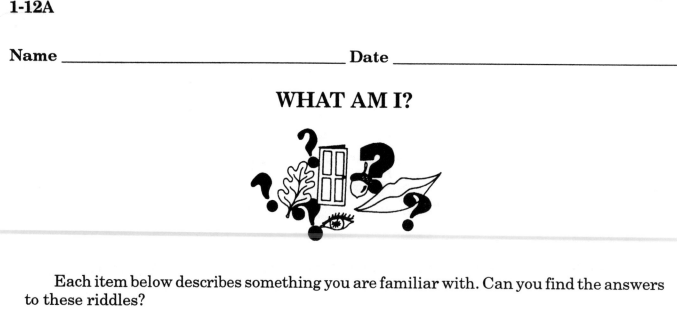

Each item below describes something you are familiar with. Can you find the answers to these riddles?

1. I have leaves, a trunk, bark, roots, and branches. What am I?

   ____

2. I have two eyes, two ears, a mouth, a nose, a shirt, and pants. What am I?

   ____

3. I have a bushy tail, fur, two eyes, two ears, and I like to eat acorns. What am I?

   ____

4. I have two eyes, two ears, a nose, a mouth, a skirt, blouse, and earrings. What am I?

   ____

5. I have a roof, floors, doors, ceilings, and people live in me. What am I?

   ____

UNSCRAMBLE THE WORDS BELOW TO FIND THE ANSWER TO EACH RIDDLE. YOU WILL NOT NEED ALL OF THE WORDS. CHECK YOUR ANSWERS.

OKOB ERTE TRMOECUP ANM SRTATOE DLYA RELIUQSR OHEUS

UNSCRAMBLED WORDS

BOOK TOASTER COMPUTER TREE MAN LADY SQUIRREL HOUSE

Name ______________________________ Date ______________________________

MAKING YOUR OWN RIDDLES

Riddles are puzzles which DESCRIBE THINGS and ASK QUESTIONS ABOUT THEM. Read item #1 below. Write your answer on the line. Then make up your own riddles for items 2, 3, and 4. Use ideas from the bottom of this page to help you make new riddles.

1. Description "I have a glass face, buttons to turn me ON and OFF, two antennae, people who stare at me day and night, and constant interruptions as I show off."

   Question "What am I?"______________________________

   Answer______________________________

2. Description______________________________

   ____

   ____

   Question______________________________

   Answer______________________________

3. Description______________________________

   ____

   ____

   Question______________________________

   Answer______________________________

4. Description______________________________

   ____

   ____

   Question______________________________

   Answer______________________________

MAKE UP RIDDLES FOR TOYS, PEOPLE, WEATHER, NUMBERS, SONGS, STORIES, ANIMALS, CARS, SPORTS, SEASONS, AND SCIENCE.

1-13A

Name ______________________ Date ______________________

WHERE DO THEY BELONG?

Cut out the pictures below and paste them in the boxes.

PEOPLE	TOYS	ANIMALS	FOOD	CLOTHES

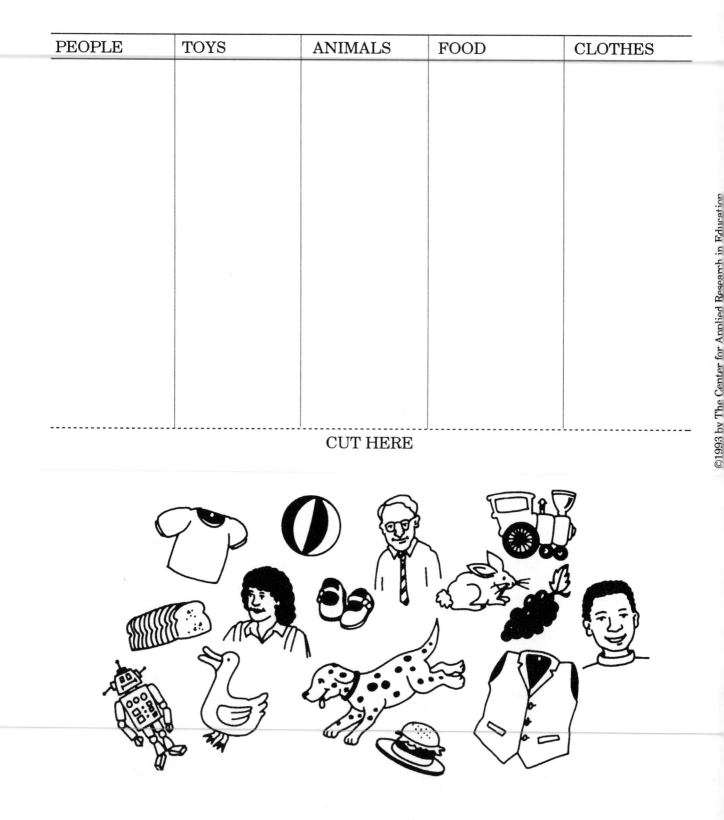

CUT HERE

Name ______________________________ Date ______________________________

WHAT DO I NEED?

MEN and WOMEN can both do many kinds of jobs. From the list of workers, choose the right one and write it in the box with his/her tools.

MUSICIAN	TEACHER
DOCTOR	CHEF
SCIENTIST	SECRETARY

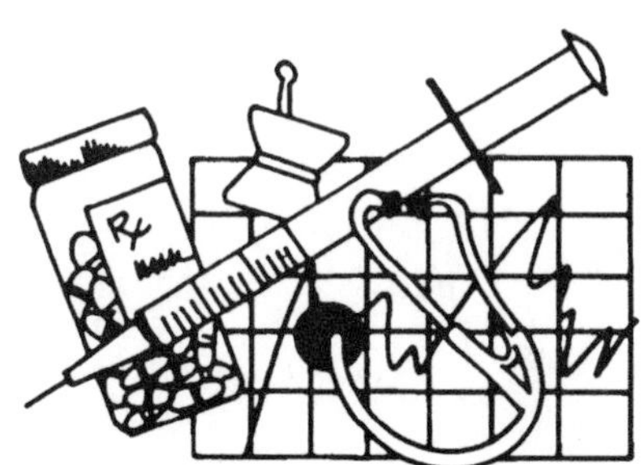

What job do YOU want to do when you grow up?______________________________

Name ______________________________ Date ______________________________

WHO ARE THE PEOPLE IN YOUR NEIGHBORHOOD?

Color the leaves on the tree using the colors of fall/autumn. Then copy the poem and learn it to say to a friend, a parent, or a group of people.

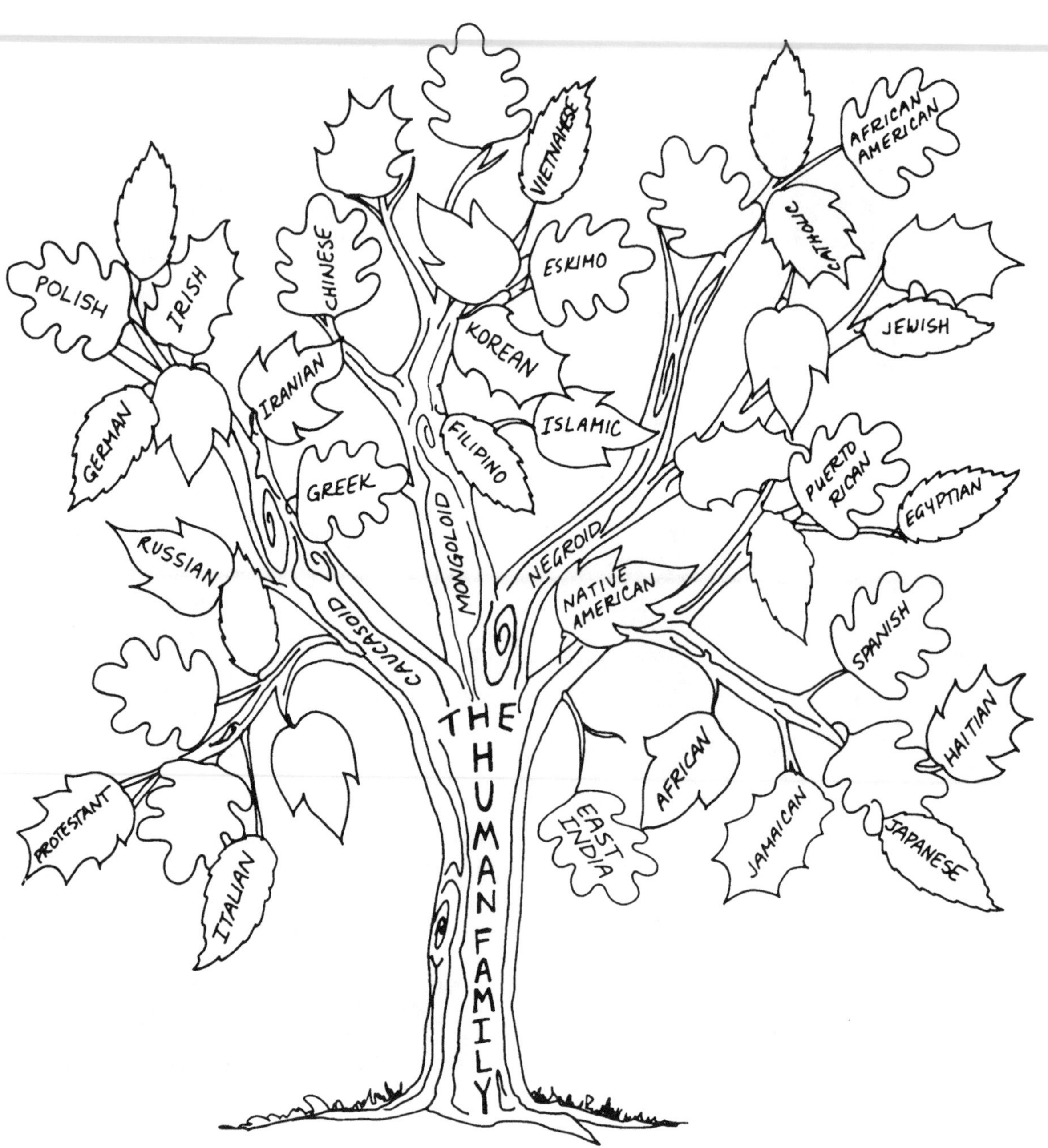

Leaves are beautiful
When autumn changes them—
Red, brown, orange,
Yellow, and deep gold.

People are beautiful
In colors that they wear—
Red, yellow, brown, pink
For young and old.
—by Saundrah Clark Grevious

Name ______________________________ Date ______________________________

IT'S GREAT TO BE HUMAN!

Human beings of all races and ethnic groups share the ability to express sadness and joy by crying or laughing. Find words which tell some of the things that people may do and how they can react to different situations. Then tell why you are glad to be human.

Laugh
Ask
Cook
Read
Wash
Paint
Kiss
Say
Thank You

S	I	N	G	Y	R	C	K	O	O	C
E	T	L	P	R	A	Y	H	D	E	A
T	A	A	G	E	N	O	S	A	E	R
I	L	U	R	A	F	D	A	N	A	K
R	K	G	Y	D	L	H	W	C	S	I
W	C	H	P	A	I	N	T	E	K	S
U	O	Y	K	N	A	H	T	Y	A	S

Write
Reason
Cry
Sing
Pray
Talk
Dance

Why I Am Glad to be Human

____
____
____
____
____
____
____
____

Name ______________________________ Date ______________________________

COSTUMES AND CUSTOMS

Native Americans used the things in nature for their daily living. Color the pictures of Native American items below:

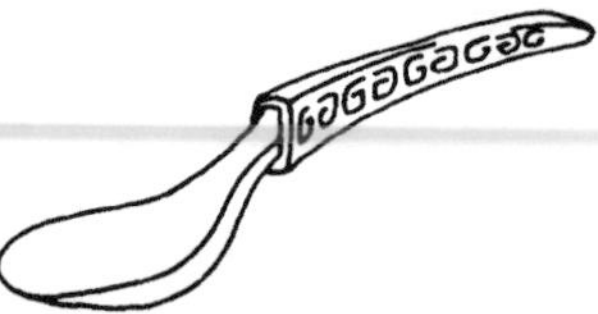

A Seminole Wooden Spoon (Woodland Indians carved spoons and other utensils from wood.)

A Sioux Carved Stone Pipe (Pipes were placed in medicine bags, along with animal and bird skins, dried herbs, and tobacco. These things were believed to have special healing powers.)

A Cheyenne Buckskin Tepee (Tepees were the homes of the Plains Indians. They were made of animal skins [buffalo, deer, and so on].)

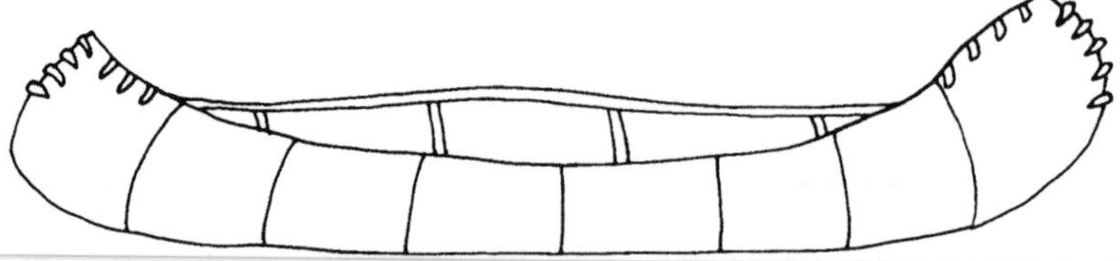

A Chippewa Birchbark Canoe (Native Americans fished in the many lakes and streams. Canoes were made from the bark of trees. Pitch or tar was used to make canoes waterproof.)

Name ______________________________ Date ______________________________

MULTICULTURAL CELEBRATIONS IN AMERICA

Add days which are important to you and your family

Culture Country	Name of Holiday Celebration	Origin Purpose	Date Season
1. Japan	Chado – The Way of Tea	Founder's Day	New Year
2. Israel Jewish	Hanukkah	Celebration of the Return of Lights to the Temple	Winter Solstice
3. African-American	Kwanzaa	First Fruits	Winter Solstice
4. India	Diwali	Festival of Lights	October
5.			
6.			
7.			
8.			
9.			
10.			

Name ______________________ Date ______________________

WHO LIVES HERE?

Take a letter from each window, the chimney, and the door of this house. Unscramble the word and answer the questions. Use your crayons to make this house pretty.

___ ___ ___ ___ ___ ___

Who lives in this house? A______________________

What does this word mean in Chinese? Jia______________________

Jia means two things in Chinese: ______________ and ______________

Name ________________________________ Date ________________________________

WE ALL LIVE HERE

A globe is a small model of the Earth. Human beings need to take care of the air, water, trees, and other things on the Earth.

The Earth is the HOME of all the people. Draw pictures of people, houses, land, water, trees, ships and other things on the globe. Then write what you can do to protect or take care of the Earth.

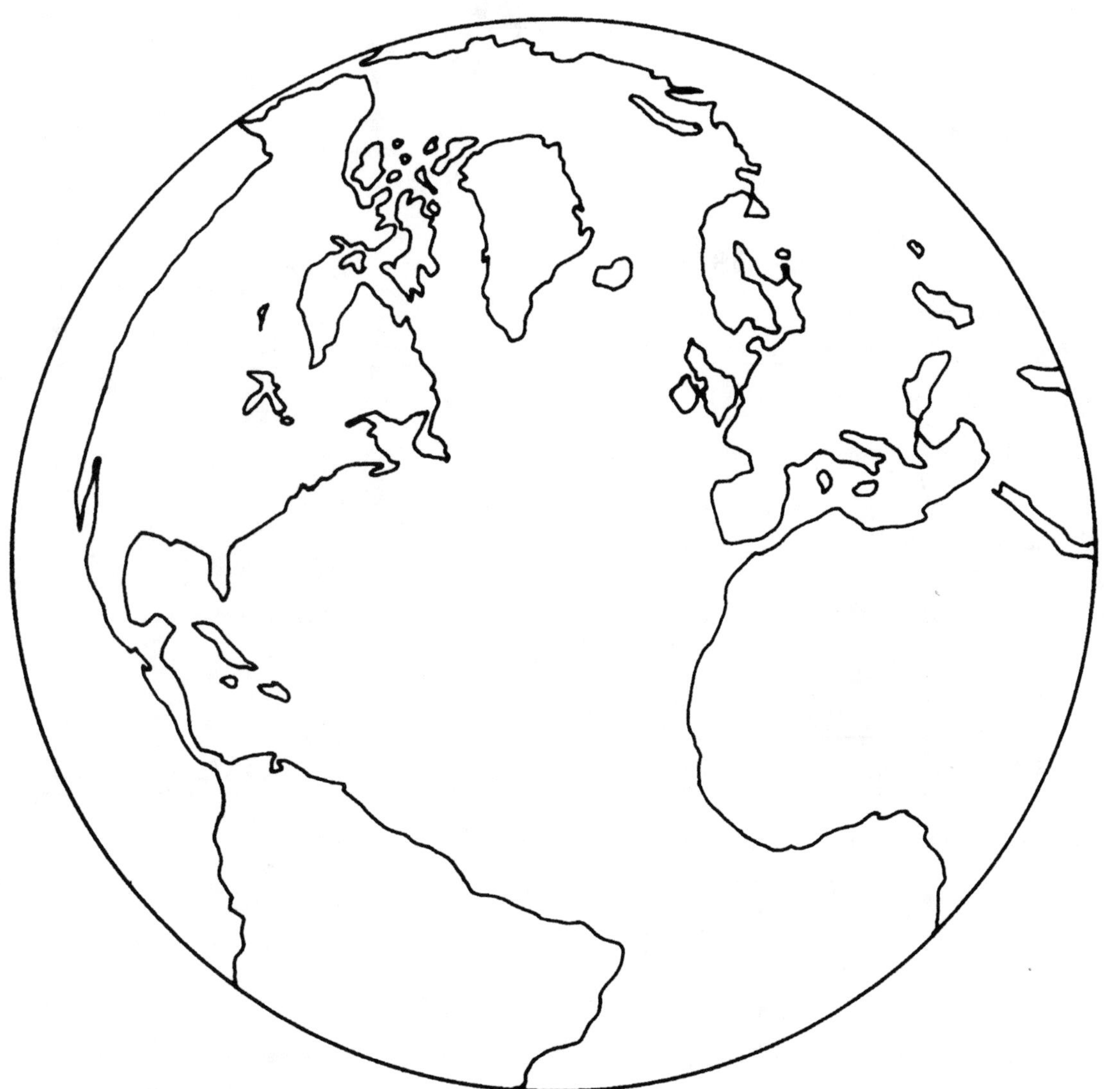

I can help take care of the Earth by____

____

____

____

1-17A

Name ______________________________ Date ______________________________

FOODS FROM GHANA, WEST AFRICA

Human beings need healthful foods from five groups. On the next page find some of these foods in the West African recipes and write them in the correct boxes below.

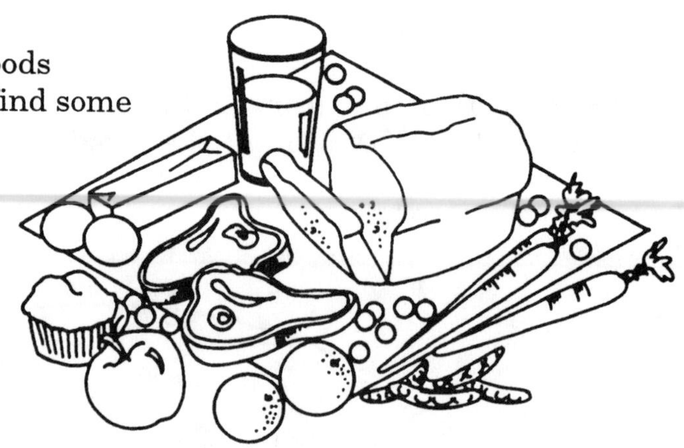

FOODS IN RECIPES FROM GHANA

MEATS	VEGETABLES

FRUITS	GRAINS/BREADS	DAIRY PRODUCTS

FIND OTHER RECIPES FROM AFRICA OR THE COUNTRY FROM WHICH YOUR FAMILY COMES. DRAW PICTURES OF SOME OF THE FOODS. MAKE A RECIPE BOOK CALLED "FOODS FROM MANY LANDS." MAKE COPIES TO SHARE WITH OTHERS.

Name ________________________________ Date ________________________________

FOODS FROM GHANA, WEST AFRICA

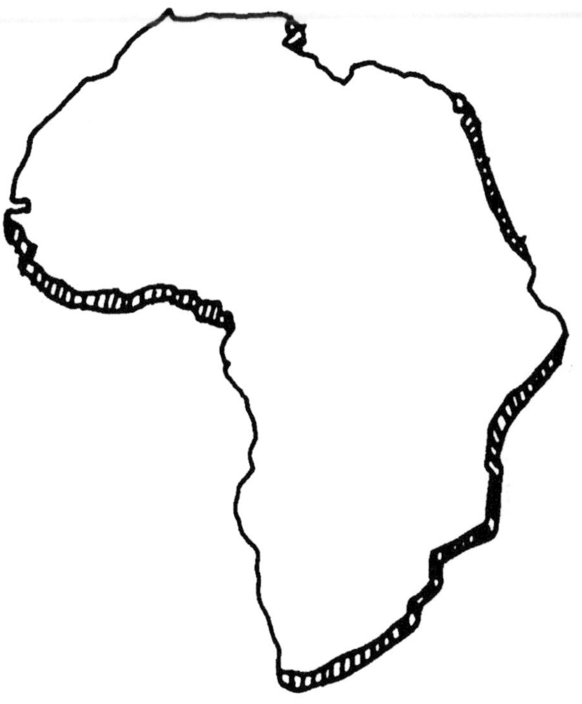

PALAVER* SAUCE

2 pounds beef stew meat cut into 1-inch pieces
3 smoked pork hocks
2 pounds torn fresh spinach or two 10-ounce packages frozen chopped spinach
2 large onions, finely chopped
2 large tomatoes, peeled and chopped
1 tablespoon grated ginger root or 1 teaspoon ground ginger
1 to 2 teaspoons ground red pepper
2 tablespoons peanut oil or cooking oil
2 hard-cooked eggs, chopped

GROUNDNUT STEW

1 2½- to 3-pound broiler-fryer chicken, cut up
3 tablespoons cooking oil
1 pound beef stew meat, cut into 1-inch pieces
2 medium onions, chopped
1 28-ounce can tomatoes, cut up
1 teaspoon salt
1 to 2 teaspoons ground red pepper
¾ cup peanut butter
Mashed sweet potatoes or hot cooked rice (optional)

FISH AND EGGPLANT STEW

1 pound fresh or frozen fish fillets
1 medium onion, chopped
1 large green pepper, chopped
2 tablespoons cooking oil
1 16-ounce can tomatoes, cut up
1 medium eggplant, peeled and diced
1 8-ounce can tomato sauce
1 cup water
1½ teaspoons salt
¾ teaspoon ground red pepper
1 10-ounce package frozen cut okra
Hot cooked rice

To cook the stews:

1. Saute all meats in cooking oil, until tender.
2. Add vegetables, spices, etc.
3. Simmer over low heat.
4. Serve with rice or potatoes.

THINK ABOUT IT!

*The word "palavra" means "talking" or "chattering" in the Portuguese language. In some African tribes the word "palaver" means "a conference." How do you think the West African recipe, Palaver Sauce, got its name?

Name ______________________________ Date ______________________________

A GREAT RECIPE FROM__________________
(Country)

SPANISH RICE AND SHRIMP FRIED RICE

Most people have heard someone say, "I like Chinese food," or "I like Mexican food." People have different tastes in foods, so have fun talking about food in small groups.

Compare the two recipes below by identifying those basic ingredients which are similar, and those which are different. Write group responses to the questions below:

#1 SPANISH RICE WITH BACON

½ pound of mushrooms
4 slices of bacon, diced
1 cup of uncooked rice
½ cup (1 medium) chopped onion
½ cup (1 medium) chopped green pepper
2 ½ cups (no. 2 can) tomatoes, cut into pieces

#2 SHRIMP FRIED RICE

12 fresh or frozen shrimp
1 beaten egg
1 tablespoon soy sauce
⅓ teaspoon pepper
2 tablespoons cooking oil
½ cup green beans sliced into 1½-inch lengths
1 medium onion, halved and sliced
½ cup sliced celery
½ cup bamboo shoots
2 cups cooked rice, chilled

COMPARE AND CONTRAST THE RECIPES

1. Which recipe would you like to prepare and eat? Explain.

____

____

2. Read the different foods in each recipe above. Write down five foods that you think will be easy to find in your supermarket.

____

____

3. Identify the ethnic origin of each recipe below:

Spanish Rice__________________ Shrimp Fried Rice __________________

Name ______________________________ Date ______________________________

MY GIFT TO YOU

Fill in the name of a special person on the Gift Certificate of Honor. Write why you are giving this gift. Decorate it with pretty colors and give it to someone who has been nice to you.

Certificate of Honor

Presented to ______________________________

in appreciation for ______________________________

____

____

____

______________________________ ______________________________

Signed Date

*Gifts do not have to cost money. Circle the words below which are gifts you can give for FREE.

A SMILE TICKETS TO A MOVIE A HELPING HAND A HANDSHAKE

A NEW CAR SPENDING TIME WITH SOMEONE MONEY LOVE

Name ______________________________ Date ______________________________

AN OPEN LETTER FROM ME TO YOU

The trees stand for the Open Letter to the Driver of the car who travels from A to H to get home. Each tree has a number which matches the scrambled words. Unscramble the words and write each one on the correct tree. Connect the dotted lines to show the driver the way home.

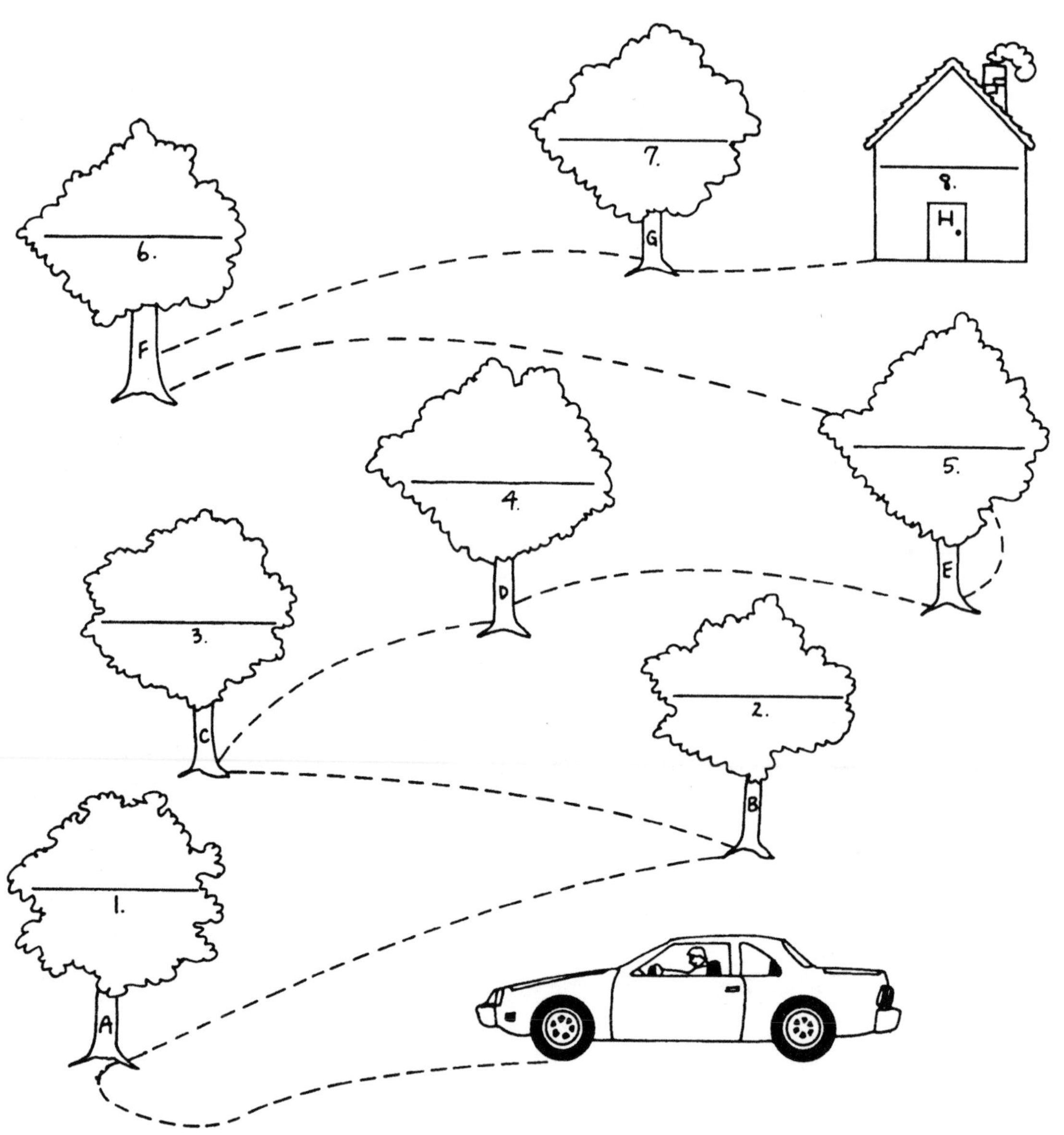

UNSCRAMBLE THESE WORDS OF WELCOME

1. MCELEOW 2. CABK 3. MI' 4. ALDG 5. OT 6. VEHA 7. OYU 8. EOHM

Your loved one travels from A-H.

Name ______________________________ Date ______________________________

WHERE ARE YOU IN YOUR NEIGHBORHOOD?

Picture yourself in your home, at the mall, post office, skating rink, bank, playground, swimming pool, visiting a friend, riding the bus, or at the ice cream parlor. There are many different places and people in a community.

Look at this picture of a neighborhood and draw yourself somewhere in it. Color your neighborhood.

Name ______________________ Date ______________________

WHO ARE YOU IN YOUR SCHOOL?

You are a STUDENT in your school. Students have a job while they are in school. Your job is to LEARN.

Explain what you are learning in each subject below. Use some of the words on the list in your sentences. Decide when you need capital or lower case letters.

Study	Math	Weekdays
Time	Library	Bedtime
Practice	Writing	Weekends
Friends	Books	Problems
Homework		

1. Reading ______________________

____

____

2. Language Arts ______________________

____

____

3. Math ______________________

____

____

4. Science ______________________

____

5. Social Studies ______________________

____

6. Art ______________________

____

7. Music ______________________

____

Name ______________________________ Date ______________________________

WHO ARE YOU IN YOUR SCHOOL?

Fill out ONE or BOTH of the identification cards. Then make a "wallet" for your cards.

My Student Identification (ID) Card

ID CARD #1 – ENGLISH LANGUAGE

Paste a Photo	______________________
	Name of Your School
	DOCUMENT · OFFICIAL · SCHOOL
	First Name · Middle Name · Last Name
	School Address (Number and Street)
	City · State · Telephone

ID CARD #2 – FOREIGN LANGUAGE

Paste a Photo	______________________
	______________________ DOCUMENT · OFFICIAL · SCHOOL
	______________________
	______________________

Name ______________________________ Date ______________________________

WE HELPED BUILD AMERICA AND THE WORLD

Choose one person from the list of disabled contributors. Locate information about how they overcame their disabilities and, in the process, made the world a better place. Work alone or with a partner to find some information on one of the persons below. Then write a response to the question.

Sarah Bernhardt

Franklin Delano Roosevelt

Barbara Jordan

Ludwig Van Beethoven

Louis Braille

Roy Campanella

DISABLED CONTRIBUTORS

1. Ludwig Van Beethoven
2. Sarah Bernhardt
3. Louis Braille
4. Roy Campanella
5. Barbara Jordan
6. Franklin Delano Roosevelt

What have you learned about the abilities of human beings to improve life for themselves and others?

____

____

____

____

____

____

Name ______________________ Date ______________________

MAKING CHOICES FOR MY LIFE

From the Choices List, choose actions which are GOOD and write them next to the REWARDS. Then choose actions which are NOT GOOD and write them next to CONSEQUENCES.

RIGHT	REWARDS	WRONG	CONSEQUENCES
1. ________	Enjoying books	1. ________	Cancer, Heart Disease
2. ________	Friendship	2. ________	Punishment
3. ________	Getting a Job	3. ________	Death
4. ________	Health	4. ________	Pain
5. ________	Happiness	5. ________	Sadness
6. ________	Vacations	6. ________	Jail
7. ________	Family Love	7. ________	Family Problems

CHOICES LIST

• Learning • Fighting • Working • Smoking • Drugs • Doing Chores • Stealing

• Not to Obey • Exercise • Friendship • Eating the Right Foods • To Listen

• Selfishness • Playing • Telling the Truth • No Friends • To Obey • Recycling

• Lying • To Help Others

(You do not have to use all of these choices)

1-21B

Name ______________________ Date ______________________

MAKING CHOICES AT HOME

From the NEEDS AND WANTS LIST find things which are necessary and NOT necessary for people to live. Write your choices on the correct list below:

NEEDS AND WANTS LIST

• Ice Cream • Earrings • Food • Pretty Clothes • Home/Shelter • Television • School • Hamburgers • Tickets to the Football Game • A Watch • Designer Tennis Shoes • A Walkman • A Job • A Letter • Exercise • Clothes • Lots of Money • Family • Friendship

(You do not have to use all of these choices)

NEEDS (Necessary for Living)	WANTS (Not Necessary for Living)
1. ______________	1. ______________
2. ______________	2. ______________
3. ______________	3. ______________
4. ______________	4. ______________
5. ______________	5. ______________
6. ______________	6. ______________
7. ______________	7. ______________

Name ______________________________ Date ______________________________

MAKING CHOICES AT SCHOOL

Unscramble the words below and write them on the pages of the open book. Place the words under the titles: STUDENTS WHO TRY and STUDENTS WHO DON'T TRY. The first ones are done for you. Check off the phrases as you find them.

TNDO PLEH FRO SKA TNDO RYT PLEH FRO SKA UTSYD

YPA ONITATENT FTREFO ON OMKERHOW

STUDENTS WHO TRY	STUDENTS WHO COULD TRY HARDER
☑ Pay attention	☑ Don't ask for help
☐ ______	☐ ______
☐ ______	☐ ______
☐ ______	☐ ______
☐ ______	☐ ______
☐ ______	☐ ______

UNSCRAMBLED PHRASES

DON'T ASK FOR HELP DON'T TRY ASK FOR HELP STUDY

PAY ATTENTION EFFORT NO HOMEWORK

Name ______________________________ Date ______________________________

MAKING CHOICES IN THE COMMUNITY

People do many things in their neighborhoods. Think of some of the things that are healthful, educational, and/or fun for families and friends to do. Write 10 of these things on the list below:

ACTIVITIES FOR FAMILIES, FRIENDS, AND NEIGHBORS

Families and friends can:

1. ______________________________
____

2. ______________________________
____

3. ______________________________
____

4. ______________________________
____

5. ______________________________
____

6. ______________________________
____

7. ______________________________
____

8. ______________________________
____

9. ______________________________
____

10. ______________________________
____

Name ______________________________ Date ______________________________

MY BEST TIMES

Share some of the BEST TIMES you have had with your family and friends by drawing pictures and writing descriptions in the boxes. Use the QUESTION WORDS to help you decide what to draw and write.

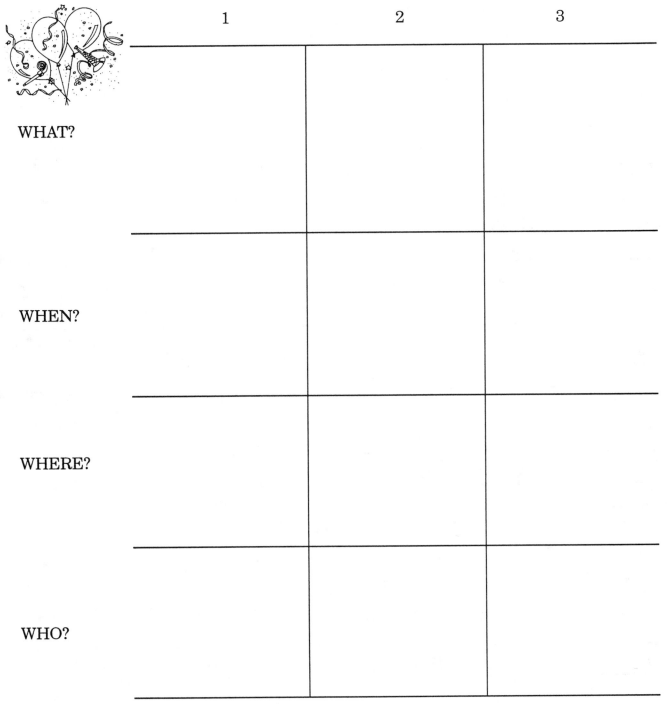

	1	2	3
WHAT?			
WHEN?			
WHERE?			
WHO?			

Now write a paragraph on another sheet of paper describing your feelings and why you felt this way during these HAPPY TIMES.

Name ______________________ Date ______________________

MY STORY

Use ideas from page 1-22A to write YOUR own story about yourself. This will be your AUTOBIOGRAPHY. Draw pictures for your story and share it with friends, family, and neighbors.

MY AUTOBIOGRAPHY

Name ______________________ Date ______________________

MY SPECIAL POEM

Write the letters of your FIRST or LAST NAME in large letters in separate boxes. Use your imagination, a dictionary, or ask your teacher for ideas for GOOD words which describe YOU. Use the sample below to help you create your special poem. Write large, dark letters.

MARK	M	Masterful	AFIA	A	Ambitious
	A	Agile		F	Fluent
	R	Reliable		I	Intelligent
	K	Knowledgeable		A	Artistic

NAME

Decorate this poem about YOU with flowers and/or geometric shapes, using crayons, markers, and/or paints. Make gifts for family, friends, and neighbors by creating NAME POEMS for them.

Name ______________________ **Date** ______________________

MY ROOTS

Complete this Family Chart beginning with yourself. Work backwards in time.

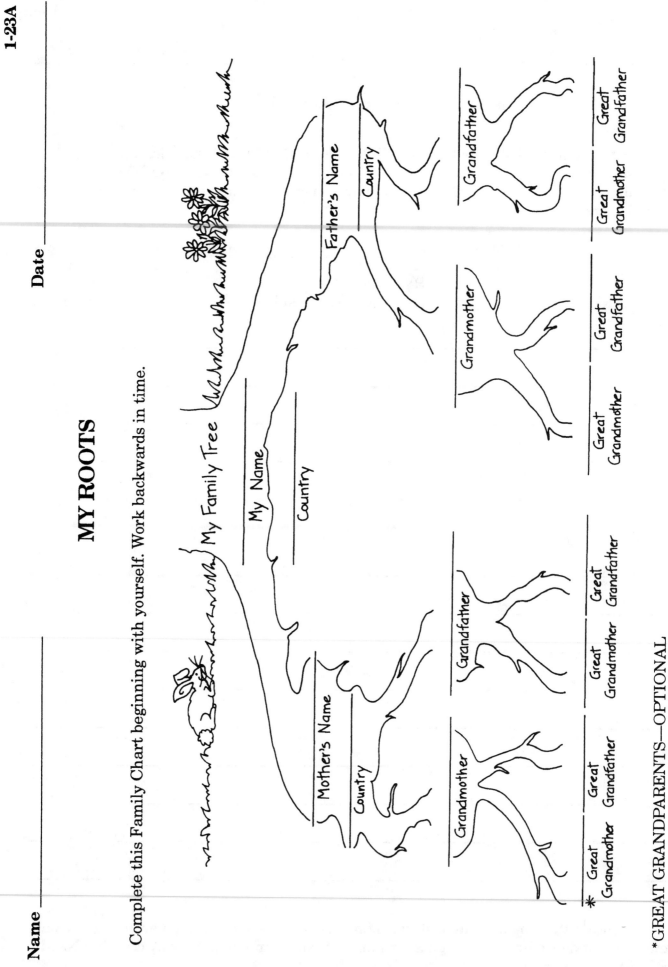

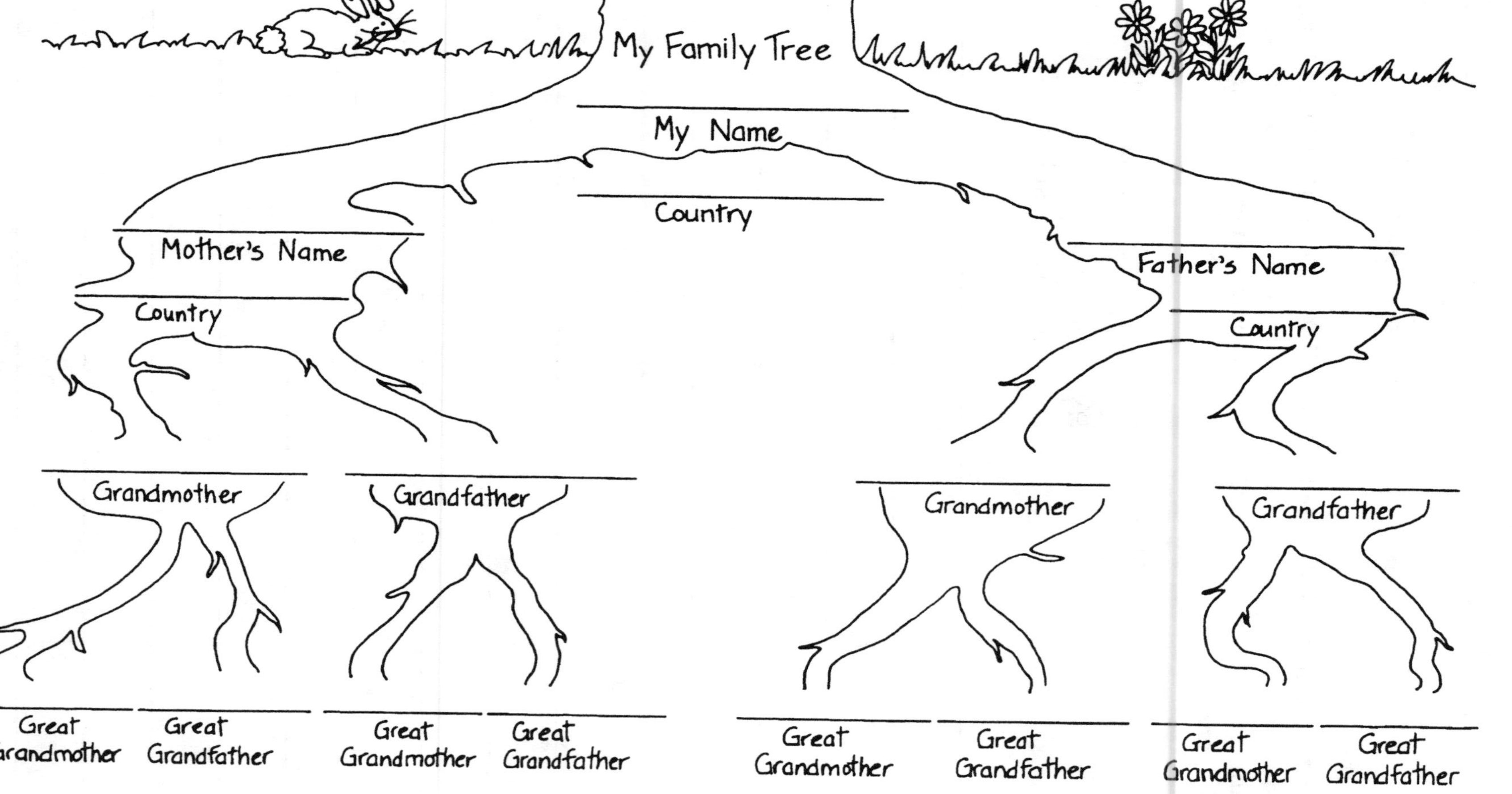

*GREAT GRANDPARENTS—OPTIONAL

Name ______________________________ Date ______________________________

FAMILIES ARE DIFFERENT

Circle some of the words below to make a (YOUR) family. Then draw and color a picture of your family and share it with others.

MOTHER	FATHER	GRANDMOTHER	
CHILD	CHILDREN	UNCLE	AUNT
ADOPTED	GRANDFATHER	FOSTER	STEP

(MY FAMILY)

Name ______________________________ Date ______________________________

FAMILY FAVORITES

Make a list of things below which show why your family is special among all others. (Do not include private family matters.)

1. List some words which are favorites in your family.

____

____

____

2. List favorite family foods.

____

____

____

3. List favorite family stories.

____

____

____

4. List favorite family times.

____

____

____

5. List favorite family games and songs.

____

____

____

Plan to compare your list with your classmates. Then take it home to share with family members.

Name ______________________________ Date ______________________________

FAMILY GRIOT

Alex Haley, author of *Roots*, listened to his aunt and grandmother tell family stories when he was a little boy. He loved the stories they told of his early African relatives. He especially liked to hear them talk about Kunta Kinte who was snatched from his African village by slave traders and brought to America. Listening to these stories made Alex curious about his African homeland and his African ancestors. So when he grew up, he searched for information about his past. He went to Africa and again he listened.

Alex Haley heard a village storyteller, a griot, recite the history of his family. The griot's mind was like a computer as he told of important events, births, deaths, slave traders, and wars. When the griot said the name, Kunta Kinte, Alex Haley knew that he had found his roots.

Do you have a griot in your family? Do you listen to people who talk about your family's history? How many things can you remember about events, celebrations, births, vacations, inventions, and surprises in your family? Become the griot in your family by listing important events and experiences.

MY FAMILY HISTORY AS TOLD BY

______________________________ FAMILY GRIOT

1. ______________________________
2. ______________________________
3. ______________________________
4. ______________________________
5. ______________________________
6. ______________________________
7. ______________________________
8. ______________________________
9. ______________________________
10. ______________________________

Section 2
MUTUAL RESPECT

INTRODUCTION

In Section 2, children will work on reproducible activities that foster the development of mutual respect. Students learn that all human beings, regardless of race, age, gender, religion, and/or national origin, are equal. As they interact in multicultural environments, children become aware of what human dignity means and become less likely to embrace racial and ethnic bias as a way of life. Too young to fully comprehend global conflicts, children are asked to observe disparities in their own relationships and those of others. Through these engaging activities, children will experience an expansion of their decision-making abilities and are guided on how to resolve conflicts which are real to them. Most importantly, students will develop respect for diverse racial and ethnic groups through a deeper understanding of man's common origin. A development of a sense of friendship and caring among all children are additional benefits from participation in these exercises in mutual respect.

Introduce the activities in this section by exploring the different types of families and languages represented in the classroom, school, and in the community. Elicit from children the reasons for the importance of communication among people who speak different languages and who come from different cultural backgrounds. Because children in any one class will have widely diverse and rich experiences, these can be used to enhance lessons in developing respect for others. Specifically, the teacher should validate the essence of the child and what he/she brings to the classroom. Children who experience acceptance can extend acceptance to others. This provides a strong basis for the development of caring, tolerance and mutual respect. The extent to which people demonstrate their love, caring, and concern for fellow human beings is shown in some of the biographies of contributors in the Appendix. These give the teacher resource information and some facts about men and women from various racial, ethnic, cultural, and religious backgrounds who fought injustices together or discovered the solutions to the social, physical, or educational problems of people. Parents, fellow teachers, family, and friends can participate in their children's learning by sharing unique artifacts, experiences, and stories with the class.

DIRECTIONS FOR SECTION TWO ACTIVITIES

Activity 2-1 ALL FAMILIES ARE______________

Children will explore varieties of human families and see similarities in them, as a basis for developing mutual respect. Discussions about families might encompass pointing out similarities in the number of children, places of birth (origin), names, interests, occupations, and neighborhoods. Note that so often these similarities cut across racial, ethnic, and cultural lines. For example, two children of different racial backgrounds might have both been born in the same city. Note that people who first meet each other usually enjoy finding that they are from the same place. Have children search for commonalities while simultaneously learning to appreciate family diversity.

Materials Needed:

- Copies of activity sheet 2-1, *All Families Are* ____________
- Pictures of multiracial families or groups of people
- Pictures of plants, animals, and objects
- Chalkboard list of various family compositions, such as:
  - — Husband and wife
  - — Remarried mother or father and children (Stepfather or mother)
  - — Foster parents and children
  - — Adopted child and parents
  - — Single parent and children
- Pencils/crayons

Directions:

1. Show children pictures of multiracial, multiethnic people involved in various activities. Show pictures of plants, objects, and animals. Discuss how people of all races, colors, and ethnic groups are alike when compared to plants, animals, and objects.

2. Ask children to look at themselves. Then have them close their eyes and think of family members with whom they spend much time. Have students open their eyes and share the good things that happen in their families. Note the differences in their experiences and backgrounds. Discuss the meaning of the word *resemblance*. Allow children to share "family resemblance" stories. Encourage every child to recognize the fact that resemblances go beyond physical characteristics.

Emotional and psychological similarities exist and should be talked about, especially with regard to children who live in foster homes and/or are adopted. For example, help the children to see how they and other family members share a love for books, for animals, for certain foods, and hobbies. Give each child an opportunity to complete this sentence: "My ____ (Dad) ____ and I are alike because we both like to ____ (read books) ____." Talk about how members of families help each other. CAUTION: Teacher awareness of possible child abuse and sources of help is necessary.

3. Show the chalkboard list of various possibilities of family compositions. Be sensitive to the needs of children who are being raised by relatives or other nontraditional familial arrangements. Ask the children to identify their family types. Write them on the board and ask students to volunteer any family types which are not written down. Include the numbers of children, extended family members and close family friends and legitimize all compositions of families. Discuss the word *good* in relation to the diverse family groups. Elicit from students the fact that it is *good* when someone cares enough about you to take care of your needs. Make a list on the board or on a chart of the children's responses to this question, "What are some words which mean the same as "good"? List them under synonyms for "GOOD." Give children the activity sheet 2-1, *All Families Are* ____________________, and have them complete it. Share the results.

LITERATURE CONNECTION: *Family Pictures: Cuardo de Familia, Story and Pictures* by Carmen Lomas Garza. The rich Hispanic culture is shared through the author's bilingual account of her childhood experiences. Intergenerational family life regarding food, games, folk-medicine, and relationships is described in English and Spanish. Children's Press, San Francisco, © 1990.

The Relatives Came by Cynthia Rylant. The fun of having family reunions; the closeness, physically and emotionally, and the celebrations of family love are shown in this humorous story. Bradbury Press, New York, © 1985. Illustrated by Stephan Gammell.

Activity 2-2A THE WORDS YOU SPEAK

Activity 2-2B KIND WORDS LIST

In this activity, children will begin to accept personal responsibility in group relationships. They will also come to understand the power that they have to make other people feel happy or unhappy. During this lesson they will be encouraged to use words to make those with whom they come into contact with feel happy instead of sad.

Materials Needed:

- Copies of activity sheets 2-2A, *The Words You Speak,* and 2-2B, *Kind Words List*
- Pencils
- A chart or chalkboard with the words NEGATIVE and POSITIVE written at the top in large letters

Directions:

1. Ask children to share some of the things which make them happy. Point out that happiness can come from the kindness people show in their conversations and actions. For example, saying nice, caring words like "Thank you," "That's a nice jacket," and "Do you want to play?" make people feel happy.

2. Encourage children to think about the words they speak and how others react to what they say. Have children explain or demonstrate various reactions to the types of words which were spoken. Explain the words *negative* and *positive.* Then make a list together on the board of words which fit into each category, i.e., CURSING, NAME-CALLING, SAYING HELLO, and ASKING IF YOU CAN HELP.

3. Ask children which they prefer, kindness or unkindness. Elicit from them WHY this is so. Then discuss WHY people use kind words (to show love, affection, concern). Finally, discuss WHY people use unkind words (because they are angry, out of control, or feel hurt or weak). Give children opportunities to share some of their experiences with giving and receiving kindness and/or unkindness.

Extend their understanding of how words people say affect the feelings of other human beings. Use the word "synonym" and explain that it means *same.*

Explain that the word "kind" is a synonym for "positive" and that "unkind" is a synonym for "negative." Give children copies of activity 2-2A, *The Words You Speak,* and activity 2-2B, *Kind Words List.* Compare completed worksheets and ask children to choose what kind of person they want to be...POSITIVE or NEGATIVE. Have them raise their hands; ask a student to count the responses, and record the results on the board or chart.

LITERATURE CONNECTION: *Mufaro's Beautiful Daughters*, written and illustrated by John Steptoe. Two sisters, one selfish and mean and the other loving and kind, are tested to see which one is better suited to be the wife of the king. Lothrop, Lee, & Shepard, New York, © 1987.

Appalachia: The Voices of Sleeping Birds by Cynthia Rylant. Illustrates the richness of the lives of mountain people as they go about their daily lives, working, sharing, worshipping, and being content with their blessings. Harcourt, Brace, Jovanovich, New York, © 1991. Illustrated by Barry Moser.

Activity 2-3A WHAT CAN YOU DO?

Activity 2-3B I CAN...

In this activity, children begin to develop an inclusive world view and recognize that all human beings have the ability to contribute to society. Students learn that people from many different places in the world are intelligent and able to give America and the world things that are useful. Have them consider the possibility that some of their foreign-born ancestors might have given something useful to the world. Ask a question, "Wouldn't it be fun to discover that the ancestors (the grandparents, great-grandparents, great-aunts, and great-uncles) of the man who invented the computer and those of the first woman to fly into space were born in countries other than America?" Rephrase the question to bring in the contributions of different races, religions, languages, and cultures. Students' consideration of the rainbow spectrum of capable people in the world should include themselves and their families as well as others in their immediate environment. Each child will discern that he/she is also able to "do something useful" and in the process gain the respect of others. The term *mutual respect* becomes more meaningful as children see the relationship between giving and receiving respect.

Materials:

- Copy of activity sheet 2-3A, *What Can You Do?*
- Copy of activity sheet 2-3B, *I Can...*
- Pictures of Michael Jordan, Larry Bird (basketball stars or other famous sports personalities)
- Pictures of people who are talented in areas other than sports
- Pencils
- Cheers (examples from high school or community cheerleaders)

Directions:

1. Show a picture of Michael Jordan, Larry Bird, and other sports figures. Define the words *respect* (to show honor, esteem, or consideration for), *talent* (a natural ability or power), *ability* (a power to do). Elicit from the students that people respect these sports stars because of their talents and abilities. Discuss the things they had to do to prepare for their careers, like learning to cooperate with

others, learning to do what's best for the team, learning the meaning of sportsmanship and, in addition, practicing on the basketball court for long hours in order to do well. Include getting their education as an important part of this list since many children aspire to be like famous athletes. Elicit from students the fact that most professional athletes work to complete their college education. Ask the children to name someone they know, like, and respect and tell why they feel this way about that person.

2. Discuss the fact that all people have talent and ability that other people can admire and respect, when they know about them. Make a list of various types of people who share their talents and abilities every day. Unlike popular sports heroes, many of these people do not have others cheering for them, but their work is very important. So, people who benefit from their work need to encourage them, give them respect, and honor them.

Ask students if they ever tell their parents how they appreciate their taking care of them, or let the bus driver who brings them to school know how they appreciate that service. Have children name other helpful men and women, such as airplane pilots, firefighters, nurses, typists, cooks, farmers, musicians, writers, librarians, teachers, artists, and so on. Discuss the fact that objects such as balls, computers, and robots can do things. But unlike people, these things have no feelings. We all enjoy watching balls bounce, zig-zag, roll, fly, pop-up, go under and over things, but balls are not human. Computers and robots help people, but they are not human either! Review the list of helpful people discussed above.

Elicit from students the fact that these and other people who help society need us to cheer them on—to make them feel like heroes. Give each child activity 2-3A, *What Can You Do?* Discuss the results. Extend the impact of this activity by asking for volunteers to make up a cheer for "Everyday Helpers." Use examples from high school or community cheerleaders. Have children learn the cheers, put movements to them, and perform them for their heroes or heroines.

3. Have children share something about their talents and abilities, such as singing, football, drawing, dancing, and so on. Emphasize academic abilities as important by praising each child for an accomplishment in class. Compliment a student who has had success in handwriting, reading, learning addition, or getting a good grade on a lesson or a test. Take this opportunity to teach the children to compliment others on their accomplishments. Praise reluctant students for achievements they might not have considered. Include peers in the praising. Extend this experience by inviting willing students to demonstrate their talents and skills for the class. Give each student activity 2-3B, *I Can...* Discuss the results.

LITERATURE CONNECTION: *Pueblo Boy* by Marcia Keegan. A 10-year-old Pueblo Indian is busy with computers, baseball, and other kinds of activities that most young boys like. Because he is proud of his

Native American heritage, he learns to do the dances and rituals of his culture. Cobblehill Books-Dutton, New York, © 1991. Illustrated with photographs by Marcia Keegan.

Activity 2-4 OTHER PEOPLE ARE SPECIAL, TOO

In this activity, children will learn the meaning of the term *mutual respect.* (DEFINITION: When two or more people honor each other and share a common regard or consideration for each other's feelings, culture, race, and language.) They will be able to give examples of admirable traits which human beings can display and which transcend race, color, religion, nationality, or language. Each child will discern that if he/she can be recognized for his/her good qualities, other people can be recognized for theirs as well. Kindness, truthfulness, helpfulness, hard work, caring, confidence, and a willingness to admit mistakes are just some of the admirable traits which students are encouraged to internalize in this activity.

Materials Needed:

- Copy of activity sheet 2-4, *Other People Are Special, Too*
- Crayons/pencils
- Stapler
- Scissors

Directions:

1. Ask children to describe something another person has done to earn their respect. As you go along, point out that admiration and respect can occur between individuals and groups for many reasons. Some reasons might have to do with a person's helpfulness, kindness, intelligence, or success.

2. Explain how respect and admiration for other people can lead to friendship and caring. When people give and receive respect and admiration, everyone benefits; no one is looked down upon. This is called mutual respect and it can and should happen between and among people of all racial and ethnic groups. Ask if any of them have friends in the class (school, neighborhood, etc.). Ask those who respond to identify reasons for their choice of a particular person for a friend. Then ask each child to tell why this person also likes him/her.

3. Have students explain how to find good things about those who are different from themselves. Also, point out the fact that people in all racial and cultural groups should and can show respect for each other. Give an example of a child's bookbag falling and the contents spilling out. Other children can show

respect by: 1. Picking up the items and helping to repack the bag or, 2. Stepping on the things which fell out of the bag and teasing the person who dropped it. Discuss both these choices and then focus on number 1.

Elicit from students the fact that kindness and respect for others should happen more often than it does because this would make our world a better place. Ask the children to show kindness toward and/or appreciation for someone who is very special to them. Give children copies of the activity 2-4, *Other People Are Special, Too.* Extend the concepts by having students work on a scrapbook, mural, and/or series of posters using "THINGS WE ADMIRE IN OTHERS" as the theme.

LITERATURE CONNECTION: *Loop the Loop* by Barbara Dugan. An old woman who is wheelchair-bound makes friends with a young girl and teaches her about aging, caring, and the love of life. Greenwillow, New York, © 1992. Illustrated by James Stevenson.

Activity 2-5A DIFFERENCES AROUND ME

Activity 2-5B PEOPLE ARE ALIKE

Activity 2-5C WHAT COLOR IS LOVE?

The foundation for developing mutual respect is deepened as students come to understand the many similarities among human beings. They will understand that no matter what color, race, religion, or ethnic group people come from, they are still alike in their emotions and reactions to certain things. Also, human beings of all cultures, races, and languages are involved in everyday activities like working, playing, showing affection, and eating. For young children, differences that cause conflicts among people fade, as they discover commonalities in their human experiences. These commonalities provide a basis for caring and concern which transcend racial and cultural differences. Furthermore, there is an emphasis on the various traits which bind human beings and set them apart, no matter what their racial or ethnic origin, from the world of animals and objects.

Finally, because human beings are special and able to reason, students are given ideas which help them think about WHY people should get along; namely, that they share ONE HOME...the Earth. Children will discern that they and other people can work together to save the Earth and keep it clean and beautiful, beginning with their own schools and neighborhoods. In addition, students will come to understand that we all need to cooperate with and be respectful of one another, if we are to survive.

Materials Needed:

- Copy of activity sheet 2-5A, *Differences Around Me*
- Copy of activity sheet 2-5B, *People Are Alike*
- Copy of activity sheet 2-5C, *What Color Is Love?*
- Multiracial/multicultural pictures of people involved in activities such as raking leaves, embracing, sitting in a classroom, or playing
- Pictures of a variety of types of animate and inanimate objects
- Real objects, i.e., toys, flowers, coins, keys, leaves, or goldfish
- Pictures of a zoo, circus, aquarium
- Pencils
- Construction paper
- Paste and scissors

Directions:

1. Ask children to think of how different they are from animals and objects. Show the pictures of animals from the circus, aquarium, or the zoo. Or show examples of real objects or goldfish. Elicit from children that, despite their various sizes, shapes, eye colors, skin colors, hair colors, religions, and languages, they are of the same species: the human race. Therefore, they have much in common; they are like each other and they are not like the animals and objects. Elicit from children the fact that because human beings have the ability to reason, they can work out ways to interact harmoniously with one another. Give each child activity 2-5A, *Differences Around Me*. Have groups of students work together to draw their own pairs of objects for comparisons. Give them an opportunity to describe the similarities and differences verbally and/or in writing.

2. Discuss the beauty of human beings, the usefulness of objects, the fun of toys, and the lovely things in the natural environment. Ask students to tell why they are happy to be human beings, rather than trees, lawnmowers, or toys. Point out that, unlike items and animals, human beings are unique and special, like poetry....the masterpieces of all the living and nonliving things in the world. Extend students' understanding to the extent that they can discern that because human beings are the highest of life-forms, they can think, reason, and learn to be good to each other. Elicit from children some of the things that happen in the world of human beings of all races and cultures and establish the fact that animals and objects are unable to carry out such functions. Give each student activity 2-5B, *People Are Alike*. Have them share the results.

3. Show pictures of different races and colors of people involved in play, work, learning, pain, traveling, and talking together. Discuss the fact that even though human beings may look very different on the outside, they often feel the same inside. Define the word *emotions*. Have the children explain how they feel inside when they get hurt and cry. Ask what color their tears are. Also, ask them to

describe the color of their blood. Elicit from students the fact that because human beings all have transparent tears and red blood, these are indications that they are the same in other ways, as well.

NOTE: Extension of these concepts into a broader study of the various systems of the human body, organ transplants, blood transfusions, and interracial families, can take place at this time. (The work of Dr. Charles Drew who discovered ways to preserve human blood in blood banks can be discussed here.) Then ask them to share how they feel inside when they are hugged or kissed, or when someone is nice to them. Point out how, no matter what they look like on the outside, they all feel the same inside when someone shows love and kindness to them. Give students activity 2-5C, *What Color Is Love?* Compare the results.

LITERATURE CONNECTION: *Black Is Brown Is Tan* by Arnold Adoff. Racially mixed parents and their children enjoy lots of family fun. Harper Row, New York, © 1973. Illustrated by Emily McCully.

Activity 2-6A SHARING FREEDOM IN AMERICA

Activity 2-6B AMERICANS COME FROM MANY PLACES

During these activities, children learn that Americans of all races, colors, and ethnic backgrounds have freedoms and rights. Mutual respect begins to build as students realize that all Americans have come from other places in the world. (Research shows that Native Americans were here before the Europeans, however. They originally crossed the Bering Straits, on a now nonexistent stretch of land, to reach the North American continent.) Children participate in lessons which demonstrate that when freedoms and rights are shared by all citizens, everyone benefits. Furthermore, in an environment of acceptance, each child learns a sense of responsibility in extending respect to others while simultaneously developing pride in his/her own cultural heritage. The American Flag, as a symbol of equality for all citizens, is used to help students cultivate the desire to share the rights it represents.

The teacher might choose to bring in information about immigration and the population of America. Such material should provide ample information for cooperative work including murals, stories, poems, drawings, and other artistic projects. In addition to the fun and satisfaction that children would derive from working cooperatively on these creative works, their efforts would highlight the beauty of the multicultural development of America. Lessons in this section feature discussions which might take two or three days. The time will be well spent, because of the importance of concepts which celebrate the international flavor of America, and lay the foundation for peace in the 21st century. Opportunities to promote human commonalities are inherent in these activities.

Materials Needed:

- Copy of activity sheet 2-6A, *Sharing Freedom in America*
- Copy of activity sheet 2-6B, *Americans Come from Many Places*
- American Flag
- Lyrics for the song, "America the Beautiful"
- Pencils
- Pictures of immigrants from around the world
- Map of the world and/or a globe
- Pictures of disabled citizens
- Cloths for use as blindfolds
- Multiracial dolls, and/or pictures of children from many races interacting together (playing, singing, reading, talking)
- Pictures of nature, trees, flowers, mountains, animals, and rainbows
- Pictures of people of many ages, races, and cultures
- Encyclopedia information about the American Flag/guidelines for use

Directions:

1. Blindfold two or three children. Allow them to take turns pointing to a place on a map or globe. Elicit from children that the Earth is the home of all human beings. Discuss the need for the people of the Earth to love and respect each other. Show pictures of multiracial groups of people or dolls. Some might be dressed in costumes from different ethnic groups. Explain that these pictures represent Americans who have all come from other places in the world. Identify America on the map or globe.

Then ask students to each name other countries from which families in America have come. Point out the fact that no matter where they came from, American citizens are all entitled to the freedoms represented by the American Flag. Give each student a copy of activity 2-6A, *Sharing Freedom in America*. Have them work in cooperative groups to complete their worksheets. Reinforce their understanding of extending freedom to others by having students exchange the flags they have cut out. Make sure that each child receives a flag.

2. Show pictures of people who are disabled (in wheelchairs or with canes). Explain the term "disabled" as one who is unable to walk, run, or see. Emphasize that this does NOT mean that the person is any less important than those who are able-bodied. See activities in SECTION ONE for additional concepts regarding the disabled. Explain the term *handicapped* as those who are physically and mentally retarded. CAUTION: Teacher sensitivity to the needs of children who are hearing

impaired, legally blind, or are in special education programs is crucial. Reduction in bias against any person, regardless of race, religion, color, national origin, age, sex, language, and/or physical and mental capabilities is a major goal in learning to respect others.

Discuss the fact that people who are disabled have the same rights and freedoms as others. Emphasize the need for all Americans to treat each other like friends. Mention specific groups of people who might often be denied their rights because of race, gender, religion, or ethnic background. Teach them the word "discrimination" based on this discussion of denying people their rights and freedoms. Explain that some racial, religious, and ethnic groups have no trouble with "discrimination" and/or prejudice in some parts of the country. However, in other sections of America their freedom is endangered. Ask the children to share their experiences with discrimination. Have students comfort each other as you explain how it helps to talk negative experiences over with those who care.

Elicit from students the fact that each person in the class is important. Demonstrate this by honoring each child with a special mini-celebration. Ideas for this might include a computer banner with the child's name and graphics to compliment his/her heritage, or post a picture of "The Student of the Week," with the intent of giving every single child his/her turn to be featured. Bring families into these activities, if desired, to enhance the impact of the celebration of cultural, racial, and ethnic diversity. Elicit from children the common need that all human beings have to be looked upon favorably by others.

3. Show a picture of a teacher with a class of students from many places. Or, refer to your own multiethnic, multicultural, multiracial students, and/or multiracial, multiethnic dolls. Such dolls are valuable in any primary play center but are very appropriate and useful in ethnically, racially and culturally homogeneous settings. Specifically, in all white, all black, and/or same culture classrooms, multiracial dolls, books with positive stories about minorities, recognition and celebration of diversity of religious beliefs, family backgrounds, places of birth, individual preferences for food and clothing, are fundamental to the stopping of prejudice before it starts.

Elicit from older children a long list of ways in which America is a richer country because of its people from many places. Encourage students to be proud of this "rainbow" of humanity called Americans. Help students to maintain pride in their family heritage and culture by sharing with them something about your background and heritage. If you are bilingual, delight your students with a demonstration of counting, reciting the alphabet, or naming items in the room in a foreign language. Give each student a copy of activity 2-6B, *Americans Come from Many Places*. Discuss the results.

Elicit from the students the need for family pride. Discuss the fact that just as we are proud of our family background, country, and nationality, we all should be even more proud of our belonging to the human family. Reemphasize the fact that people are alike in that no matter where they come from or what their ethnic/racial background, they have in common their need for food, clothes, and houses. Help students draw the analogy between the houses or apartments that they live in, as places of safety and shelter, and the Earth all humans live on, as a place for safety and shelter.

The Earth is the ONLY PLANET on which humans can survive and that makes it necessary for every person to learn to get along with people who are racially and culturally different from himself/herself. In addition to learning to care about each other, the citizens of the globe must learn to care for the Earth. Have children make a list of the things which each of them can do to help take care of the air, water, land, and other natural resources. Have them volunteer answers to the question, "What would happen to human life if there were no clean water, soil, or air?" Discuss the answers.

Use pictures of nature and people to extend the concept of the beauty in diversity in the natural environment and the beauty of the rainbows of people who inhabit the Earth. Emphasize the common human needs which bind all people and make them "brothers and sisters beneath the skin." Extend this concept to include the work of civil rights volunteers. See Activity 3-16B. Explain this phrase that teaches people to care about each other as human beings, despite race and color. Play the song, "America the Beautiful."

4. Have different students describe the pattern or design of the American Flag (colors, stripes, and so on). Show pictures of the flag from the encyclopedia and have students note that there are guidelines and rules for using this national symbol. Discuss how the flag serves as a BOND for its people of many races, colors, religions, languages, and ethnic backgrounds. Give each student another copy of activity 2-6A, *Sharing Freedom in America.* Extend this activity to include cooperative, creative activities. Students can suggest artistic ways to depict immigration and the popularity of America. Analyze the results.

LITERATURE CONNECTION: *Mom Can't See Me* by Sally Hobart Alexander. A story of the joy which fills the life of a blind author, as told by her daughter. A positive account of the ability of her mother to live a normal life. She cooks, reads stories to her children, dances, cleans house, plays ball, and rides a bike for two, and when she makes a mistake, they laugh about it. Macmillan, New York, © 1990. Photos by George Ancano.

The Chalk Doll by Charlotte Pomerantz. A Jamaican mother shares stories of her childhood with her daughter. Lippincott, Philadelphia, © 1989. Illustrated by Frane Lessae.

I Pledge Allegiance by June Swanson. A historical analysis of the words of the Pledge and the evolution and expansion of the text. Important events in the growth of the nation are included, as the author discusses the people, places, and the laws regarding recitation of the pledge to the American Flag. Carolrhoda Books, Minneapolis, © 1990. Illustrated by Rick Hanson.

Activity 2-7A HOW ARE YOU FEELING?

Activity 2-7B WE CAN BE FRIENDS

Children will appreciate the diversity found among the members of the class and learn to accept and enjoy their common responsibilities in creating happy environments. They take note of the fact that males and females of all races, cultures, colors, ethnic groups, religions, ages, and physical capabilities, have feelings. In this context, students discern that each person has the power to make others feel happy, rather than sad. Many other opportunities for helping students understand cause and effect are woven throughout these experiences. Lessons in how to give and receive respect are important concepts for young people to internalize and carry with them as their world widens. Equipping young children with tools to resolve conflicts in their own immediate environments improves their outlook on the future and prepares them for their roles as responsible citizens. In the process of internalizing these concepts, students develop new friendships, positive attitudes towards various ethnic groups, and insightful decision-making skills.

Materials Needed:

- Copy of activity sheet 2-7A, *How Are You Feeling?*
- Copy of activity sheet 2-7B, *We Can Be Friends*
- Crayons and/or markers
- Popsicle sticks or firm cardboard strips
- Scissors
- Pencils
- Pictures of people of different races and ethnic backgrounds enjoying the same kinds of things, such as books, games, celebrations, cooking, worshipping, talking, and the like
- Liberators and Survivors Day and a film, "The Liberators." (The story of blacks who rescued Jews during the Holocaust) See Bibliography (Optional)
- Civil Rights Movement—Mini-Biographies of blacks, whites, and Jews who fought and often died for equal rights for African-Americans. See Appendix
- Pictures of people of different races and ethnic groups working together for freedom
- Chart paper for a "Words Which Welcome" Chart

Directions:

1. Discuss the fact that mutual respect can be given. For example, all humans have the same kind of beginning to their lives. Everyone was born of a mother and has the need to have someone care for him/her until adulthood. Also, all human beings like to be happy. When they are happy they have the same kinds of expressions. Have children dramatize how they feel when something pleasant happens to them. Note the positive facial expressions, body language, and so on.

Elicit from children the fact that human beings are special and unique because they can also show their feelings when they don't like something. Note that people in all races, colors, and ethnic groups have similar types of negative facial expressions and body language when they are unhappy or displeased. Have children dramatize how they feel when something unpleasant happens to them.

2. Show pictures of different races of people enjoying the same kinds of things. Have students suggest words which fit beneath each of the following headings in order to verify human commonalities and preferences. Explain that people of all races and colors share the same kinds of LIKES and DISLIKES.

(Sample Ideas)

LIKES	DISLIKES
1. Birthdays	1. War
2. Other people	2. Crime
3. Peace	3. Pain
4. Love	4. Hate
5. Cars	5. Accidents
6.	6.
7.	7.
8.	8.

Continue by emphasizing human commonalities in the ways that people are ALIKE by using the heading:

HUMAN BEINGS ARE ALIKE

1. People of all colors were born rather than being hatched.
2. People of all colors and races were helpless at birth.
3. People of all colors and races have blood. Blood types can be exchanged among different races.
4. People of all races, languages, and colors....
5. Adults of all nationalities have to.....

6. Boys and girls all over the world like to.....
7.
8.

Have students complete the statements and discuss these as good reasons for being kind to one another and feeling like we ALL belong to the same human family. Give each student a copy of activity 2-7A, *How Are You Feeling?* Give children time to play with their puppets and get closer to the various emotions experienced by human beings. Take note of reluctant students who might need encouragement from you and his/her classmates.

3. Elicit from students the role they have in creating a happy classroom atmosphere. Ask them what they can say to others to make them feel happy. Explain to young children the importance of being honest and real in expressing our feelings. Discuss the words *violence* and *fighting*. Have children give examples of reasons why people fight with guns, words, bombs, or fists. Discuss how many disagreements are over little things which are not "life and death" situations. Two children might have a fight over a pencil, for example. Or two adults might disagree over how much money to spend on a new coffee pot. Help children to discern that words and actions which hurt others create unhappy feelings or emotions, while kind words and actions create happy feelings and friendships. Discuss the importance of talking about problems, rather than fighting and arguing. Ask students to use these solutions at home and in the community, as well as in the classroom. A carryover into the larger, global society is expected.

NOTE: Students and their families might be aware of specific conflicts among various racial, ethnic, cultural, and/or religious groups in their communities. Use historical realities to help diffuse tensions that might have spilled over into the classroom. See Multicultural Mini-Biographies in the Appendix about blacks, whites, and Jews who cared enough to fight and often die for each other's freedom. While there are only names of four civil rights workers, use these as motivation for encouraging children to read and write research reports on their contributions. See Research Report Form in the Appendix. These are examples and can be adapted to fit the various conflicts which might occur between and among people of other racial and ethnic groups.

4. Elicit from children the roles that they can play in helping people in their neighborhoods to get along better. Discuss how children of different colors, religions, languages, and ethnic groups work and play together in schools and neighborhoods every day. Ask students if children can help adults learn to be better neighbors. Give each student a copy of activity 2-7B, *We Can Be Friends*. Extend the impact of this lesson by having students act out this scene. Encourage them to use their own dialogue and actions in which name-calling, gossip, and other words which cause conflict and hurt are contrasted with words of apology and kindness.

Follow this experience with a discussion about words which "welcome" people and make them feel happy and accepted. Place the list of words, such as "Please," "Thank you," "May I help you?" and "Welcome," in a prominent place in the room. Share the results of this activity with other classes, families, and community groups.

LITERATURE CONNECTION: *Maxie* by Mildred Kantrowitz. A woman feels lonely and depressed until her neighbors let her know that they need her. Four Winds Press, New York, © 1970. Illustrated by Emily A. McCully

Tar Beach by Faith Ringgold. An African-American girl dreams of flying over her Harlem neighborhood. The author combines fact and fiction as she relates the efforts of this family to overcome hardships and the father's struggle to become a member of the workers' union. Crown Publishers, New York © 1991. Illustrated.

Activity 2-8A **LANGUAGES ARE FUN**

Activity 2-8B **INTERPRETING THE ENVIRONMENT FOR MULTICULTURAL CLASSMATES**

Activity 2-8C **LANGUAGES ARE DIFFERENT**

Activity 2-8D **ORDERING CHINESE FOOD FOR LUNCH**

Activity 2-8E **ART AND LANGUAGES**

Mutual respect is enhanced as English-speaking students experience how it would feel to be in a foreign country and not know the language. Foreign language students will welcome the opportunity to share their knowledge in environments where they are often shy and reserved because they have not yet mastered the English language. Participation in this activity will foster multicultural understanding, as all students learn how people lose control over their lives when they cannot communicate their needs and wants. More importantly, during these excursions into foreign languages, students will begin to assume the responsibility for opening up the lines of communication with those who are different from themselves.

The activities are adaptable and can be altered to meet the needs of the various ethnic, racial, and cultural groups represented in the class. Mutual respect will continue to develop among students as they work in cooperative groups on these and other activities. For example, several lessons encourage students to identify the English and foreign language words for familiar items. Others challenge the children to use prior knowledge of math and language concepts to enhance their understanding of numbers and words in new languages. Each activity presents opportunities for family and community members to participate.

Materials Needed:

- Copy of activity sheet 2-8A, *Languages are Fun* (6 pages)
- Copy of activity sheet 2-8B, *Interpreting the Environment for Multicultural Classmates*
- Copy of activity sheet 2-8C, *Languages Are Different*
- Copy of activity sheet 2-8D, *Ordering Chinese Food for Lunch* (2 pages)
- Copy of activity sheet 2-8E, *Art and Languages*
- Markers or pencils
- Chinese characters (numbers)
- Egyptian Hieroglyphics
- Chalkboard
- Restaurant menu or a picture of one foreign language list in the Appendix/ FL dictionaries and/or books
- Bilingual resource people (parents, students, teachers, etc.)
- Map or globe
- Multicultural artwork (books, encyclopedias, posters, etc.)
- Paintings of landscapes, houses, flowers, still life of bread, fruit, cheese, and so on)
- Family Name Origins (the Appendix)

Directions:

1. Have two children try to get a message to each other without using words in order to demonstrate the need for language. Give them these written words or whisper in their ears messages such as, "Please bring that hat to me" or "Can you go out to play after school?" Also, ask a bilingual child to speak to the others in his/her language. Students will have fun as they see how difficult it can be to communicate without knowing the language others are using. Discuss how important it is for people to understand each other if they are trying to ask someone a question, buy a hamburger, or make hotel reservations on the telephone.

Give each child copies of activity 2-8A, *Languages Are Fun.* There are six pages, each highlighting one word in English. The children are asked to find three foreign words for a person, an animal, a day of the week, and so on. (See Appendix for [FL] foreign language lists.) Students will enjoy trying to pronounce the foreign language words for familiar things like SATURDAY, HOUSE, BIRD, TUESDAY, MOTHER, RED, etc. They will also have fun finding their Ghanaian names in the appendix and recording them in activity 2-8A.

Provide many opportunities for students to use the list in the Appendix, and other foreign language resources to increase their knowledge. Also, help them to identify, on a map or globe, some of the countries in which these languages are spoken. For example, the language of Gujarati is spoken in the country of India, Tagalog and Bikol in the Philippines, Spanish in Spain, Mexico, Puerto Rico, Colombia, etc., French in France, Canada, Haiti, etc., and Chinese in the country of China. Ask students from other countries to share these and other words in their native languages. Invite parents and community members to participate. Work with students to prepare interview questions for visitors.

2. Discuss foreign languages, especially those that might be spoken by students in the classroom. Ask students to demonstrate their language by naming some familiar items in the room in their foreign language. Have students label items, such as books, chairs, the clock, cabinets, computers, and so on in several different languages. Give each student a copy of activity 2-8B, *Interpreting the Environment for Multicultural Classmates.* Assist them as they work in small groups with FL (Foreign Language) lists, foreign language dictionaries, and Family Name Origins (see Appendix).

3. Have students work in cooperative groups to learn the meanings and pronunciation of foreign language words. Help them to point out similarities and differences in the types of letters and sounds. Ask all students to demonstrate their knowledge of foreign language words by reading LOVE, PLAY, WORK, FAMILY and FUN in a foreign language. Have them identify these words in the following languages: English, Gujarati, Tagalog, Chinese, French, and Spanish. Have them add other words and languages. Also, have students from other countries teach these words in their languages.

All students, English and foreign language, will have fun with this activity. An environment of acceptance is increased as students from diverse cultural, ethnic, and/or racial backgrounds interact. Also, normally shy immigrant students' self-esteem visibly rises, as they teach others AND watch their English-speaking classmates laugh and struggle with the pronunciation of foreign words. Give each student a copy of activity 2-8C, *Languages Are Different.* Ask students in small cooperative groups to share the outcome of their work together. Encourage them to compare and contrast the configuration of the various characters, letters, and sounds of the languages.

Extend this activity by labeling objects in the room with titles in as many different languages as possible. Give students opportunities to write out easy words in Egyptian hieroglyphics. Celebrate the diversity AND the common need for human beings to be able to communicate with each other.

4. Show a restaurant menu, or a picture of one. Ask students what it is used for. Discuss their experiences eating out. For example, what do you have to do once you come to the table in a restaurant? (Answer: Sit at the table, read the menu,

give the waiter your order, wait for your food, eat, pay for the food, and so on.) Ask the students to describe what would happen if they went to a French (Russian, Kenyan, Mexican, Italian) restaurant and the menu were written in French. Discuss the importance of either knowing the language or having someone interpret the menu. Give each student activity 2-8D, *Ordering Chinese Food for Lunch.* Ask students why the foods are written vertically on the Waiter's Ticket. Have students total the cost of the lunch and compare their answers. Also, have them share the results of writing Chinese characters.

5. Extend this excursion into foreign languages into the area of multicultural artwork. Show children pictures/paintings of everyday things that people all over the world use and/or need. Invite children to work in cooperative groups to find foreign language words for familiar items. Here children will also recognize the universality of the enjoyment of artwork. Provide them with pictures of artwork from various cultures and try to recreate models of vases, masks, faces, and so on. Then have them locate specific foreign language words for their own creations of things people in cultures see, use, and draw in paintings, such as houses, food, flowers, etc. Give each student activity 2-8E, *Art and Languages.* Have group decisions on where to display their work. Plan to do research and find other examples of art by people from many cultures. Invite parents and members of the community to participate.

> **LITERATURE CONNECTION**: *The Day of Ahmed's Secret* by Florence Parry Heide. An Egyptian boy goes through the bustling streets of Cairo delivering bottles of fuel to his customers. The flavor of the culture is imparted as he relates to others while on his route. At night he shares a wonderful surprise with his family. Lothrop, Lee & Shepard Books, New York, © 1990. Illustrated.

Activity 2-9A **COUNTING IN CHINESE IS FUN**

Activity 2-9B **DO YOU KNOW CHINESE NUMBERS?**

Activity 2-9C **FOREIGN NUMBER WORDS PUZZLE**

Activity 2-9D **HOW MANY BALLOONS?**

Activity 2-9E **FIVE FINGERS IN ANY LANGUAGE**

In this series of math activities, students will expand their knowledge regarding the need for calculation systems in all cultures. Moreover, the foundation for mutual respect is strengthened as students experience intriguing number symbols and practice counting in English and other languages. Understanding the commonalities among various languages, while simultaneously experiencing the universal need for computation, are significant student outcomes.

Materials Needed:

- Copies of activity sheets:
  2-9A, *Counting in Chinese Is Fun*
  2-9B, *Do you Know Chinese Numbers?*
  2-9C, *Foreign Number Words Puzzle*
  2-9D, *How Many Balloons?*
  2-9E, *Five Fingers in Any Language*
- Foreign Language Lists of Numbers (see Appendix)
- Pencils
- Crayons or markers
- Scissors

Directions:

1. Ask children to join together in counting aloud to the number 10. Explain that people all over the world count to 10 and higher, just as we do in America. Show children a few numbers in Spanish, Chinese, Swahili, etc., on the chalkboard. Have them compare the English numbers to the foreign language numbers (words and/or symbols).

2. Discuss the need for numbers in every culture. Ask students to think of ways in which people use numbers. For example, to keep track of the number of students in a classroom, to know the amount of money it takes to buy food, to ask for the gallons of gas needed for the car, to count the number of days in the week, or the number of weeks in the month, are only a few of the ways numbers are used.

3. Ask students who are bilingual to share what they know about numbers in their languages. They might write numbers on the board. These children could act as teachers as the class completes the activity sheets in this series.

4. Give children activity sheet 2-9A, *Counting in Chinese Is Fun*. Place some of the symbols on the board. Have foreign language "teachers" help their classmates to pronounce number words.

5. Distribute activity sheet 2-9B, *Do You Know Chinese Numbers?* Have students use their new knowledge to complete this activity.

6. Pass out activity sheet 2-9C, *Foreign Number Words Puzzle.* Ask students to read the number words for ONE, TWO, THREE, FOUR, and FIVE in three foreign languages. Then have them cut the languages and the number words out and mix them up. Have them work in pairs or small groups to arrange the numbers in the correct boxes beneath each language.

7. Give children activity sheet 2-9D, *How Many Balloons?* Reinforce the concept that people of all nationalities have to use numbers every day. Discuss some of the places and times numbers are used. For example, in buying food, clothing, and paying for services. These things happen in every country and in every culture.

8. Distribute activity sheet 2-9E, *Five Fingers in Any Language.* Emphasize the fact that all human beings, no matter what their racial or ethnic background, have five fingers on each hand. (NOTE: If necessary, discuss situations in which individuals might not have four fingers and one thumb on each hand because of birth defects, accidents, war, etc.) Provide opportunities for students to locate the information they need on the Foreign Language List in the Appendix.

LITERATURE CONNECTION: *Amigo Means Friend* by Louise Everett. The fact that best friends can speak different languages is shown in this easy-to-read story. Troll Associates, Mahwah, New Jersey, © 1988. Illustrated by Sandy Rabinowitz.

Activity 2-10 LETTERS, NUMBERS, AND WORDS ARE DIFFERENT

This activity reinforces the value of similarities and differences among human beings in the world. Also, it gives children exercises in discernment and practice in foreign languages, as a basis for increasing their development of mutual respect.

Materials Needed:

- Copy of activity sheet 2-10, *Letters, Numbers, and Words Are Different*
- Pencils
- Drawing paper
- Crayons or markers

Directions:

1. Give each child the activity 2-10, *Letters, Numbers, and Words Are Different.* Define the words *similarities* and *differences.* Have students note the shapes

and configurations of the pairs of items in the boxes. Do the first box together. Then ask students to complete the worksheet and draw their own pairs of objects for comparing and contrasting. Encourage them to look around the classroom for ideas.

2. Give children an opportunity to identify the foreign language symbols in the last box on the activity sheet. Ask them to recall the numbers for four and five in Chinese from activities 2-9A and 2-9B.

LITERATURE CONNECTION: *26 Letters and 99 Cents* by Tana Hoban. Photographs of everyday items and coins depicting similarities and differences. Instructional and entertaining. Greenwillow Books, New York, © 1987.

Puniddles by Bruce McMillan and Brett McMillan. Easy-to-solve riddles and puns are presented in photographs of everyday things. Macmillan, New York, © 1982.

Activity 2-11A PEOPLE ARE INTERDEPENDENT

Activity 2-11B SET YOUR TABLE FOR COMPANY

Activity 2-11C WHAT'S TO EAT?

In this section, children learn more about the value of respect by observing how people of every race, religion, and culture need each other. Also, they will be able to discern the beauty and excitement inherent in diversity while finding security and validity in commonalities which cause human beings to come together in times of emergency, or during times of celebration. In addition, students learn that, in the world of business, people do not usually worry about the color, race, or ethnic origin of the person whose goods and services they need. Through these lessons, the children observe that the community and the school are richer because of the various cultures of people who, by their very presence, share their heritage. Finally, the concept of extending hospitality to people of diverse racial, cultural, and ethnic origins is used to further advance the children's skills in reducing conflicts in their own environments.

Materials Needed:

- Copy of activity sheet 2-11A, *People Are Interdependent*
- Copy of activity sheet 2-11B, *Set Your Table for Company*

- Copy of activity sheet 2-11C, *What's to Eat?*
- Crayons/pencils
- Scissors
- Cardboard and/or construction paper
- Markers
- Tongue depressors
- Paper plates and napkins
- Poster paper/oaktag
- Glue
- Construction paper/different colors
- Recipe books, take-out restaurant menus, and magazines with food suggestions from different cultures
- Pictures of a variety of people of different races and colors
- Multiracial dolls (optional)
- Photographs of students (school pictures)
- Name tags*

Directions:

1. Have students find multiracial pictures of people in magazines and newspapers. Discuss the beauty of the differences among the various types of people. Have them imagine how boring it would be if every person in the world looked alike, spoke the same language, lived in the same type of house, or had the same skin, hair, and/or eye color. Then, elicit from the children things which all human beings have in common, even though they are from different racial, ethnic, and cultural backgrounds. Discuss the similarities in moods: happiness, sadness, anger, surprise, and so on. Also, talk about basic human needs of food, clothing, and shelter, affection, friends, work, etc.

2. Show some pictures of the recent natural disasters which have occurred in America: fires, earthquakes, floods, and hurricanes. Ask children how caring people helped the victims of these tragedies. Explain the insignificance of race, color, culture, or religion when it came to human beings in these crisis situations, receiving and giving help. Recall the word "INTERDEPENDENT." Have students note how diverse groups of human beings need the same kinds of things in order to live. Emphasize the fact that people should not think about the color or race of the person when it comes to getting or giving a job, providing a service, or helping in an emergency.

Give each student a copy of activity 2-11A, *People Are Interdependent.* Extend this concept by listing ways in which students depend upon each other. Some ways might include: Planning and painting a mural, partners or team members in a sport, singing a song, playing board games, and the like. Encourage students to applaud themselves, if they are already involved in interdependent activities. Have them give specific examples.

3. Discuss the ways in which human beings live their lives, because they are not animals or flowers. Some examples include these: Human beings get paid for doing their jobs, write and record music for audiences, play team sports, and cele-

brate religious holidays and birthdays. To strengthen the basis for the development of mutual respect among the various cultures in the class, discuss the commonality of human birth and growth. Use multiracial dolls versus children to demonstrate how real people grow, no matter what their racial, religious, or cultural background. Elicit from children the reasons that dolls do not grow. This foundation for respecting and understanding others can be further strengthened by pointing out that all people share a similar life cycle: birth, a period of living, and death.

Write the words MUTUAL RESPECT, JEALOUSY, LOVE, SELFISHNESS, HATE, SHARING, FRIENDSHIP, and FIGHTING on the chalkboard. Ask children to choose only the words which make people happy and tell why. Have students come to the board and cross out the words which make people unhappy. Begin to write and post the "good" words on large posters around the room. Add other "good" words as often as possible.

4. Discuss the fact that it is natural for human beings to live in groups, rather than alone. So, they should treat each other in positive (right), rather than negative (wrong) ways. Elicit from children that this is called MUTUAL RESPECT. Help students to see the "good" or "positive" words as useful in their everyday lives. Encourage them to look at the "good" words and choose from among them, as they work and play with people of diverse racial, religious, cultural, and ethnic backgrounds. Use the "good" words continually, as a conflict resolution strategy. Help children identify sources for "good" words, such as the thesaurus, conversations, feelings, and so on.

5. Elicit from children the ways that they have fun in their families, i.e., celebrations of birthdays, holidays, and so on. Note the similarities in preparing for guests, such as shopping for food, cooking, and setting the table. Ask students to pretend that they are inviting each other's families and friends for dinner. Give each student activity 2-11B, *Set Your Table for Company*. Explain that item 14 is an example for them to follow. Have them share the completed worksheets in small groups.

6. Give each student activity 2-11C, *What's to Eat?* Have them work together to plan a menu for their guests. Provide them with the materials they would need to make larger versions of the worksheet table settings. Have the children collect the items they need to create attractive table settings. Have recipe books with menus from many ethnic groups available for the completion of the worksheet. Extend the concept of hospitality by planning a real multicultural feast. Invite parents to participate.

CELEBRATE THE RACIAL, CULTURAL, AND NATIONAL ORIGIN OF EACH CHILD IN THE CLASSROOM. MAKE IT SPECIAL: Plan to honor a child, a family, and/or a cultural group on a daily, weekly, bi-monthly, or monthly basis. Use this opportunity to present specific information which would make each child proud of his/her background, family, and/or heritage.

*(A special poster or chart with slots for changing names and photographs can be made for this purpose.)

LITERATURE CONNECTION: *The Park Bench* by Takeshita Fumiko. Diverse groups of people visit the park each day as told from the viewpoint of the park bench. A Japanese and English bilingual edition. Kane/Miller, New York, © 1989. Illustrated by Mamoru Suzuki. Translated by Ruth A. Kanagy.

Neighborhood Odes by Gary Soto. A Spanish-American poet celebrates neighborhood life by writing of the diverse experiences of the people who live there. He writes of fireworks, music, snow, the water sprinklers, tennis shoes, and relationships. Harcourt, Brace and Jovanovich, New York, © 1992. Illustrated by David Diaz.

Activity 2-12A GOOD MORNING

Activity 2-12B GOOD NIGHT

Children will experience diversity and have fun with their peers as they practice speaking to each other in different languages. In addition, there will be an extension of concepts in multicultural understanding, as students internalize the commonalities among the languages, the common need to communicate, and the common need that people of all cultures have for pleasant greetings. It is expected that there will be a carry-over into the community, as children take these new greetings home to share with family and friends.

Materials Needed:

- Copy of activity sheet 2-12A, *Good Morning*
- Copy of activity sheet 2-12B, *Good Night*
- Drawing paper
- Markers or crayons
- Foreign Language List and/or books
- Scissors

Directions:

1. Explain the similarities among human beings which indicate that people of different races, religions, and nationalities greet each other by saying, "Good Morning" or "Hello." Have students greet each other. Elicit from children the fact that people make each other happy when they speak pleasantly and that

this is a good way to start each new day. Point out the fact that the smiles and happy expressions, which usually accompany greetings, just add to the joy.

2. Pronounce several foreign language words for "hello" or "good morning." Pronounce these words together. Use the Foreign Language List in the Appendix and/or foreign language dictionaries. Indicate some of the countries where the languages are spoken. Swahili is a language spoken in several African countries, for example. Jambo or Salamu are words for "hello" in Swahili and can be used at any time. The students will learn the Swahili word for good morning, "Habari za asubuhi," on the worksheet.

3. Give students copies of activity 2-12A, *Good Morning*. Pronounce the words together. After they complete the worksheet and practice saying the greetings, have them choose one or two of them to memorize and illustrate. Have students draw pictures of themselves, and/or people of different ethnic groups, speaking to others at the beginning of the day. Elicit from children the types of expressions the people will have on their faces.

4. Give students copies of activity 2-12B, *Good Night*. Discuss the fact that people of every race, culture, and ethnic group have pleasant words that make people feel good at the end of the day. Pronounce the words together. After they complete the worksheet and practice the greetings, have them choose one or two of them to memorize and illustrate. Have students draw pictures of themselves and people of various ethnic backgrounds exchanging greetings, at the end of the day. Elicit from the children the types of expressions the people will have on their faces.

Extend this activity by having children take the greetings home and share them with their families. Also, encourage the children to add to their collection of greetings and countries of origin. A good cooperative activity would be for students to collect several commonly used sentences in several languages. For example, "How are you?" "What is your name?" "Come and play with me."

LITERATURE CONNECTION: *Jambo Means Hello: Swahili Alphabet Book* by Muriel Feelings. A vision of East African tribal life is given using the national language of the countries of Uganda, Kenya, and Tanzania. A pronunciation key is included. Dial, New York, © 1981. Illustrated by Tom Feelings.

Activity 2-13A AN AMERICAN CLASSROOM

Activity 2-13B MY CLASS STORY

Activity 2-13C BOOKS IN EVERY LAND

Activity 2-13D AMERICANS—ALL

In this series of activities, mutual respect will become natural for students as they develop an intrinsic world view and consider their multicultural backgrounds. Their understanding of the diversity among human beings is enhanced as they portray six imaginary classmates in pictures and stories. Students will give these "classmates" characteristics and write class stories which could parallel their own multicultural experiences. Also, students will think about the necessity of education for all children in a lesson which focuses on the importance of reading. Ideas for encouraging children to pursue academic excellence by regularly reading from a broad range of literature are included.

Students encounter the historical reality of the immigrant status of all Americans and, as a result, think about their roles in helping to promote peace. They come to understand that no one group has a claim on America; it belongs to all of us. Finally, students will discern that, like our country, this ONE EARTH has to be SHARED by the people of various hues, religions, cultural, and ethnic groups. Primary students come to understand that to act unkindly towards others results in fighting, not peace. Therefore, they learn that MUTUAL RESPECT and treating others kindly is the only WISE course of action.

Materials Needed:

- Copy of activity sheet 2-13A, *An American Classroom*
- Copy of activity sheet 2-13B, *My Class Story*
- Copy of activity sheet 2-13C, *Books in Every Land*
- Copy of activity sheet 2-13D, *Americans—All*
- Pencils
- A sample class story on a chart or written on a chalkboard (see sample)
- Crayons or markers
- Foreign Language Lists and books
- Various types of books (texts, stories)
- Drawing paper
- Globe and/or map of the world
- Pictures/films of school children in other lands, the subjects they have to learn, the length of school days and year

Directions:

1. Discuss the various groups of people in class and where their ancestors might have come from. Give children copies of activity 2-13A, *An American Classroom,* and point out that all across the country, boys and girls of different

races, colors, religions, and cultural backgrounds go to school together. Ask students to color the pictures of the six children to reflect different races and cultures. Then have them make up background information about each of the six children. They might include: age, gender, hair and eye color, favorite books, friends, native land, language, and family. Ask someone to volunteer to read the Class Story below:

"Our Class Story"

We have fun in our classroom. In our room most of us speak English, but we have students from many foreign countries; we're all learning together. See our six friends? Rita was born in Colombia and she speaks Spanish. Hagos is from Eritrea, a region in Africa. He speaks Tigrinya. Sung is from Korea; can you guess his native language? My other friends are from India, Norway, and Russia. Arti speaks Gujarati, Erika speaks Norwegian, and Sasha (he) speaks Russian. We counted the number of countries of the people in our class. There are 25 children. They and their families are from eight different foreign countries. We found all of these places on the big globe in the library, including the United States. We all live in America now and we're happy to be American citizens.

Our teacher was born in Mississippi and she helps us to learn more about English and other languages. We're also learning to count in Swahili and Chinese. Xin is helping us learn to write Chinese characters. We're reading about the different holidays, games, and native costumes of people all over the world. It's fun learning about different cultures and languages. We're going to have a big party for our class. There will be music, dancing, costumes, and food. Would you like to come?

Ask students to share information about their places of birth, languages, and holidays. Have them use some of this information, and ideas from the sample "Our Class Story" above, to complete the next activity.

2. Give students the activity 2-13B, *My Class Story,* and ask them to write something about themselves and their experiences with people in the classroom. Encourage them to share their stories with each other, family, and friends.

3. Elicit from students the reasons that people go to school. Give all children an opportunity to add comments regarding the need for education in order to get jobs, to survive on their own, to help other people, and to contribute to society. Then ask what they think other boys and girls their age might do during the weekdays in Spain, Korea, and other foreign countries. Discuss the importance of education for young people in every land. Show pictures of school children in other countries. If possible, get specific information about the types of subjects they learn, the length of the school day, the length of the school year, school uniforms, and other things which might be compared to American schools.

Elicit from children the fact that boys and girls from other lands would have to learn some of the same things they are learning. Ask students if they can name some things that all boys and girls learn. As they name such things as reading, math, science, writing, have them share what it would be like for them if they did not know these things. Discuss the words "literate" and "illiterate" and talk about the fact that people have to know how to read and compute in order to buy or create food, houses, clothing, and other basic human necessities.

4. Show children many types of books such as picture books, encyclopedias, dictionaries, and textbooks. Have students look at foreign language lists/books. Discuss the types of books, and the various languages that books are written in. Have them compare some of the foreign language texts to English texts. In an effort to help all students achieve academic excellence, encourage them to read on their own everyday. Offer incentives for reading outside of class, such as contests and prizes. Cite the public library as well as the school library as sources of recreational reading materials. Provide opportunities for students to discuss their books with you and each other.

Compare reading to running, which is good exercise for keeping the heart strong. Have students think of reading as an exercise for the mind, to keep it strong and alert. Adopt the motto—"Read for Your Life!" Have students say it and write it on posters. Give students activity 2-13C, *Books in Every Land.* Solicit the help of parents in starting reading programs for their children. Use librarians as resource people.

5. Explain that America is a land of many different people who all can share in its freedoms. Tell students that no one ethnic group owns America because all of its citizens, or their ancestors, have come from some other land. Therefore, all United States citizens should respect the rights of other Americans. NOTE: Information about the Civil Rights Movement of the 1960s can be used to extend the concept of equal rights. See the Mini-Biographies of Martin Luther King and Malcolm X, and references to Michael Schwerner, James Chaney, Andrew Goodman, and Viola Luizzo in the Appendix. Even young children can see that it is unfair to keep people from drinking from a public water fountain, eating in a restaurant, or riding on a bus just because of race or skin color. Elicit from children what is fair and equal treatment for people, of all races and colors, who want to use public places.

Compare and contrast how people of different races showed respect for each other before, during, and after the Civil Rights Movement. For example, before the Civil Rights Movement, boys and girls of different races had to go to different schools. In addition, African-Americans could not use public bathrooms, unless there was a sign which read BLACK or COLORED. Elicit from children that people of many races, colors, and religions worked to fight injustice and make sure that every American citizen has equal rights. Today, there are no signs WHITE or BLACK. American citizens of all races, colors, and ethnic groups can now use restaurants, bathrooms, water fountains, schools, and hospitals. Ask children how they can help make sure these freedoms remain. Also, elicit from children ways that they can show mutual respect and friendship for each other in the classroom.

6. Show children a world map or a globe and discuss the many different continents, climates, and people who inhabit the Earth. Pinpoint America as a place where people from long ago, even Native Americans, came to live. Define the word "immigrant." Explain that some immigrants, like the Pilgrims, came from England by choice and others, like the African slaves, were forced to come. (Grades 2 and 3 might discuss "immigration" and how people from many countries are on "waiting lists" to come to America.) NOTE: It is thought that Native Americans immigrated to North America by way of a strip of land which no longer exists. (Bering Straits)

7. Ask students how they would feel if they gave a party and the guests began to fight with each other and destroy the furniture, walls, and appliances. Elicit from students the idea that human beings are guests of the Earth and that they MUST care about each other and stop fighting. People everywhere would enjoy life better if they learned to respect each other. Give students activity 2-13D, *Americans-All.* Encourage them to use the words in the directions to help them complete the activity. Have them make up riddles and try them out on other students. Emphasize the concept that since we are all immigrants AND guests of the Earth, we should always welcome other immigrants and use our best manners when we are in their company.

LITERATURE CONNECTION: *I Hate English* by Ellen Levine. A Chinese girl's refusal to learn English until she finds that she often understands and speaks it. The fact that she continues to use her native Chinese language, even after learning English, promotes cultural pride. Scholastic, New York, © 1989. Illustrated by Steven Bjorkman.

Activity 2-14A THE FORMS OF ANIMALS AND THINGS

Activity 2-14B HUMAN FORMS ARE ALL ALIKE

Activity 2-14C HUMAN BEINGS LAUGH AND CRY

In this series of activities, students will note that human beings have the same basic physical characteristics. Through making comparisons and finding similarities, they learn that all human beings have the same kinds of emotional reactions to external and internal stimuli. Mutual respect develops as diverse student populations identify with similar physical and emotional reactions to their environments. Students experience a carry-over from their appreciation of beauty in the natural environment, to a deeper understanding and appreciation of the beauty of diversity among human beings. The theme of human commonalities, however, transcends the diversity and provides children with leverage as they come into contact with human beings from all over the world in their schools and communities. Diversity and commonality in the larger society are reflected in smaller multiracial family units. Children of different races are sometimes born or adopted. Whether the parents are of the same race or different races, these are families with people of different races living together harmoniously.

Materials Needed:

- Copy of activity sheet 2-14A, *The Forms of Animals and Things*
- Copy of activity sheet 2-14B, *Human Forms Are All Alike*
- Copy of activity sheet 2-14C, *Human Beings Laugh and Cry*
- Paste and scissors
- Pillowcase for concealing small objects, including geometric shapes
- Geometric shapes (pairs) in several colors
- Drawing paper
- Pictures of a variety of animals, objects, and people
- Pictures of people showing different emotions
- Pictures of racially mixed parents and children
- Chart paper

Directions:

1. Ask students if they can tell the difference between a cat and a book in the dark and to explain why they can. Have them look around the room and name other pairs of objects which can be identified in the dark. Play a game in which students can demonstrate their skills of discernment. Allow them to reach into a pillowcase which contains several small objects. Without looking, they should be able to identify some of the items. Give all students who want to try this an opportunity to guess what the objects are.

2. Ask students to describe the shapes and size and color of some of the items in the room, such as the desks, bulletin boards, books, computers, maps, chairs, clocks, and so on. Follow this by asking them how they could identify these same things if the room were totally dark. Most children would volunteer that things can be identified by shape but not by color. Discuss the value of having light to see the things we use AND the beauty of the differences in shapes and colors of objects,

animals, and flowers. Give students activity 2-14A, *The Forms of Animals and Things*. Have them complete this and share their findings.

3. Have students describe specific things about the human form (shape). Elicit from students that as with nonhuman things, there are specific shapes and features like the nose, eyes, head, legs, and arms that can be used to identify the human form. Mutual respect develops as children see common physiological features among themselves and their peers; features that distinguish all of them, despite diversity in skin color, races and ethnicity, from nonhuman objects. Use pictures and real objects to compare the human form to other forms. Begin a discussion of the skeletal system. (Optional)

4. Mix pairs of geometric shapes in with the objects in the pillowcase. Ask for volunteers to find shapes which can be placed together or which match just by the way they feel. Have children find objects which are just alike in size and shape, but not in color. Now, have someone volunteer to reach in the bag and pull out geometric shapes that are the same.

See if children can identify triangles, circles, and so on. Have them note that they can discern shape, but not color. Elicit from students that the same is true for human beings. Basic human forms are alike. Give students activity 2-14B, *Human Forms Are All Alike*. Elicit the insignificance of skin color, language, national origin, and religion with regard to human qualities.

5. Describe some very common human traits that have nothing to do with skin color, race, gender, age, national origin, or culture. Elicit from children the kinds of emotions that people of all racial and ethnic groups express. Ask students if animals or plants display any of these emotions.

6. Ask students to think of the kinds of things they do everyday that other human beings all over the world do. Discuss a few human activities and have students work in small groups to make lists of things pertaining to work, play, and worship.

7. Give students activity 2-14C, *Human Beings Laugh and Cry*, to complete. They may use words from their small group lists, from discussions, or make up new ones. On separate paper, have each of them draw pictures of people of many colors, religions, and languages involved in the activities they have written about on their worksheets. Answers will vary and could include: People of all races can SLEEP, PLAY, READ, SING, WALK, SMILE, TALK, CRY, LAUGH, EAT, WRITE, etc. Encourage children to think of as many answers as possible. They can share them. Display their drawings and worksheets.

LITERATURE CONNECTION: *Shawn Goes to School* by Petronella Brienburg. The story of a little boy's first day in nursery school! The period of adjustment is something children of diverse backgrounds can relate to. HarperCollins, New York, © 1973. Illustrated by Errol Lloyd.

Activity 2-15A WE ARE NEIGHBORS

Activity 2-15B WHAT IS FRIENDSHIP?

The cultural richness in racially mixed neighborhoods and schools is observed by students in these lessons. That the people in these areas are economically, and sometimes socially, interdependent is indicated. When students consider the businesses and services available to the residents of a community, they note that there is little concern about the race, religion, or culture of the providers. In neighborhoods, people want to live and survive by having their basic needs met. Specifically, people of every ethnic, racial and cultural origin have basic needs of food, clothing, and shelter. Sometimes emergencies happen and these basic needs are threatened or destroyed. In many of these cases neighbors help each other and don't stop to think about race or ethnic origin. They work together to solve their problems because they have the same kinds of basic needs. These activities provide opportunities for children to develop cause and effect skills as they explore the reasons and results of their own actions and those of others.

Respect for diverse groups of people develops further as children interact with each other as neighbors in the school environment, and learn to put racial and ethnic differences aside. It is rewarding for students to find that superficial differences can be put in their proper perspective and that they can learn to care for each other, without regard to race, color, religion, language, ethnic background, or culture. From such experiences, friendships can develop.

Materials Needed:

- Copy of activity sheet 2-15A, *We Are Neighbors*
- Copy of activity sheet 2-15B, *What Is Friendship?*
- Colorful pictures of people in neighborhood settings such as buildings, houses, stores, gas stations, fire station, etc.
- Scissors and glue
- Construction paper
- Crayons/markers/pencils
- Paper for writing stories
- Building blocks, miniature trees, animals, and houses for building a neighborhood

Directions:

1. Begin with the question, "How many of you have taken a walk around your neighborhood and what did you see?" Listen and record as many responses as possible on the chalkboard under the headings:

PEOPLE BUSINESSES HOUSES APARTMENTS NATURE

Have them write experience stories about their neighborhoods, even if they have not walked around. Some students might respond that they have been driven to various places in the family car. List these, as well. Give opportunities for sharing and illustrating the stories. Display the stories in the classroom and/or in the community.

2. Discuss the different races of people who live in the neighborhood around the school and possibly on the same blocks with students in the class. Allow children to talk about classmates who are their neighbors. Have them share stories about pets, experiences with special events on their block, and times when they've played together. Suggest some exciting neighborhood happenings like block parties, street games, ice-cream vendors, Girl Scout cookie sales, etc. Elicit from students the multiracial, multiethnic, multicultural participation in these events.

3. Show pictures of houses, buildings, businesses, fire stations, doctors' offices, and post offices. Ask children if they have ever heard a siren or air raid warning signal. Discuss the fact that these sounds indicate that there is trouble, or provide warnings to people that there is a possibility of danger and that they should prepare to go to a place of safety. Have children share experiences with emergency sirens and/or vehicles. For example, some children might have heard rescue squad, police, or fire truck sirens. Others might know someone who has been taken to the hospital in an ambulance or a police car. Maybe there has been a fire, flood, or storm which made it necessary for families to quickly leave their homes.

Ask students if they have heard about the fires and earthquakes in California where many people lost their homes. Discuss how neighbors helped each other during these emergencies. Elicit from students the fact that people tend to forget about race, culture, and ethnic background in times of trouble. They help each other because everyone has the same need to feel safe. In order to survive people need houses to live in, food to eat, and clothes to wear. Many people who live far away often send food, clothes, and money to help those who have lost their homes and other basic needs. They are good neighbors, even though they live far away.

Give each child a copy of activity 2-15A, *We Are Neighbors*. Discuss the results and have children read their sentences. Extend the impact of these concepts by giving students the opportunity to cooperatively plan and build a replica of their neighborhood. Encourage them to make multiracial people to place in the community. Invite parents and friends to see their work.

4. Ask children for responses to the question, "What is friendship?" Allow each child to respond. Have students share specific activities friends do together and how these shared experiences create bonding and make the friendship better. For example, friends can have good times together and help each other in times of trouble. Children might want to tell about specific examples of games, trips, and

other fun times they've had with a friend. Ask if friends ever fight. Then tell the story of the "Toymaker" to the class.

"The Toymaker"

> A puppeteer made two puppets. He dressed one in red and white polka dots and the other one in red and white stripes. At first the puppets played and had fun together. Then one noticed that the other one was different. He then thought that he was better, so a violent fight began. The puppeteer entered to stop the argument and the fight. The puppets asked him which one of them he loved better. The argument was settled when the puppeteer said the following things, "I love you both. You see, I made you. One of you is my left hand, the other is my right hand. Both of you belong to me. You're part of me. So, by fighting, you've harmed yourselves and you've made yourselves and me very unhappy. Now that you've hurt each other so badly, don't you think it's time to apologize to each other and then all of us will be happy again?" The puppeteer shows the puppets making up.

Elicit from children the reasons that the puppets become friends again. One suggestion might be that they have much in common because they were made by the same person and are part of him. Another reason is that they are both loved. Have students look for other reasons for the renewed friendship in the story, and apply these learnings to solving real conflicts in the classroom and/or community. Elicit from students ways that people of different races and religions can stop fighting, begin talking, make up with each other, and be happy living together. Assess real life conflicts that have taken place in the class or neighborhood and help children write a play, a skit, or a story similar to "The Toymaker." Plan to publish the play for parents to read in the school paper, or have students perform it for parents and/or community groups.

5. Have children work in cooperative groups to make "Friendship" books. Provide them with magazines from which they can choose pictures of people from a variety of racial, cultural, and ethnic groups. Have them cut pictures out and paste them on pages which have the following types of sentences:

1. A friend will love you at all times.
2. A friend is there when you need him or her.
3. A friend will never be ashamed of you.
4. A friend will give you his or her best.
5. A friend will not hurt you.
6. A friend will not stay angry with you.

Encourage creativity by having students use crayons, markers, and other things to decorate their books. Ask students if parents and other adults can be their friends. Have them support their opinions with specific reasons, examples, and details.

6. Encourage children to make up their own sentences which reflect the relationships they have with friends. Also, ask them to get ideas for friendship sentences from the magazine pictures. Finally, elicit from children the idea that in order to have friends, each person has to BE A FRIEND. Use their friendship books to discuss how people can develop friendships. Give each child a copy of activity 2-15B, *What Is Friendship?* Have them address the envelope and give it to a friend. CAUTION: Teacher should be aware of shy students who might need friends. Make sure that every student receives a Friendship Card. OPTION: Ask the children to take the card home and share it with friends and family.

LITERATURE CONNECTION: *Abuela* by Arthur Dorros. The richness of Hispanic culture is shared with readers as a little girl and her grandmother take a fantasy trip over the city. Their "flying" experiences are captured in English and in Spanish. Dutton Children's Books, New York, © 1991. Illustrated by Elisa Kleven.

Fly Away Home by Eve Bunting. A young boy and his dad are homeless and have to live in an airport, along with other homeless people. They know how to blend in and not be noticed. Hopes for a better life are seen as a bird, who is trapped in the terminal, gets free. Clarion Books, New York, © 1991. Illustrated by Ronald Himler.

Activity 2-16A BRINGING HOME THE BACON

Activity 2-16B PEOPLE HAVE THE SAME NEEDS

Activity 2-16C ALL PEOPLE NEED _______ ?

Through comparisons of basic human needs among diverse groups of people, children will develop a foundation for mutual respect. The common quest for food, water, clothing, and shelter, those things which human beings of all races and cultures need, are important elements which children can identify as crucial to their own survival. Therefore, students, through close observation of human commonalities, will discern that the rejection of others who are very much like themselves is unwise, unkind, and unrewarding.

While involved in these activities, children will absorb rich and meaningful information regarding the interdependence of people of different cultures. Specifically, they will learn that producers of goods and services and consumers of goods and services need each other. An understanding of these concepts form the basis for positive intercultural relationships. Through these activities, even very young children can relate to the plight of people in areas of famine. They can also understand that respect for other human beings encompasses a concern for their survival. Thus, information about food being taken to the starving people of famine stricken Somalia will provide good examples for students who are learning what it means to care about other people, despite their culture, race, religion, or nationality.

Materials Needed:

- Copy of activity sheet 2-16A, *Bringing Home the Bacon*
- Copy of activity sheet 2-16B, *People Have the Same Needs*
- Copy of activity sheet 2-16C, *All People Need________?*
- Pencils
- Crayons, markers, paints, etc.
- Pictures of farms, farmers, tractors, supermarkets, trucks
- Pictures of harvests and food processing
- Pictures of houses, clothing, and food from many cultures
- Charts to show interdependence
- Information about people helping each other during natural disasters
- Construction paper
- Scissors and glue
- Pictures of multicultural groups of military and civilian people from America, Germany, France, the Red Cross, CARE, United Nations, working together in Somalia in East Africa to help those who are starving
- Pictures and/or stories of crisis in which people help others (homeless, elderly, sickness, crime)

Directions:

1. Ask students if they have ever been really hungry and what they did about it. Explain that, all over the world, there are people who do not have enough food. Emphasize that people must have food, if they are to live healthy lives. Elicit from children how those who are strong can help others. Show pictures of multiracial, multinational troops of marines and soldiers helping the starving people of Somalia in East Africa. Discuss how human beings who help each other are showing respect for human life.

2. Have students name some workers who see to it that human beings have the food that they need to live. Discuss the various types of people who bring food to supermarkets. Mention the farmers', food manufacturers' and food processors' roles. Show pictures of farms and various transportation vehicles which take food to markets. These may include refrigeration cars, trucks, trains,

and planes. The use of planes, tanks, and other military equipment and personnel are sometimes required to get emergency supplies of food to people in famine areas. Discuss the interdependence of the farmers who plant, the workers who harvest, the truck drivers who deliver, the food processors, the people who pack, and the people who buy and eat the food. Use a chart to show this INTERDEPENDENCE. Define the words PRODUCER and CONSUMER as those people who produce or provide goods and services and those people who buy goods and services.

HUMAN BEINGS ARE INTERDEPENDENT
(PEOPLE NEED EACH OTHER)

FARMERS

HARVEST WORKERS   PRODUCE BUYERS   TRUCK DRIVERS

STORE OWNERS   STORE MANAGERS   EMPLOYEES   CONSUMERS

3. Ask children to share some of their experiences with grocery shopping. Use the chart to emphasize how the food gets to the supermarket and how their parents have to earn money from someone else in order to buy food. Have students note the various races and cultures of the people on the chart. Give students activity 2-16A, *Bringing Home the Bacon*. Elicit from students the meaning of this expression and how it came about. (Suggest that the need for someone to work and earn the money to buy food for his/her family is one meaning.) Emphasize the concept of INTERDEPENDENCE regarding the need for people to have food to eat. Have children read their responses to the question regarding the importance of race and color in bringing food to people.

4. Ask children to identify those things that are necessary for living. Then ask them to identify those things which human beings can do without. Elicit from students the difference between the items which are NEEDS and those which are WANTS. Emphasize human common needs which exist for African-Americans, European-Americans, Native-Americans, Hispanic-Americans, Asian-Americans, and so on. All people need to eat, wear clothes, and have a place to live. Help students to discern that people do not NEED televisions, toys, jewelry, in order to survive. However, people do need water and food in order to live.

Elicit from children the fact that the basic needs of all people can be met only if we all work together to protect the Earth's natural resources. Ask students to suggest ways that individuals from all races and ethnic groups can help take good care of the Earth. Write their suggestions on the chalkboard beneath these headings:

TAKING CARE OF THE

LAND	WATER	AIR	FOOD
1.	1.	1.	1.
2.	2.	2.	2.
3.	3.	3.	3.

Give students activity 2-16B, *People Have the Same Needs.* Ask students to use ideas from the list above to help them respond to the writing assignment at the bottom of the activity sheet. Have them share their written responses. Challenge the students to think about what could happen to human beings in America and the rest of the world, if we do not protect the land, water, and air. Elicit from them the fact that food supplies could be harmed and that people around the world might not have the food they need to live. Discuss what they can do to help.

5. Write the word HEALTH on the chalkboard and draw a circle around it. Ask students to tell what the word means to them. Some might suggest that health means not being sick, having the strength to run, or being able to lift heavy things. Write their responses outside the circle. Elicit from students what one has to do to have HEALTH. Some might suggest eating the proper foods, exercising regularly, and so on. If students do not mention sleep, write this outside the circle and explain the importance of rest in the lives of all human beings, regardless of their age, racial, ethnic, or cultural origin.

Help children to understand that, like food and exercise, rest is important to the health of each person's body and mind. When people have had enough rest, they think better, they are happier, and they are more successful in school and at work. Ask children to share their experiences when they or someone in their family has not had enough sleep. Discuss their responses in the context of the words *cross, mean-tempered, sleepy-head,* and *lazy.* Ask students how to solve this problem.

Give students activity 2-16C, *All People Need __________ ?* Have them color the picture and complete the sentence. Share the results.

NOTE: A lesson in classification would greatly enhance student understanding of the various common basic needs of all human beings. Have students form groups to identify and draw examples of FOOD, CLOTHING, and SHELTER. To demonstrate and re-emphasize that these are needs for people all over the globe, have students cut out and paste pictures of basic human needs on a large world map. Display the map in the school and/or in the community.

LITERATURE CONNECTION: *At the Crossroads* by Rachael Isadora. Children of a South African Township shantytown anxiously await the return of their fathers. They sing and plan, as they prepare for the homecoming of the men who have been away working in the mines for nine months. Greenwillow, New York, © 1991. Illustrated.

The Rag Coat by Lauren Mills. An Appalachian girl wears her special quilted coat to school and is teased by her classmates. She wins their friendship with her accounts of how the coat belongs to all of them. Little, Brown, Boston, © 1991. Illustrated by Dennis Nolan.

Activity 2-17A EVERYONE LIKES TO PLAY

Activity 2-17B FRIENDLY RAINBOWS

Activity 2-17C LET'S PLAY

Activity 2-17D PUZZLES AND FRIENDS

This series of activities will promote the concept of the universality of playfulness in human beings. Children are encouraged to choose friends to play with in a variety of games. Mutual respect is advanced during interaction on the playground, at the game table, at school, at home, etc., as children learn that people of all races, colors, and ethnic groups like to have fun. Furthermore, as they play together, children's curiosity about each other is satisfied and their learning about and appreciation of each other as individuals is increased. Children will discern that playing is fun and makes people happy, like feeling sunshine and seeing recurring smiles. In addition, they will compare the varieties of colors, ethnic groups, races, and cultures represented in the class to a beautiful rainbow. As they relate to peers in a nurturing classroom environment, children will learn to enjoy the benefits of diversity and, simultaneously, relish their commonalities as human beings.

Materials Needed:

- Copy of activity sheet 2-17A, *Everyone Likes to Play*
- Copy of activity sheet 2-17B, *Friendly Rainbows*
- Copy of activity sheet 2-17C, *Let's Play*
- Copy of activity sheet 2-17D, *Puzzles and Friends*
- Pencils
- Scissors
- Patches of cloth/felt—many colors
- Blunt needles
- Thread—one color
- Hole puncher
- Lists of things that people enjoy
- Lists of things that people do not enjoy

Directions:

1. Give students an opportunity to tell about their favorite games and/or what they like to do to have fun. Encourage them to talk about favorite toys, hobbies, and musical instruments that reflect their cultural heritage. Then, note the similarities and differences in the choices they make, which have nothing to do with their racial or cultural backgrounds.

2. Point out that people in families, neighborhoods, schools, and businesses, all over the world, like to play. Have students identify things that have little or nothing to do with playing. Elicit from children the fact that playing is fun. (NOTE: Professional sports is a good example of people who earn large sums of money to PLAY, and others pay large sums of money as they have fun watching athletes PLAY.) Ask students to describe how people act when they play.

3. People who are involved in playing smile, laugh, and do other things which indicate their joy. Give students opportunities to share different types of games that they know about and/or have played. Have students compare and contrast the responses of people when they are playing and their actions when they are involved in more serious or less enjoyable activities like TAKING A TEST OR TAKING OUT THE GARBAGE. Elicit from children the fact that people of different races and cultures respond similarly when they are NOT PLAYING. Give children copies of 2-17A, *Everyone Likes to Play.*

4. Ask how many children have ever seen a rainbow. Compare the varieties of students in the class to the beauty of the many colors in a rainbow. Discuss the beautiful eyes, skin colors, hair, and clothing. Extend this concept and reinforce each child's pride in his/her heritage by having them make their own "Rainbow Quilt." Provide each child with a felt square to decorate and personalize with his or her own name. Punch very small holes on the edges and have children work cooperatively to sew their quilt together. Elicit from students the fact that the different colors in the quilt and the decorations celebrate their racial, cultural, and ethnic diversity, while the one color of the thread used to sew the patches together celebrates their human commonalities. Just as the many squares of the quilt are bound by the thread, human beings are bonded by their friendship. Display the Rainbow Quilt in a special place in the school and/or community.

5. Extend the concept of human commonalities, which cause human beings to desire to play and enjoy the company of other people, to include human LIKES and DISLIKES. For example, the human dislike for war, hate, and pain transcend color, race, and ethnicity. The same is true of the human enjoyment of peace, love, and health. Encourage children to think about human LIKES and DISLIKES that transcend race, color, religion, and ethnic origin. Plan a time when the students can do some of the activities they have chosen.

Ask the questions: WHAT ARE HUMAN LIKES? WHAT ARE HUMAN DISLIKES? and HOW ARE HUMANS ALIKE? Discuss their responses and write them on the board. Give children activity 2-17B, *Friendly Rainbows*. Encourage students to use their own personal responses to complete the worksheet. Provide additional help for those who need it by using ideas from the list below:

HUMAN LIKES	HUMAN DISLIKES	HOW HUMANS ARE ALIKE
1. Birthdays	1. War	1. Birth process
2. Feeling safe	2. Feeling unsafe	2. Blood types
3. Toys	3. Not sharing	3. Need for friends
4. Beautiful things	4. Feeling unliked	4. Grown-ups care for children
5. Music	5. Fighting	5. Need for food, home, clothes
6. Food	6. Pain	6. Need for family

Have children read their sentences and share their drawings from this two-page activity.

6. Discuss the fun children can have playing together, especially if they choose people who like to do the same things they like to do. Name several types of games and ask them to raise their hands to choose a favorite. Note that choices have nothing to do with the person's ethnic background, religion, race, or color. Explore several games from different cultures to include in the instruction. Give children activity 2-17C, *Let's Play*.

7. Give children activity 2-17D, *Puzzles and Friends*. Encourage small group play and exchange of ideas.

LITERATURE CONNECTION: *Playtime in Africa* by Efual Autherland. Happy times are found in play for children of every land. The fun of children in Africa doing the same kinds of things that children in other lands do is shown in photographs and poetic text. Atheneum, New York, © 1968. Photographs by Willis E. Bell.

Roxaboxen by Alice Mclerran. Children work and play together to build a town of their own. Based on memories of real life experiences. Lothrop, Lee & Shepard, New York, © 1991. Illustrated by Barbara Cooney.

Wheels by Shirley Hughes. An African-American boy and a Hispanic boy play on their bikes in a neighborhood full of children. A story of friendship and competition. Lothrop, Lee & Shepard, New York, © 1991. Illustrated.

Activity 2-18A FRIENDS IN THE RAIN

Activity 2-18B FRIENDS IN THE SUNSHINE

Activity 2-18C YOU ARE MY SUNSHINE

In this series of activities, children will observe that in certain situations people often need other people. They learn that a person's racial or cultural background has little to do with his/her basic human needs. In addition, they see that people of diverse ethnic backgrounds work together to help meet the needs of other human beings. Furthermore, as children interact with each other, they begin to appreciate and enjoy friendships which can occur among people who are different. They will also understand that human beings of different races and cultures can help each other through difficult times and protect one another from the rain (pain) of life. Learning to care about others is an important concept which develops as children begin to accept and appreciate their human commonalities.

Materials Needed:

- Copy of activity sheet 2-18A, *Friends in the Rain*
- Copy of activity sheet 2-18B, *Friends in the Sunshine*
- Copy of activity sheet 2-18C, *You Are My Sunshine*
- Multiracial pictures of people helping others (doctors, teachers, volunteers)

Directions:

1. So often, people find themselves caught in the rain with no umbrella. Ask students if they would share, if they had an umbrella and it started to rain. Allow time for them to tell why they would or would not let someone else get beneath their umbrella.

2. Draw an analogy between rain and some types of problems which can happen to people. Discuss the need for help when a person is sick, hungry, locked out of a car, lost, or hurt. Ask students if people should refuse help from someone because of skin color, race, or religion. Turn the question around the other way and ask if people who are able to give help should refuse because of skin color, race, or religion of the needy. Ask children how they feel when stormy weather with flashes of lightning and claps of thunder comes. Have them compare fear and concern to the joy of seeing the sun come out again. Elicit from students the joy that all people feel when they have trouble and others come to help.

3. Ask children to name some emergencies which different people might experience such as: fires, floods, accidents, and illness. Have them identify possible sources of help, such as firefighters, police officers, or doctors. Ask, "Who would you call if your house were on fire?" Follow with the statement, "Would you check to see what race or color the firefighters were, or would you let them put out the fire?" Discuss this and make sure that all students understand that the need for help in time of trouble makes people forget about unimportant things and leads them to think about survival. The age, religion, color, culture, race and/or ethnic group becomes much less important than the fact that some human beings need help and other human beings can give that help.

Give students activity 2-18A, *Friends in the Rain.* NOTE: The foreign languages all say the same as the English words, "Friends in the Rain." The foreign languages are: French, Gujarati, Korean, and Spanish.

4. Discuss the meaning of friendship. True friends care about each other in happy times and in sad times. Ask students to share some of their experiences with friendships. Make a list of some of the activities which friends can participate in, such as parties, camping, picnics, swimming, sleepovers, telephone conversations, going out for ice cream, shopping, singing songs, laughing and crying together. Give students activity 2-18B, *Friends in the Sunshine.*

5. Draw an analogy between sunshine and different types of happy experiences people can have together. Discuss what happens when friends share good times at the beach, amusement park, or the playground. When the sun shines people feel warm and good! Ask students how it feels inside when they do something nice for someone. Compare and contrast this to their feelings if they should do something mean. Discuss the good feelings of kindness and respect towards others. Give students activity 2-18C, *You Are My Sunshine.*

Have students compare the feelings they get when the sun comes out after a rain to that of giving and/or receiving kindness and respect to others. Mention the fact that in places of business, organizations, and schools, people contribute to "Sunshine Clubs" which give gifts to fellow workers who are sick or are having some kind of trouble. Show commonalities among human beings by noting the fact that people of all races, colors, religions, often have a need for help from others.

LITERATURE CONNECTION: *Harry and Wily and Carrothead* by Judith Caseley. Born with a missing left hand, Harry proves that he is just like any other regular child. Greenwillow Books, New York, © 1991. Illustrated.

Jake and Rosie by Patricia E. Lillie. Rosie's best friend Jake is worried that she will never return. She has a surprise for him. Greenwillow Books, New York, © 1989. Illustrated.

Activity 2-19A A VISIT TO THE POST OFFICE

Activity 2-19B IT'S A BEAUTIFUL MORNING

Courtesy, as an extension of the concept of mutual respect, will be the focus of these activities. Students will understand that people can make choices as to how they relate to other human beings. They will observe that kindness towards others is mutually beneficial and that people can contribute to positive environments in which to live, learn, work, and play. There is an emphasis on the sense of responsibility human beings should have, as they come into contact with each other in the community.

Materials Needed:

- Copy of activity sheet 2-19A, *A Visit to the Post Office*
- Copy of activity sheet 2-19B, *It's a Beautiful Morning*
- Pencils
- Crayons or markers
- Pictures of people of different racial and ethnic groups
- Pictures of a community with a U.S. Post Office

Directions:

1. Have students look at pictures or recall various races and cultures of people who live in their neighborhoods or go to school with them. List the many kinds of jobs which men and women do. Point out that disabled and elderly people also contribute to society by working in meaningful jobs such as telephone operators, police officers, nurses, bus drivers, teachers, business managers, chefs, gas station attendants, post office clerks, waiters, salespersons, and school principals.

2. Discuss the words *polite* and *courteous*. Have children describe what happens when people wait in long lines, in crowded stores. Point out that many times a person might impatiently push ahead of others. Discuss the results of such behavior. Give students activity 2-19A, *A Visit to the Post Office*. Discuss the results.

3. Have children verify the fact that people of many ethnic backgrounds see each other in various places in the community. Ask how they should act when they find themselves in the same place, at the same time, with someone who is of a different race or color. Record their responses and categorize them under headings which reflect students' reactions to and attitudes towards people of various races and cultures.

KIND RESPONSES	UNKIND RESPONSES
1.	1.
2.	2.
etc.	etc.

4. Ask children to describe the way they like to begin their mornings. Elicit from them how important it is for people in the family to greet each other pleasantly. Many people leave their houses in the morning to go to work, run errands, and/or exercise. Sometimes people are pleasant and speak to each other. Sometimes people are not pleasant. Ask children which kind of person they want to be. Give students activity 2-19B, *It's a Beautiful Morning.* CAUTION: This is a good place to warn children about the danger of speaking to, accepting candy from, or going with a STRANGER! Discuss this concern and the results of the completed activity.

> **LITERATURE CONNECTION**: *Julian, Secret Agent* by Ann Cameron. Julian, along with his brother and friend, pursue some criminals whose pictures they saw in the post office. Random House, New York, © 1988. Illustrated by Diane Allison.
>
> *Katie Morag and the Two Grandmothers* by Mairi Hedderwick. A bluff, hearty, unrefined grandmother and a refined grandmother adjust to each other when they visit Katie on a Scottish island. Little, Brown, Boston, © 1986. Illustrated.

Activity 2-20A DIFFERENT KINDS OF JOBS

Activity 2-20B LEARN TO SWIM FIRST

Mutual respect for people in the world of work will be developed in these activities. Many children have seen only men work in certain jobs. In today's world, women work in jobs in which they have not always been allowed to work. However, some barriers remain and people have to be aware of the fact that women, as well as men, should have equal opportunity in the workplace. During these lessons, students learn that gender, age, ethnic group, or race should not be a factor in hiring people to do meaningful work. Students will learn the importance of equal opportunity, cooperation, and responsibility in the world of work.

Materials Needed:

- Copy of activity sheet 2-20A, *Different Kinds of Jobs*
- Copy of activity sheet 2-20B, *Learn to Swim First*

- Pencils
- Crayons
- Lists of various types of jobs
- Multiracial pictures of people (men, women, seniors, disabled) at work
- Pictures of people swimming in various locations, at the beach, and in a swimming pool at home

Directions:

1. Ask children if they know of women who work. Have them share some of the kinds of jobs these women do. Explain that years ago women who worked outside the home were criticized. Then discuss the fact that, until recently, there were certain jobs that only men were allowed to do, such as airline pilot, road construction, electrician, and the military. Have students add to this list jobs which both men and women do in today's society. Give students activity 2-20A, *Different Kinds of Jobs*.

   Extend the impact of this lesson by having children share the kinds of jobs their parents do. Emphasize women who work in jobs which have historically been male dominated. Also, point out that there are men who work in jobs which have historically been dominated by females.

2. Show pictures of people swimming and ask students if they know how to swim. Allow them to share how they learned. Make it clear that people have to learn techniques for water safety as well as for having fun in the water. Elicit from children the fact that swimming teachers must know how to teach the many steps their students need to know, such as BREATHING, TREADING THE WATER, MAKING STROKES, KICKING, and DIVING. Discuss water safety rules, such as making sure that someone else is present before going into the water, staying out of the deep end until treading is mastered, never diving into any body of water unless the depth is known, and so on.

3. Indicate that there are many good swimming teachers and that some are men, some are women, some are young and some are old. Help children discern that a person's age, gender, race, culture, or color does not make a difference in their ability to do a job well. Give each child a copy of activity 2-20B, *Learn to Swim First*. Elicit from children the importance of learning water safety.

LITERATURE CONNECTION: *Helping Out* by George Ancona. Through his photographs, the author shows that children enjoy helping grown-ups with different kinds of jobs. Clarion Books, New York, © 1985.

Clean Your Room, Harvey Moon! by Pat Cummings. Harvey has no choice but to obey his mother's demand to pick up his toys and dirty clothes or he cannot watch cartoons. Bradbury Press (Macmillan), New York, © 1991. Illustrated.

Activity 2-21 THE GARDEN IS SWEET

Having an attitude of respect for human beings with disabilities will emerge as students complete this activity. Children will understand that all types of people, including the physically challenged, use their senses to enjoy the beauty of nature. Children are encouraged to broaden their horizons and elevate the worth of people who are not always considered important in the larger society. Because of lessons which are designed to reduce or eliminate prejudice, children will emerge with a more wholesome outlook on life. Ideas for long-term lessons on the systems of the human body are included for those who wish to use physiology to provide a deeper understanding as to the futility of racial and ethnic bias. As a result of their participation in these activities, it is expected that there will be a carry-over of positive attitudes into the children's relationships with diverse groups of people.

Materials Needed:

- Copy of activity sheet 2-21, *The Garden Is Sweet*
- Pencils
- Pictures of disabled and able-bodied people of all races, nationalities, and ages involved in a variety of activities
- Fresh flowers, plants, or herbs and/or pictures of gardens
- Cologne or air freshener
- Musical instruments (bells, sticks, triangles, drums, castanets, keyboard, tambourines)
- Pictures of the inside of the human body (heart, lungs, muscles)—use science and/or reference books
- Films about the human body

Directions:

1. Have a sprig of parsley, a bouquet of flowers, a can of air freshener, or a bit of cologne in the room. Have students close their eyes. Spray a little of the cologne or freshener away from the children. Or allow them to pass the parsley or flowers around. (CAUTION: The teacher should be aware of any allergies among students [pollen, herbs, etc.] and take necessary precautions.)

2. Ask the children to imagine what life would be like if they did not have their sense of smell. Think about various kinds of disabilities, such as being confined to a wheelchair, loss of sight, hearing, a leg, arm, or speech. Have children share any personal experiences with people who are sight-impaired, hearing-impaired, or physically disabled. Discuss whether these forms of disabilities would prevent people from enjoying the smell of fresh bread, perfumes, or spices. Have

children think about how the disabled can still enjoy many things in the world, including a flower garden, because of their remaining senses.

Encourage children to think about their own visible responses (body language, smiles, etc.) when they see or smell flowers. They might imagine themselves walking among flowers and stopping to smell them. Explain that people with muscular dystrophy, or the loss of limbs, or with diseases which confine them to wheelchairs, can go among the flowers and enjoy looking at and smelling the blossoms. Give children activity 2-21, *The Garden Is Sweet*. Discuss the results. Extend the impact of this activity by asking all to share what makes them happy.

3. Extend these concepts by devising similar lessons for the other senses. Note the following activities which help students to understand the sense of SOUND.

Have children clap their hands to the rhythm of a fast or slow beat. Musical instruments like bells, sticks, drums, triangles, keyboard, tambourines, and castanets, can be used to enhance the affect of the sounds. Ask children to notice that they are responding to the SOUNDS THAT THEY HEAR WITH THEIR EARS. Discuss the function of the ear as an important organ that human beings have to help them understand the things around them. Have children name different types of sounds, other than musical. For example, dogs barking, footsteps, mother calling, wind blowing, doors slamming, etc. Ask children to recall all of the senses and talk about their functions. Show pictures of various types of people and ask if the functions of the senses change or stay the same with differences in race, religion, gender, or physical abilities.

4. Extend these concepts further by investigating the sense of TASTE with the students. Note the ideas below:

> Explain that under normal circumstances what you are going to ask would not be polite, but that you are teaching a lesson. Ask students to stick out their tongues, just for a couple of seconds. Ask them to notice the color of each other's tongues. Have one student write the color of everyone's tongue on the board. Then ask students to make up a sentence which informs people that every human being, no matter what his or her race or skin color, has a PINK tongue. Ask if anyone knows why the tongue is so important to human beings. Elicit from students the fact that the taste buds in the human tongue help people to TASTE the foods they eat. Discuss the fact that people who are physically disabled have the same ability to taste as people who are able-bodied. Investigate specific functions of the tongue.

Elicit the different purposes of the tongue in human beings. (The tongue helps people make the sounds of words. Because people have tongues they can taste. The tongue is also important in helping to chew and swallow food.) Explain that the tongue is part of the digestive system, the way food is processed in our bodies. Show the multiracial pictures of people involved in eating and/or conversing. Also, ask children to observe each other at lunchtime. Have children note that all humans react in similar ways to things because they share in common their senses of smell, sound, taste, touch, and sight. (NOTE: Indicate when appropriate that there are people who have experienced loss or impairment of one or more of their senses. Explain that even in these cases, some senses remain and these people can still function.)

NOTE: DEVISE SIMILAR LESSONS FOR THE SENSES OF TOUCH AND SIGHT. (See Section One.) Learning about systems of the human body helps to combat racial and ethnic bias.

5. Emphasize the fact that all human beings are alike beneath the skin. Tell children that all hearts have the same number of chambers, all lungs have air passages, all muscles have fibers, and all the organs and systems of the body work the same way in humans regardless of their ethnicity or race. Have students look at the pictures of the human body in science and/or reference books. Discuss the wonder of the human body and its functions. Show films which explain details of how the various systems work. To extend this study further, locate information on the following:

THE HUMAN BODY

- Cells
- Tissues
- Organs
- Skin
- Muscles
- Respiratory System
- Nervous System
- Blood
- Circulatory System
- Digestive System
- Skeleton

LITERATURE CONNECTION: *Where's Chimpy?* by Bernice Rabe. A little girl with Downs Syndrome searches for her lost stuffed chimpanzee. A story of the normal feelings and concerns of a special child. Albert Whitman & Company, Niles, Illinois, © 1988. Photographs by Diane Schmidt.

What If You Couldn't...?: A Book About Special Needs by Janet Kamien. Readers become more aware of some of the problems of the disabled. Scribner, New York, © 1972. Illustrated by Signe Hanson.

Activity 2-22 SAY THANK YOU WITH A FLOWER

In this activity children relish the joy of their own humanity and that of others by showing gratitude. Learning that various racial and cultural groups have in common ways of saying "Thank you," "I love you," "I appreciate you," give children cause to celebrate. Children will develop a deeper understanding of the concept of gratitude, as they investigate various foreign language words for "Thank you" and

"Flower." In addition, children develop a sense of responsibility as they learn to put racial, ethnic, and cultural differences aside, when it is time to give a gift and/or say "Thank you" to someone special. The internal joy that students will feel while preparing a gift for someone else is a significant ingredient in the development of mutual respect.

Materials Needed:

- Copy of activity sheet 2-22, *Say Thank You With a Flower*
- Pictures of people holding flowers
- Crayons or markers
- Scissors
- Pencils
- Foreign Language Lists and dictionaries

Directions:

1. Discuss the pleasant feeling people get when someone says thank you. These words are beautiful in English and in any other language. For example, in Spanish people thank others by saying *gracias*, in French they say *merci* and in Russian, thank you is pronounced, *spah-see-bah*. Ask students why these expressions of thanks are so beautiful. Elicit from children the fact that caring is demonstrated between and among people who show gratitude and appreciation to others.

2. Point out that giving gifts is another way of saying thank you or showing appreciation. Ask children to think of someone they would like to thank with a special celebration. Have them think about what it would take to plan a party or a feast for this person. Encourage them to think of other ways to honor this person. Maybe the gift could be tickets to a basketball game, a special vacation, or a dinner at a restaurant. Explain that gifts which do not cost money are often the best kinds. Suggest a lovely flower.

Give children activity 2-22, *Say Thank You With a Flower*. Ask them to pronounce and trace the foreign language words for flower. Introduce and define the word *synonym* as a word which means same. Explain that the word *signature* is a synonym for the word's written name. Explain that a person's signature is important and should be added to his or her thank-you note. Encourage children to give their flowers to a very special person. Some children might want to write a note to accompany the flowers.

3. Ask children if they have ever received gifts for their birthdays, Christmas, Hanukkah, Kwanzaa, Diwali, or other special occasions. Have them tell how they showed appreciation to the person(s) who gave them the gift. Have them indicate if someone else had to remind them to say thank you. Note that expressions of thank you exist in all cultures and that people should NOT have to remind the

receivers of gifts to say "thank you"; that is the responsibility of the person who accepted the gift.

4. Define the word "responsible" for students by giving examples with which they can identify. Ask this question, "Has anyone ever asked you to do a job, like clear the table, take the garbage out, or hang your coat up?" Allow students to respond. Indicate that those who did the job were responsible because they did what they were asked to do. Explain that they are also dependable. Give them opportunities to share times when they have shown responsibility. Extend this to include their ability to assume responsibility in saying thank you when someone has done something nice for them. Connect the students' understanding of the need to show appreciation to their understanding of the concept of mutual respect. For example, two people who have been kind to or given gifts to each other can both say thank you. This demonstrates mutual respect.

LITERATURE CONNECTION: *The Wednesday Surprise* by Eve Bunting. Anna teaches her grandmother to read, to the delight of the entire family. Clarion Books, New York, © 1989. Illustrated by Donald Carrick.

Activity 2-23A PLANTING THE SEEDS OF PEACE

Activity 2-23B GLOBAL RAINBOWS

Activity 2-23C WHAT IS AMERICA?

In these activities, children come to understand that people can work together to get the things they all want and need. Mutual respect comes from a deeper understanding of shared hopes and dreams. Children see that the quest for peace is not confined to one race or ethnic group but that it is the wish of human beings around the world. This common goal creates an ongoing sense of brotherhood. Young children can start planting the seeds of peace now, in the interest of their future. As they work on lessons which cultivate kindness and respect for others, students see that they can help spread hope, joy, love, harmony, and friendship once they begin to understand and respect each other. Finally, during these activities the concept of mutual respect will be extended to include individual rights and decision-making. Students will read short descriptions of how different people define America and learn something about the democratic process, as they make a choice and vote on the definitions. Through this, they understand that in a free country, people have a right to their individual opinions and can vote to express them, without feeling afraid. Because they're learning to resolve conflicts together, opportunities for children to make value judgments regarding lying or telling the truth are provided. Finally, the children participating in these activities will emerge as emissaries; a spectrum in the global rainbow which is necessary for spreading peace and harmony into the larger world.

Materials Needed:

- Copy of activity sheet 2-23A, *Planting the Seeds of Peace*
- Copy of activity sheet 2-23B, *Global Rainbows*
- Copy of activity sheet 2-23C, *What Is America?*
- Foreign Language Lists
- Multiracial groups of people
- A globe
- Crayons or markers
- Pencils
- Seedlings for trees and flowers, soil
- Recording of music for the song "My Country 'Tis of Thee"
- Ballots for Activity 2-23C (optional)

Directions:

1. Ask children how they would react in a number of situations. For example, what would they do if someone they loved went away, or if they saw a plane crash, or a beautiful rainbow or sunset. Discuss the similarities in the reactions of different types of people in the classroom. Point out that other human beings around the United States and the world would have the same kinds of reactions. They would be sad if a loved one went away, or if they saw a plane crash. They would be happy if they saw a lovely sunset. Encourage students to talk about beautiful things they have seen and enjoyed. Draw an analogy between enjoying beautiful things and enjoying beautiful or kind people. Emphasize the word "kind" and discuss how important it is to be nice to others.

Write the words "peace" and "harmony" on the board. Give children an opportunity to explain what it means to them. Elicit from children the fact that people of all races, colors, religions, cultures, and languages want to have peace. Ask children why all types of people want peace and what they think is the best way to get peace. Help discern that people have to treat each other with kindness in order to get along. For example, to have a friend you have to be a friend, or to have peace you have to offer peace, are necessary truths for all of the children to grasp. Have students work together to find words which can be used to create harmony and peace among people. Write the words on the board for use with the following activity. Or you might want to give students the worksheet to take home and bring back at a later date. Give each child a copy of activity 2-23A, *Planting the Seeds of Peace*. Have them collect words of kindness and peace from as many sources as possible. Compare and contrast the results.

Extend the impact of this activity beyond the children's home and school environments. Discuss how human beings of all races and colors want wars to stop and peace and harmony to spread throughout the world. Explain how human beings can make choices not to fight or go to war, but to look for peaceful ways to solve differences.

2. Write the word "truth" on the board. Ask the students to explain what it means. Give each child an opportunity. Help reluctant students by having them each use the word in a sentence. Ask children to share some of their experiences with telling the truth. Discuss REWARDS (internal and external). Have children give the word which is the opposite of truth. Write the word "lying" on the board and elicit from students that lying causes problems for people. Ask them to describe some of their experiences with lying. Compare and contrast emotions and behavior as a result of lying to those which occur as a result of telling the truth. Discuss which feeling they prefer. (Students can share stories of others who have gotten into trouble by not telling the truth.) Write the word "consequences" on the board. Explain that it means that people have to accept what happens to them after they have chosen to act or behave a certain way. Elicit from children that their parents and those of all cultures want their children to tell the truth, to have friends, and to stay out of fights. Give each child a chance to express his/her choice in regards to telling the truth or lying.

3. Discuss how respect for people of many different racial and cultural backgrounds can help promote peace. Have the students interlock their arms and form a circle. (Place the globe in the center of the circle, if desired.) Elicit from the children the fact that they will grow up and relate to people from many different continents and countries of the world. Explain that the classroom and their culturally mixed neighborhoods are great examples of the larger world. Ask students what they might show other boys and girls about making friends with people from different races and cultures. Have students sing the song "My Country 'Tis of Thee." Follow this experience with a planting of symbolic seeds of peace. NOTE: Have children plant rea seedlings for trees or flowers in a special place around the school or in the community.

4. Explain how young people are the hope for the future. If, in their own worlds at home, at school and in their communities, they can show caring and respect for others, there is hope for peace. Give each student a copy of the activity 2-23B, *Global Rainbows*. Have them select several words from the worksheet and use them in sentences and/or stories about ways to get along with those who are from a racial, cultural, or ethnic background other than their own. Elicit from children that while the globe in the center of the floor is symbolic for the whole Earth, they as children of many races and colors are symbols of hope for the future.

5. Extend the concepts of mutual respect by placing emphasis on individual rights. Elicit from students the fact that, in America, people have a right to express

their opinions and beliefs without feeling afraid that someone will hurt them. Discuss an issue that students can relate to, such as taking five minutes away from their recess period. Invite oral opinions, then place votes under the words YES and NO on the board. Explain that the majority wins and relate that to methods used to elect American presidents, senators, congressional representatives, governors, and mayors. Ask students to mention other issues that are important for citizens to vote on. Give examples, such as smoking in public places, laws to keep the air clean, health services for citizens, money for education, keeping the roads safe, and so on. Ask students to think about the kind of country America is and to tell why they feel happy to be an American citizen.

6. Ask students if they know the "High Five" sign. Have two students demonstrate raising their right hands and (instead of shaking hands) clapping their open palms together. This is a sign many people use to demonstrate their agreement on something. Encourage students to compliment each other on their American citizenship by giving high-five signs. Then discuss how each citizen can do something responsible to help keep America free. Elicit from children the meaning of the word "vote" as making a decision or choice. Suggest that VOTING is one main way of keeping America free and that each citizen, of every racial, cultural, and ethnic background, should exercise his/her right to express opinions which are important to his/her life and the life of every other citizen. Have children relate their differences of opinion on several issues.

Define the words: "melting pot" as a blending of different races and cultures into one, "salad" as separate ingredients which keep their own flavor even though they are in one container, and "patchwork quilt" as lots of pieces of colorful cloth sewn together with common thread to form one large cover. Give students activity 2-23C, *What Is America?* and ask them to work in small groups until the activity is completed. Give students separate ballots, if desired. Select a committee to count the votes. Have someone announce the winning vote and ask all students to record the results on their worksheets. Explain to the class that they have, as American citizens of different racial, cultural and/or ethnic backgrounds, participated in the democratic process by expressing their individual opinions and exercising their rights to vote.

PLACE THE FOLLOWING WORDS ON CHARTS AND/OR THE BOARD FOR READY REFERENCE

• Friendship • Harmony • Hope • Love • Truth

Challenge the children to define the words and add to the list as frequently as they wish.

LITERATURE CONNECTION: *Potatoes, Potatoes*, written and illustrated by Anita Lobel. Children learn of the pain and futility of fighting and war, as two brothers become leaders in rival armies. Harper Row, New York, © 1967.

Activity 2-24 KISSES AND HUGS

In this activity, children reflect on the meaning of affection and consider its mutual benefits. By internalizing synonymous words for love and eliminating those which are indicative of conflict, children garner the tools that they need to accept people of different races, ethnic groups, and cultures. The intent of this lesson is not to encourage physical contact, but to help all children to understand that there are certain positive behaviors which reinforce each other. Using the analogy of "friendship," children are asked to find words which are "best friends"; words which belong together **and** have a positive effect on people. Students use higher-level thinking skills as they discern that there are negative words which are also "best friends" but they do not meet the criteria for reinforcing positive human behaviors. Children will note that people of all racial and ethnic groups can relate to the analogy of friendship, caring, and affection. As these "best friend" words connote positive attitudes among children, they easily translate into acts of mutual respect and in the giving and receiving of kindnesses.

Materials Needed:

- Copy of activity sheet 2-24, *Kisses and Hugs*
- Pencils
- Picture of a military tank with a gun or a toy gun with toy bullets
- Multiracial pictures of people involved in friendly activities

Directions:

1. Share with children your experiences with a best friend. Then give them a chance to tell about best friends. Elicit from students that best friends are loyal and try to make each other happy. Explain that loyal means that they will not stop being friends over little disagreements or problems. Loyal also means that they will stand up for each other when someone picks a fight with one or the other. Tell the class that words can be best friends. Use the examples below to help with the explanation.

2. Ask children to place their fingers over their lips. Then ask the question, "What do lips do?" Allow them to respond and list what they say on the board. They might respond, "Lips kiss," or "Lips speak," etc. Elicit from children that people can make each other feel good by the kind of words they speak.

3. Ask children to hold their arms out and make a circle with them. Then ask the question, "What do arms do?" Write their responses on the board. They might respond, "Arms hold babies," or "Arms hug," among other things. Elicit from children that people can make each other feel good by holding and touching. (Teacher sensitivity and awareness to the needs of children who might be abused is crucial...a discussion of how to protect themselves from improper touching might be necessary in this lesson.)

4. Hold up a picture of a military tank with a large gun attached. Also, show a toy gun with several toy bullets. Then ask the question, "What do guns and bullets do?" Write their answers on the board. They should respond, "Guns and bullets kill." Elicit from children that guns, bullets, and killing do not make people feel good. Because people can be hurt or can die from guns, bullets, and killing, these words do not belong on the Best Friends list. These words have a connotation of pain, violence, and/or death. They do not meet the criteria for our "Best Friends" list.

5. Write the words KISS, HUG, GUNS, KILL on the board. Ask children to decide which words belong together. Have a volunteer write the words which belong together in a circle.

6. Elicit from children which words make people feel good and which words make people feel bad. Indicate that people of all races and cultures want to get rid of all the things which cause people to feel bad, fight, and/or be unhappy. Have a volunteer go to the board and mark a big **X** on the words that make people feel hurt, scared, or unhappy. Explain that "Best Friend" words which belong together must ALSO make people feel good, in order to be written on the pictures in the next activity. Give each child a copy of activity 2-24, *Kisses and Hugs*. Compare and contrast the results and share them with family and friends. Have students develop an ongoing list of "Best Friend" words.

Extend the impact of this activity by having children make large posters with magazine pictures which show people from various racial and ethnic backgrounds enjoying sports, music, theater, etc. Have children write positive words which are BEST FRIENDS all around the pictures. Make certain that they are very colorful. Display them in the school and all around the community. Share feedback from responsive family, friends, and community members.

LITERATURE CONNECTION: *Jenny* by Beth P. Wilson. The story of a little girl's experiences with her family and friends, her dreams, and her prayers for peace. Macmillan, New York, © 1990. Illustrated by Dolores Johnson.

Name ______________________________ Date ______________________________

ALL FAMILIES ARE ________

There are many different types of human families: two-parent, single-parent, foster, adoptive, and many more. Complete the sentence below. Then draw and color a picture of your family.

The many different types of families are all ______________________________.
(Fill this blank with a word which makes sense to you.)

Name ______________________________ Date ______________________________

THE WORDS YOU SPEAK

Words that people speak are like raindrops, they can soak in. Unkind words can cause hurt feelings. Pleasant words help people to treat each other kindly. Can you think of any good thoughts and kind actions to write on the clouds? One is done for you.

Name ______________________________ Date ______________________________

KIND WORDS LIST

Human beings should be kind to each other. If people say nice things, others feel good. Circle only the words that make other people feel happy. Cross out the words which make people feel unhappy.

You have very nice parents.

Your whole family is nice.

You're my friend.

Get out of here.

I'll help you.

A Smile

You're stupid.

The hero in this book reminds me of you.

Come to dinner!

Please

Mind your own business

Fighting

Hey, I waited for you. Want to play?

I know how you feel.

I really don't care.

I like you.

Thank you.

I like your outfit.

I'm glad to be with you.

Name ______________________ Date ______________________

WHAT CAN YOU DO?

Balls of all sizes, shapes, and colors can roll and bounce.

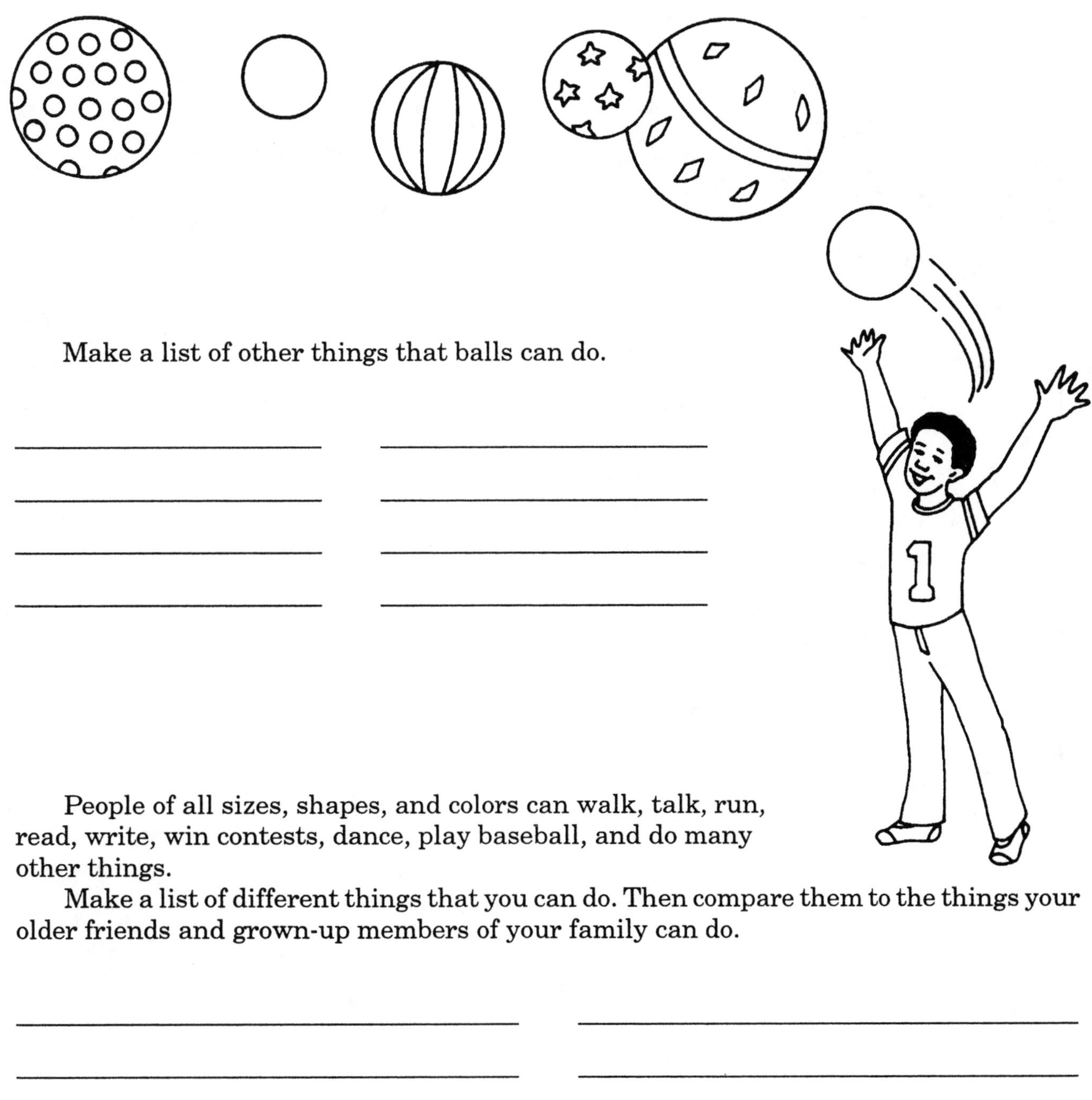

Make a list of other things that balls can do.

______________________ ______________________

______________________ ______________________

______________________ ______________________

______________________ ______________________

People of all sizes, shapes, and colors can walk, talk, run, read, write, win contests, dance, play baseball, and do many other things.

Make a list of different things that you can do. Then compare them to the things your older friends and grown-up members of your family can do.

______________________ ______________________

______________________ ______________________

______________________ ______________________

______________________ ______________________

______________________ ______________________

Name ________________________________ Date ________________________________

I CAN...

What are some of the things you do very well? Think of a time, place, or special event when you have been happy about your ability to succeed. Were others there to share in your joy? Tell about your special talents below.

Draw a picture of your special event or talent on the back of this sheet.

Are you good at soccer or basketball? Have you received a high grade on a spelling test? Are you a singer, basketball player, dancer, or writer?

Name ______________________________ **Date** ______________________________

OTHER PEOPLE ARE SPECIAL, TOO

Trace the letters/words. Write your own "good thoughts" in the empty boxes. Make a book, or cards, of good thoughts for different people. Use paints or crayons to decorate your work. Give these gifts to a special someone at home, in your classroom, or in your community.

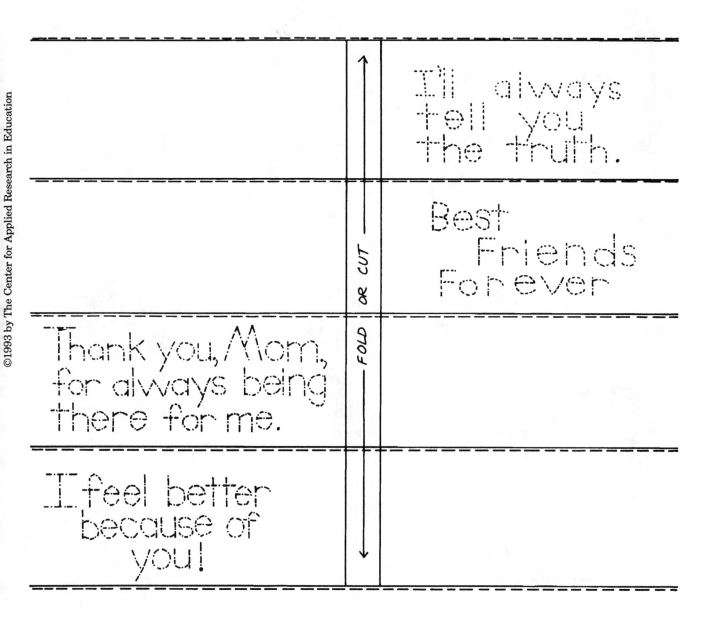

	FOLD OR CUT	
		I'll always tell you the truth.
		Best Friends Forever
Thank you, Mom, for always being there for me.		
I feel better because of you!		

2-5A

Name ______________________________ Date ______________________________

DIFFERENCES AROUND ME

Compare the pictures of people, animals, and objects. Write the words which complete the statement about differences. Then draw your own pairs of pictures to compare and contrast.

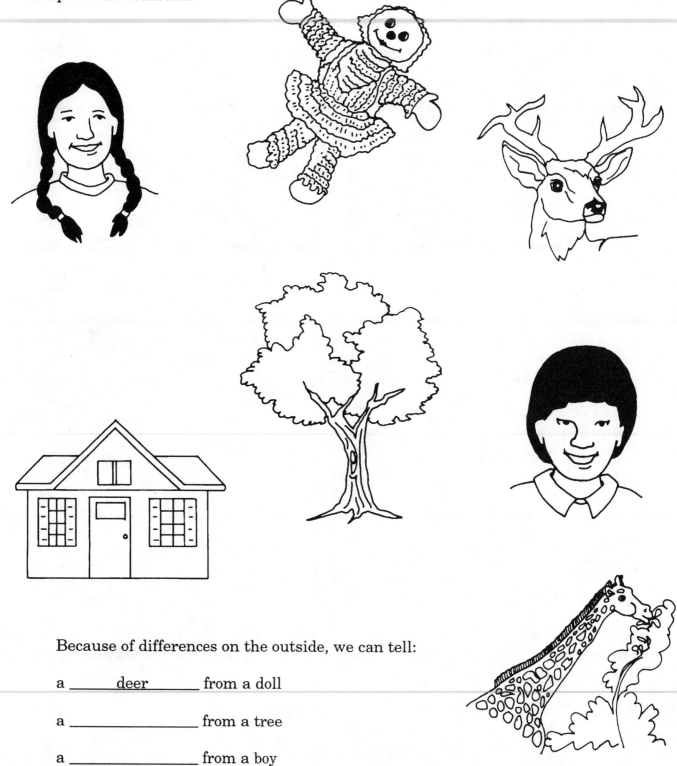

Because of differences on the outside, we can tell:

a ____deer____ from a doll

a ______________ from a tree

a ______________ from a boy

Name ______________________ Date ______________________

PEOPLE ARE ALIKE

People are more alike than they are different. Look at the pictures. Then fill in the blanks of each sentence with different words for PEOPLE. (PEOPLE—human beings, mothers and fathers, men and women, boys and girls.)

FILL IN EACH BLANK WITH SYNONYMS FOR THE WORD "PEOPLE"

1. Who kisses children good night?______________________
2. Who walks on two legs?______________________
3. Who thinks, reads, and can use a computer?______________________
4. Who cooks, eats, makes beds, and shops?______________________
5. Who sings, plays basketball, and goes to school?______________________
6. Who gets married, has children, and works?______________________

Name ______________________________ Date ______________________________

WHAT COLOR IS LOVE?

The Earth is like one BIG HOUSE for all of the people of the world to SHARE. People of all races, religions, and languages need to care about each other for we are all neighbors. Color clouds surrounding the Earth with the colors of your choice.

Now write a few sentences that explain what the completed picture means to you.

____

____

____

____

Name ______________________ Date ______________________

SHARING FREEDOM IN AMERICA

Answer the four questions that show that the American Flag is a symbol of freedom for all of its citizens.

Read the sentences that tell what the COLORS, STRIPES and STARS stand for. Then cut out and give the flag to another person.

1. Can you pick one person whose family owns America?

   YES NO (Circle One)

2. Are Americans many different colors and races?

   YES NO (Circle One)

3. Do all Americans, of all races and colors, want others to care about them?

   YES NO (Circle One)

4. Do all races and colors of Americans want freedom?

   YES NO (Circle One)

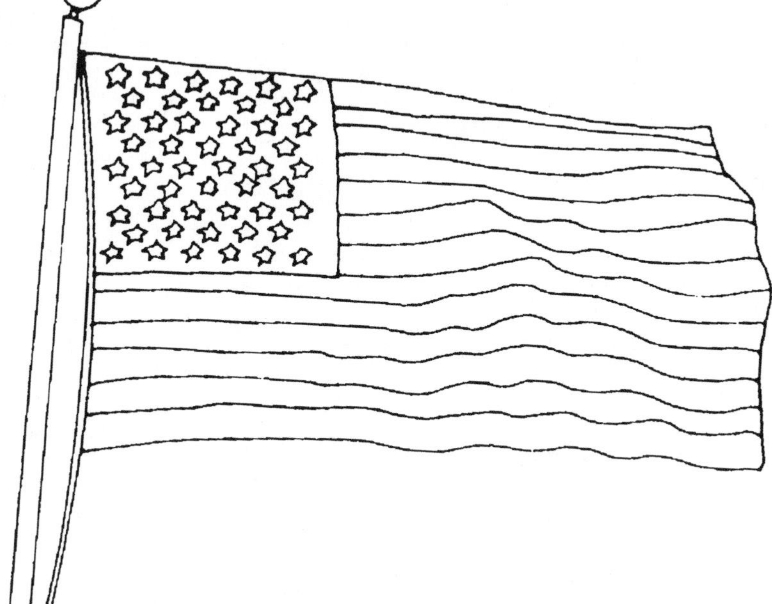

- Red is for COURAGE
- White is for PURITY
- Blue is for JUSTICE
- The Stripes are for the original 13 states
- The 50 Stars are for the 50 States in the United States (U.S.) of America
- CUT OUT
- GIVE the symbol of freedom to another person by giving him or her an American Flag
- Shake hands and smile when you give and receive your Flag

2-6B

Name ______________________________ Date ______________________________

AMERICANS COME FROM MANY PLACES

Many people have been born in America. Some of them can remember that their parents or grandparents were born in other countries. Talk to your classmates, your teacher, your friends, and other people to find out when, why, and how they and their families came to America. Trace the outline of the continents on the world map.

Name ______________________________ Date ______________________________

HOW ARE YOU FEELING?

Show the different kinds of feelings that people can have by drawing SAD, HAPPY, ANGRY, and SURPRISED expressions on the faces below. Color, cut out, and paste the faces on popsicle sticks. Use them for puppets as you play with your friends.

People of all races and colors have the same kinds of feelings.

Name ______________________________ Date ______________________________

WE CAN BE FRIENDS

Read the story and cut out the puppets. Then act out the scene with some of your friends and classmates.

Name ______________________________ Date ______________________________

LANGUAGES ARE FUN

Read the English words for COLORS, DAYS OF THE WEEK, FAMILY MEMBERS, and HOUSE at the top of each of the following pages. Then use the Foreign Language Lists in the Appendix to find the same words in other languages. Write the foreign language word in the box with the NAME of the language and the COUNTRY. This one is done for you.

SATURDAY

Write the word for SATURDAY in three new languages. Remember to identify the language of each new word. Use the Foreign Languages Lists in the Appendix.

	LANGUAGE/COUNTRY	NEW LANGUAGE CHOICE
1.	Spanish	Sábado
2.	Swahili	Jūmamosi
3.	Japanese	Do-yōbi

Name ______________________________ Date ______________________________

LANGUAGES ARE FUN

TUESDAY

Write the word for TUESDAY in three new languages. Remember to identify the language of each new word. You may want to make up a new page for each of the other days of the week.

LANGUAGE/COUNTRY	NEW LANGUAGE CHOICE
1.	
2.	
3.	

I'm from Ghana. My name is Kwabena because I was born on a Tuesday.

The people of Ghana often name their children for the day of the week on which they were born. What is your Ghanaian name? ______________________________

Name ______________________________ Date ______________________________

LANGUAGES ARE FUN

FAMILY MEMBERS

Write the word for different members of a FAMILY in three new languages. Choose the word mother, father, sister, brother, girl, or boy. Remember to identify the country of each new word.

LANGUAGE/COUNTRY	NEW LANGUAGE CHOICE
1.	
2.	
3.	

Name ______________________________ Date ______________________________

LANGUAGES ARE FUN

HOUSE

Write the word for HOUSE in three new languages. Remember to identify the language of each new word.

LANGUAGE/COUNTRY	NEW LANGUAGE CHOICE
1.	
2.	
3.	

Name ______________________________ Date ______________________________

LANGUAGES ARE FUN

RED

Write the word for the color RED in three new languages. Remember to identify the language of each choice. You may want to make up new pages for other colors.

LANGUAGE/COUNTRY	NEW LANGUAGE CHOICE
1.	
2.	
3.	

Name ______________________________ **Date** ______________________________

LANGUAGES ARE FUN

BIRD

Write the word for BIRD in three new languages. Remember to identify the language of each choice.

	LANGUAGE/COUNTRY	NEW LANGUAGE CHOICE
1.		
2.		
3.		

Have fun finding foreign language words for many other things. Where will you go for help?

Name ______________________________ Date ______________________________

INTERPRETING THE ENVIRONMENT FOR MULTICULTURAL CLASSMATES

Label each item below in two different languages. Work with your classmates to label other items in as many languages as are represented in your class.*

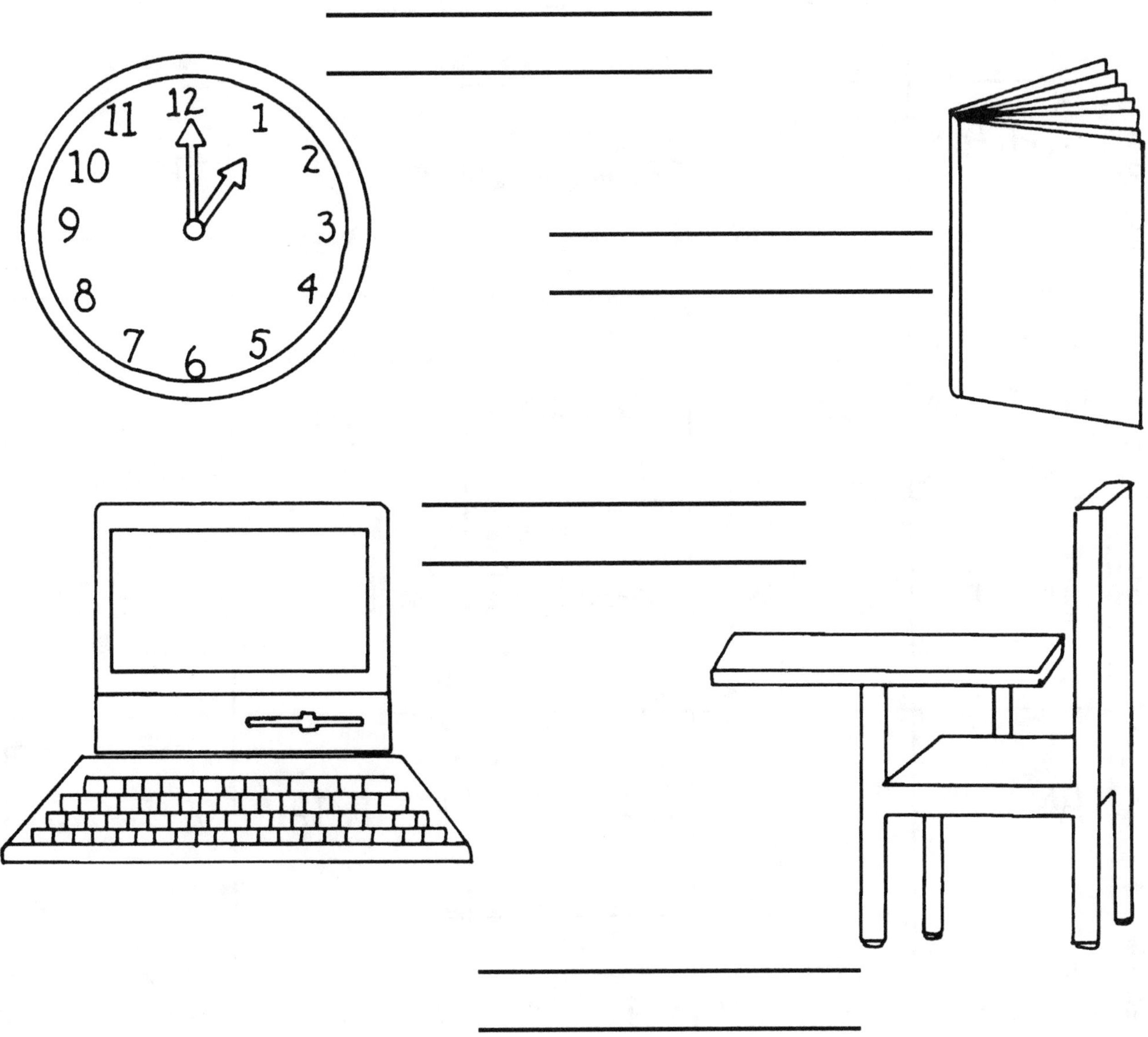

*Use the Foreign Language lists in the Appendix and foreign language dictionaries.

Name ______________________ Date ______________________

LANGUAGES ARE DIFFERENT

Look at the foreign language words for LOVE, PLAY, WORK, FAMILY, and FUN. Use your pencil to trace the letters, shapes, and lines. Try to pronounce the words.

	LOVE	PLAY	WORK	FAMILY	FUN
1. GUJARATI	[illegible] (PYAR)	રમવું (RAMVU)	કામ (KUM)	કુટુંબ (KUTUMBE)	મજા (MAJA)
2. TAGALOG	WALANG-IBIBIGAY	LARO	KASAWKASAW	NANAYAT TAYTAY	MASAYA
3. FRENCH	AMOUR	JOUER	TRAVAILLE	FAMILLE	AMUSEMENT
4. SPANISH	AMOR	JUGAR	TRABAJAR	FAMILIA	DIVERSIÓN
5. CHINESE	愛 ài	玩 wán	工作 gōng zuò	家庭 jiā tíng	玩笑 wán xiao

Now discuss with your classmates which words sound alike and which sound different.

Name ______________________________ Date ______________________________

ORDERING CHINESE FOOD FOR LUNCH

Four friends want to buy lunch in the Sunny Glen Chinese Restaurant. You are a waiter or waitress. What would you suggest for each person? Copy the choices in Chinese onto your ticket. Write each choice from top to bottom.

CHINESE LUNCH MENU

1. Chicken with Cashew Nuts

腰 果 鸡
yāo guǒ jī

2. Chicken with Broccoli

甘 蓝 鸡 (鷄)
gān lán jī

3. Sweet and Sour Chicken

甜 酸 鸡 (鷄)
tián suān jī

4. Lemon Chicken

柠 檬 鸡 (鷄)
níng méng jī

5. Chicken with Mixed Vegetables

蔬 菜 鸡 (鷄)
shū sài jī

6. Sweet and Sour Pork

甜 酸 猪 肉
tián suān zhū ròu

7. Pork with Garlic Sauce

猪 肉 蒜 汤
zhū ròu suàn tāng

8. Beef with Broccoli

甘 蓝 牛 肉
gān lán niú ròu

ALL YOU CAN EAT FOR $4.95

Name ______________________________ **Date** ______________________________

ORDERING CHINESE FOOD FOR LUNCH

One customer's order is written for you. Add the total cost of lunch on your Waiter's Ticket.

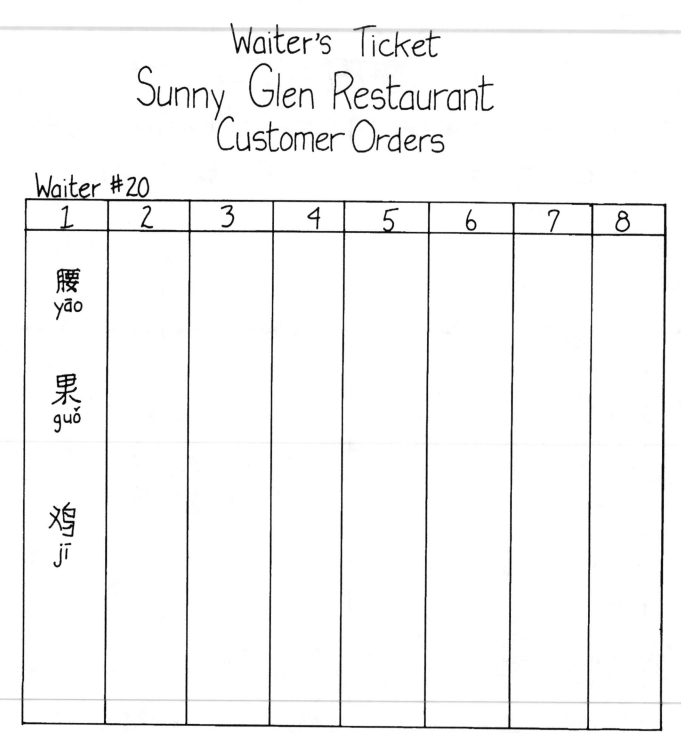

Waiter's Ticket
Sunny Glen Restaurant
Customer Orders

Waiter #20

1	2	3	4	5	6	7	8
腰 yāo 果 guǒ 鸡 jī							

Total Cost $ ________

Name ______________________________ Date ______________________________

ART AND LANGUAGES

Trace the English word for each item below. Then use the Foreign Language Lists to find new foreign language words for the same items. Draw and color all pictures.

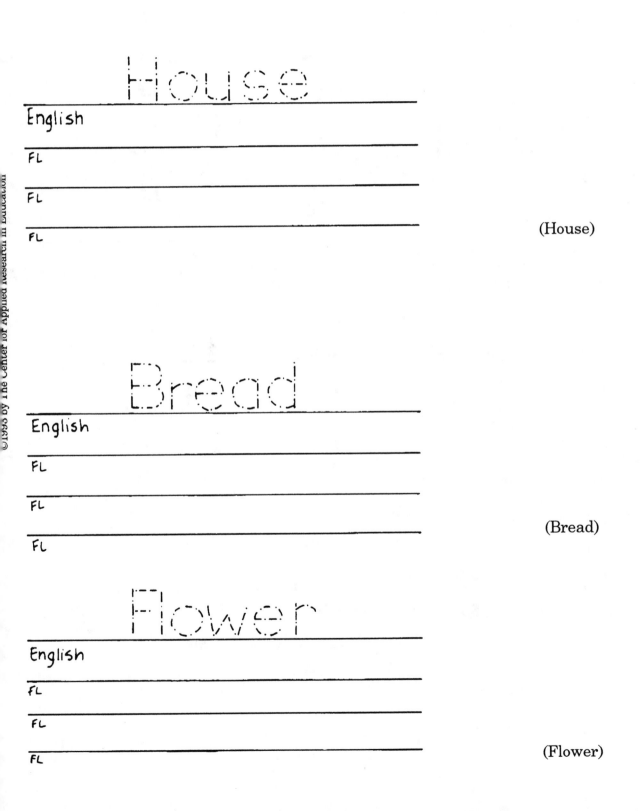

House
____
English
____
FL
____
FL
____
FL

(House)

Bread
____
English
____
FL
____
FL
____
FL

(Bread)

Flower
____
English
____
FL
____
FL
____
FL

(Flower)

Name ______________________ Date ______________________

COUNTING IN CHINESE IS FUN

Count to ten in Chinese by using the pronunciation key. Trace the first five numbers. Then write the numbers 6 to 10 by yourself.

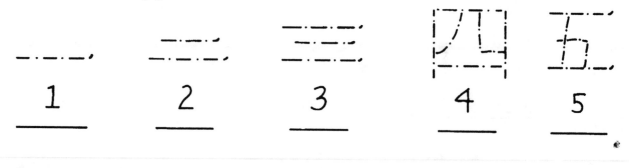

1	2	3	4	5	6	7	8	9	10
一	二	三	四	五	六	七	八	九	十
yī	èr	sān	sì	wǔ	liù	qī	bā	jiǔ	shí

Copy the numbers from 1 to 10 in Chinese. Trace the first five numbers. Then write the numbers 6 to 10 by yourself.

一	二	三	四	五
1	2	3	4	5

____	____	____	____	____
6	7	8	9	10

Name ______________________ Date ______________________

DO YOU KNOW CHINESE NUMBERS?

Write the Chinese numbers for each English number on the balls. Use the Chinese sounds and characters on the previous page to help you. Then decorate the five balls, cut them out, and show them to someone at home.

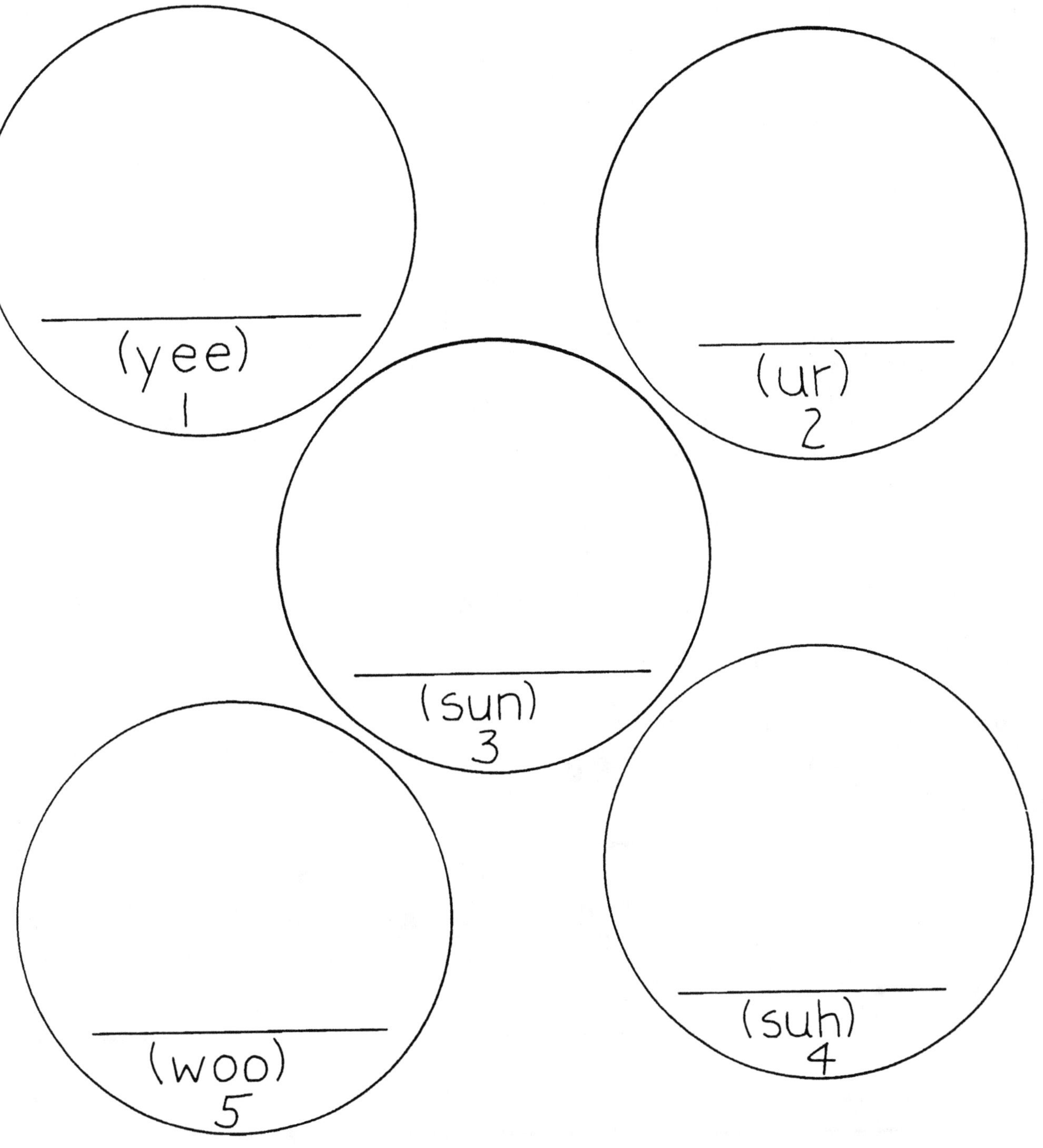

Name ______________________ Date ______________________

FOREIGN NUMBER WORDS PUZZLE

Read the number words from ONE to FIVE in Spanish, French, Swahili, and Russian. Cut out each language and number word. Mix them up and then see if you can place the correct numbers with the language from which it comes.

CUT HERE CUT HERE

English	one	two	three	four	five
Spanish	uno	dos	tres	cuatro	cinco
French	un	deux	trois	quatre	cinq
Swahili	moja	mbili	tatu	ine	tano
Russian	ah-deen	dvah	tree	chyeh-tir-yeh	peey hat

CUT HERE

Place the foreign language number words in the right boxes.

	Spanish	English	French	Swahili	Russian
1	1	1	1	1	1
2	2	2	2	2	2
3	3	3	3	3	3
4	4	4	4	4	4
5	5	5	5	5	5

Name ________________________________ **Date** ________________________________

HOW MANY BALLOONS?

Write the number words for ONE, TWO, THREE, FOUR, and FIVE on each balloon in two foreign languages. Count in Japanese, spoken in the country of Japan, and Bikol, spoken in the Philippines.

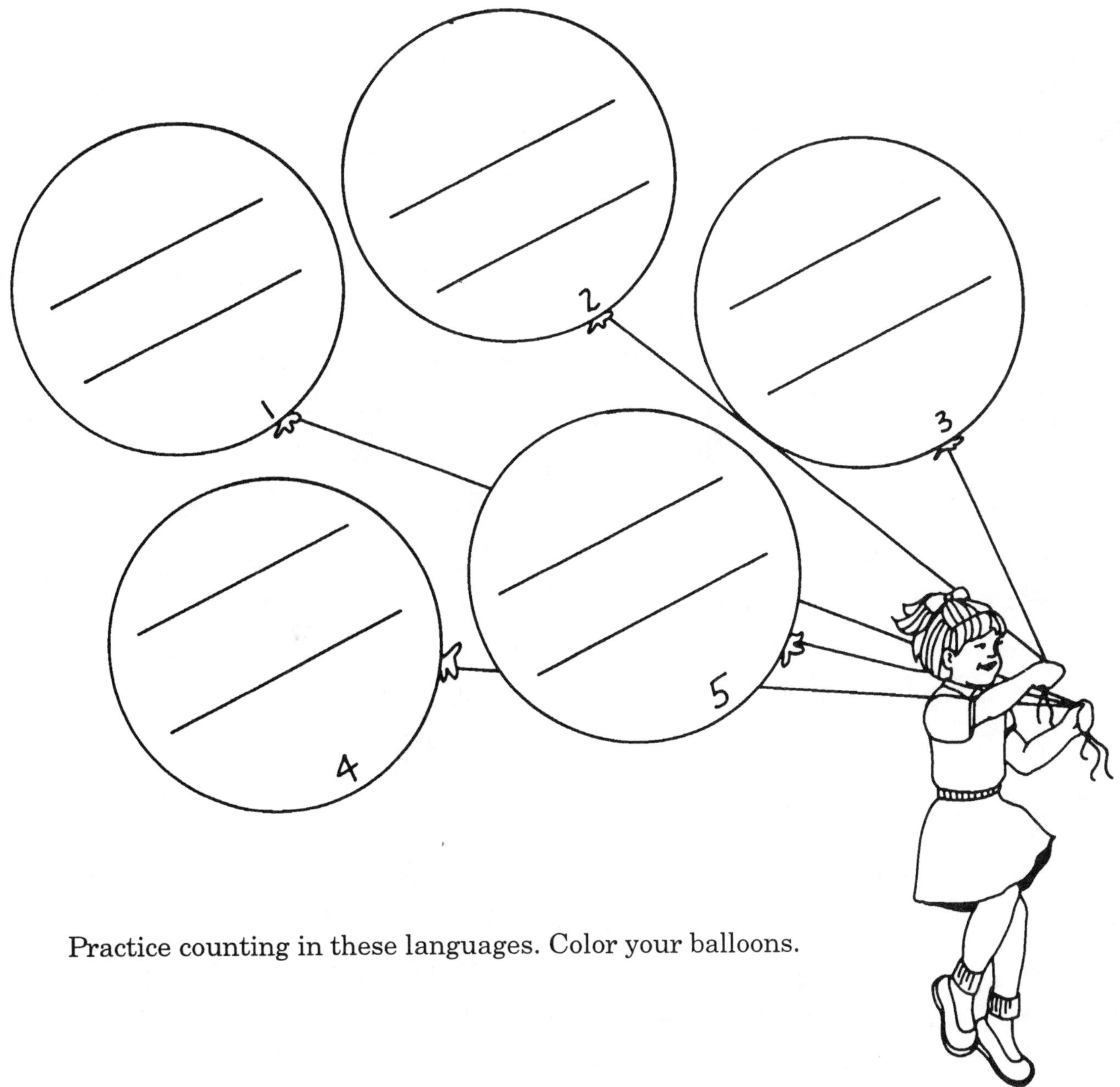

Practice counting in these languages. Color your balloons.

*See Foreign Language lists in the Appendix.

2-9E

Name ______________________ Date ______________________

FIVE FINGERS IN ANY LANGUAGE

People all over the world have five fingers on each hand. Count from ONE to FIVE in SWAHILI and TAGALOG. Use the Foreign Language List. Color the hand and design rings for each of the five fingers. The first one is done for you.

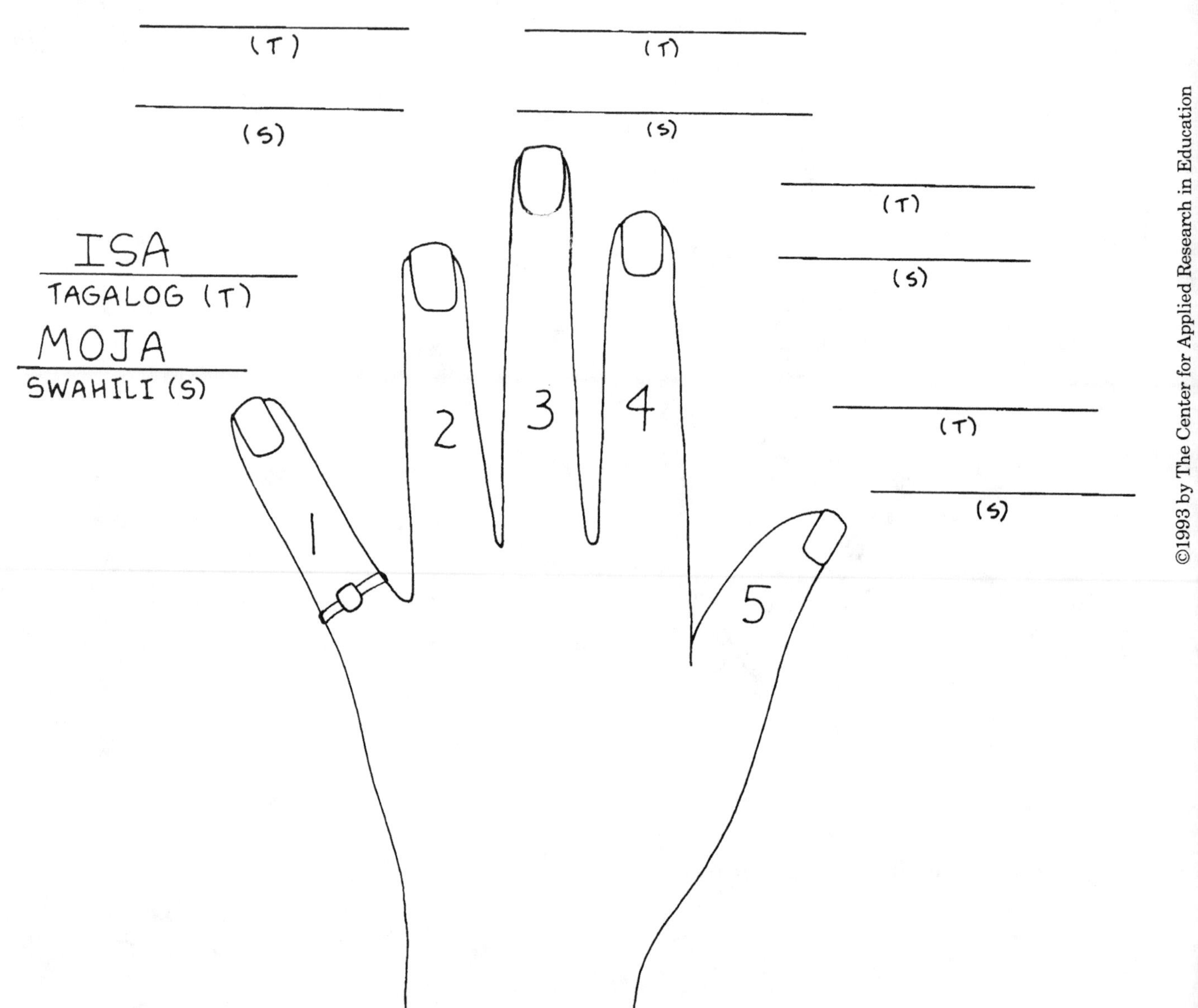

Name ______________________________ Date ______________________________

LETTERS, NUMBERS, AND WORDS ARE DIFFERENT

Look at the two items in each box below. If the two items are just like each other, circle the word ALIKE. If they are not like each other, circle the word DIFFERENT.

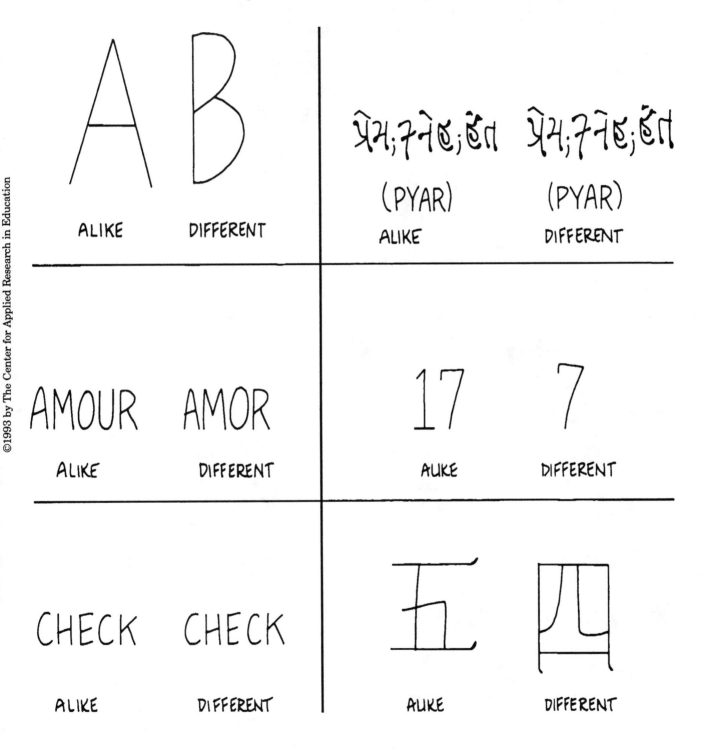

A B ALIKE DIFFERENT	प्रेम;स्नेह;हेत प्रेम;स्नेह;हेत (PYAR) (PYAR) ALIKE DIFFERENT
AMOUR AMOR ALIKE DIFFERENT	17 7 ALIKE DIFFERENT
CHECK CHECK ALIKE DIFFERENT	五 四 ALIKE DIFFERENT

Now draw your own pairs of objects and explain why they are alike or different.

Name ________________________________ Date ________________________________

PEOPLE ARE INTERDEPENDENT

Consumers are people who buy goods and services. Producers are people who make or provide goods and services.

People need each other. This means that people are INTERDEPENDENT. Draw lines to MATCH the CONSUMERS and PRODUCERS to show that they do NEED each other. One is done for you.

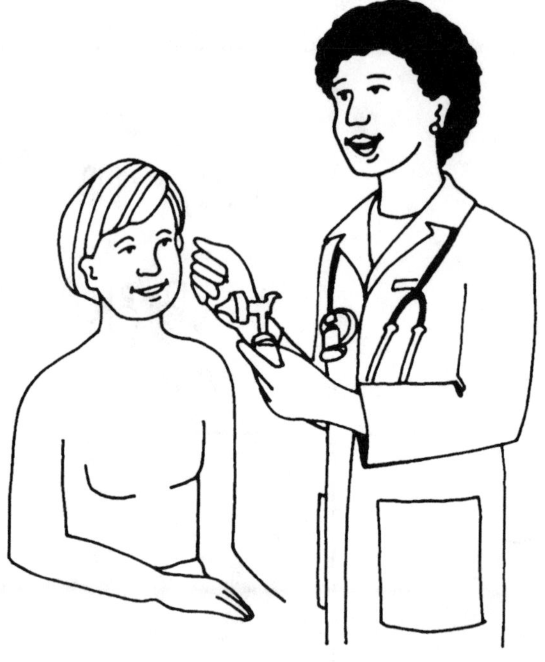

Doctors	Makers of cloth
Grocers	Glassmakers
Bus Drivers	Pilots
Students	Riders of buses
Makers of airplanes	Teachers
Drinkers of milk, juice, water, etc.	Farmers
Tailor	Sick people

Name ______________________ Date ______________________

SET YOUR TABLE FOR COMPANY

Set your table for guests of many races, colors, and languages. Use only your best dishes and glasses. Find all the plates and glasses that are UNSAFE for your guests and place an X on them. Write only the numbers from the SAFE plates and glasses on the lines on the tablecloth.

Name ______________________________ Date ______________________________

WHAT'S TO EAT?

Decorate the table setting below or make larger plates, forks, spoons, knives, napkins, and placemats for you and your guests. Then work with some of your classmates to plan a delicious menu/meal that people from different cultures can enjoy. You can plan meals for BREAKFAST, LUNCH, or DINNER.

MAKE A LARGER TABLE SETTING FROM CONSTRUCTION PAPER, CARDBOARD, AND TONGUE DEPRESSORS.

THE MENU

______________ ______________ ______________

______________ ______________ ______________

______________ ______________ ______________

Name ______________________________ Date ______________________________

GOOD MORNING

Have fun saying "GOOD MORNING" in four different languages. Cut out the new words and paste them on separate cards. Practice saying these greetings to your classmates and family members. Add other greetings to your collection.

GREEK

1. Kal-eemehra

PORTUGUESE

2. Bom dia

SWAHILI

3. Habari za asubuhi

KOREAN

4. Annyong ha se yo

Name ______________________________ Date ______________________________

GOOD NIGHT

Have fun saying "GOOD NIGHT" in four different languages. Cut out the new words and paste them on separate cards. Practice saying these greetings to your classmates and family members. Add other greetings to your collection.

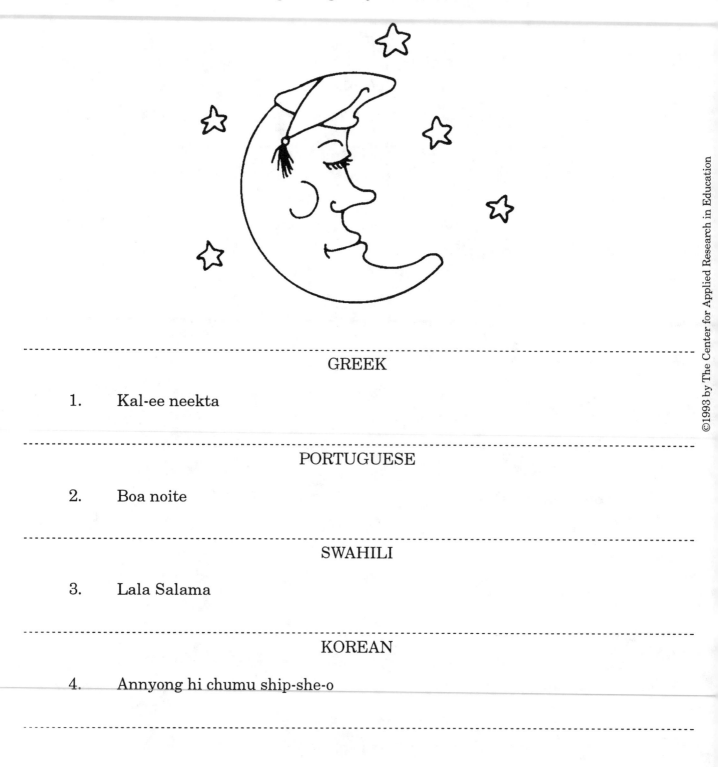

GREEK

1. Kal-ee neekta

PORTUGUESE

2. Boa noite

SWAHILI

3. Lala Salama

KOREAN

4. Annyong hi chumu ship-she-o

Name ______________________________ Date ______________________________

AN AMERICAN CLASSROOM

Girls and boys of many different races, nationalities, cultures, and languages go to school in American classrooms. These children learn and have fun together. Use your crayons or markers to color the pictures.

Pretend that you know something about the children in the pictures. Then write a story about the fun they have working and learning together.

WRITE YOUR STORY ON THE NEXT PAGE.

2-13B

Name ______________________ Date ______________________

MY CLASS STORY

Make up places of birth, ages, addresses, favorite toys, books, and other interesting things about the children in this class. Include information about their teacher and the things that they are learning in the class.

___

___

___

___

___

___

___

___

___

___

___

Now have fun sharing your pictures and story with your classmates, teacher, and family.

Name ______________________ Date ______________________

BOOKS IN EVERY LAND

Children all over the world read books in their own language. Write the word BOOK in four NEW languages. Make sure you put the word BOOK in another language on the picture. Then complete the sentence below.

1. ______________________
2. ______________________
3. ______________________
4. ______________________

Complete the sentence below by writing ONE of the words in the blank.

______________________ for your life!

- Sing
- Kick
- Read

Name ______________________________ Date ______________________________

AMERICANS—ALL

Who was already living in America when the people from the old world came? Which group of new immigrants was forced to come as slaves? Who came seeking freedom? Read the name of each group below. Then write a description to share with others.

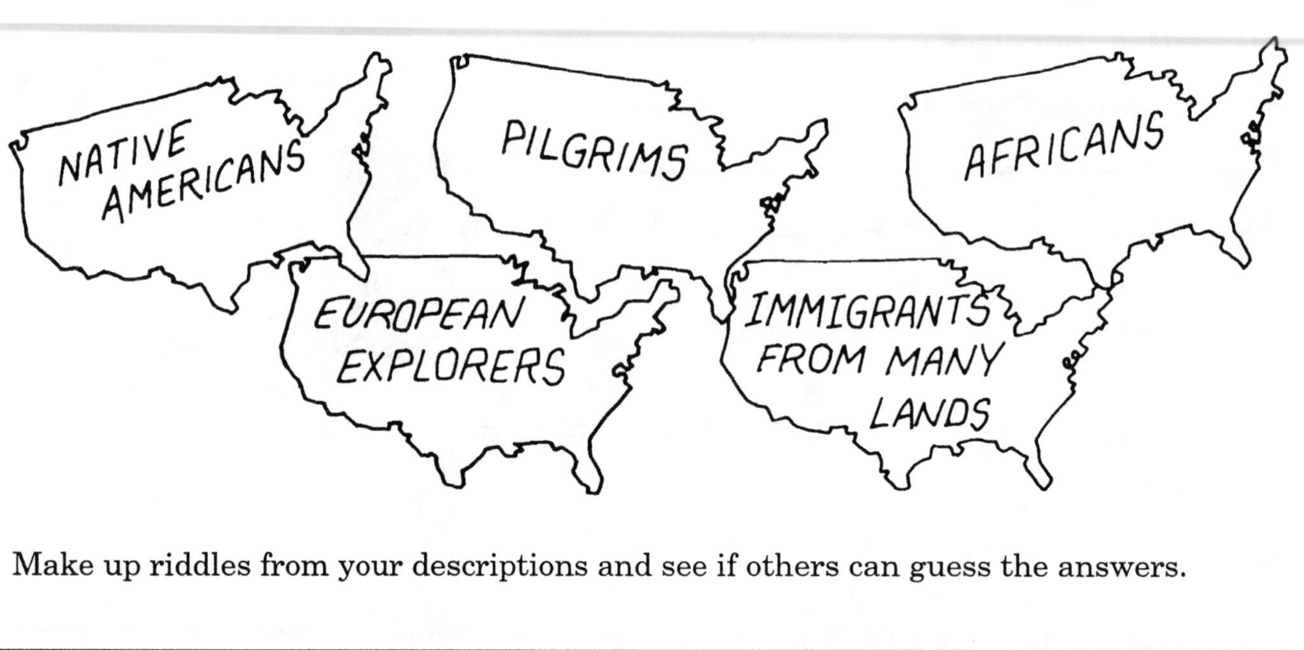

Make up riddles from your descriptions and see if others can guess the answers.

---

1. PILGRIMS.....YOUR DESCRIPTION:

---

2. EUROPEAN EXPLORERS....YOUR DESCRIPTION:

---

3. NATIVE AMERICANS....YOUR DESCRIPTION:

---

4. AFRICANS......YOUR DESCRIPTION:

---

5. IMMIGRANTS FROM MANY LANDS....YOUR DESCRIPTION:

Name ______________________________ Date ______________________________

THE FORMS OF ANIMALS AND THINGS

The world around us is beautiful, exciting, and fun because of the many different shapes and colors of animals and things. Color the pictures and find the name of each item on the Word Search puzzle.

S	T	R	A	W	B	E	R	R	I	E	S
J	U	I	C	E	I	B	M	X	G	H	D
B	L	U	E	W	H	A	L	E	G	O	I
I	E	S	R	O	H	L	O	G	E	R	R
R	A	C	B	A	L	L	T	G	W	S	B
D	B	U	T	T	E	R	F	L	Y	E	Y

Name ______________________________ **Date** ______________________________

HUMAN FORMS ARE ALL ALIKE

Sizes and skin color may change, but human forms all have the same shape. Cut out the human form and the different faces. Place the faces on the form, one at a time. Do they all fit?

YES NO (Circle one)

Name ________________________ Date ________________________

HUMAN BEINGS LAUGH AND CRY

All human beings, no matter what their color, religion, or culture, do many of the same kinds of things. Write 10 words that tell how people of all races and nationalities are the same.

PEOPLE OF ALL RACES CAN:

1. ________________________
2. ________________________
3. ________________________
4. ________________________
5. ________________________
6. ________________________
7. ________________________
8. ________________________
9. ________________________
10. ________________________

Name ______________________________ Date ______________________________

WE ARE NEIGHBORS

Neighbors help each other in times of need. Cut out the shapes below and use them to make something that someone else needs. Then write the name of the item on the line. Complete the sentence to explain why this item is needed by all human beings.

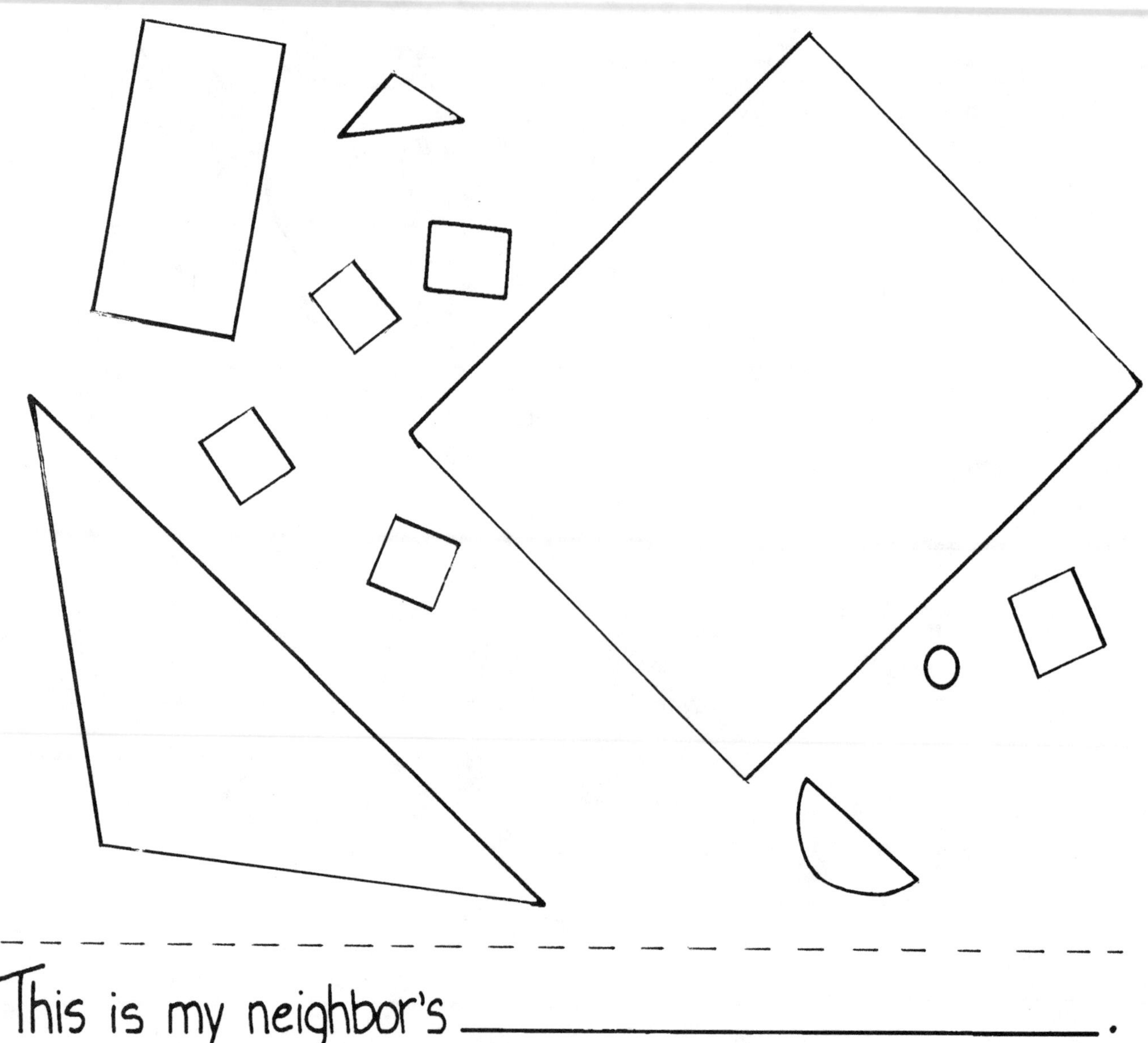

This is my neighbor's ______________________.

My neighbor needs the... ______________________

because... ______________________

____

Cut on the broken line. Paste sentences on your new worksheet.

Name ______________________________ Date ______________________________

WHAT IS FRIENDSHIP?

People of all races, colors, and cultures need to feel wanted by other human beings. Make someone you know feel happy by giving him/her a special note.

Write a ONE SENTENCE GIFT on the card below. Decorate it with flowers, shapes, etc. Use some of the ideas in the boxes or create new sentences.

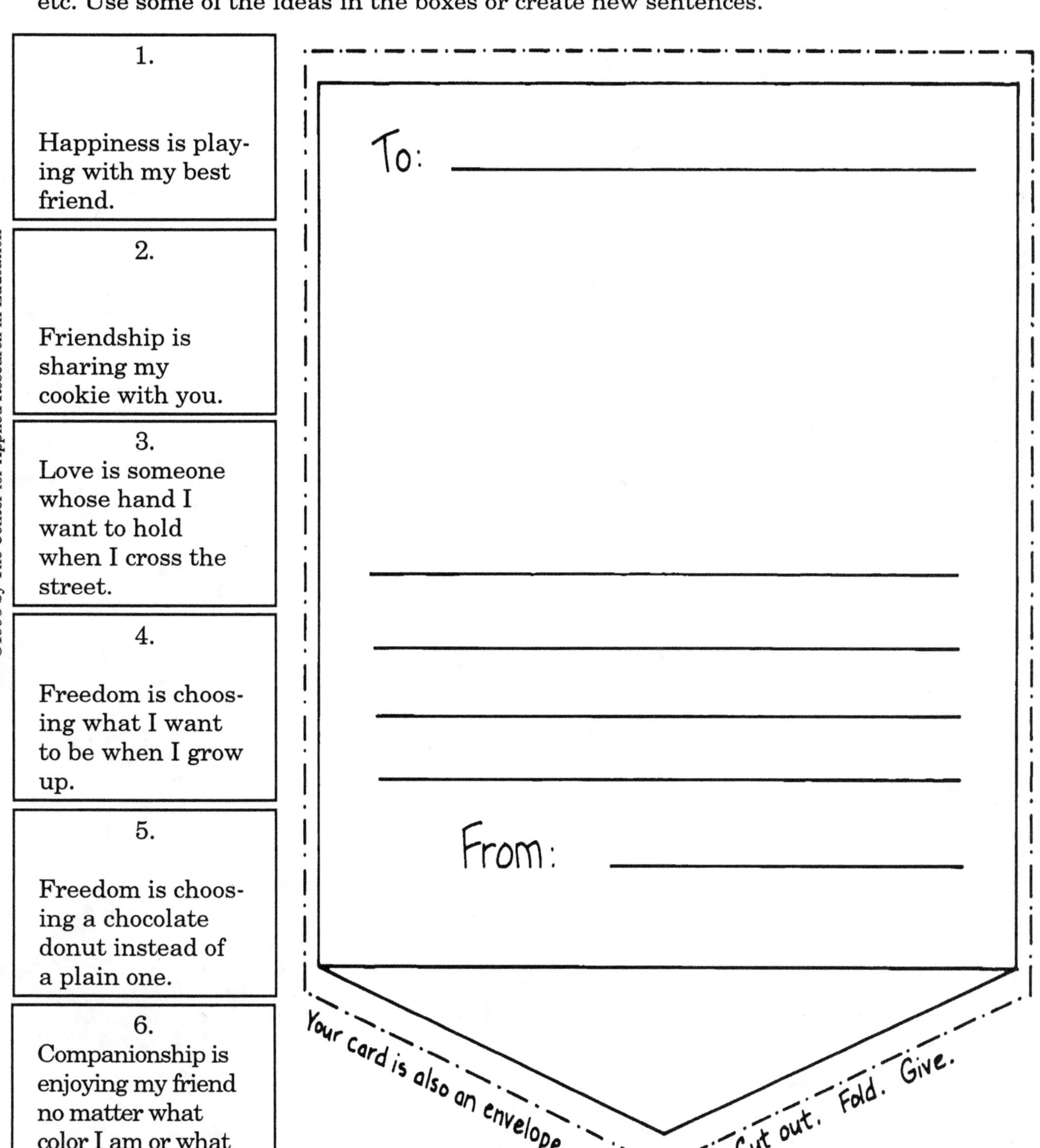

To:
From:
Your card is also an envelope.
Cut out. Fold. Give.

1. Happiness is playing with my best friend.

2. Friendship is sharing my cookie with you.

3. Love is someone whose hand I want to hold when I cross the street.

4. Freedom is choosing what I want to be when I grow up.

5. Freedom is choosing a chocolate donut instead of a plain one.

6. Companionship is enjoying my friend no matter what color I am or what color he/she may be.

2-16A

Name ______________________________ Date ______________________________

BRINGING HOME THE BACON

Look at the different foods below. Place an X on the lines next to those people who can help get food for us to eat. Color the foods.

Truck Driver ____ Butcher ____ Grocer ____ Farmer ____

Father ____ Mother ____ Teacher ____ Cook ____ Mailman ____

Think about this: What race or color does a person have to be to bring food to others? ____________________

Name ______________________________ Date ______________________________

PEOPLE HAVE THE SAME NEEDS

Unscramble the words. Then write each word under the correct picture.

1. ofod ______________________________
2. uohse ______________________________
3. cethlso ______________________________
4. tarwe ______________________________

______________________________ ______________________________

______________________________ ______________________________

Color the pictures. Then write a few sentences telling why people want to take care of the land, water, and air. Also tell how you can help take care of the Earth.

Name ______________________________ Date ______________________________

ALL PEOPLE NEED ______________ .

Human beings need food in order to live. Connect the dots below to find out something else that all people need.

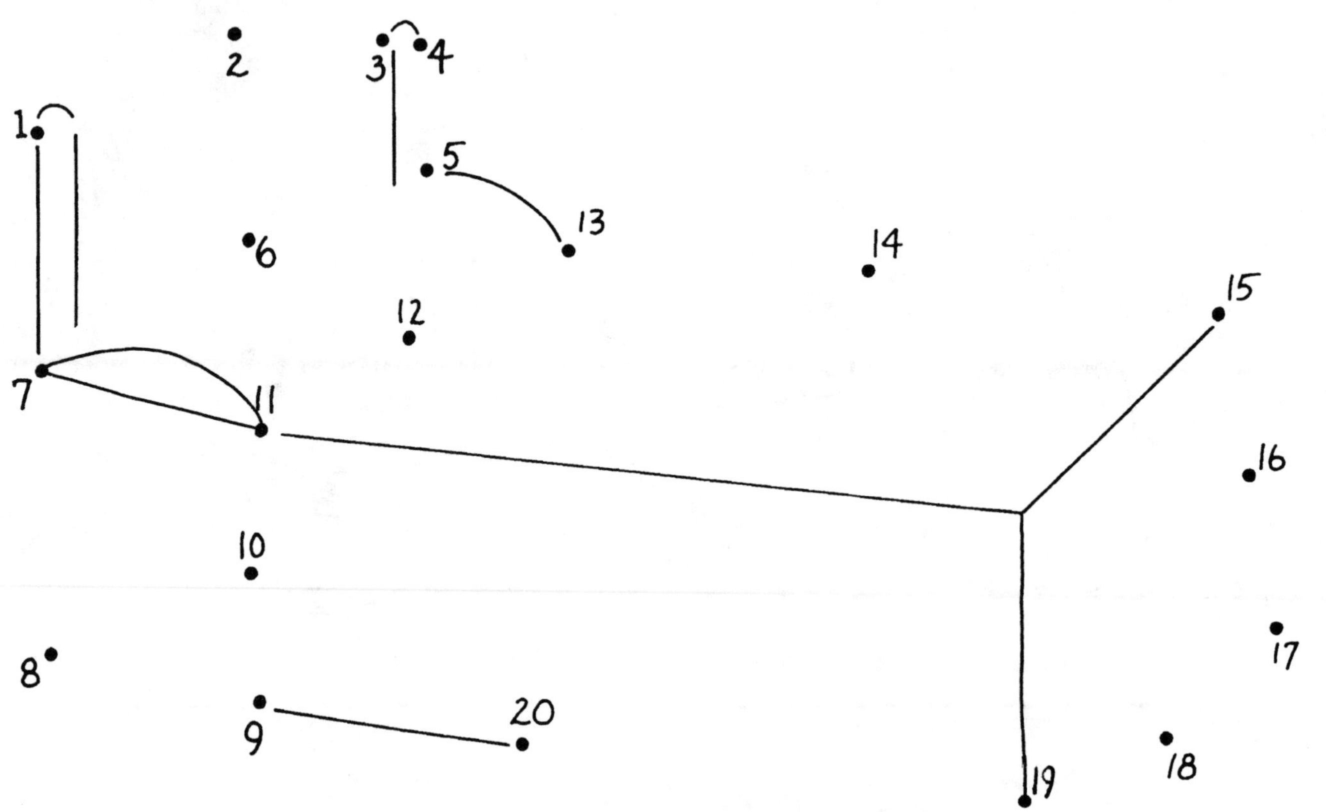

Write the five-letter word in the title above. Then use it to complete the sentence below:

I'm tired, I want to go to __ __ __ __ __ .

Now make a design on the bedspread and fill it with bright colors.

Name ________________________________ Date ________________________________

EVERYONE LIKES TO PLAY

The faces of people, the clothes they wear, their hair and eyes are all different colors, just like a rainbow. Having friends and classmates from different cultures, races, and religions can be fun. Choose a friend and invite him/her to do an activity with you.

Circle the names of the games and activities that you and a new friend might want to do.

RUNNING	JUMPING	MAKING MOVIES
YELLING	TICKLING	WATCHING VIDEOS
DOLLS	SWIMMING	COLLECTING SNAILS/FROGS
COOKING	BASKETBALL	MAKING FACES
HIKING	READING	GARDENING
WASHING DISHES	DANCING	BUILDING BLOCKS
READING COMICS	FISHING	EXPLORING
RHYMING	LAUGHING	GETTING DIZZY
SKATING	STILT WALKING	MARBLES
BASEBALL	SINGING	BOARD GAMES
CLIMBING TREES	PLAYING FRISBEE™	FOOTBALL
FLYING	DIGGING	FLYING KITES
HOPSCOTCH	BLOWING BUBBLES	TUG-OF-WAR
JUMPING ROPE	*PIG LATIN	RIDDLES
TONGUE TWISTERS	SHOVELING SNOW	TAKING OUT THE GARBAGE

*PIG LATIN— Take off the initial consonant of a word, put it at the end of the word and attach the sound of "ay" behind it. This playful way of talking is sometimes used to tell secrets to someone while in the presence of a third party.

Can you read this sample of PIG LATIN?	"ooday	ooyay	etgay	isthay?"
	Do	you	get	this

Name ______________________________ Date ______________________________

FRIENDLY RAINBOWS

Human beings of all races, colors, and religions have some things that they LIKE and other things that they DISLIKE. Write FIVE things under each heading. Then use these and other ideas to write sentences (on the next page) that tell how all human beings are ALIKE.

FIVE THINGS HUMANS LIKE

1. ______________________________
2. ______________________________
3. ______________________________
4. ______________________________
5. ______________________________

FIVE THINGS HUMANS DISLIKE

1. ______________________________
2. ______________________________
3. ______________________________
4. ______________________________
5. ______________________________

Name ______________________________ Date ______________________________

FRIENDLY RAINBOWS

Write five sentences telling how human beings of all races and colors are ALIKE.

1. ______________________________
____
____

2. ______________________________
____
____

3. ______________________________
____
____

4. ______________________________
____
____

5. ______________________________
____
____

On the back of this sheet, draw a picture of different types of people enjoying the same kinds of things.

2-17C

Name ______________________ Date ______________________

LET'S PLAY

Invite a friend to do a fun activity with you. Circle the words which show some things you and your new friend can do together.

Let's Look at a Book

Let's Color

Let's Sing

Let's Make a Puppet

Let's ______________________________

Write your own idea here and draw a picture to go with it.

Name ________________________________ Date ________________________________

PUZZLES AND FRIENDS

Make a puzzle by drawing lines on the picture to make puzzle pieces. Cut the pieces out and put them together with a friend.

2-18A

Name ________________________________ Date ________________________________

FRIENDS IN THE RAIN

Fill in the blanks below and color the picture.

How many people are under the umbrella? ____________________

Count the number of legs you see. ____________________

Write the word which describes the weather. ____________________

Trace the foreign language words. ____________________

What do you think the foreign language words say? ____________________

____

Name ______________________________ Date ______________________________

FRIENDS IN THE SUNSHINE

Fill in the blanks and color the picture.

How many girls are in the picture? ______________________________

How many boys are in the picture? ______________________________

How many foreign languages do you see? ______________________________

What do you think the foreign language words say? ______________________________

____

Compare this picture with the one on the previous page? How are these two pictures alike? How are they different? ______________________________

____

Name ________________________________ Date ________________________________

YOU ARE MY SUNSHINE

How do you feel when you are standing in the sunshine?

You can be the sunshine in someone's life by doing something to make him or her happy. Circle only the pictures and words which show what you can do to make another person feel warm and happy.

SMILE

HIT OR KICK A PERSON

"YOU CAN'T PLAY WITH US!"

"I'LL HELP YOU!"

"THANK YOU FOR THE FLOWER."

FROWN

Name ______________________________ Date ______________________________

A VISIT TO THE POST OFFICE

Some children fight about being FIRST IN LINE. Why is that so important? Read the story below. Then answer the question.

Two smiling ladies, in bright summer clothes, talked softly as they waited in line at the post office. The younger of the ladies held a small child in her arms. The older lady leaned on a cane.

"May I help you?" The clerk behind the counter asked. "You can go first," the lady with the baby told her neighbor. "Oh, no. You go first," the older woman answered.

Who do you think should go first? Why? ______________________________

____

____

Color the pictures of the postal worker, the clerk, and the two neighbors.

Name ______________________________ Date ______________________________

IT'S A BEAUTIFUL MORNING

The way people speak to each other in the morning sets the tone for the whole day. You decide what the people in the story should say to each other.

The sun was warm, the wind was blowing softly, and mothers decided that it was a good morning to walk their babies. What will the mothers say to each other as they meet?

Circle the words the mothers might say to each other:

"Good morning." "What a cute baby." "Get out of the way!"

"What are you doing in this neighborhood?" "Hello, I'm.... What is your name?"

"It's a lovely morning, isn't it?" "Your baby is ugly".

"Have a bad day." "Have a good day." "I'm glad to meet you."

Now, on a separate sheet of paper write the rest of the story. What happens next? Do the mothers go shopping, to the park, or to the school to pick up other children?

Name ______________________________ Date ______________________________

DIFFERENT KINDS OF JOBS

Men and women can work in many of the same jobs today. Circle jobs that BOTH males and females can do. Then answer the questions in your own words.

DOCTOR LAWYER MUSICIAN GARBAGE COLLECTOR LIFEGUARD
ELECTRICIAN GARDENER FARMER PRESIDENT HAIRDRESSER
PRIEST MINISTER GROCER DANCER ACTOR WINDOW WASHER
FIREFIGHTER SENATOR WRITER COOK NUN COACH
ENGINEER BUS DRIVER TRUCK DRIVER TYPIST
BASKETBALL PLAYER COMPUTER PROGRAMMER
MAILPERSON POLICE OFFICER SALESPERSON
TAILOR TELEPHONE OPERATOR SECRETARY
BUSINESS PERSON LIBRARIAN PHOTOGRAPHER
RABBI

1. Are there jobs listed above that a man CANNOT do? Write the job(s) on the lines and explain why a man cannot do this work.

____

____

____

2. Are there jobs listed above that a woman CANNOT do? Write the job(s) on the lines and explain why a woman cannot do this work.

____

____

____

3. Are there jobs listed above that a person could be TOO OLD to do? Write the job(s) on the lines and explain why someone can be too old to do this work.

____

____

____

4. If a man or woman can do a job, should his/her race, color or age matter? Circle YES or NO.

Name ________________________________ Date ________________________________

LEARN TO SWIM FIRST

Joan is in trouble in the swimming pool. Circle the name of the ONLY person who is trained to help. Then write some things that Joan could do before **she** goes into the pool again.

SWIMMING TEACHER   CASHIER

LAWYER   POSTAL CLERK

LIBRARIAN

Before Joan goes back into the swimming pool she should ________________________

____

____

Name ______________________________ Date ______________________________

THE GARDEN IS SWEET

Write the word YES next to the pictures of those who can enjoy the flowers in the garden. Write the word NO next to those things that cannot see, smell, or touch the flowers. Color the flowers and the people.

Name ______________________________ Date ______________________________

SAY THANK YOU WITH A FLOWER

Sometimes someone helps you and you want to say THANK YOU. Color this rose and give it to someone special. Trace the word FLOWER in six languages. Then sign your name to your gift.

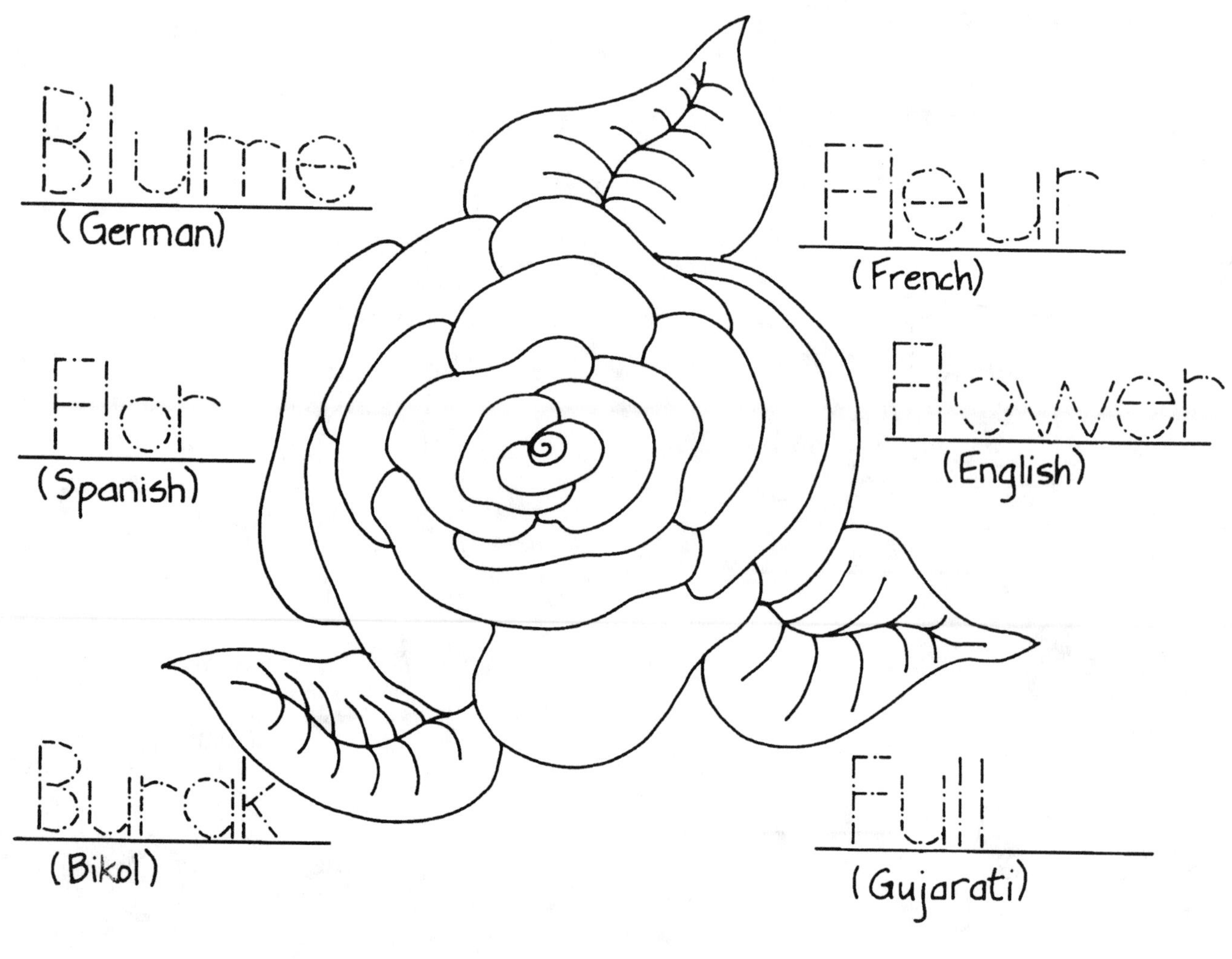

Your Signature ______________________________

Name ____________________ Date ____________________

PLANTING THE SEEDS OF PEACE

What if all seeds gardeners planted were words of kindness? Collect words of kindness, love, and caring from friends, family members, teachers, and other students. Write each kind word on the lines near the "PEACE SEEDS" in the ground.

Plant a garden of peace by writing each word in the soil. Then write answers to the questions.

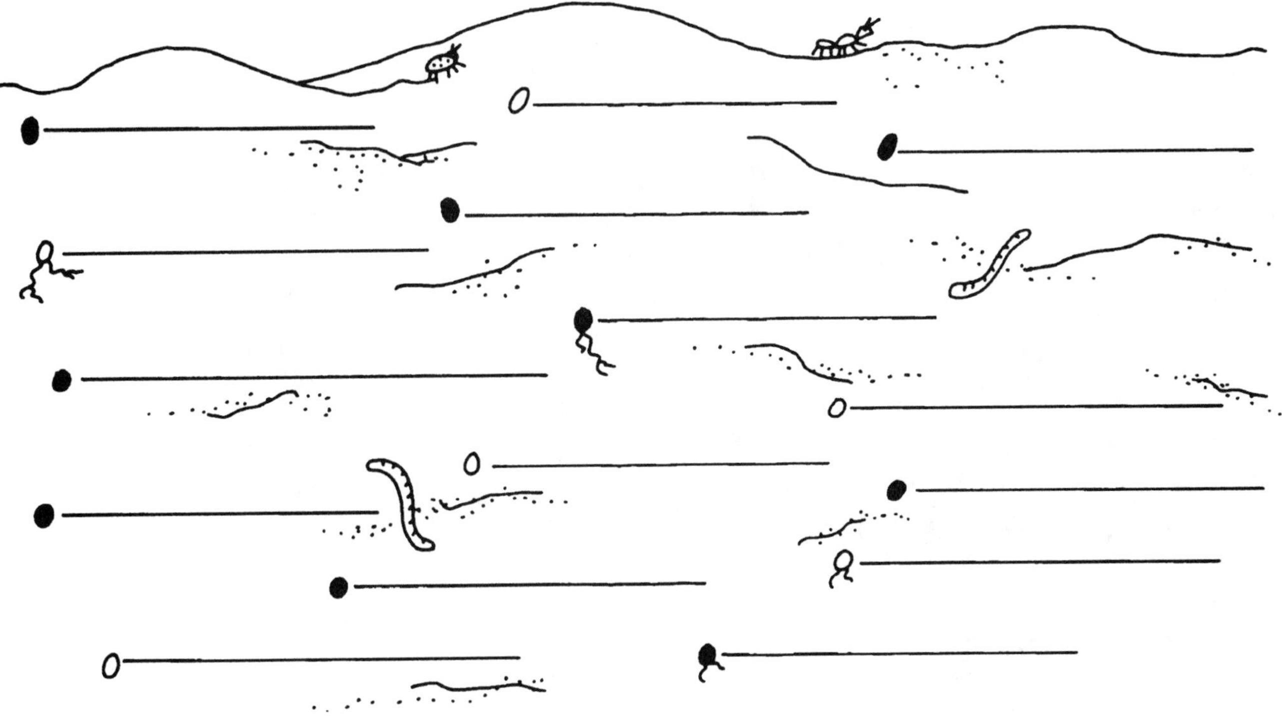

1. What if every ray of sunshine and every raindrop made your "peace seeds" grow? What kinds of things will you have in a garden where only kind words are spoken?

   ____

   ____

2. How many "peace seeds" did you collect from others? ____________________

3. How many "peace seeds" did you think of by yourself? ____________________

4. Have you said something kind to someone today? Circle one. YES NO

Name ________________________________ Date ________________________________

GLOBAL RAINBOWS

Rainbows are symbols of peace and hope all over the world. People of all colors, races and nations want to get along with each other. Circle ONLY the words which give human beings HOPE and PEACE.

Write a foreign language color word on each band on the rainbow. Color your rainbow of peace. Use the Foreign Language List in the Appendix.

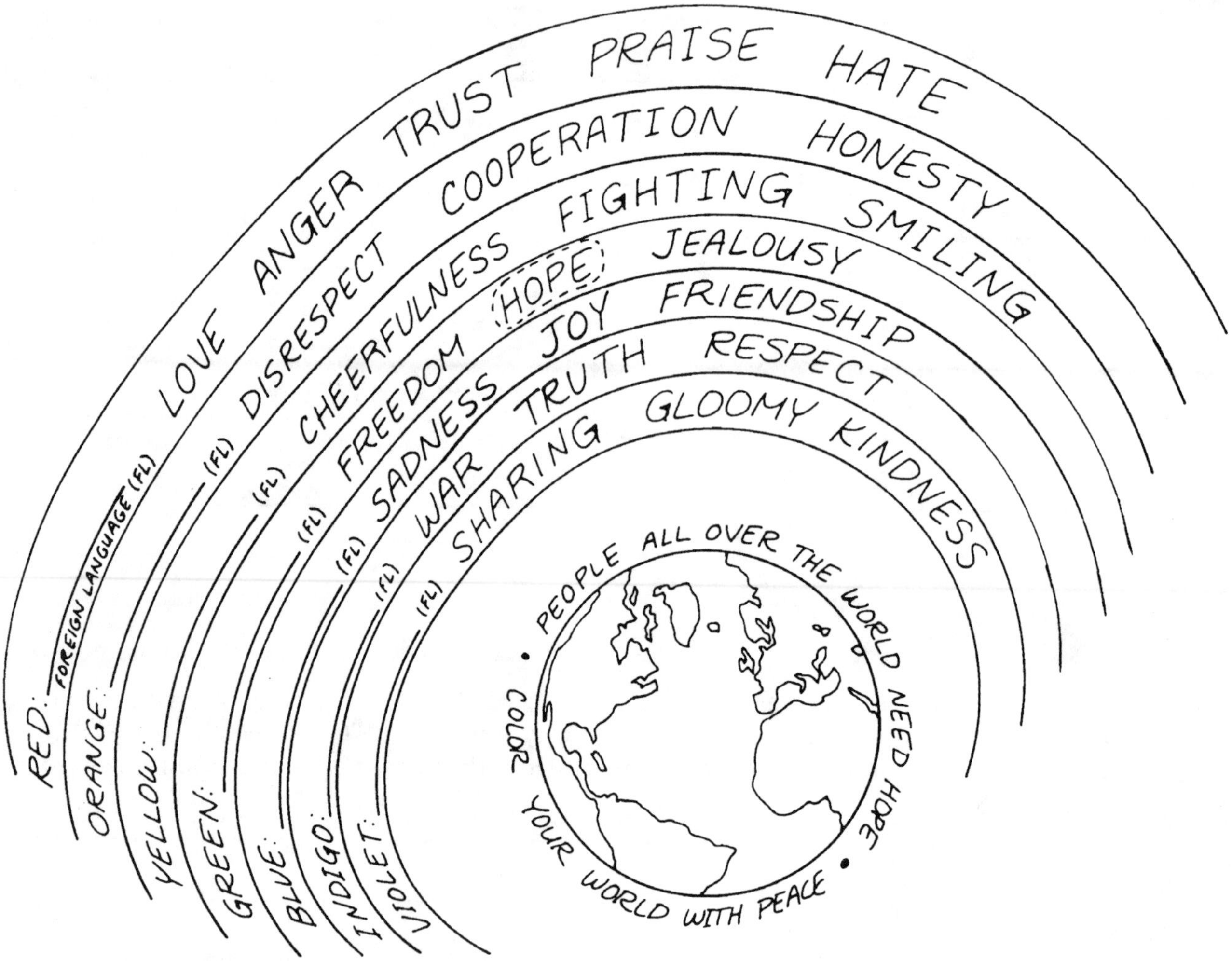

LOVE ANGER TRUST PRAISE HATE

(FL) DISRESPECT COOPERATION HONESTY

(FL) CHEERFULNESS FIGHTING SMILING

(FL) FREEDOM HOPE JEALOUSY

(FL) SADNESS JOY FRIENDSHIP

(FL) WAR TRUTH RESPECT

(FL) SHARING GLOOMY KINDNESS

RED: FOREIGN LANGUAGE (FL)

ORANGE:

YELLOW:

GREEN:

BLUE:

INDIGO:

VIOLET:

• PEOPLE ALL OVER THE WORLD NEED HOPE • COLOR YOUR WORLD WITH PEACE

Name ____________________ Date ____________________

WHAT IS AMERICA?

Read the passages below and think about what America means to you. Talk with some of your classmates and make your decision among the three choices which describe our country.

America is...

Choice #1 A Melting Pot

Have you ever smelled a delicious pot of soup or stew? If so, like many other people, you enjoy the aroma of all of the ingredients blending, almost melting together. Because all of the different vegetables, spices, noodles, meat, and liquid are cooked together, the separate flavors make ONE great taste. Some people say that America, with all of its different races, colors, religions, languages and nationalities of citizens, is like a melting pot. What do you think?

Choice #2 A Bowl of Salad

Have you ever eaten a salad? If so, you know that each ingredient has its own special flavor. People who like salads enjoy the separate flavors of the salad greens, tomatoes, carrots, cucumbers, onions, beets, celery, peppers, and other things. The dressings and croutons (crispy cubes of toasted bread) add additional tastes. Some people say that America, with all of its different races, colors, religions, languages and nationalities of people, is like a salad. What do you think?

Name ______________________________ Date ______________________________

WHAT IS AMERICA?

Choice #3 A Patchwork Quilt

Have you ever seen a quilt or watched someone make one? If so, you can see that many shapes and colors of cloth are sewn together to make a beautiful wall hanging, or cover for a bed, chair or sofa. Cloth from someone's old dress, a piece of a baby's nightgown, a patch from a man's shirt, leftover fabric from curtains, etc., often have meaning for the person making a quilt, as he/she sews the patterns together with a common thread. Some people say that America, with all of its different races, colors, languages, and nationalities of individuals, is like a patchwork quilt. We're all different, but we are bound together by our common human needs of food, shelter, rest, and work. What do you think?

VOTE FOR YOUR CHOICE ON A BALLOT OR
BY PLACING AN "X" IN ONE OF THE BOXES BELOW:

CHOICE #1 ☐ AMERICA IS A MELTING POT

CHOICE #2 ☐ AMERICA IS A BOWL OF SALAD

CHOICE #3 ☐ AMERICA IS A PATCHWORK QUILT

THEN COLOR THE PICTURE OF YOUR CHOICE WITH BRIGHT COLORS.

COMPARE YOUR VOTE TO THOSE OF OTHERS AND TALK ABOUT THE REASONS FOR YOUR CHOICES.

Record the final class vote below:

America is a: ______________________________

Winning number of votes ______________

Name ______________________________ Date ______________________________

KISSES AND HUGS

KISSES and HUGS are the best of friends because they are often done at the same time AND they MAKE PEOPLE FEEL GOOD. Look at the words in each line below and find words which are best friends. Write the BEST FRIEND words on the lips and arms. See how many you can find. One is done for you.

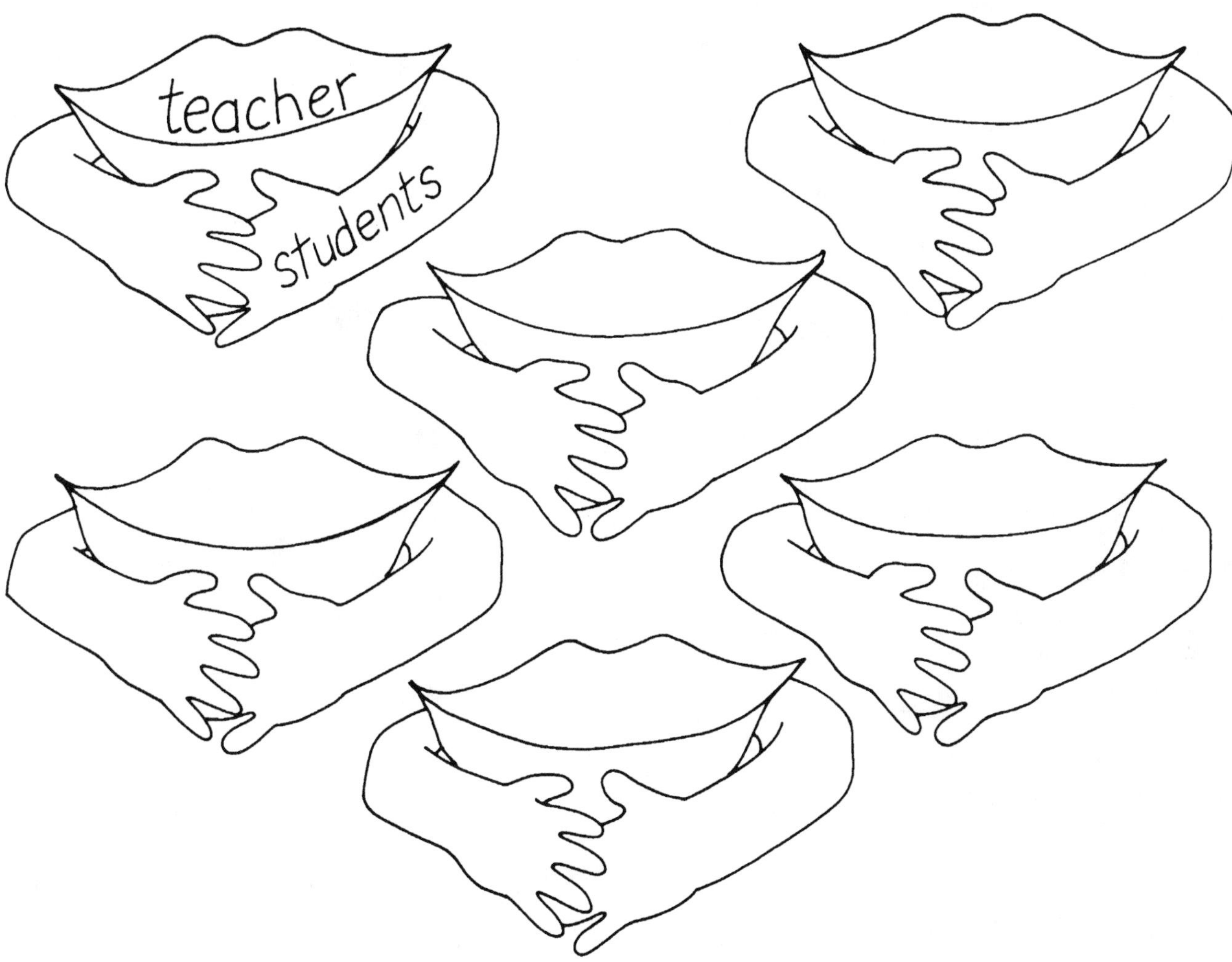

1. light cake (students) pages sun books birthday (teacher)
2. faces cookies tree me smiles you milk leaves fear
3. paper gun moon tears pencil stars bullets anger
4. feet movies fingers parent shoes popcorn hands baby
5. peace ice friends work truth home love cream hate

Section 3

MULTICULTURAL CONTRIBUTIONS

INTRODUCTION

In Section 3, children will identify contributors from various racial and ethnic groups who have helped mankind. They will understand that human beings of all races, cultures, and ethnic groups are intelligent, industrious, and capable of contributing to society. Many members of minority groups, including African-Americans, Native Americans, Asian-Americans, and women, have often been left out of what is known as American history. These activities are designed to fill in some of the gaps left by these omissions. Because this section considers the contributions of groups which are representative of all Americans (Native, European, Hispanic, African, and Asian), children will develop a deeper understanding of what the term *multicultural* really means. Moreover, it will become clear to students that the term embraces all that concerns these groups of human beings, including their customs, traditions, religions, and holidays. Again, the goal here is to highlight the fact that contributions to civilization, and more specifically to America, have always transcended race, culture, and nationality and that people from all of these groups, based upon their humanity, have much in common. Furthermore, members of all groups have been and are intellectually capable of helping society. To further emphasize this truth, the teacher should feel free to insert contributors from races and cultures that reflect the multicultural mix of the classroom. Some activities identify the race, cultures, and ethnicity of contributors throughout, others identify the racial, cultural and/or ethnic origins of one, two, or none. This provides further opportunities for whole class, small group, and/or individual research. The Literature Connection feature at the end of each activity is designed to extend the multicultural concepts presented in the lessons and to help children get in touch with their own feelings about those who are different from themselves.

To introduce these activities, use multiracial pictures to demonstrate the fact that America is made up of people from many different places on the Earth; they vary in language, skin color, and nationality. Explain the fact that America was built by people of many cultures and that some of their ancestors might have had much to do with providing for the needs of citizens today. For the benefit of students' ongoing study and immersion in these concepts, it is suggested that an in-class library be organized. At the very least, such a library would include books, pamphlets, pictures, audiovisual materials, and news articles, with information about people from diverse ethnic and racial backgrounds. Moreover, a broad range of occupations, including inventors, scientists, civil rights leaders, politicians, doctors, engineers, musicians, artists, writers, and athletes should be reflected in the collection. Most importantly, an effort to balance race, gender, and disabilities in these selections is crucial. The school librarian and/or public library should be able to provide such materials for use over an extended period of time.

In addition to an in-class library, a permanent place to display information about multicultural contributors can be established. Whether it is a bulletin board, showcase, or a table, items should be changed periodically with the children's understanding that it is THEIR area. The teacher's efforts to expose his/her students to the technological, medical, scientific, literary, and social advancements which have occurred because of the contributions of many different races and cultures will be greatly enhanced by including the children in the planning and maintenance of the area. As a result of their exposure to and participation in these activities, students will grow in their knowledge of contemporary and historical contributions and, simultaneously, experience great respect for people of diverse racial, ethnic, and cultural backgrounds. A special form for teaching children to do minimal research is included in the Appendix.

DIRECTIONS FOR SECTION THREE ACTIVITIES

Activity 3-1 THEY HELPED BUILD AMERICA

In this activity children will see the connection between the needs and wants that individuals and groups have and the ability of others to provide them. These providers can be called **contributors**, since they have the intelligence and the resources necessary to make products, or organize services, to meet people's needs. Children will also see that providers or contributors come from many racial, cultural, and ethnic groups.

Materials Needed:

- Copy of activity sheet 3-1, *They Helped Build America*
- A list of familiar "Needs and Wants" and a place for the names of contributors
- Pencils
- Crayons or markers
- Multiracial pictures of contributors for copying and/or display
- Encyclopedia information about various contributors
- Activity 1-21B, *Making Choices at Home*

Directions:

1. Show the list of Needs and Wants on Activity sheet 1-21B (Section One), *Making Choices at Home*. Have the children extend the items on the list and categorize them. Identify contributors for each item. Share multicultural contributors' pictures and biographies.

2. Ask students to describe some services and items people use daily. For example, people use telephones, traffic lights, doctors, airplanes, and repair people. Elicit from children how life would be without these things, in order to stress their importance.

3. Discuss the fact that people who provide for the needs and wants of others are called contributors. Ask students to complete activity 3-1, *They Helped Build America*. Have them share information from all worksheets with the class.

4. Extend this activity by having students make a bulletin board display of multicultural contributors to America. Emphasize the roles of women, as well as men, in science, law, medicine, education, art, music, and civil rights. Share the display with other classes and members of the community.

LITERATURE CONNECTION: *Great Americans* by Mary Jane Fowler and Margaret Fisher. Historical and contemporary contributors are described in biographical sketches, drawings, and photographs. Men and women of diverse backgrounds who made contributions to science, music, art, health, civil rights, and education are shown as outstanding Americans. Gateway Press, Grand Rapids, Michigan, © 1988. Illustrated by Lee Brown and Ellen Osborn.

Activity 3-2 CRASH! BANG! OUCH!

Traveling by car is a daily experience for many American citizens. Traffic control is fairly easy because of lights at the intersections of streets. Children will learn about the work of Garrett A. Morgan, the African-American man who invented the first traffic light. In addition, they will learn that symbols are necessary in communicating nonverbal safety messages to people of diverse cultural backgrounds.

Materials Needed:

- Copy of activity sheet 3-2, *Crash! Bang! Ouch!*
- Pictures of traffic lights and other safety signs for drivers and pedestrians
- Pencils
- Crayons or markers
- Information about Garrett A. Morgan, African-American inventor of the traffic light (See World Book Encyclopedia, © 1982)
- Information about the invention of the automobile, including pictures of Henry Ford, cars, and so on
- Information about traffic safety and the invention of seatbelts, windshield wipers, etc.

Directions:

1. Ask students to describe some of their car trips. Have them share experiences with near accidents. Ask them to imagine what could happen on city streets if there were no traffic lights to give signals for cars to STOP or GO. Elicit from children information about safety in driving and the need for people to have training before they get behind the wheel of a car. Teach SAFETY FIRST! Examine other types of nonverbal signs and determine how they help keep drivers and pedestrians safe. For example, the signs showing silhouettes of school children with books, or deer crossings.

2. Show pictures of different modes of transportation, for example, car, bus, train, boat, submarine or airplane. Discuss the crowded streets during peak travel hours and busy airports. Elicit from children that the potential for accidents is

very high, especially when people are not careful. Help them to understand the need for order when people are being transported by private cars, mass transportation vehicles, including airplanes, ships, buses, and trains.

Have students identify several ways that people who travel by various vehicles can be safely transported. For example, all drivers, engineers, and pilots must take lessons and get licenses. All vehicles must be kept in good operating condition and drivers, engineers, and pilots have to obey all rules and regulations. In addition, there must be some kind of method for controlling ground traffic, as well as air traffic. With these controls people can be safe as they travel. Elicit from children the importance of seatbelts, turn signals, road signs, and windshield wipers. Encourage students to do some research on the origin of these and other safety features.

3. Explain that a very intelligent person saw the need to control the flow of traffic at intersections. So he invented a special light signal to help the many drivers of ground vehicles (including motorcycles and bikes) to take turns moving into the intersection. Show the pictures of Garrett A. Morgan. Discuss his ability to see a need and work to save lives by solving traffic problems.

4. Give students activity 3-2, *Crash! Bang! Ouch!* Have them complete both sheets and share their findings. Elicit from students the ordinal numbers for the vertical arrangement of the lights: red, first; yellow, second; green, third. Read some of the life story of Garrett A. Morgan.

5. Extend this activity by having students do minimal research to discover who invented the automobile. Elicit from them the fact that inventors see "needs" and think of ways to fill them. Use the encyclopedia and other resources to help children see that people from many different places contributed to the development of the modern-day car. Among these people were Henry Ford, Charles Brady King, Ransom Eli Olds, and Alexander Winston. Have children read information and draw pictures that show the multicultural development of the car and other vehicles. Elicit from them why the traffic light was so important after the invention of motor vehicles. Also, use this opportunity to emphasize the concept of interdependence, as people of diverse racial, ethnic, and cultural backgrounds work to provide citizens with things which will improve their lives. Display the results of this activity.

LITERATURE CONNECTION: *I Read Symbols* by Tana Hoban. Various signals which help with traffic safety are shown. Greenwillow Books, New York, © 1983. Illustrated with photographs.

Activity 3-3 TALK, TALK, AND MORE TALK

In this activity, students will learn about the work of the very intelligent Scottish-American, Alexander Graham Bell. They will see the importance of the need for people to be able to communicate over long distances, that is, beyond the normal range of the human voice. In addition, they will understand how difficult it was to get messages to others before the invention of the telephone. Children will also learn that the human body often provides clues for scientists as they do their research. For example, Alexander Graham Bell knew a great deal about the structure of the human ear and based his invention of the telephone on his expertise as a teacher of the deaf. This lesson provides opportunities for class research in the ways sound travels through the air.

Materials Needed:

- Copy of activity sheet 3-3, *Talk, Talk, and More Talk*
- Pencils
- Crayons
- Encyclopedia information about Alexander Graham Bell, the Scottish-American inventor of the telephone
- Two or more unconnected telephones of various types

Directions:

1. Show pictures of people talking. Point out that talking is an important way to communicate information, feelings, and concerns. Explain how teachers and students must talk in order for learning to occur.

2. Discuss how people who are far away from each other can talk together. Without saying the word "telephone," give students activity 3-3, *Talk, Talk, and More Talk*. Show pictures and read about Alexander Graham Bell, when they complete the activity.

3. Extend concepts by having children research Bell's work with deaf children. Encourage them to compare Bell's knowledge of how the ear works with his ability to invent the telephone. Give students a chance to examine telephones in the classroom. Extend this activity by having the class do research on the human ear to discover how they are able to hear the sounds around them. Children who have auditory problems and use hearing aids might serve as resource persons. They become contributors.

LITERATURE CONNECTION: *Let's Find Out About Telephones* by David C. Knight. An easy to understand explanation of how the telephone works. Franklin, Watts, New York, © 1967. Illustrated by Don Miller.

Activity 3-4 EVERYONE NEEDS SHOES

In this activity, students will come to appreciate the brilliant work of Jan E. Matzeliger, the African-American inventor of the shoe-lasting machine. Without his invention, people would still have to wait weeks and months to get a pair of shoes made.

Materials Needed:

- Copy of activity sheet 3-4, *Everyone Needs Shoes*
- Scissors and glue
- Drawing paper
- Blunt needles and coarse thread (optional)
- Flannel (optional)
- Encyclopedia information about Jan Ernst Matzeliger, an African-American inventor (World Book, © 1986, Vol. 13)

Directions:

1. Ask students to examine their own shoes and those of their classmates. Discuss where they got their shoes and how long it took to buy them. Compare and contrast shoe sizes and styles.

2. Point out that long ago, people had to have their shoes made by hand, one at a time. Because of this, they had to wait weeks and months to get one pair of shoes. Compare and contrast the time it took to make one pair of shoes to the number of shoes which can be made in one hour, or in a day, with the shoe-lasting machine. Ask students which they would prefer, hand-made or machine-made shoes.

3. Give students an opportunity to see how difficult it must be to make a pair of shoes by hand. Have them complete the 2-page activity 3-4, *Everyone Needs Shoes*. Discuss the amount of time it took to cut out the pieces from the worksheet and glue them onto drawing paper. Elicit from students the difficulty of trying to make a real pair of shoes. Study the shoe-lasting machine. Then read something about Jan Matzeliger's life. (OPTIONAL: Allow students to attempt making a shoe from flannel. Discuss their experiences.)

4. Extend the impact of this activity by planning a trip to a shoe repair shop. Ask the cobbler to demonstrate how he repairs soles and uppers on his sewing machine and how much time it takes. Elicit from children how it must have been for a cobbler in early America to do this sewing by hand.

LITERATURE CONNECTION: *Whose Shoe?* by Margaret Miller. A wonderful collection of shoes worn by athletes, dancers and just everyday people. There's fun in guessing who wears each shoe. Greenwillow New York, © 1991. Color photographs.

Shoes for Everyone by Barbara Mitchell. The story of Jan Matzeliger's success in developing the shoe-last, despite the hardships of loneliness, prejudice, and poverty. Carolrhoda Books, Minneapolis, © 1988. Illustrated by Hetty Mitchell.

Activity 3-5 MAKING PROGRESS IN AMERICA

In this activity, children will consider familiar, everyday things and discuss the fact contributors have made the lives of everyone easier, because of their genius and willingness to work hard. Point out the multiracial, multicultural characteristics of contemporary and historical contributors.

Materials Needed:

- Copies of activity sheet 3-5, *Making Progress in America*
- Pencils
- Books and pictures of contributors
- Pictures of or sample household items, foods, spaceships, doctors, engineers, etc.
- Encyclopedia information
- Magazine pictures
- Coupons with pictures of cereal, fruit, etc.
- Sale flyers of electronic equipment, household goods, food, etc.
- Glue
- Scissors

Directions:

1. Have children observe pictures of familiar things. Or, they may use their imaginations to think of goods and services that people need. Discuss how life would be without refrigerators, lights, books, music, weather satellites, trains, typewriters, and computers. Assign individual and group reports on the usefulness of these and other contributions.

2. Explain that people who invent the things we use, and provide the services we need, are contributors, builders, makers of progress. Discuss the work of doctors, newspaper reporters, seamstresses, and the like. Have students share what they know about these occupations. Invite speakers in to enhance student understanding and to encourage them to think about their goals.

3. Discuss the fact that when America was new, people of many different racial and ethnic backgrounds made things which others needed. The same is true today. Post a chart on which students can write about and/or paste pictures of

items that people use everyday. Ask children to feel free to glue pictures of computers, shoes, clocks, spaceships, planes, trains, food, etc., on the chart. Use this as a way to begin discussions about how life is better because of the things individuals from different racial and ethnic origins have invented.

4. Give students activity 3-5, *Making Progress in America.* Have them complete this page and share the results. ANSWER KEY: 1. Jan Matzeliger, 2. Major Robert H. Lawrence, 3. Dr. William James Mayo, 4. Alexander Graham Bell, 5. Phyllis Wheatley, 6. Benjamin Banneker, 7. Garrett A. Morgan, 8. Sally Ride, 9. Charles Birdseye, 10. Dr. Elizabeth Blackwell. See encyclopedia information about several contributors. Make sure to point out their racial and/or ethnic backgrounds. Show students how to do a mini-biography on a person of their choice.

5. Have students add to their permanent multicultural display. Encourage them to be aware of the contributions of women, the disabled, Native Americans, Asian-Americans, Hispanic-Americans, and other ethnic groups which might not have been honored at this point. Elicit from children why it is important to recognize the work of people from various cultures. Continue to emphasize the fact that human beings from all racial and ethnic groups have helped to improve life for people in America and the world.

> **LITERATURE CONNECTION**: *Dreams into Deeds: Nine Women Who Dared* by Linda Peavy and Ursula Smith. Nine women of diverse backgrounds fulfill their dreams by contributing to society, despite outside pressures. Charles Scribner's Sons, New York, © 1985. Photographs.

Activity 3-6 WHAT COULD TOMMY BE READING?

The focus of this activity is on encouraging students to begin reading about contributors on their own. The multicultural contributions of Americans provide fascinating information. Many people have been inspired to invent because they have been exposed to stories of people who saw a need and found a way to fill it. Students in your class might be future inventors. Encourage all children to do independent reading and writing about various contributors and plan a brief oral report for presentation. These reports can be illustrated. Because today's students will be living in a global society, investigating the lives and contributions of races and cultures other than their own is crucial. This is especially true if students are attending school in racially and/or ethnically homogeneous environments. An important motivator for students of various racial and ethnic backgrounds is to make certain that literature, films, news articles, magazines, and textbooks reflect positive things about their heritage.

Materials Needed:

- Copy of activity sheet 3-6, *What Could Tommy Be Reading?*
- Many books, films, pictures, etc., on multicultural contributors
- List of multicultural contributors on a chart and/or chalkboard
- Pencils
- Paper
- Pictures
- Encyclopedia information
- Multicultural biography and report forms (see Appendix)

Directions:

1. Display pictures and books of multiracial, multiethnic contributors in a special place in the classroom. Label the area with a meaningful title, such as "Builders of America" or "Books About American Contributors." Use strategic moments during the day to read interesting portions of the lives of contributors to students. If, at any time, children find information they want to share, allow time for this, as well.

2. Give students an opportunity to borrow books, pictures, and so on, from the in-class library. Keep a list of names and contributions they have read about on a chart or the chalkboard. Ask the students to add new names and contributions as they locate them. Caution students to balance their inclusions of males, females, and members of various racial, cultural, and ethnic groups.

3. Ask children to name at least one person who has made a contribution to America. Allow more, if the students wish to volunteer information about additional contributors. Encourage students to consider the contributions of family, friends and members of the community, as well as historical contributors.

4. Give students activity 3-6, *What Could Tommy Be Reading?* Have them copy names from the chart, the chalkboard, the books they are reading, Activity 3-5, the Appendix, and/or other sources. Assist children in developing critical thinking skills by having them infer and hypothesize based on evidence that contributions to civilization have been and are multicultural. For example, have the children state this hypothesis, "If people of many races have made contributions....then we should see many races of people on stamps, in books, on posters, on television, in art galleries, and so on." Based on these experiences, the students will discern the need to learn about and promote the work of long-neglected contributors. Allow time for sharing new information and drawing conclusions.

5. Extend the concept of the value of reading to increase knowledge. Establish multicultural reading periods. Have children share one new thing they learned with the class. Give them a choice to share orally, through drawings, and/or

through writing. The results of these experiences can be used in the Multicultural Display Area, and/or shared with family and the community.

> **LITERATURE CONNECTION**: *Famous American Indians* by L. Edmond Leipold, Ph.D. Exciting stories of Native Americans of historical and contemporary significance. It is suggested that the teacher read to the students. T.S. Denison and Company, Minneapolis, © 1967.
>
> *Famous Puerto Ricans* by Clarke Newlon. Contributions to government, art, literature, music, education, sports, and political reform are discussed through the lives of several Puerto Rican leaders. Dodd, Mead & Co., New York, © 1975. Photographs.

Activity 3-7A CHOOSE A NAME TO WIN THE GAME

Activity 3-7B CHOOSE A NAME TO WIN THE GAME—ANSWER KEY

Children will use prior knowledge to play a game which reinforces what they have learned and gives information about new contributors, as well. Opportunities for students to see themselves and others as contributors are inherent in the concepts presented.

Materials Needed:

- Copies of activity sheet 3-7A, *Choose a Name to Win the Game* and activity sheet 3-7B, *Choose a Name to Win the Game—Answer Key*
- Scissors
- Construction paper
- Glue
- Brads for dial
- Multicultural contributors' lists
- Multicultural books
- Encyclopedia information

Directions:

1. Discuss the contributions of several women and men who are American citizens. Give children time to share new information. Continue to stress the multiracial, multiethnic, multicultural nature of contributions to the growth of America. Whenever possible, mention the fact that people in other parts of the world have the same needs as Americans. Elicit from students the concepts of local, national, and global interdependence.

2. Explain the concept of contributions regarding contemporary as well as historical figures. Encourage children to see people in their homes, school, and

communities as contributors. Have children ask each other questions about their hobbies and talents and cite these as contributions to their home and school environments.

Discuss possible needs for the classroom, their homes, or the community and ask students what they can do to meet these needs. For example, there could be a need for a container for "recycling" in the classroom. One child or several children can cooperate in "inventing" such a container from an empty box. At home, possibly, there is a need for a special place to put the car keys or the mail. Have students brainstorm about needs and ways in which they, as contributors, can fill them. When they have "invented" and/or "created" things to help others, have them work on ways to promote or "sell" (share) their inventions or services.

IDEAS FOR STUDENT INVENTIONS: An original T-shirt, personalized placemats, family flags or coat-of-arms, an original necktie, and the like. Extend this to include services students can provide, such as delivering newspapers, mowing lawns, babysitting, and the like.

3. Give students copies of activity 3-7A, *Choose a Name to Win the Game,* and 3-7B, *Answer Key.* They can cut out the game and glue it onto construction paper. Dials can be made and they can play the game alone or with a friend. Encourage further research on these and other contributors. Elicit from children the fact that most contributors did many more things than those shown on the worksheets. Students can make up their own multicultural games, share them with other classes, and become contributors in the process. Use the *Answer Key* to enhance the discussion on interdependence, intelligence that transcends race, culture, ethnicity, etc. Then clarify the functions and usefulness of each contributor's work.

LITERATURE CONNECTION: *Space Challenger: The Story of Guion Bluford* by Jim Haskins and Kathleen Benson. A biography of the first African-American astronaut, his resisting of efforts to discourage him from reaching his goal, and his 1983 flight on the space shuttle Challenger. Carolrhoda Books, Minneapolis, © 1984.

Activity 3-8 DOCTOR SEWS UP A HUMAN HEART!

Doctors and other healthcare workers contribute very much to the progress of humanity. Children will see that contributions are not always material things that we can touch. Doctors help people to feel better when they are sick. Emphasize the intelligence of doctors and others who help people maintain their health. Point out that people of minority groups, including women, are doctors. An African-American, Dr. Daniel Hale Williams, was concerned about the needs of human beings and performed a new type of surgery to help them. This new surgery was the first heart operation in history.

Materials Needed:

- Copy of activity sheet 3-8, *Doctor Sews Up a Human Heart*
- Biography and pictures of Dr. Daniel Hale Williams
- Multiracial pictures of doctors
- Books about medical doctors
- Pictures of the heart
- Pencils
- Crayons

Directions:

1. Discuss how doctors contribute to the community by helping families stay healthy. Show pictures of male and female doctors of many racial and ethnic groups. Elicit from children the various special areas that doctors can choose to practice in. For example, most students have been to a doctor who cares for children, a PEDIATRICIAN. Some might know about the doctor who delivers babies, an OBSTETRICIAN. Others might have heard of an OPHTHALMOLOGIST, a doctor who treats the diseases of the human eye. Have the children create a multicultural, multiracial display of contributors to the medical profession.

2. Emphasize the difficult schoolwork that medical students have to do in order to become doctors. Discuss the classes, long hours of work in hospitals, tests, and so on. Elicit from children the fact that doctors continue to do very hard work even after they complete medical school and when they start their practices.

3. Explain the word *risk*. Talk about new procedures that doctors attempt in order to save lives. Give students activity 3-8, *Doctor Sews Up a Human Heart*. Discuss the seriousness of the operation, and how this new procedure helped people who have heart problems today. Elicit from students the racial origin of Dr. Daniel Hale Williams. Have them do research, or provide the answer, if necessary.

> **LITERATURE CONNECTION**: *The Heart Man* by Louise Meriwether. The story of the young African-American surgeon who performed the first open heart operation. Prentice-Hall, Inc., Englewood Cliffs, New Jersey, © 1972. Illustrations by Floyd Sowell.

Activity 3-9 EXTRA! EXTRA! READ ALL ABOUT IT!

In this activity, children will learn about the importance of the printed word. They will see how several contributors improved mass communication of news and other types of printed information. In addition, students will be able to see the value in the invention of the computer, typewriter, printing press, and modern paper-making procedures. How these inventions impacted on the distribution of many types of books for education, health, and so on can be brought out during this activity.

Materials Needed:

- Copy of activity sheet 3-9, *Extra! Extra! Read All About It!*
- Pictures of typewriters, computers, a printing press
- Books, newspapers, etc.
- Crayons
- Encyclopedia information about the history of mass media
- Stamp pad with ink
- Individual rubber letters of the alphabet
- Large sheets of white paper for printing words and sentences
- Examples of different kinds of writing, such as hieroglyphics, calligraphy, etc.
- Soap, water, and paper towels

Directions:

1. Demonstrate the procedure for using a computer and allow students to use it. Explain rules and have sign-up sheets. Discuss the many kinds of computers and how and where they are used today. Display pictures of computers and typewriters in banks, schools, businesses, libraries, and in homes. Include multicultural pictures of male and female inventors and/or consumers of computers and/or typewriters. Use a camera to take pictures of students in their computer laboratory. Display these as examples of multicultural consumers.

2. Have children look at the books around them, and the ones they are reading. Discuss the printing press as used in the mass production of books and newspapers. Compare these improved technologies to the printing of a book by hand (i.e., scrolls and manuscripts) versus doing it on a computer. Plan a class project to demonstrate these two ways of writing a book.

3. Ask students to imagine what life would be like without newspapers, books, computer software (for word processing), magazines, games, films, and so on. Allow them to print words and sentences with individual rubber letters and a stamp pad. Have them compare this process to the printing press and discuss which they prefer and why.

4. Give children copies of activity 3-9, *Extra! Extra! Read All About It!* Follow up with plans to publish a class newsletter/newspaper.

5. Extend the impact of these experiences by having students try to make paper, and write Chinese characters and Egyptian hieroglyphics. Invite parents in to assist with and/or teach these skills.

LITERATURE CONNECTION: *Black on White and Read All Over: The Story of Printing* by Albert Barker. The author traces the development of written communication from the discovery of methods of making paper by the Egyptians and Chinese to the invention of the printing press. Julian Messner, New York, © 1971. Illustrated by Anthony D'Adamo.

Activity 3-10 WE WORKED TO HELP MANKIND

Children will learn more about how the needs and wants of people function as stimuli for inventions. After the invention of many items, including the telephone, other people added something to make them even better. Students will understand the real meaning of the words "interdependence" and "multicultural contributions," as they see how people of many races and cultures prepare the telephone for use in homes, hospitals, schools, and businesses. Use children's prior knowledge of telephones to highlight the interdependence of workers who manufacture, install, and repair telephones. Also discuss the roles of telephone operators, sales persons, and so on. Finally, students will see the value of contributors working together to improve inventions, as in the case of the two men of different races who worked to make the telephone what it is today. Discuss the value of making long distance telephone calls and how this makes ours a "global" society.

Materials Needed:

- Copy of activity sheet 3-10, *We Worked to Help Mankind*
- Pictures of, or actual items, which were invented by one person and modified by someone else
- Crayons
- Pencils
- Books about multicultural contributions
- Encyclopedia information

Directions:

1. Explain how several inventors may sometimes work on improving or perfecting one invention. One person invents something. Then another person sees a need to improve it. Give the example of Thomas Edison inventing the light bulb and Lewis Latimer inventing the filament for the light. The filament is what makes the light bulb burn for long periods of time. Elicit from students that the European-American background of Thomas Edison and the African-American background of Lewis Latimer are important so that people can see that people of different races

and nationalities are intelligent and capable. However, their inventions/contributions are even more important than the color of their skins to the people who use the telephone. Elicit from children why this is true.

2. Ask children to recall the invention of Alexander Graham Bell. Years after he invented the telephone, Granville T. Woods, an African-American, invented the transmitter which made long-distance communication possible. Alexander Graham Bell was Scottish-American. Help students to infer that people of different races, nationalities, and cultures can work on the same inventions and make them better.

3. Have students complete activity 3-10, *We Worked to Help Mankind.* Have children think of other inventions which are important to people. Discuss changes that might have taken place to improve these things. Invite parents, older students, other school personnel, and members of the community to share their inventions, and tell about the help they might have received from people who are different from themselves.

> **LITERATURE CONNECTION**: *Negroes Who Helped Build America* by Madeline Stratton. African-American contributions to science, civil rights, music, business, military, medicine, government are told through the biographies of historical and contemporary leaders. Ginn and Company, Boston, © 1965. Illustrated.

Activity 3-11A PEOPLE NEED TO TRAVEL

Activity 3-11B PEOPLE NEED TO TRAVEL ANSWER KEY

The need to travel is common among people of diverse racial and ethnic origin. Transportation workers are contributors, and they do their jobs in homes, schools, businesses, and other parts of communities everyday. This activity will help children not only to see the work of the people around them as contributions but to also discern the interdependence of the ticket sellers, commuters, and drivers. Because they can relate so closely to transportation, children should begin to see themselves and other "everyday people," as contributors in their own environments.

Materials Needed:

- Copies of activity sheet 3-11, *People Need to Travel*
- Pencils
- Crayons
- Pictures of various types of vehicles

- Multiracial pictures of pilots, bus drivers, conductors, engineers, and astronauts
- Encyclopedia information

Directions:

1. Explain that every person who helps someone else is a contributor. Ask students to share times when they have helped someone. Have them recognize the contribution itself and their roles as contributors.

2. Point out that people in the community need to get to their jobs, to stores, and other places each day. Ask children to think about the hundreds of people in many racial and ethnic groups who are driving cars, cabs, trains, and buses in order to take people where they want to go.

3. Identify pilots of planes and captains of ships as contributors to the transportation needs of commuters. Ask children to describe some of their experiences as travelers. Elicit from children the fact that the skills of the people who operate these vehicles are more important than their racial and/or ethnic background. Again, emphasize the interdependence of people who need and people who provide transportation. Have children add multiracial pictures of transportation workers to their Multicultural Display Area.

4. Give children activity 3-11, *People Need to Travel* to complete. Ask children to color the vehicles. Some children might want to draw people in these pictures, or draw their own original transportation scenes. Display them in the classroom, the school, and/or in the community.

LITERATURE CONNECTION: *Wilbur and Orville Wright: The Flight to Adventure* by Louis Sabin. The childhood of the inventors of the airplane, their family experiences, education and events leading up to their achievement. Troll Associates, Mahwah, New Jersey, 1983. Illustrated by John Lawn.

A Balloon for Grandad by Nigel Gray. A young boy's balloon flies out of a window. He is unhappy until his father suggests that the balloon is traveling to his grandfather's. Franklin Watts, New York, © 1988. Illustrated by Jane Ray.

Dragonwings by Laurence Yep. The story of a flying machine built by a Chinese immigrant and his son in San Francisco. Harper Publishers, New York, © 1975.

Big Mama's by Donald Crews. A man who grew up in Newark, New Jersey remembers the summers of his childhood, spent at his grandparents' home in Cottondale, Florida. Many children can relate to the adventures of a train ride, running around without shoes, and big family meals. Greenwillow Books, New York, © 1991. Illustrated.

Activity 3-12A AFRICAN ART

Activity 3-12B CHINESE ART

Activity 3-12C NATIVE AMERICAN ART

Activity 3-12D SPANISH ART

This series of activities helps children to see the universality of artistic expression among human beings. When art is shared with others, the joy is mutually beneficial and the artist, the contributor, has helped others. Children will begin to think of their potential as contributors because they are offered many opportunities to express themselves artistically in their classrooms. (A display of art and artifacts from many cultures would provide excellent indirect multicultural instruction.)

Materials Needed:

- Copy of activity sheet 3-12A, *African Art*
- Copy of activity sheet 3-12B, *Chinese Art*
- Copy of activity sheet 3-12C, *Native American Art*
- Copy of activity sheet 3-12D, *Spanish Art*
- Books on art from many cultures
- Art encyclopedias
- Crayons
- Markers
- Paints and brushes
- Scissors and glue
- Construction paper
- Clay
- Yarn—different colors
- Artifacts from different cultures
- Art museum posters, brochures, reproductions, and the like
- Picture books

Directions:

1. Discuss the words *talents, skills,* and *artistic ability*. Show children a variety of types of art in the art encyclopedias and/or multicultural books on art. Observe the many kinds of art shown in picture books, community murals, showcases, etc. Discuss the colors, textures, shapes, and the talents and skills of the artists.

2. Motivate and encourage children to draw. Give them opportunities to express themselves artistically through various media, such as finger paints, clay,

crayons, papier-mâché, cutting/pasting, weaving, etc. Have them evaluate each other's final products. Point out the enjoyment of the work: conversation, movement of hands and eyes, and smiling during production. Encourage children to identify themselves as artists, as contributors. Display their art in special places, at home, in school, and/or in the community.

3. Explain that people of every racial, ethnic, and cultural group have different talents and skills. Many individuals in these groups have made artistic contributions to America and the world. Show students examples of authentic artwork from art museum collections. Children who have visited art shows and museums can share their experiences. Some children might have paintings at home that they can describe. (Do not encourage bringing artwork from home, unless security is guaranteed.)

4. Provide students with experiences in working with art from different cultures. Also, there are many different forms of art, such as broad categories of things which people of many races and cultures MAKE and DO. For example, people make objects with color, design, and balance for others to look at, enjoy, and use. Jewelry, ornaments, pottery, paintings, and tools fall into this group. Then there are artistic ideas, sounds, and actions which provide special experiences to readers, listeners and observers. Great poetry, novels, stories, music, and plays fall into this category. Moreover, the raw materials which go into the creation of artistic things require talent and ingenuity.

Elicit from children the fact that artistic talent occurs among the people of all races, cultures, and nationalities. Display pictures of works of art, tools, architecture, inventions, and play music from different cultures. Add works that reflect cultures of particular groups in your classroom.

5. Pass out activity 3-12A, *African Art*. Explain that art is a part of daily life in Africa. This mask combines human and animal features. Find examples of other African art in the art encyclopedias, artifacts, pictures, and books. Have students make masks or pyramids from clay.

6. Give students activity 3-12B, *Chinese Art*. Explain that this Chinese Ginger Jar is only one kind of Chinese art. Show other kinds in art encyclopedias, artifacts, pictures, and books. Have students do Chinese bamboo brush painting.

7. Distribute activity 3-12C, *Native American Art*. Have them color the background and the people and animals on the worksheet. If desired, students can make a replica of this basket in clay, let it dry and then paint it. Or, if possible, obtain materials for weaving and allow children to make real baskets in class.

Explain that Native American art grew out of their daily needs. For example, the woven basket is one of the types of basket weaving created by the California and Nevada tribes for food storage, for water, and sometimes for cooking. The Apache's principal art was decorative basketry. Consult art encyclopedias, books, pictures, for more information about Native American art. Also, students can make pottery from clay or weave yarn into small replicas of blankets.

8. Give students activity 3-12D, *Spanish Art.* Paint and stitchery were combined as artists developed this crown and Spanish coat of arms. Consult the art encyclopedias, books, etc., for additional examples of Spanish art. Have students make piñatas from papier-mâché and/or use empty walnut shells to make castanets for dancing.

9. Allow students to explore art from other cultures through investigation of various art books. Some interesting art projects might include:

Origami—Japanese art of folding paper to form animals or flowers
Sculpture—Replicas of African masks, jewelry, utensils, animals, emblem, etc., in clay
Dolls—Yugoslavia
Corn-cob–Donkeys—Venezuela
Bear—Russian
Balancing Fisherman—Portugal
Tepee & Moccasins—Native American
Twirling Yo Yo—The West Indies
Paper Cuts—Chinese

LITERATURE CONNECTION: *Childcraft: The How and Why Library,* Volume 11. Detailed directions of how to make many different types of arts and crafts. Multicultural illustrations and concepts. Use as many ideas as possible in order to extend the concepts and the positive multicultural experiences, as children of diverse backgrounds work together on these artistic creations. Worldbook-Childcraft International, Chicago, © 1982.

The Legend of the Indian Paintbrush by Tomie de Paola. The story of how lovely flowers sprang from an Indian Brave's paintbrush to decorate the lands of Wyoming and Texas. Putnam Books, New York, © 1988. Illustrated.

Activity 3-13A STAMPS FOR HEROES AND HEROINES

Activity 3-13B POSTERS FOR UNKNOWN AMERICAN HEROES

Activity 3-13C T–SHIRTS FOR SPECIAL CONTRIBUTORS

Children's understanding of the multiracial, multiethnic contributions to humanity will be reinforced in this activity. Present the contributions of men and women who have lived in the past. Also, present the work of contemporary contributors, including members of the various branches of the United States armed forces.

Materials Needed:

- Copy of activity sheet 3-13A, *Stamps for Heroes and Heroines*
- Copy of activity sheet 3-13B, *Posters for Unknown American Heroes*
- Copy of activity sheet 3-13C, *T–Shirt for Special Contributors*
- Pictures of contributors from the past and present
- Multicultural Contributions List from the Appendix
- Books about scientists, educators, businessmen and women, artists, musicians, doctors, lawyers, athletes, civil rights leaders, politicians, military personnel
- Pictures of military medals
- Information about the "Liberators and Survivors Day"—December 17
- Crayons and/or markers
- Posterboard and/or drawing paper
- Scissors
- Timeline which has spaces to write in minority contributions

Directions:

1. Ask children to identify Abraham Lincoln and George Washington. Most children will know that they were United States Presidents. Ask them to identify Lewis Latimer or Sally Ride. They might not be able to identify the African-American inventor of the long-lasting filament for the light bulb or the U.S. female astronaut.

2. Discuss the fact that people of every race and culture who make contributions to society should be honored, just as presidents are recognized for their work. Explain that many men and women from different minority races and cultures have not received recognition for their work in American history books. Elicit from children how this can be corrected. Display a timeline which shows well-known contributors and the dates of their contributions. Leave spaces for the addition of minority contributors and the dates of their contributions.

3. Show multiracial, multicultural pictures of members of the United States military services. Highlight the work of men and women who have fought and died

to protect our country. Also, elicit from students the good will that our troops show when they go to help people in other countries. Discuss the Persian Gulf War and Somalia, two places where American troops gave their lives and contributed their time to helping human beings of other cultures. Ask children how the men and women of the military can be honored as a result of their contributions. Discuss some of the existing rewards, such as the Purple Heart, etc.

Show children information about military people who have helped in other wars. For example, a troop of black soldiers rescued 20,000 Jews from concentration camps in Germany during World War II. Describe the special film called *The Liberators* which tells the story of this rescue mission. Describe the special proclamation, "Liberators and Survivors Day," which has been designated to honor the African-Americans (The Liberators) and the Jews (The Survivors). This multicultural celebration will be held every December 17.

Inform students that they can bring recognition to one or more contributors by designing a stamp, a bumper sticker, or a poster for him or her. Plan a "Recognition Day" for these contributors. Invite parents, other classes, and community residents to the celebration.

4. Give students activities 3-13A, *Stamps for Heroes and Heroines*, and 3-13B, *Posters for Unknown American Heroes*. On activity 3-13A, students are to list four relatively unknown people and their contributions. Then, they are to do further reading and/or research on two of these people. Encourage children to imagine how it would be if people were to ignore special things that they have done, for example, making a gift for someone, helping someone who is sick, etc. Ask them to try and make "forgotten" contributors popular by making the BEST stamp or poster; large, beautiful pictures of the person, with great words and lovely, bright colors. Explain that when they do their best to create wonderful designs, they are helping to bring respect to neglected contributors. Analyze the results of this two-page activity. Try to publish and/or display some of the work.

5. Extend the impact of this activity by having students vote on the two best designs for the above activity. Solicit the help of parents and other volunteers in making T-shirts which bring attention to multicultural contributions. Give each child a copy of activity 3-13C *T–Shirt for Special Contributors*. Plan to have representatives from African-Americans, Hispanic-Americans, Asian-Americans, and European-Americans on the shirt. Have students wear the shirts proudly, as often as possible, in the interest of racial, cultural, and ethnic harmony. Be prepared to share these ideas with other classes and schools.

LITERATURE CONNECTION: *Shortchanged by History: America's Neglected Innovators* by Vernon Pizer. Stories of people of different racial and ethnic backgrounds who have made great contributions to America but have not been properly recognized for their work. (It is suggested that teachers select and read information to the students.) G.P. Putnam's Sons, New York, © 1979. Illustrated by Catherine Stock.

Activity 3-14A NATIVE AMERICAN CONTRIBUTIONS

Activity 3-14B NATIVE AMERICAN CLASSIFICATION CHART

In this activity, children will understand that when contributions last for many years, they have been very worthwhile. From the list of inventions, techniques, and natural elements which have been introduced by Native Americans, students will come to appreciate their contributions.

Materials Needed:

- Copy of activity sheet 3-14A, *Native American Contributions*
- Copy of activity sheet 3-14B, *Native American Classification Chart*
- Books and encyclopedias on Native American life before the Europeans
- Information about Indian reservations, including addresses of some of the schools
- Pictures of everyday things which originated from Native Americans
- Pencils
- Paper

Directions:

1. Explain that the quality of American life would not be as advanced as it is were it not for the contributions of Native Americans, African-Americans, European-Americans, Asian-Americans, Hispanic-Americans, etc. Emphasize, however, that Native Americans were the first Americans and, as such, they shared much of what they learned with all those who came after them.

2. Discuss some of the things which Americans use every day that were introduced to us by Native Americans, such as corn or maize, leather, herbal medicines, canoes, road-building, pottery, etc. Use books to extend the list which develops during the discussions.

3. Suggest that students plan to pay tribute to Native Americans as they develop their stamps and posters. Help them to set up a Traveling Display of Native American Contributions. The intent is to inform others of the many things that people use every day that are a result of the genius of Native Americans. The

display can consist of artwork, games, maps, posters, designs for stamps, picture books, etc.

4. Give children activities 3-14A, *Native American Contributions,* and 3-14B, *Native American Classification Chart.* Read the directions with the class, defining difficult words such as NATURAL, MAN-MADE, and PROCEDURAL. Then allow students to work alone or in pairs to complete the chart.

5. Extend the impact of this lesson by investigating the present condition of most Native Americans. Elicit from children ways that Americans can begin to show concern for and help to provide equal rights, justice, and freedom to Native Americans. Suggest that students write letters to Native American children. They can also write their opinions to the editors of local newspapers. Define the word *reservation.* Discuss the questions "Are Native Americans free?" "What happened to their land and why?" Share student responses with other classes, family, and community. Older students might want to do more reading and research.

LITERATURE CONNECTION: *Ladder to the Sky: How the Gift of Healing Came to the Ojibway Nation* by Barbara Juster Esbensen. The story of why the Ojibway people must now use herbal medicines for healing from sickness and death. Little, Brown, Boston, © 1989. Illustrated by Helen K. Davie.

When Clay Sings by Byrd Baylor. Creative illustrations and effective word images depict methods of traditional pottery-making. Scribner's (Macmillan), New York, © 1987. Illustrated by Tom Bahti.

Activity 3-15A MULTICULTURAL RIDDLES

Activity 3-15B MULTICULTURAL RIDDLES— ANSWER KEY

Children will enjoy playing this game of riddles. No penalties exist, only rewards, for if they do not know the answers this is motivation for finding them. Not only will students experience increased levels of confidence in their own potential as contributors, but they will develop respect for people of diverse backgrounds who have made historical and contemporary contributions. In that these riddles are easy to formulate, multicultural contributors which reflect the population in the classroom and in the surrounding community can be added, at any time. Encourage students to include male and female citizens whose contributions are not always recognized. Provide them with materials which give information about men and women from various racial and ethnic groups who may be disabled or beyond the age of retirement.

Materials Needed:

- Copy of activity sheet 3-15A, *Multicultural Riddles*
- Copy of activity sheet 3-15B, *Multicultural Riddles—Answer Key* (Save both activities for later use)
- Cardboard to make a dial (optional)
- Markers
- Score sheet
- List of Multicultural Contributors
- Books, encyclopedias
- A display area for multicultural contributions

Directions:

1. Discuss the definition of the word *contributor.* Ask students to name the discoverer of electricity. Most children will respond "Benjamin Franklin." Ask students to name the U.S. Vice President from 1928 to 1933. Few children will be able to name Charles Curtis, a Native American, who served as the 31st United States Vice President under President Herbert Hoover. He was both a U.S. Congressman and a Senator. Post information about Charles Curtis on a chart or bulletin board, in preparation for activity 3-15A. Charles Curtis was a successful lawyer before he began his political career. Explain how politicians contribute to society.

2. Elicit from students the reasons for studying multicultural contributions to America. One reason is to help children from many cultures see their own worth and potential. Children more clearly understand that they, too, can be successful, when people from similar races and backgrounds are recognized and honored for their contributions. Also, have students find out about the kinds of contributions which have been made by members of their cultural/racial groups by interviewing relatives and reading books.

3. Give students copies of 3-15A, *Multicultural Contributions* and 3-15B, *Multicultural Contributions—Answer Key.* Help children answer the first question. It is suggested that the teacher hold on to these completed activity sheets for future use.

4. Extend this activity by having the children make up their own riddles about people in their families, communities and cultures. Use the Multicultural Lists in the Appendix and other resources. Have students distinguish between contemporary and historical contributors in terms of dates, places, and types of contributions.

LITERATURE CONNECTION: *Dancing Tepees: Poems of American Indian Youth* by Virginia Driving Hawk Sneve. The sacredness of the spoken word is preserved in the chants, stories and songs of contemporary poets. Holiday House, New York, © 1991. Illustrated by Stephen Gammell.

Activity 3-16A PIECING A PEACE QUILT

Activity 3-16B BROTHERS AND SISTERS BENEATH THE SKIN

In this activity, children will have another chance to recognize and honor more contributors who have not been praised by society. Everyone feels good inside when people who have helped others receive some kind of thank you. Point out the friendly atmosphere which exists when people are celebrating; when they are honoring people who have made contributions. There is no time for arguing or fighting. When multicultural groups of people are given credit for helping to build America, there is a sense of brotherhood and an atmosphere of peace. Some of the diverse groups of people who were active in promoting civil rights laws will be highlighted as important contributors.

As a result of these activities, students will be able to identify many people of different racial, ethnic, and cultural origins who cared about the freedoms of African-Americans and other minority citizens. Moreover, students will be able to cite presidents, civil rights leaders, lawyers, and others who worked to eliminate segregation in public places in America. All children will come to understand the meaning of the words "brotherhood" and "equal rights" and adjust their attitudes and behaviors, accordingly. This will occur largely because they can make decisions about their own worth and that of their peers, as they interact in the nurturing environment of the classroom.

Materials Needed:

- Copy of activity sheet 3-16A, *Piecing a Peace Quilt*
- Copy of activity sheet 3-16B, *Brothers and Sisters Beneath the Skin*
- Crayons and/or markers
- Multicultural lists of contributors
- Books, encyclopedias and pictures of diverse groups of contributors
- Pictures of and information about civil rights workers
- Newspaper and magazine articles about the people and places involved during the civil rights struggle
- Speakers (parents, community members, lawyers, etc.) who can share information about civil rights
- Pencils
- U.S. postage stamps in honor of several minority contributors
- Information about Nobel Peace Prize recipients/a picture of a Nobel Prize certificate

Directions:

1. Explain to children that society usually rewards people who make life better for others. Show books and pictures which identify well-known contributors to medicine, art, politics, civil rights, law, music, education, technology, and so on.

2. Show students U.S. postage stamps with pictures of minority contributors. Show a Nobel Prize form. Cite examples of things which are done to honor famous scientists, educators, doctors, inventors, politicians, and military personnel. Sometimes buildings, parks, streets, and monuments are named after contributors. Nobel Prizes are given to others. For some, their pictures are placed on stamps and scholarships are given in the names of other contributors.

3. Ask students to recall how good it makes them feel when they give a gift, or say thank you to someone who has been nice to them.

4. Tell students that there are many people who have not been recognized for their work. Explain that they have a chance now to make a special quilt to honor some contributors who are not so famous, but who deserve thanks and recognition from those who have benefited from their work.

5. Give children activity 3-16A, *Piecing a Peace Quilt.* Discuss how this quilt will make the contributors feel inside. Plan to do a larger cloth replica of the quilt. Invite parents and members of the community to participate. Display students' completed worksheets and the completed quilt.

6. Show pictures of some famous civil rights leaders, such as Martin Luther King, Malcolm X, President Lyndon B. Johnson, President John F. Kennedy, Robert Kennedy, Rosa Parks, and so on. Then read the names of less famous people who gave their lives for the rights of African-Americans to be free and equal. Among those contributors who are not so well known are: James Chaney, Andrew Goodman, and Michael Schwerner. These three young men of different racial, ethnic, and religious backgrounds were killed in the state of Mississippi, as they worked to help blacks register to vote. Viola Gregg Luizzo, a young mother, was killed in Alabama as she worked to help African-American Freedom Fighters. James, an African-American, Viola, Andrew, and Michael, who were white, acted as brothers and sister. They ignored skin color and thought only about the rights of all Americans to gain the freedoms guaranteed by the U.S. Constitution.

Elicit from children that men, women, teenagers, and children from various racial, ethnic, and religious backgrounds, fought and died for the rights of African-Americans and other minorities to be free. Discuss the fact that Rosa Parks, an African-American woman, started the Civil Rights Movement when she refused to go to the back of a bus. Also, define the role of Martin Luther King, the leader of the movement. He used nonviolence to fight injustice. Have children compare and contrast the rights of African-Americans before and after the Civil Rights Movement. Invite parents and grandparents of various races and cultures to come and share their experiences during the civil rights struggle.

7. Show a picture of Martin Luther King and ask the students to identify him. Show a picture of Malcolm X and ask students to identify him. Read short biographies of both men. (See Appendix.) Then elicit from children how the men were alike and how they were different. Have them make a list of the work and accomplishments of both men. Provide materials which tell why Malcolm X changed his name from Malcolm Little, why he and Martin Luther King had different opinions about how to gain equal rights for blacks in America, and why, after he went to Mecca, Malcolm X changed his mind and believed, like Martin Luther King, that people of all races and cultures should live peacefully with each other. Give each child a copy of activity 3-16B, *Brothers and Sisters Beneath the Skin.*

Invite speakers from families and the community in to share their personal experiences, and/or read to the children from literature which tells about the civil rights struggle, and/or reinforces the fact that all people are and should be treated equally. Elicit from children the fact that every American has to continue to help make certain that all citizens are free. Read about Coretta Scott King, the widow of Martin Luther King. Discuss how she still works to help people of different races and cultures get along together.

LITERATURE CONNECTION: *The Patchwork Quilt* by Valerie Flourney. Tanya helps to unite her family's past and present by completing a quilt started by her grandmother. Dial, New York, © 1985. Illustrated by Jerry Pinkney.

In Search of Peace by Edith Patterson Meyer. The history of the Nobel Prize, founded by Swedish multimillionaire Alfred Nobel, is told. Winners of Nobel Peace Prizes from 1901 to 1975 are highlighted. It is suggested that the teacher select and read portions to students. Abingdon, Nashville, Tennessee, © 1978. Illustrated by Billie Jean Osborne.

Selma, Lord, Selma by Sheryann Webb and Rachel West Nelson. Two African-American women recall their childhood experiences during the Civil Rights Movement. They tell their story to Frank Sikora. They reveal that it is also the story of America and that the civil rights struggle was a multicultural, multiracial, multiethnic, and an intergenerational effort. University of Alabama Press, Tuscaloosa, © 1980.

Activity 3-17A THE AFRICAN CONNECTION

Activity 3-17B AFRICAN WORD SEARCH

Opportunities for counteracting negative portrayals of the roles of African-Americans in the building of America and the world are presented in this activity. Furthermore, while American history books have always told the slavery part of the history of African-Americans, there has been little, if anything, about the fact that most black Americans are descendants of ancient African royalty. African-Americans have a glorious history which extends back in time to the continent of Africa. Some of this history includes Africa's contributions to the advanced sciences, architecture, geometry, literature, economics, art, and the many languages of the world. These activities will expose students to some of the truths about Africa's and African-Americans' heritage of intellectual prowess, wealth, and accomplishments.

It is suggested that the teacher read the information on the worksheets with the students. Concepts and strategies are adaptable to include the contributions of other ethnic, cultural, and racial groups represented in the class. The overall intent is to give every child a good, positive feeling about his/her ancestry. This provides a basis for the building of self-esteem, high-expectations, and intrinsic motivation; necessary ingredients for literacy and success in life.

Materials Needed:

- Copy of activity sheet 3-17A, *The African Connection*
- Copy of activity sheet 3-17B, *African Word Search*
- Books on ancient Africa
- Pictures of the Great Pyramid and the Sphinx
- Pictures of African kings and queens
- Maps of the continent of Africa
- African art
- Pictures of African-Americans (descendants of African Royalty)
- Encyclopedia and other sources of information about Africa

Directions:

1. For very young children emphasize the intriguing stories of African royalty, some of the fascinating information about the Great Pyramid and the Sphinx, and show the connection between Americans of African descent and the kings and queens of ancient Africa.

2. Second- and third-graders might find some of the information in books and on maps interesting to look at and/or read. Also, encyclopedia entries will describe

specifics about ancient and modern life on the African continent. Details about the many different types of people, the wide ranges of customs and culture (including food, clothing, marriage, and family), education, religion, art, and music, are only a few of the things students will learn as they study maps, pictures, and read passages about Africa. Again, the connection between former American slaves and African royalty should be made. Plan visits to the library to enhance learning. (Read portions of the book listed below in the Literature Connection: *Understanding Africa* by E. Jefferson Murphy...Also, read information from the *International Library of Negro Life and History,* edited by Charles Wesley, © 1969. Encourage students to do additional reading and research on the wealth of ancient African empires and the beginning of European contact which led to the slave trade.

3. Give students activity 3-17A, *The African Connection.* The two-page "A Few Facts About Ancient Africa" sheet can be read orally, with the teacher. The "Think About It" section can also be done with the teacher.

4. Have students do activity 3-17B, *African Word Search.* Point out the fact that people from all over the ancient world came to study in the libraries of the city of Timbuktu.

5. Give students opportunities to draw pictures of the Great Pyramid, the Sphinx, and other things (hieroglyphics, architecture, thrones, etc.) which represent the advanced society from which African-Americans have come. Provide materials for some of these items to be made from clay, papier-mâché, etc.

6. Extend the concepts which verify the roles many African-Americans have assumed in the building of America. Expose children to books, charts, maps, encyclopedias, and other materials which reveal the contributions of African-American poets, politicians, scientists, doctors, ironworkers, teachers, inventors, shoemakers, etc. Have children read about the building of America and insert positive facts which show how African-Americans participated in the fight for our country's freedom during the Revolutionary War and the Civil War. One example is that Crispus Attucks, an African-American, was the first person to die in the Revolutionary War. Concepts in this activity can be adapted to include the roles that other cultural, ethnic and racial groups played in the growth of America and the world.

LITERATURE CONNECTION: *The Afro-American* by Howard Smead. One of a series of books on The Peoples of North America. Specific sections of the text verify the fact that the ancestors of most black Americans lived in the wealthy West African empires of Ghana, Mali, and Songhay. It is suggested that the teacher read and interpret information about these flourishing civilizations for young students. See the chapter "From Freedom to Slavery" on pages 19-30. Other chapters deal with significant historical and contemporary facts about the positive roles and hardships of Americans of African descent. Chelsea House, New York, © 1989. Photographs and drawings.

Understanding Africa by E. Jefferson Murphy. That Africa is a continent of diversity is the focal point of this book. It contains rich information about America's growing awareness of Africa as a continent of enlightenment and "rich tradition..." It is suggested that the teacher read and interpret portions of Chapter Four for young students. Entitled "The Glory of Ancient Africa," this chapter highlights the skills, the advanced commercial enterprises, the wealthy and powerful kingdoms of the Sudan, and cities in Mali, namely, Timbuktu and Gao which were very powerful and wealthy. Details about the rise and fall of these empires, the abundance of gold, the exchange of ambassadors, and the educational advancement are described on pages 75-96. The connection between the ancient royal heritage of African-Americans and their history as descendants of slaves is described in Chapter Five, "Europe Discovers Africa: The Colonial Conquest" on pages 97 to 117. Thomas Y. Crowell, New York, © 1978. Illustrated by Louise E. Jefferson.

Ashanti to Zulu: African Traditions by Margaret Musgrove. A lovely collection of paintings of 26 African tribes in acrylics, watercolors and pastels. Each painting is accompanied by text which accurately depicts the diversity in ceremonies, customs and celebrations of each group. A 1977 Caldecott Award winner. Dial Books for Young Readers, New York, © 1976. Illustrated by Leo and Diane Dillon.

Activity 3-18A MULTICULTURAL CONTRIBUTORS TO SCIENCE

Activity 3-18B MY MULTICULTURAL WORD SEARCH

These activities continue the presentation of the concept that no one race or culture is superior to the other. Moreover, it develops children's appreciation of America as a world-class country because of the work of many different types of people who have immigrated to America from places all over the globe. Children will make up their own puzzles by choosing contributors from various cultures. As they observe the fact that man's progress can be attributed to Europeans, Asians, Africans, Hispanics, and people of mixed racial heritage, they will place themselves somewhere within these groups and discern that they, too, have the potential and the responsibility to contribute.

Materials Needed:

- Copy of activity sheet 3-18A, *Multicultural Contributors to Science*
- Copy of activity sheet 3-18B, *My Multicultural Word Search*
- Multicultural lists of contributors
- Pencils
- Multicultural pictures of scientists
- Encyclopedia information
- Books

Directions:

1. Remind children of the many areas in which men and women have contributed. For example, contributions have been made to science, literature, technology, art, music, sports, economics, politics, etc. Show pictures of people who have helped America and the world. Emphasize the fact that males and females have invented useful things and provided needed services. Sarah Josepha Hale, a European-American journalist and editor, convinced President Lincoln to designate the last Thursday in November as Thanksgiving. Dr. Mae Jemison, an African-American astronaut, engineer and physician, participated in a recent space flight on the shuttle Discovery. Dr. Lise Meitner, a European-American nuclear physicist, found that the atom could be split and release huge amounts of energy. Nuclear reactors, based on her findings, provide much of the electricity used today.

2. Ask students to name some scientists that they have heard or read about. Show pictures of additional scientists such as French scientist Charles Pravaz who invented the hypodermic syringe; the European-Americans, Orville and Wilbur Wright, who invented the airplane; Lun, the Chinese scientist who invented paper; Benjamin Banneker, the African-American, who invented the first clock in America; Native Americans who developed a method of watering plants called irrigation. If pictures of people are not available, show drawings of some inventions, such as the hypodermic syringe used for giving injections of medicine, or irrigation systems on farms. Discuss these and other scientific contributions and how they have helped improve the lives of all human beings. Elicit from children the multicultural and multinational backgrounds of scientists. Give children activity 3-18A, *Multicultural Contributors to Science.* It is suggested that the teacher guide students through the reading and completion of this activity. Have them use the lists in the Appendix and other resources to complete the chart.

3. Discuss the rights that students have to make choices. Then give them an opportunity to choose words from various sources to complete activity, 3-18B, *My Multicultural Word Search.* Use the completed worksheets you have saved from activity 3-15, lists from the Appendix, books, charts, encyclopedias, etc. Reproduce

the results for a class Multicultural Word Search booklet. These can be shared with other classes, friends, family, and the community.

4. Extend the impact of this activity by setting up a mobile which shows multicultural contributors. Any artwork, reports, posters, and other things created by students should be a part of the display. Balance the exhibit in terms of age, gender, disabilities, race, and ethnicity. Share this "Traveling Multicultural Display" with other classrooms and with various organizations in the community. Include local contemporary and historical contributors, if possible.

LITERATURE CONNECTION: *Lasers: Humanity's Magic Light: The Encyclopedia of Discovery and Invention* by Don Nardo. An account of the various scientists who were involved in the development of the laser. Among them were Alexander Graham Bell, Albert Einstein, and Norman French. Lucent Books, San Diego, California, © 1990. Illustrations and photographs.

Activity 3-19 NATIVE AMERICANS HELP NEWCOMERS

Children will see the relationship between learning about the contributions of many races and cultures and higher levels of respect between and among diverse groups of people. Another important understanding is that of the responsibilities of citizenship. Every American can be a good citizen and make a contribution by working to improve the society. How? By following the example of Native Americans who helped the Pilgrims and explorers. Volunteering to help newcomers to this country is one way of helping to make neighborhoods and communities better. Higher-level thinking skills are involved as children are encouraged to think about the meaning of freedom in regards to the plight of Native Americans who live on reservations.

Materials Needed:

- Copy of activity sheet 3-19, *Native Americans Help Newcomers*
- Lists of Native American contributions
- Drawing paper
- Mini-Research Report form (Appendix)
- Crayons or markers
- Pencils or pens
- Encyclopedia information
- Books

Directions:

1. Discuss how people feel when they move to a new state, city, town, or school. Point out the need for help in locating places to shop, banks, post offices, and making new friends. Elicit from children the need for people to adjust and learn to get along in their new surroundings. Discuss the fact that people who are already there can contribute to the comfort of newcomers by being friendly and helpful.

2. Native Americans helped Europeans to adjust to a new way of life in America. They showed explorers and Pilgrims methods of farming, trapping, fishing, and hunting. In addition, they showed the newcomers a new type of food, corn, or maize. Today, corn is a staple part of almost every American family's diet.

3. Food was not the only thing with which Native Americans helped the newcomers. Give students an opportunity to read about other kindnesses which the Indians showed to the Pilgrims and explorers. Have students extend their understanding of how contributions which are valuable last over the years. Investigate some of the things that Native Americans shared with newcomers that still exist today. For example, Native Americans introduced newcomers to tanning processes (making leather from animal skins), making popcorn, making roads, weaving blankets, making pottery, and so on. Evidence that people still use these and other skills taught by Native Americans proves that their contributions were very valuable.

4. Ask children to complete activity 3-19, *Native Americans Help Newcomers*. Have them share the results of this activity. Elicit from students that they can make a contribution by welcoming new students into the classroom. Some ways of helping new classmates to feel comfortable might include smiling, shaking hands, giving tours, playing at recess, sitting at the lunch table, introducing to others, inviting to parties, doing homework together, etc.

5. Extend the concepts of this activity by having students do a mini-research report on Native Americans. Help them to formulate the hypothesis, "If Americans are free, then they can live anywhere in the country they want to live." Elicit from students whether or not Native Americans living on reservations are really free. Have students answer this question based on readings and discussions. Allow time for them to write opinions and letters to newspapers regarding their findings. Younger children can draw pictures of themselves and Native American children playing together at school, at home, or at the playground. Also, find addresses of reservations so that students can become pen pals with Native American children. Share the results of these activities with other classes, family members and community organizations.

6. Older children might be interested in pursuing the search for freedom for Native Americans and/or other groups of people who have experienced and are still

experiencing inequality in America. Elicit from children the fact that, as long as some of us are denied our freedom and rights, none of us is totally free.

LITERATURE CONNECTION: The World Book Encyclopedia, Volume 10, "American Indian," pages 108 to 138. An account of the existence of the first inhabitants of the Americas thousands of years before Europeans arrived. Information on all aspects of Native American life and the extent to which they went to welcome and assist the newcomers. It is suggested that the teacher select specific portions to read to young children. Many activities, in addition to those listed above, can be developed based on this information. World Book, Inc., Chicago, © 1983. Illustrated.

Activity 3-20 ORIGIN OF NATIONAL AND INTERNATIONAL SPORTS

Sports as a form of entertainment, relaxation, and exercise exists in countries all over the world. In this activity, children will learn that the origin of several familiar American sports can be traced to other nations. Therefore, positive attitudes toward people of diverse racial and cultural groups will continue to develop, as students see that all types of people participate in, listen to, or watch athletic events as a form of personal enjoyment. As in other activities, children will discern that common interest in sports brings people of various racial, ethnic, and cultural groups together.

Materials Needed:

- Copy of activity sheet 3-20, *Origin of National and International Sports*
- Pictures of several types of sports equipment
- Names of various sports on a chart
- Sports magazines and/or newspapers
- Books about sports in different lands
- Encyclopedia information
- Construction paper
- Scissors
- Glue

Directions:

1. Discuss sports as a favorite pastime for people in countries around the world. One game, rugby, which is similar to football, is played in Australia, France,

Great Britain, New Zealand, Japan, Canada, Ireland, Scotland, South Africa, Wales and England. Another game, squash, similar to handball but is played with a racket, is popular in America, Mexico, Canada, some countries of South America, Australia, and New Zealand. Curling is a game played on level sheets of ice. The object is to push large stones towards targets. This game originated in Scotland and the Netherlands. It has been popular in Canada and parts of the United States, including Alaska. There are many other sports. Ask students to share their favorite sport and tell why it's important to them. Elicit from students how sports help people of all races and cultures to relax and have fun, as they participate themselves or watch talented and skillful athletes compete.

2. Give children copies of activity 3-20, *Origin of National and International Sports.* Discuss the multicultural characteristics of American sports and the fact that many games which are played in America come from other countries.

ANSWER KEY:

BASKETBALL—America, Springfield, Massachusetts 1891
BASEBALL—England; Originally was a game called "Rounders," 1600's
FOOTBALL—America, Eastern United States, Mid 1800's
GOLF—Scotland; Based on the Roman game Paganica, 1100
HOCKEY—Canada, 1865
KARATE—India, 400 B.C., Later Japan, 1600's
LACROSSE—Canadian Indians, Mid 1800's
SOCCER—China, 400 B.C.; Romans, 200 A.D.
TENNIS—French, 1100's or 1200's
PING PONG—England (Table Tennis), Late 1800's
NOTE: Native-Americans played games with rubber balls before European contact.

3. Plan a class booklet of "Favorite Sports." Ask children to bring in multiracial pictures of athletes who are involved in their favorite sport(s). Give opportunities for cutting and pasting the pictures into a sports booklet. Also, ask students to write brief notes to accompany the pictures. Students from foreign countries can be encouraged to bring in pictures, books, and equipment which provide information about different games played in their cultures. Have students exhibit their booklets and other information on the "Traveling Multicultural Display."

4. Give students opportunities to meet in small groups to read and talk about sports. Boys and girls who are involved in team sports or have a special interest in athletics can serve as leaders of these groups. Have students compare and contrast certain games. For example, they might discuss the similarities and

differences in the games of rugby, soccer, and football. Ask students to share their own athletic skills by planning a demonstration of their knowledge and accomplishments in certain sports. An optional activity could be to have students find ways to honor the various participants in the Special Olympics.

Some of the additional sports which can be researched or illustrated are as follows: tennis, croquet, swimming, canoeing, judo, water polo, ice skating, skiing, and fencing. Encourage independent reading by highlighting the lives of unusually skillful athletes such as Arthur Ashe, the first African-American tennis player to win the championships at Wimbeldon and the U.S. Open.

5. Extend the impact of this activity by giving the students opportunities to play some of the games from different countries and cultures. Encourage creativity by helping them to adapt games to reflect available equipment, etc.

LITERATURE CONNECTION: *Games Children Play: Ball Games* by Ruth Oakley. A description of historical and contemporary games children in various countries play with balls. Leather, yarn, and rubber are some of the materials used in balls for games played in such countries as Belgium, Britain, Haiti, Austria, etc. Marshall Cavendish, New York, © 1989. Illustrated by Steve Lucas.

The Guinness Book of Sports Records: 1991, edited by Mark Young. An alphabetical list of the many different competitive sports around the world. The origin of the games, the way they are played, the champions and their records, the Olympics, and the various countries participating in these sports are described. This record of international sports is filled with black and white photographs. It is suggested that the teacher select portions to read with the children. Facts on File, New York, © 1991. Photographs.

Name ______________________________ Date ______________________________

THEY HELPED BUILD AMERICA

Write the name of the person who made these contributions next to the correct pictures on the third page. Color each picture.

Norbert Rillieux found a way to refine sugar. (African-American)

Dr. Myra Adele Logan was the first female surgeon to operate on the heart. (African-American)

Orville Wright and his brother Wilbur invented the first airplane. (European-American)

Name ______________________ Date ______________________

THEY HELPED BUILD AMERICA

Dr. Mae Jemison is a medical doctor, engineer, and an astronaut. She was a member of the shuttle crew, Discovery, on her first trip. (African-American)

Thomas Edison invented the record player. (European-American)

Dr. Lise Meitner found that atomic energy could give out a lot of electricity at one time. (European-American)

Name ______________________________ Date ______________________________

THEY HELPED BUILD AMERICA

Men and women of many different races and ethnic groups have helped America to be a great country. Because of their work, people who live in America can get help when they are sick, need to fly a long distance, want to listen to a record, or eat pie.

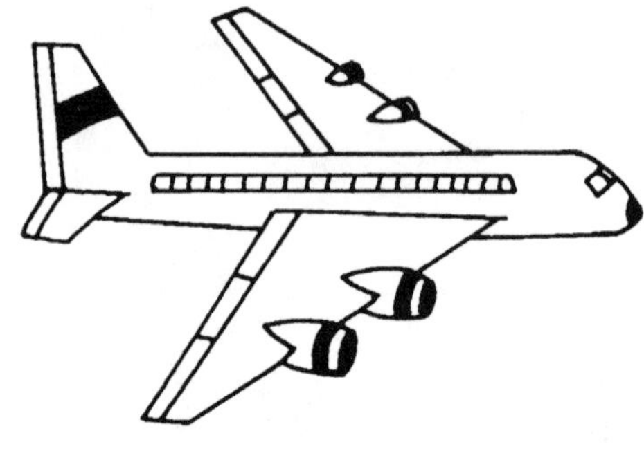

______________________________ ______________________________

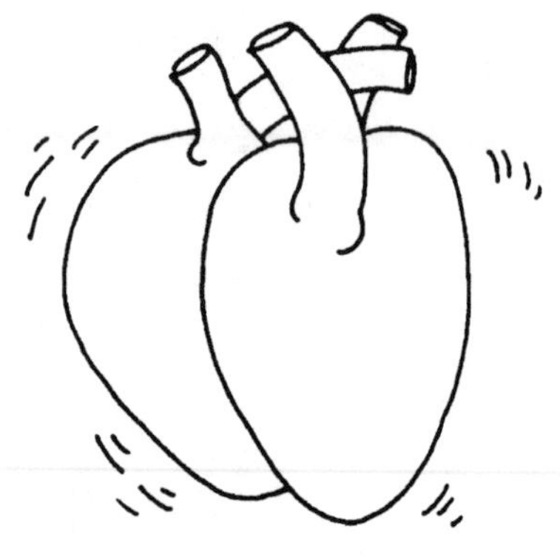

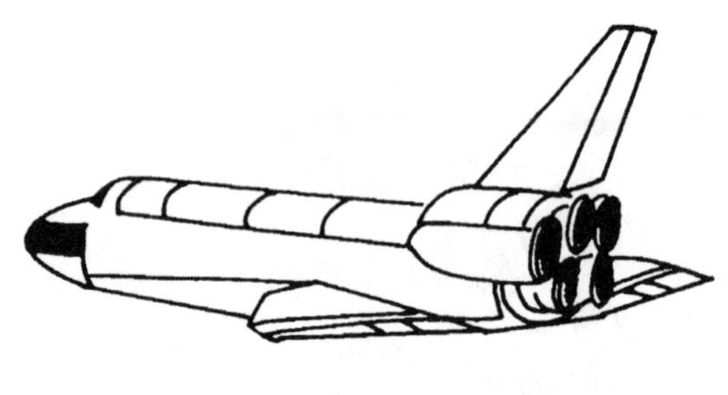

______________________________ ______________________________

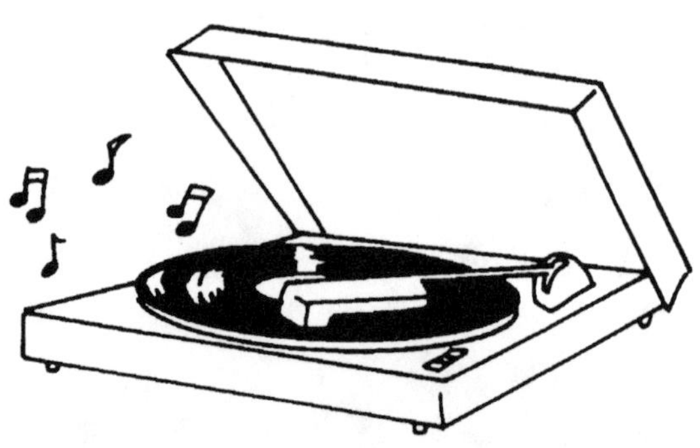

______________________________ ______________________________

Name ________________________________ Date ________________________________

CRASH! BANG! OUCH!

Until Garrett A. Morgan invented the traffic light, drivers had to guess at the right time to drive across the street. Color the picture of the accident and the angry people.

Circle the words that tell how it was for drivers BEFORE the invention of the traffic light:

SAFE UNSAFE FUN SCARY GUESSWORK ANGER

Name ______________________________ **Date** ______________________________

CRASH! BANG! OUCH!

The traffic signal has three lights. Each light means something important. Match the words which tell the right meanings for each light. Then color them.

YELLOW	STOP
GREEN	BE CAREFUL/WATCH
RED	GO

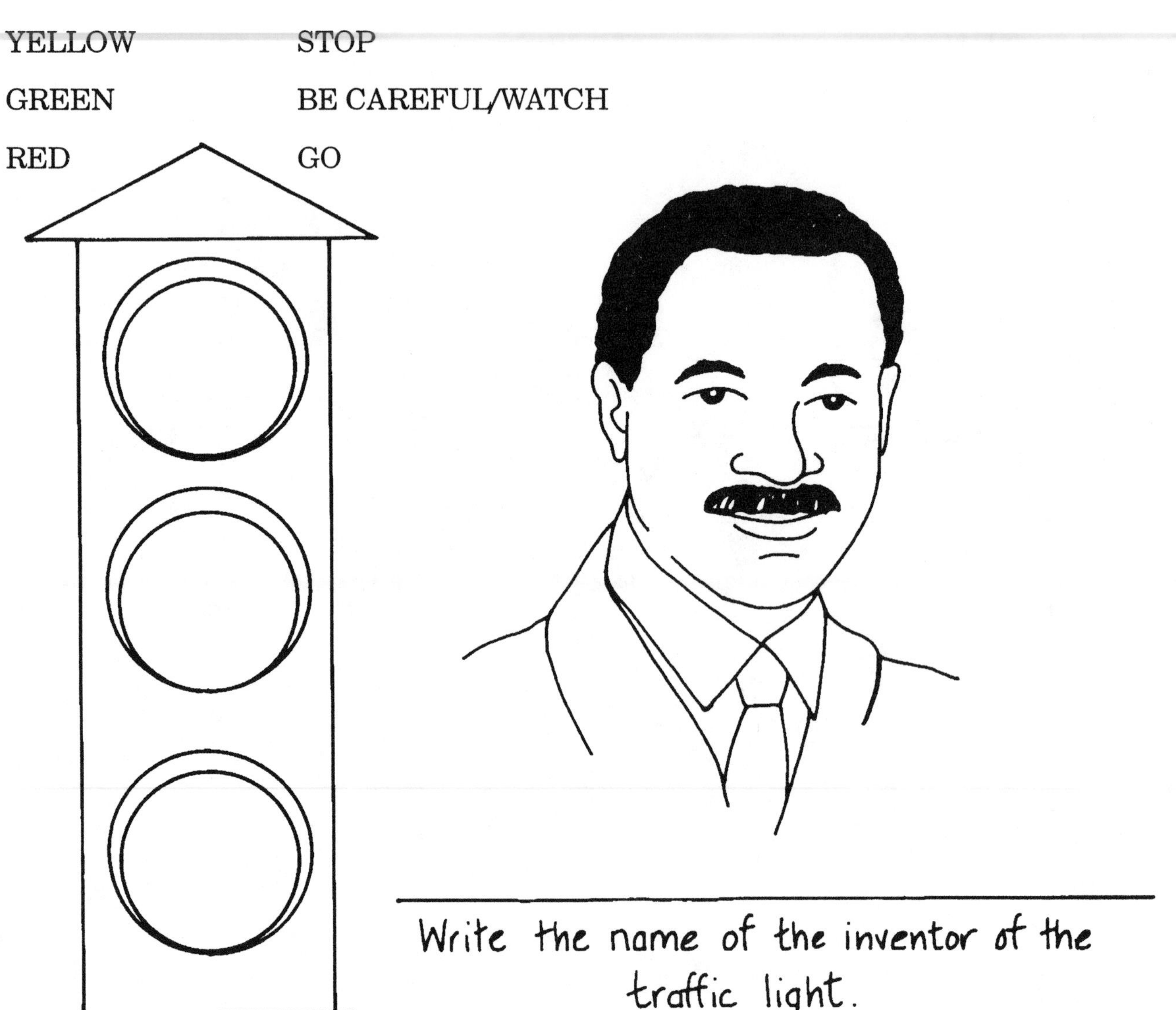

Write the name of the inventor of the traffic light.

Circle the words that describe how driving improved AFTER the invention of the traffic light.

SAFE FOR DRIVERS AND WALKERS　　NO GUESSWORK　　UNSAFE

Garrett A. Morgan (African-American)

Name ________________________________ Date ________________________________

TALK, TALK, AND MORE TALK

People like to talk. Sometimes they talk to people close to them. Other times they talk to friends and family who are far away. Connect the dots and discover a popular talking device.

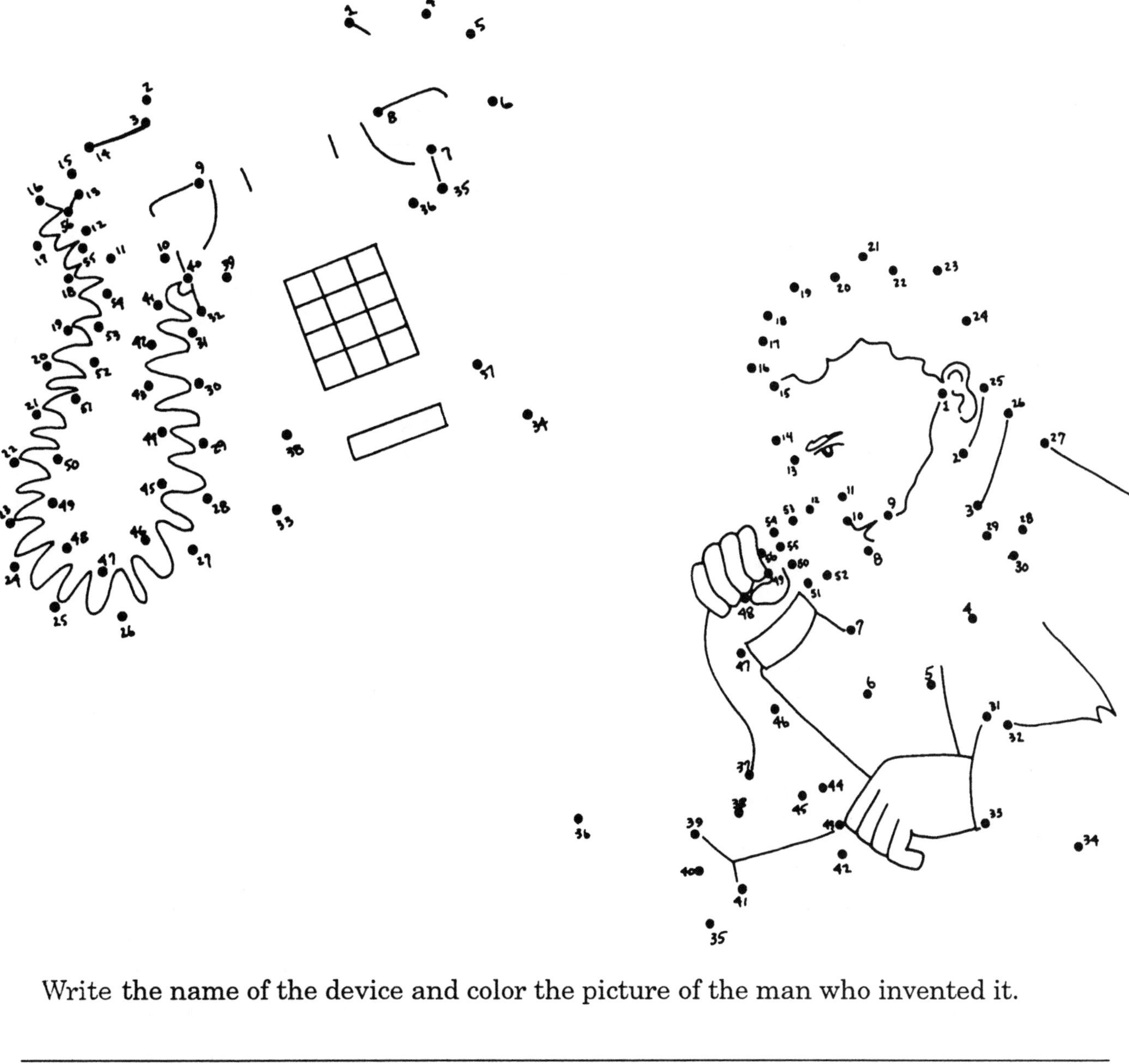

Write the name of the device and color the picture of the man who invented it.

____

____

____

Alexander Graham Bell (European-American)

Name ______________________________ Date ______________________________

EVERYONE NEEDS SHOES

Today, you can buy as many pairs of shoes as you want in a matter of minutes. Long ago, people had to wait several months to have a pair of shoes made by hand.

Cut out the pieces of this shoe and glue them on plain paper. How many minutes did this take? ______________ minutes.

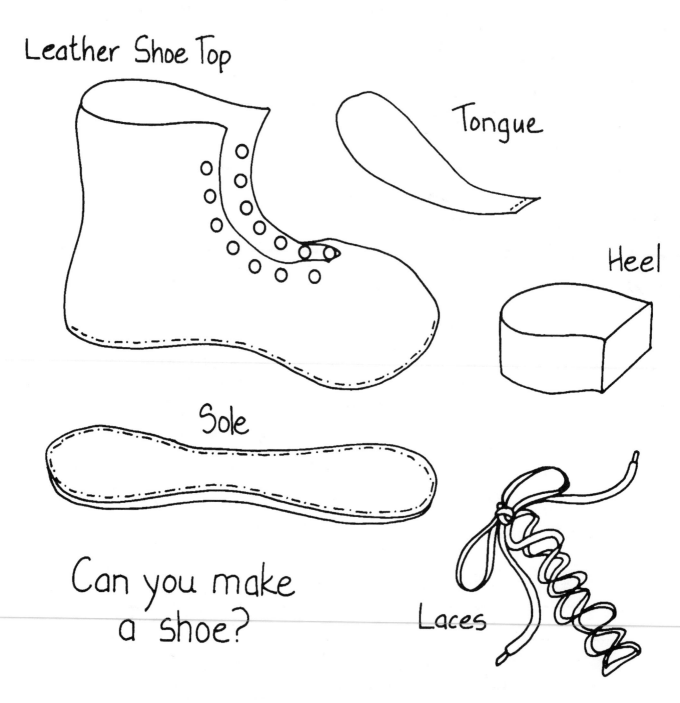

Leather Shoe Top

Tongue

Heel

Sole

Can you make a shoe?

Laces

Name ______________________________ Date ______________________________

EVERYONE NEEDS SHOES

Color the picture Jan Matzeliger. He made a machine which sewed the leather tops of shoes to the soles in just a few minutes. It was called a shoe-lasting machine.

Jan Matzeliger, 1852-1889
The inventor of a shoe-lasting machine which revolutionized the construction of shoes.
(African-American)

Trace the shoe-lasting machine.

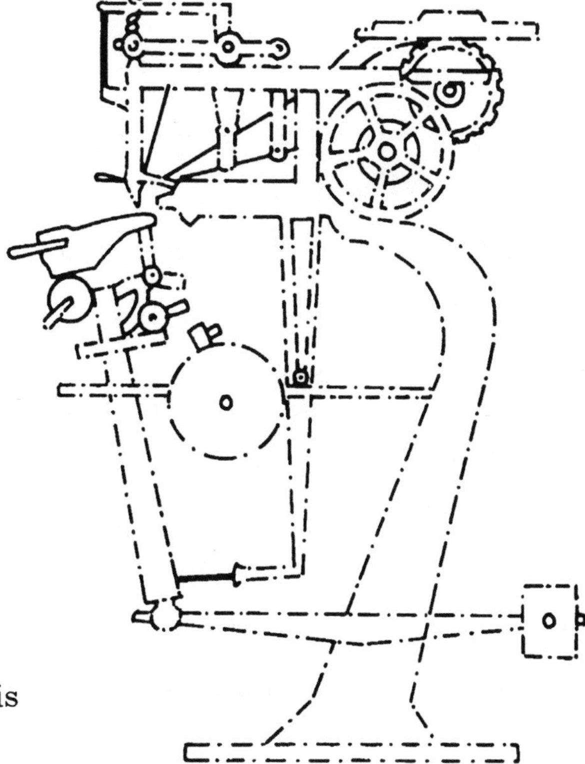

Jan Matzeliger's own drawing of his lasting machine.

Name ______________________________ Date ______________________________

MAKING PROGRESS IN AMERICA

Many different kinds of people made America a great country. Someone made a clock, another person made the traffic light, someone else invented the telephone. All of these things made life better for everyone.

Write the correct names beneath each sentence.

1. He helped many people get shoes.

____

2. He wanted to travel to the moon.

____

3. If you were sick, he could make you better.

____

4. People can talk on the telephone because of his work.

____

5. She wrote poetry about freedom and George Washington.

____

6. He made the first clock in America.

____

7. His invention of traffic lights made crossing the street safer.

____

8. She was the first American woman in space.

____

9. He invented a way to freeze vegetables and other foods.

____

10. She was the first woman doctor in America.

____

Name ____________________ Date ____________________

WHAT COULD TOMMY BE READING?

List the names of different American contributors who could be in Tommy's book:

1. ____________________
2. ____________________
3. ____________________
4. ____________________
5. ____________________
6. ____________________
7. ____________________
8. ____________________
9. ____________________
10. ____________________

Name ______________________________ Date ______________________________

CHOOSE A NAME TO WIN THE GAME

Cut out the game along the dotted line. Make a dial to attach to the center, then play the game with 2 or 3 other people. When the dial is turned to an invention, players try to guess the name of the inventor. Check the ANSWER KEY (3-7B) to see if your answers are correct.

Name ______________________________ Date ______________________________

CHOOSE A NAME TO WIN THE GAME—ANSWER KEY

1. Kay C. Bennett is a Native American writer and a doll maker. Kay is short for Kaibah.

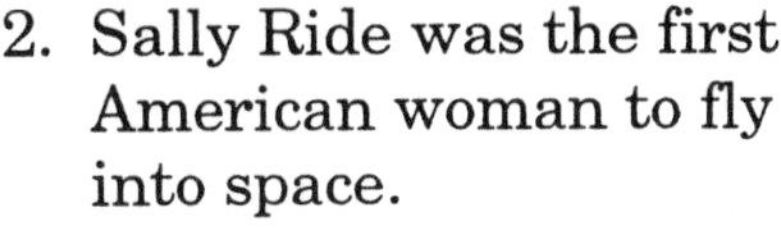

2. Sally Ride was the first American woman to fly into space.

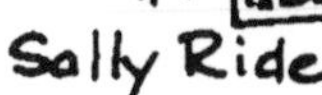

3. Benjamin Banneker invented the first clock in America.

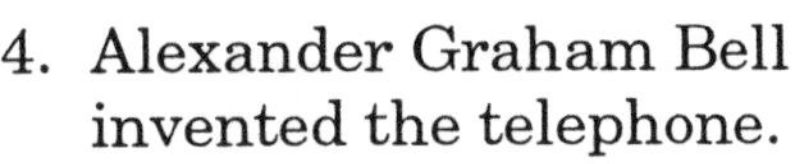

4. Alexander Graham Bell invented the telephone.

5. Thomas Edison invented the first record player.

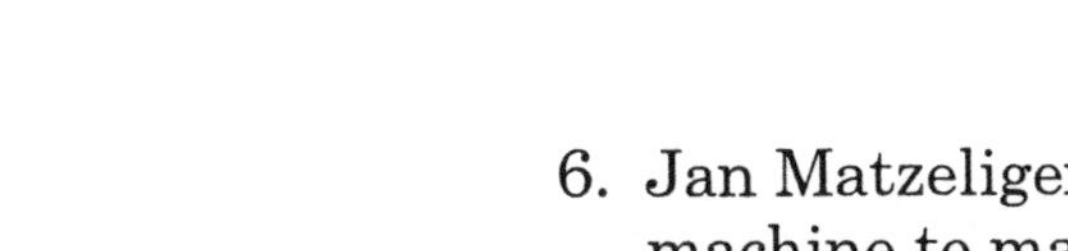

6. Jan Matzeliger invented a machine to make shoes faster.

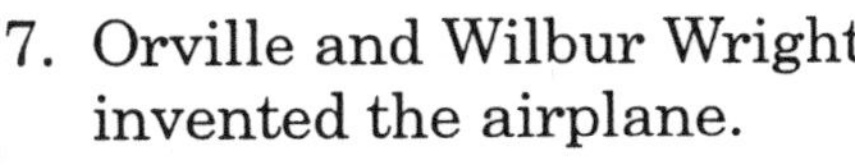

7. Orville and Wilbur Wright invented the airplane.

8. Ieoh Ming Pei designed the John F. Kennedy Library.

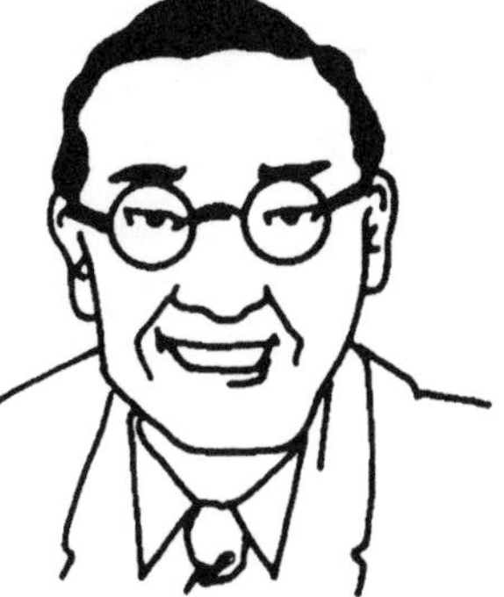

Name ______________________________ Date ______________________________

DOCTOR SEWS UP A HUMAN HEART

Dr. Daniel Hale Williams was the first person to operate on the human heart. He sewed up a cut in a man's heart. The man lived!

Color the picture of Daniel Hale Williams. Then write a sentence telling how he helped other people.

____

____

____

Daniel Hale Williams, 1858-1931
The founder of Provident Hospital of Chicago in 1891. He performed the first successful open heart surgery in 1893.

Name ______________________________ Date ______________________________

EXTRA! EXTRA! READ ALL ABOUT IT!

Color the pictures of the inventors and their inventions and answer each question.

J. Mauchly and J. Eckert invented a fast way to process information. They invented the computer in 1946.

Have you ever used a computer?

Circle your answer: YES NO

Christopher Sholes invented the typewriter in 1867. He wanted a fast method of communicating information to others.

Can you type?

Circle your answer: YES NO

Johannes Gutenberg invented the printing press in 1440. He wanted to help large numbers of people communicate via the printed page, (newspapers, books, and magazines).

Is it important for you to know how to read and write? Circle your answer and write a sentence telling WHY it is important for you to know how to read and write. YES NO

____

____

Name ________________________________ Date ________________________________

WE WORKED TO HELP MANKIND

People of many cultural, racial, and ethnic backgrounds invented things needed by others. Often, one person would develop something very exciting. In later years, another person would add something else to the original item and end up improving upon the original invention.

Read the information below. Place the names of the correct scientists, or contributors, under their invention.

Lewis Latimer....His invention helped lights to burn longer.

Thomas Edison....He made it possible to read at night.

Granville T. Woods...He made long-distance telephone calls possible.

Alexander Graham Bell...His invention helped people talk to others without visiting in person.

INVENTION: The electric light bulb

INVENTOR: ________________________________

INVENTION: A long-lasting filament, a very thin wire for use in electric bulbs

INVENTOR: ________________________________

INVENTION: The telephone

INVENTOR: ________________________________

INVENTION: A long-distance transmitter, a device which transfers sounds

INVENTOR: ________________________________

Name ______________________________ Date ______________________________

PEOPLE NEED TO TRAVEL

It's shopping day, moving day, vacation time, or you have to get to school. People of many colors, races, and religions have to get from one place to another. People of many colors, races, and religions can help you get to where you want to go. See the next page for the answers.

Unscramble the names below. Write them near their vehicles.

1. EDFIRN OR VETIREAL ________________ OR ________________
2. OPILT ______________________________
3. CTRKU RIEVDR ______________________________
4. USB REIVRD ______________________________

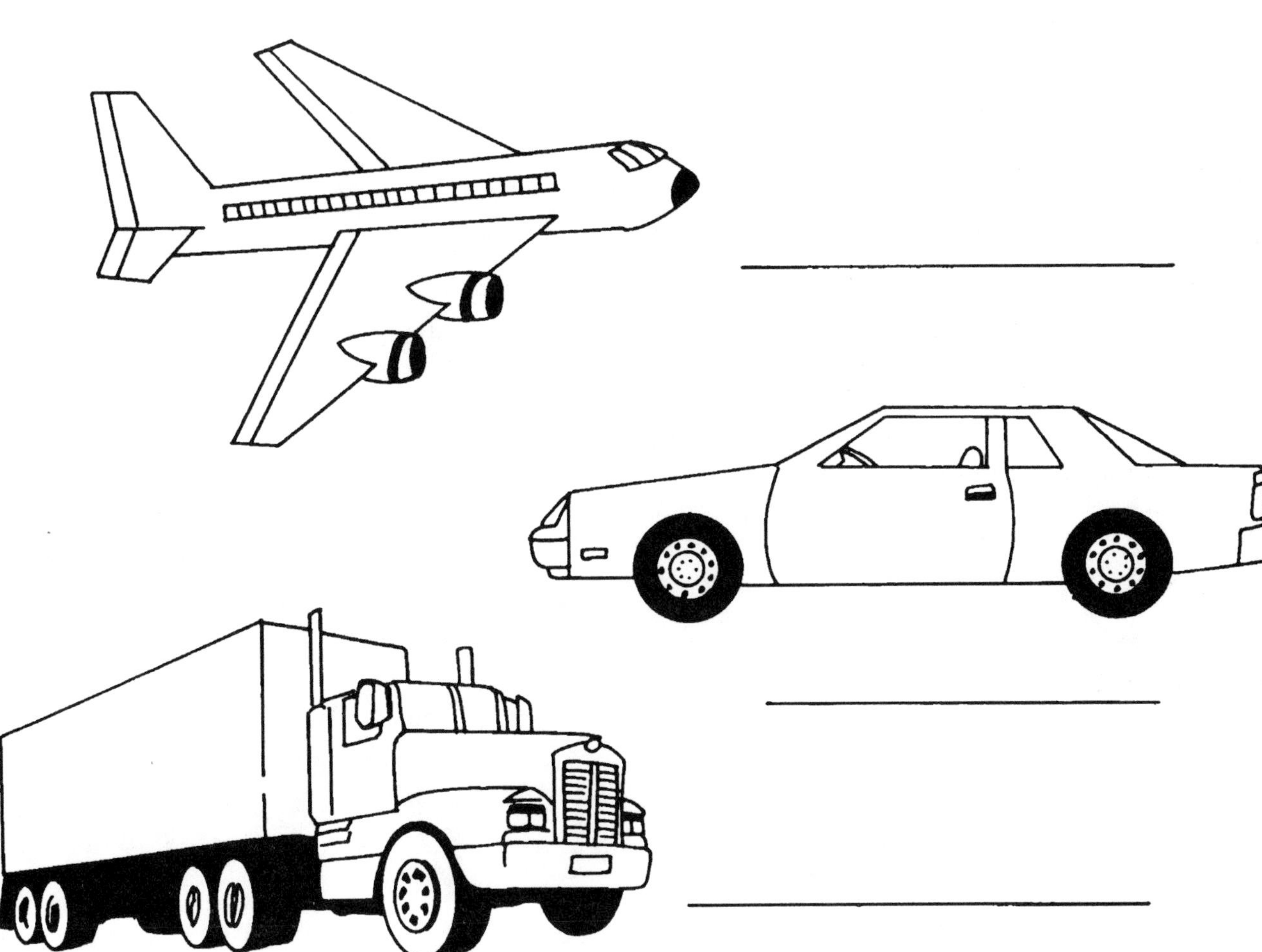

Name ______________________________ Date ______________________________

PEOPLE NEED TO TRAVEL

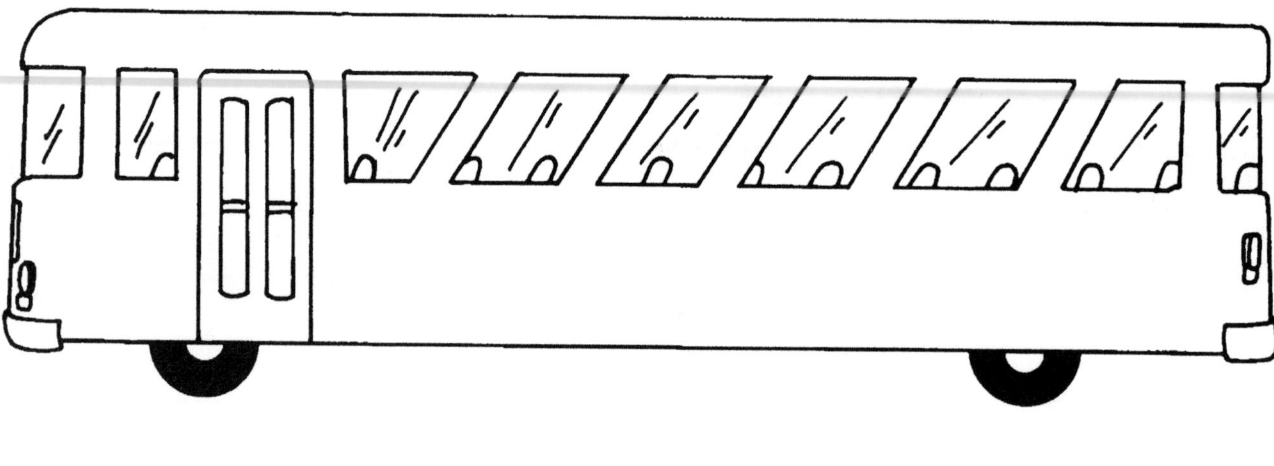

____

Think about this: What race, color, or religion does the person who helps you have to be? Aren't you glad when he/she helps you get to the place you want to go? Have you smiled at the person who has helped you?

CHECK YOUR ANSWERS: 1. Friend or Relative 2. Pilot 3. Truck Driver 4. Bus Driver

Name ______________________________ Date ______________________________

AFRICAN ART

- Paint It
- Frame It
- Hang It

Bakwele dance mask from the Congo

Name ______________________________ Date ______________________________

CHINESE ART

Decorate with many flowers.

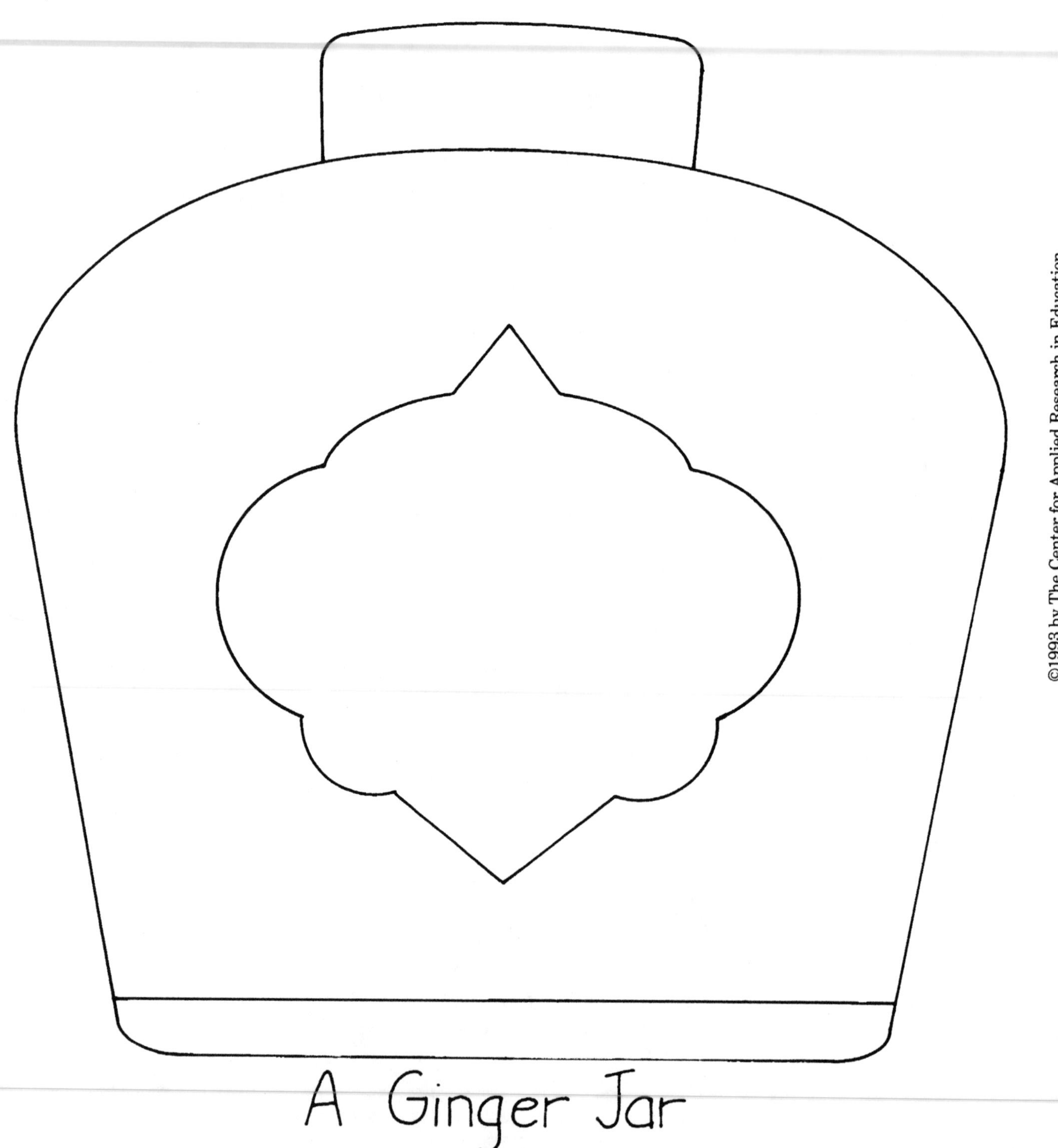

Name ______________________________ Date ______________________________

NATIVE AMERICAN ART

Color, cut out, string, and wear this tambourine.

A TAMBOURINE DRUM

NORTHWEST COASTAL TRIBES

MADE OF PAINTED WOOD AND SKINS

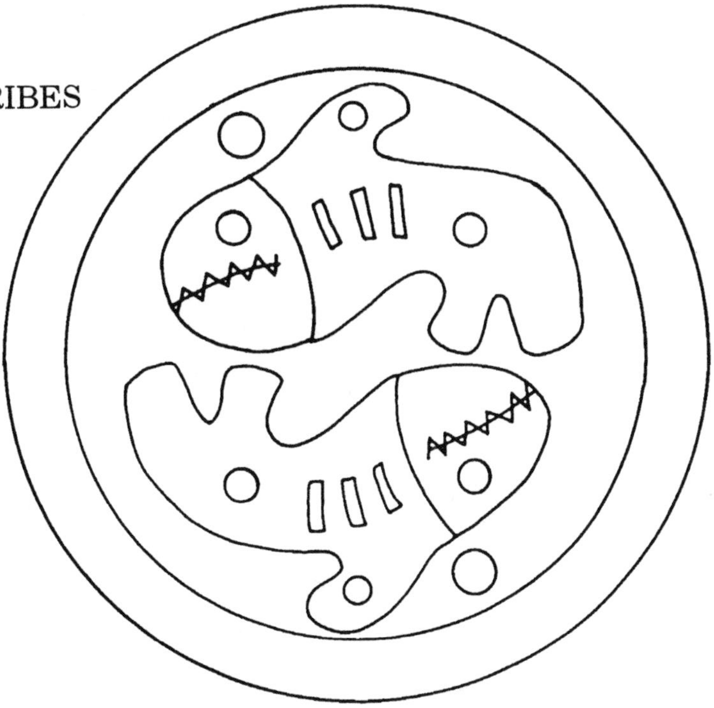

Color this picture of a basket, or form one out of clay. Then paint people and animals on it.

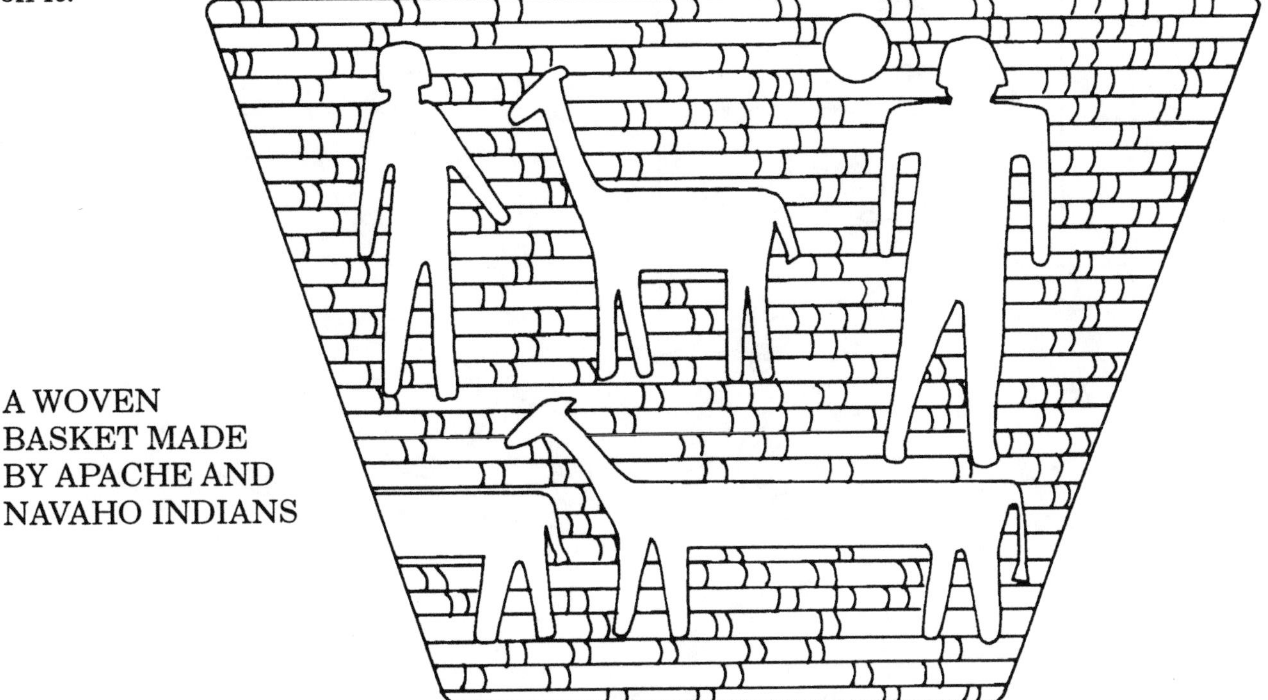

A WOVEN BASKET MADE BY APACHE AND NAVAHO INDIANS

Name ______________________________ Date ______________________________

SPANISH ART

A Crown and Coat of Arms

Color and share.

This shield is made of leather.

Name ______________________________ Date ______________________________

STAMPS FOR HEROES AND HEROINES

Americans of many races and colors have helped make the country great. Some are famous and their names and pictures are on stamps and in books. Find the names of new American heroes and heroines. Write their names and the contributions that made them famous on the lines below.

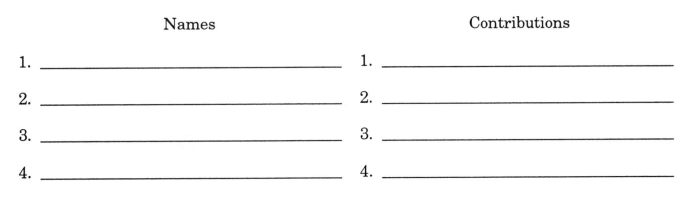

Names	Contributions
1. ______________________	1. ______________________
2. ______________________	2. ______________________
3. ______________________	3. ______________________
4. ______________________	4. ______________________

Choose two people from the list for your stamps. Decorate each stamp and submit to the U.S. Postal Service. Maybe they will publish your work.

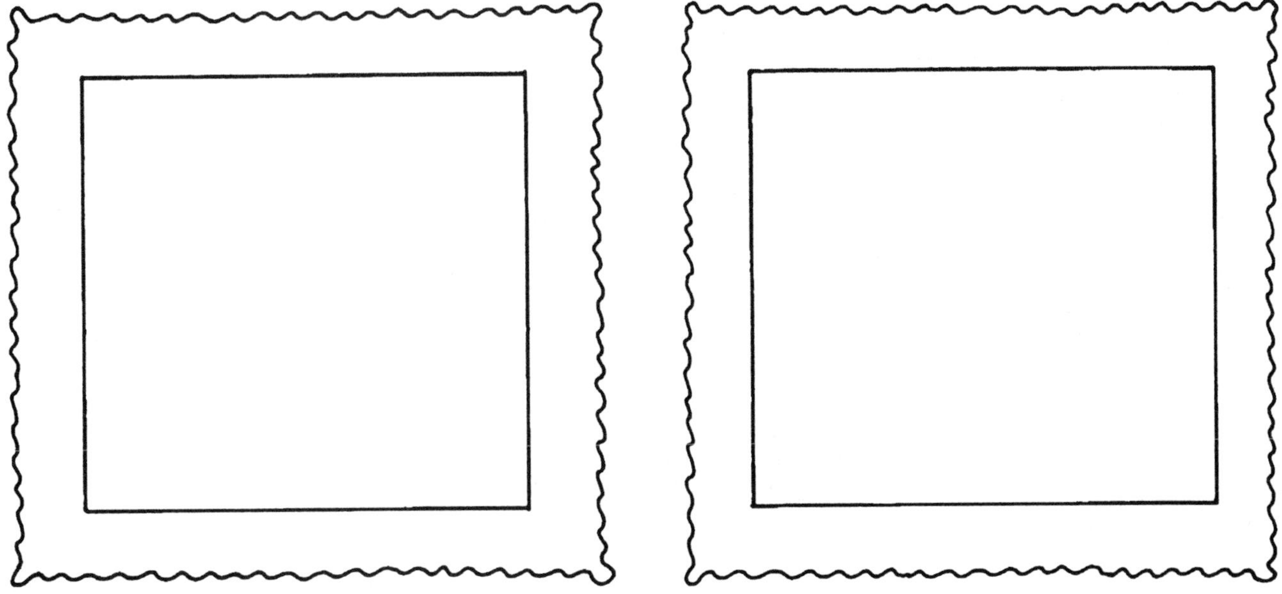

Name ______________________________ Date ______________________________

POSTERS FOR UNKNOWN AMERICAN HEROES

Write a short sentence or phrase that honors a man, woman, or child who has done something great for America. Use crayons or magic markers to draw a picture to go with your sentence. Cut your poster out and share it with others. Use your slogan or sentence on a T-shirt.

Sentence or Phrase:

____

____

My Poster...

Name ______________________________ Date ______________________________

T–SHIRT FOR SPECIAL CONTRIBUTORS

WRITE A CLEAR, MEANINGFUL SLOGAN ON YOUR T-SHIRT TO HONOR A CONTRIBUTOR WHO HAS MADE AMERICA A BETTER PLACE TO LIVE.

Name ________________________________ Date ________________________________

NATIVE AMERICAN CONTRIBUTIONS

(Before the Europeans)

The value of the contributions of a person, or of groups of people, can be seen when their inventions are used for many, many years. Native Americans had already developed methods of farming, tanning, and metalworking before Europeans arrived. Materials from the natural environment were turned into useful products which helped to make life better for them. Native Americans shared these contributions with the newcomers.

DIRECTIONS: Choose 10 items, for a total of 30, from each list. Identify GOODS or PROCEDURES that are used today. Then classify the items as NATURAL, MAN-MADE, or PROCEDURAL in Activity 3-14B. Circle the items you choose.

LIST 1

wool, cloth, baskets, snowshoes, mittens, bows, arrows, buckskin, leather, canoes, ceramics, sculpture, pottery, boxes, copper, pots, jewelry, blankets, spoons, drums, masks, furs, shields, clubs, textiles, tools, dwellings, tortillas, hominy, totem poles, looms, art

LIST 2

weaving, grinding, cutting, chopping, scraping, carving, farming, hunting, mining, sculpturing, trading, spinning, milling, metal working, drawing, painting, tanning, trapping, tracking, baking, boiling, fishing

LIST 3

stone, wood, bone, feathers, goat hair, cowhide, acorns, cotton, corn (maize), buffalo hides, shells, wool, brush, wood fibers, tree bark, clay, gold, silver, turquoise, birds, seeds, nuts, fruit, seaweed, cattle, horses, pumpkins

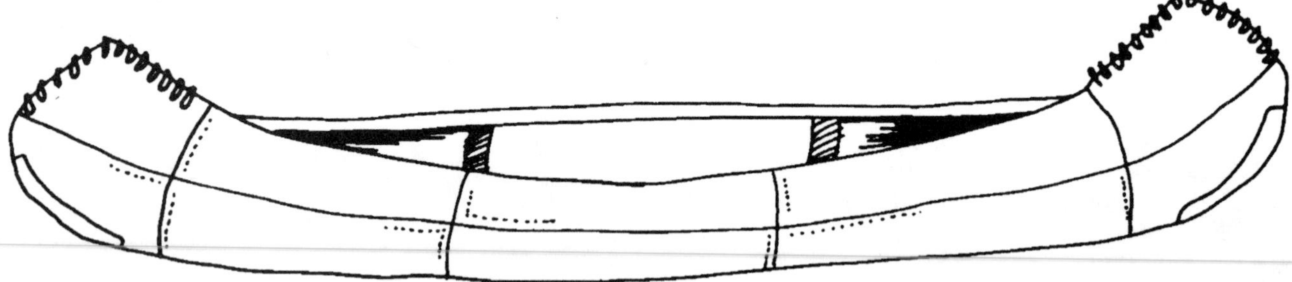

Name ______________________________ Date ______________________________

NATIVE AMERICAN CLASSIFICATION CHART

NATURAL	MAN-MADE	PROCEDURAL
1.	1.	1.
2.	2.	2.
3.	3.	3.
4.	4.	4.
5.	5.	5.
6.	6.	6.
7.	7.	7.
8.	8.	8.
9.	9.	9.
10.	10.	10.

THINK ABOUT IT—Write your thoughts below:

1. How valuable were the contributions of Native Americans to people? Which items are most useful today?
2. What can we learn about caring for the natural environment from Native Americans?
3. Most people do not think about the origin of the things they use in everyday life. Do you think it is a good idea to recognize those who have made contributions which make life better for others? Why or why not?
4. Which of the items above are used by your family and friends or people in the neighborhood?

____

____

____

____

Name ______________________________ Date ______________________________

MULTICULTURAL RIDDLES

Play this game of riddles alone or with a partner. The object of the game is to select the correct person by choosing a number on the dial. Correct answers are worth 5 points each.

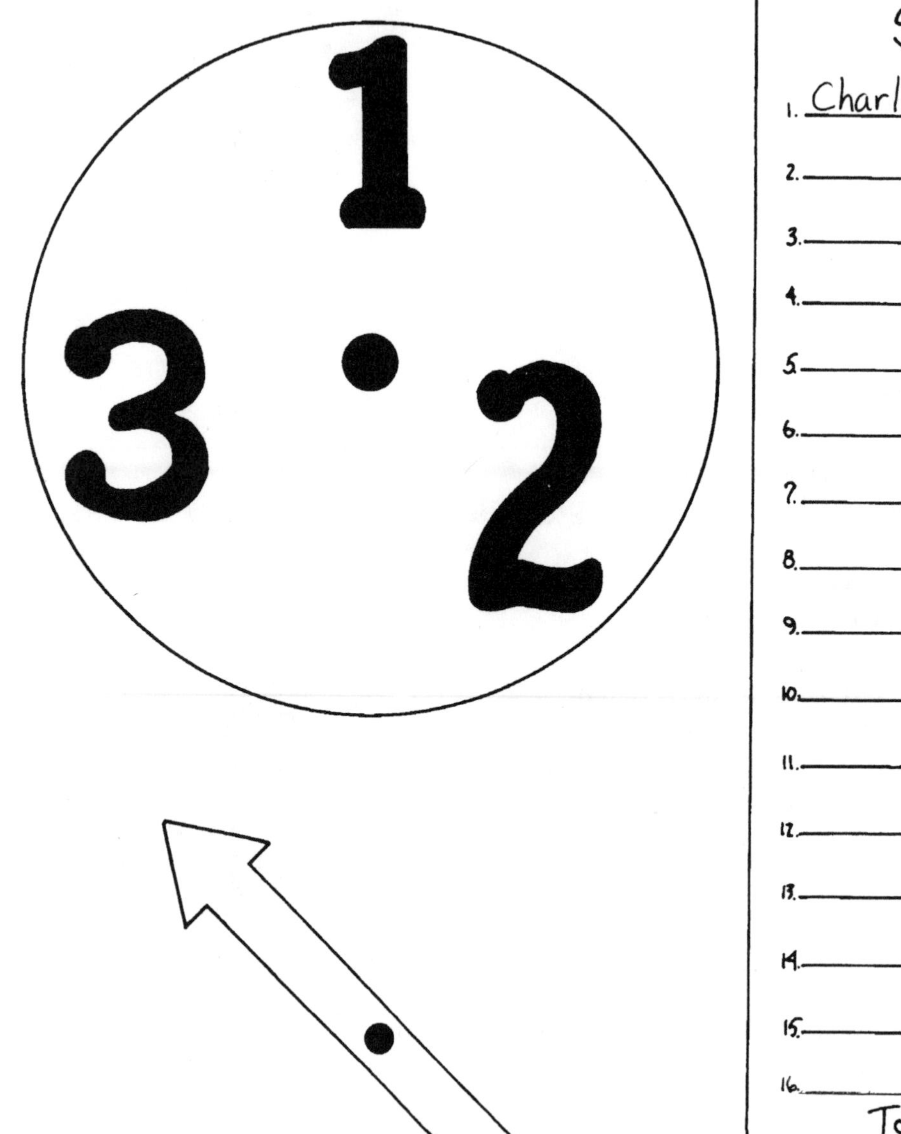

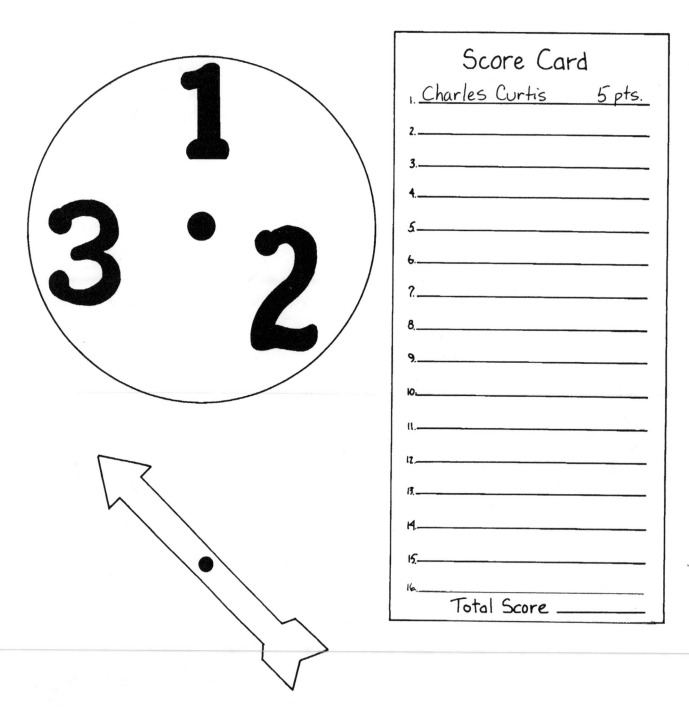

Score Card

1. Charles Curtis 5 pts.
2. ____________
3. ____________
4. ____________
5. ____________
6. ____________
7. ____________
8. ____________
9. ____________
10. ____________
11. ____________
12. ____________
13. ____________
14. ____________
15. ____________
16. ____________

Total Score ________

Name ______________________________ Date ______________________________

QUESTIONS FOR MULTICULTURAL RIDDLES

Read each question. Then guess the right answer.

1. He was Vice President of the United States from 1928 to 1933. He served under President Herbert Hoover. Who was he?
    1. William Hastings
    2. Charles Curtis
    3. Jim Thorpe

2. He performed the first successful open heart surgery. He founded Provident Hospital in Chicago, Illinois.

    Who was he?

    1. George Samuels
    2. Michael Jordan
    3. Daniel Hale Williams

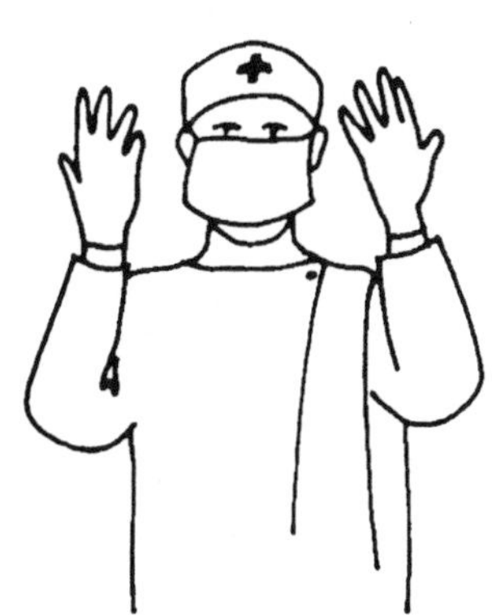

3. She helped to save many lives with her research work on bone marrow and tuberculosis.

    Who was she?

    1. Florence Joyner Griffin
    2. Florence Sabin
    3. Jane Eyre

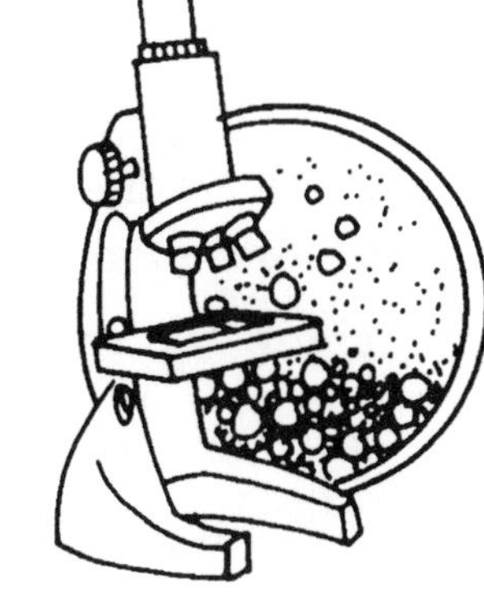

4. He invented the electric light bulb, the phonograph and many other items to help advance civilization.

    Who was he?

    1. Thomas Edison
    2. Hulk Hogan
    3. Jesse Owens

5. She organized health care and protection against dangerous working conditions for working people.

    Who was she?

    1. Nancy Brown
    2. Clara Hale
    3. Alice Hamilton

Name ______________________________ Date ______________________________

QUESTIONS FOR MULTICULTURAL RIDDLES

6. She won the 1963 Nobel Prize for her work in nuclear physics. Who was she?
   1. Harriet Tubman
   2. Maria Goeppert-Mayer
   3. Charlotte Ray

7. He made the first clock in America and planned the layout of the capitol of the country, Washington, D.C. Who was he?
   1. Benjamin Banneker
   2. Nathan Bedford Forest
   3. Larry Bird

8. He invented the bicycle in 1816. Who was he?
   1. Orville Wright
   2. Karl Von Sauerbronn
   3. Elijah McCoy

9. She was the first female to operate on the heart. Who was she?
   1. Ida B. Wells
   2. Myra Adele Logan
   3. Toni Morrison

10. These two brothers invented the airplane. Who were they?
    1. John and Andy Wilson
    2. Herb and Charles Goodman
    3. Orville and Wilbur Wright

11. He helped to save many lives and prevent the crippling effects of polio with his development of the polio vaccine in 1953. Who was he?

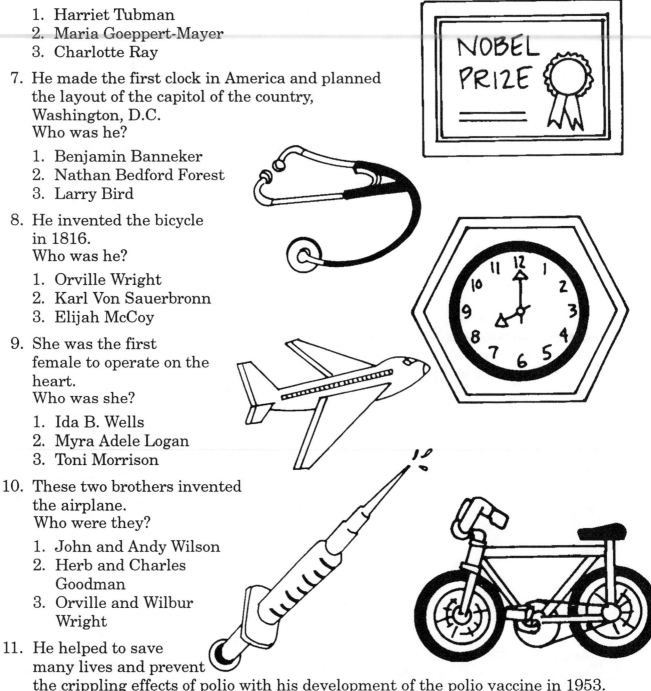

Name ________________________________ Date ________________________________

QUESTIONS FOR MULTICULTURAL RIDDLES

1. Abraham Lincoln
2. Jonas Salk
3. Dan Quayle

12. Without his invention shoes would still be made by hand, and people would have to wait a long time to get shoes.

    Who was he?

1. Jan Matzeliger
2. Lyndon Johnson
3. Christopher Sholes

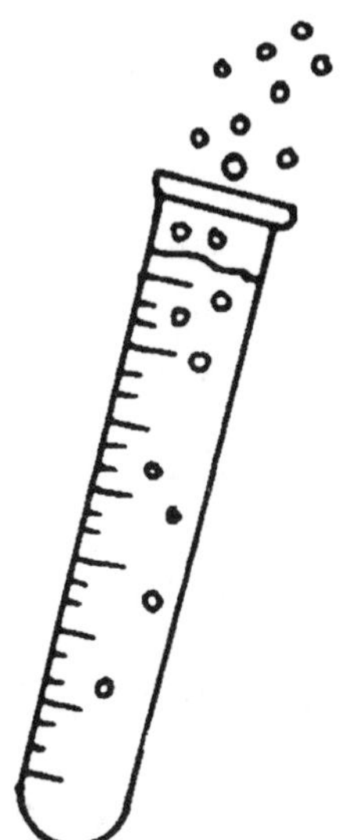

13. She discovered radium in 1890. This substance in used in the treatment of cancer.

    Who was she?

1. Alexandria Bell
2. Marie Curie
3. Mary Beth Browning

14. He developed a method for preserving food by quick-freezing.

    Who was he?

1. Charles Birdseye
2. William Tucker
3. James Baird

15. Because of his invention of the telephone, people can talk to others in the same town, in different states, or in foreign countries in a matter of minutes.

    Who was he?

1. Anthony Burns
2. Alexander Graham Bell
3. Johannes Gutenberg

16. He proved that the blood of human beings could not be identified by race. He found a way to preserve or save blood in banks so that it could be used in transfusions.

    Who was he?

1. Paul L. Dunbar
2. Dr. Charles Drew
3. John Brown

Write more riddles using the Multicultural Contributions Lists in the Appendix. Also, do research and expand the lists to include more recent multiethnic contributors.

Please save the completed copies of 3-15A for future activities.

3-15B

Name ______________________________ Date ______________________________

MULTICULTURAL RIDDLES—ANSWER KEY*

There are 16 riddles in the game, Multicultural Riddles. These answers correspond by number to the riddles.

1. Charles Curtis...Native American

2. Daniel Hale Williams...African-American
3. Dr. Florence Sabin...European-American
4. Thomas Edison...European-American
5. Dr. Alice Hamilton...European-American
6. Dr. Maria Goeppert-Mayer...German-American
7. Benjamin Banneker...African-American
8. Karl Von Sauerbronn...German
9. Dr. Myra Adele Logan...African-American
10. Orville & Wilbur Wright...European-American
11. Dr. Jonas Salk...European-American
12. Jan Matzeliger...African-American
13. Marie Curie...Polish and French
14. Charles Birdseye...European-American
15. Alexander Graham Bell...Scottish-American
16. Dr. Charles Drew...African-American

*NOTE: There are other contributors on the lists in the Appendix. Make up more riddles using these lists. Also, continue to increase your knowledge of the multiethnic contributions to civilization by doing your own research.

Please save this sheet for future use.

Name ________________________________ Date ________________________________

PIECING A PEACE QUILT

Statues and monuments have been made, portraits have been painted, and poems, songs and stories have been written to honor people who have helped society. A way to show honor for several people at one time is to make a patchwork quilt. Each person has a patch designed just for him/her. Then all the patches are sewn (or pieced) together. Make a multiethnic quilt of American contributors.

Identify twelve contributors from various ethnic groups. Use the Appendix or other sources for your choices. Design a patch for each contributor. Then write the names of the people you have chosen on the patches and decorate them.

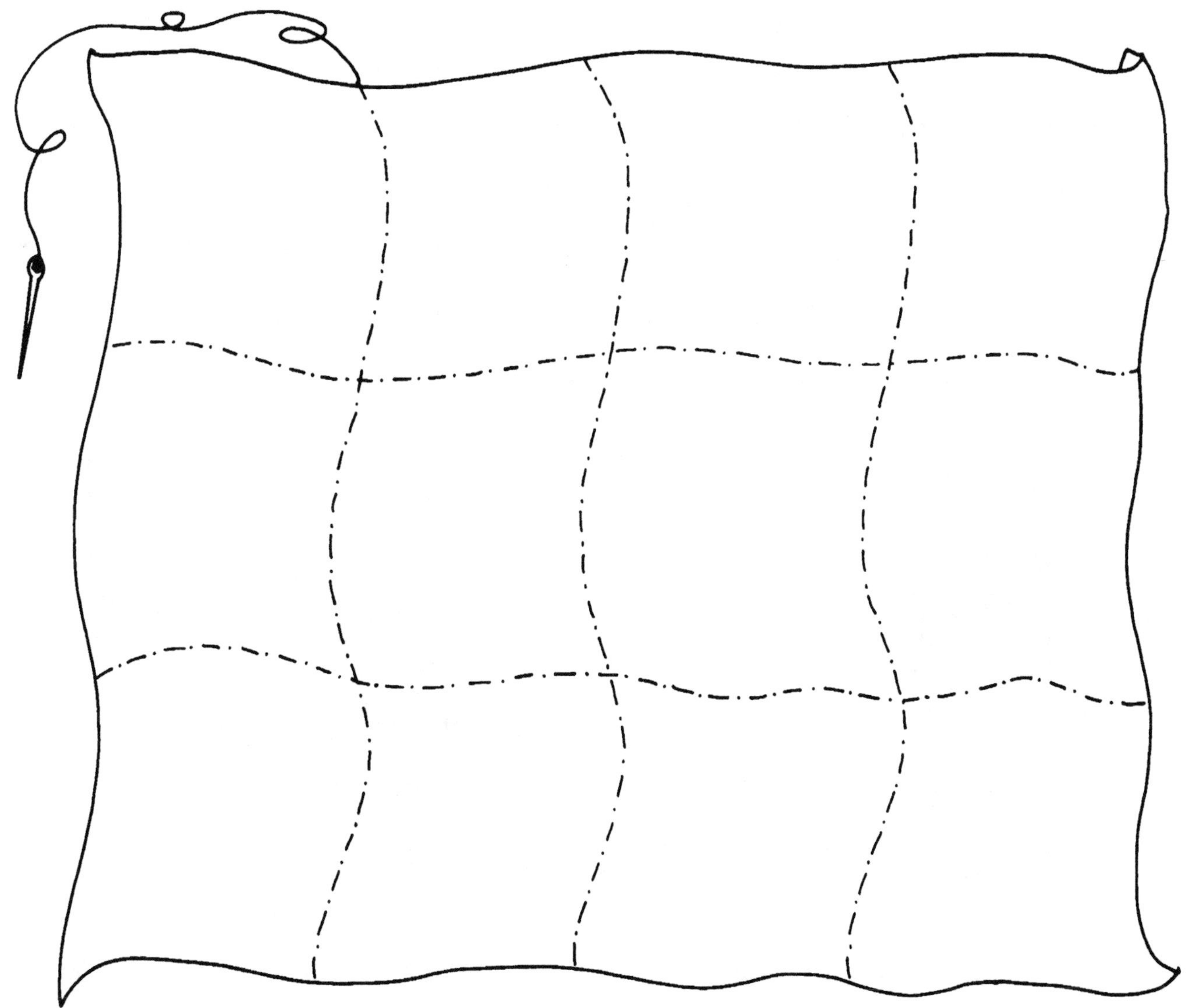

Choose one or two of the contributors you admire and pay tribute to each of them in some other special way.

Name ______________________________ Date ______________________________

BROTHERS AND SISTERS BENEATH THE SKIN

People of many different racial, ethnic, and religious backgrounds have worked to make America a place where each person can be free. Circle the names of the people in each sentence below. Then write each name on the ladder which leads to equality, justice, and freedom.

Martin Luther King helped Rosa Parks and others to sit anywhere they wanted on a public bus. He gave his life in the fight for freedom.

Viola Gregg Liuzzo drove civil rights volunteers to Selma, Alabama so that she and others could join them in a march to freedom. She was killed. She gave her life so that others could be free.

James Chaney, Michael Schwerner, and Andrew Goodman helped people gain the right to vote. They all died. They gave their lives to help others gain freedom.

Name ______________________________ Date ______________________________

THE AFRICAN CONNECTION

A FEW FACTS ABOUT ANCIENT AFRICA

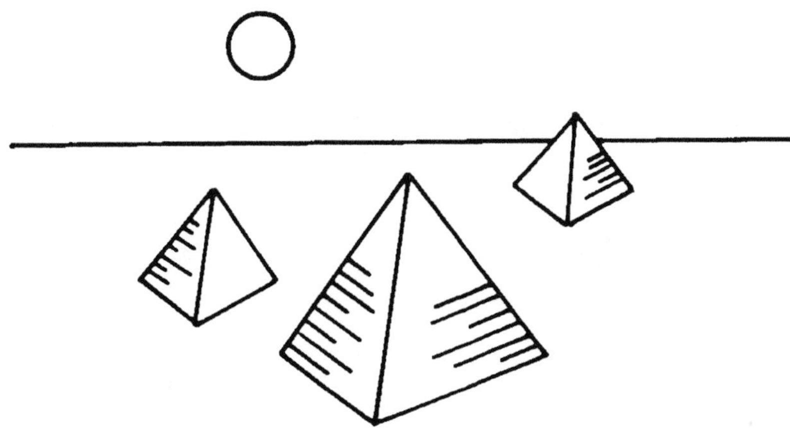

Directions: Read the information. Then complete the exercise below:

One of the Seven Wonders of the World is the Great Pyramid of Egypt. History shows that Egypt and other countries on the continent of Africa were great centers of learning. Math, science, literature and other forms of education began with people who lived in ancient Africa. Most African-Americans are descendants of these ancient African people and countries.

- There were African kingdoms of great wealth and highly developed civilizations. Among these advanced countries were:

  1. Egypt 2. Ghana 3. Timbuktu 4. Mali 5. Songhay 6. Sudan

- Mansa Musa ruled Mali, one of the largest empires in the world. He brought western Sudan under a unified system of law, protected routes, and expanded his rule to include such cities as Timbuktu, a great learning center.

- Kings of Ghana displayed great wealth, for example:

  King Teraminen was a powerful ruler who could put thousands of warriors into battle. His pages held gold-mounted swords and shields, the sons of the princes of the empire sat on his right hand with strands of gold plaited in their hair. Excellent breeds of dogs wore collars of silver and gold.

  King Kanissa'ai, a seventh-century ruler, owned one thousand blooded horses, each of which had three personal attendants and slept only on carpets. Their halters were ropes of silk.

- The Great Pyramid of Egypt, one of the Seven Wonders of the World, was built by Cheops. His knowledge of geometry and architecture was amazing.

Name ______________________________ Date ______________________________

THE AFRICAN CONNECTION

- Abderrahman Es-Sadi was a Sudanese writer who described the history of West African civilizations. He gave glowing accounts of trade, university centers, the rulers, and the basic culture of the people.
- Despite their enslavement, blacks were full participants in the discovery, exploration and settlement of the New World. Furthermore, history shows that the descendants of these African slaves became contributors to the development of Europe and America.

Write YES or NO in the blank next to each statement:

1. ______ Some animals in Africa wore gold and silver and slept on carpets, to show the wealth of the rulers.
2. ______ The ancestors of most American blacks were African.
3. ______ The builder of the Great Pyramid was European.
4. ______ Many Americans are the descendants of kings and rulers of great learning centers in western Africa.
5. ______ People who were slaves made valuable contributions to America and the world.

THINK ABOUT IT

- If your ancestors had been kings and queens, would you want to know about it? If so, how could you discover the truth about your history?
- Africa has been called the "dark continent." Now that you know there were great educational centers in cities like Timbuktu, how would you rename Africa?
- There are many things which are in use today which were invented or developed by people of African ancestry. Do you know of some of them? How are our lives better today because of the work of people of African, Asian, European, and Hispanic origin?
- America is different, special, and advanced among the nations of the world. Could it be that the nation has benefited from the genius of all of its many races and cultures of people?

Name ______________________________ **Date** ______________________________

THE AFRICAN CONNECTION

Study the map of ancient West Africa on this page. Think about how you would answer each question. Then trace the outline and color the different kingdoms and the picture of the king and queen.

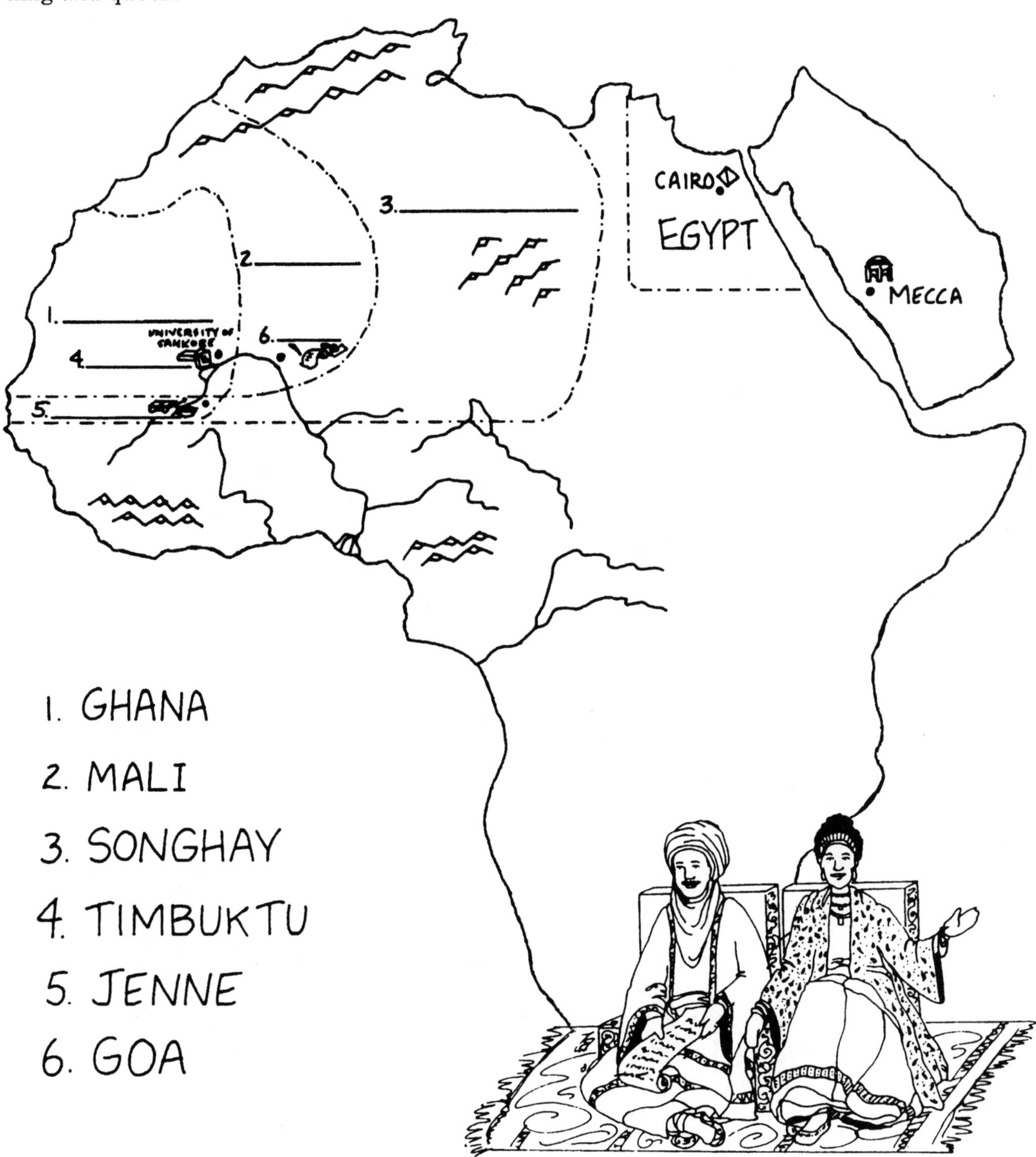

Name ______________________________ Date ______________________________

AFRICAN WORD SEARCH

Now that you are filling in the gaps in your knowledge of multicultural contributions, try your skills at making a word search. Read the African Connection on the Student Information pages. Then solve the African word search with the people and places on this list of African history facts. Finally, make a word search for contributors of many different races and cultures. Share it with your classmates.

Find the following items in the puzzle below:

1. Timbuktu
2. Cheops
3. Egypt
4. Ghana
5. Sudan
6. Songhay
7. Great Pyramid
8. Teraminen
9. Mali
10. Mansa Musa
11. Kanissa'ai

U	T	K	U	B	M	I	T	C	H	E	O	P	S	T
K	A	N	I	S	S	A	A	I	N	A	D	U	S	P
X	E	C	S	T	E	R	A	M	I	N	E	N	A	Y
F	M	A	N	S	A	M	U	S	A	M	A	L	I	G
T	D	D	I	M	A	R	Y	P	T	A	E	R	G	E
I	Y	A	H	G	N	O	S	G	H	A	N	A	B	D

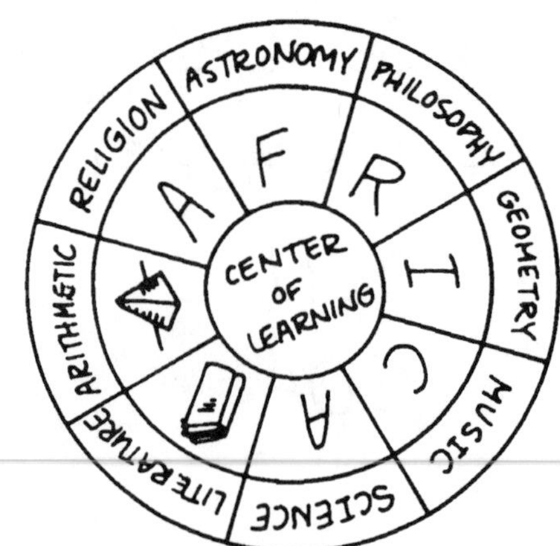

Did you find all of the words in the puzzle above? Now make your own Word Search Puzzle from lists of contributors in the Appendix and/or the Multicultural Riddles (3-15A)

Name ______________________________ Date ______________________________

MULTICULTURAL CONTRIBUTORS TO SCIENCE

Locate scientists, inventors, and doctors who have made contributions to science and technology in America and the world. Consider other areas of contribution at any time.

AFRICAN-AMERICANS	DUTCH	GERMAN	NATIVE AMERICANS
Benjamin Banneker	Zacharias Janssen	__________	__________
Built first American clock 1753	Invented compound microscope	Invented bicycle	Developed irrigation techniques
Dr. Myra Adele Logan	__________	Dr. Maria Goeppert-Mayer	__________
First female to operate on the heart	__________	Nuclear Physicist Nobel Prize 1963	__________

ASIAN	EGYPTIAN	FRENCH	POLISH	SCOTTISH
Ts'ai Lun	__________	__________	Marie & Pierre Curie	__________
Invented paper	__________	__________	__________	Invented telephone

Use the information in the Appendix, what you have learned in class, and/or other resource materials to complete this chart. Also, make new charts with headings which will reflect other ethnic groups.

Name ______________________________ Date ______________________________

MY MULTICULTURAL WORD SEARCH

Identify at least 12 contributors from activity sheet 3-15A to complete this list. Then use these names to create your MULTICULTURAL WORD SEARCH below:

List your puzzle items here:

1. ________________ 2. ________________ 3. ________________

4. ________________ 5. ________________ 6. ________________

7. ________________ 8. ________________ 9. ________________

10. ________________ 11. ________________ 12. ________________

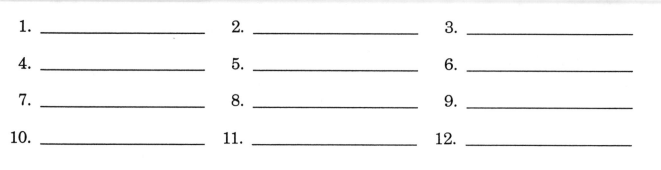

Write your multicultural contributors/contributions on the puzzle grid below. Fill in blank boxes with various letters of the alphabet. Share your puzzle with your classmates.

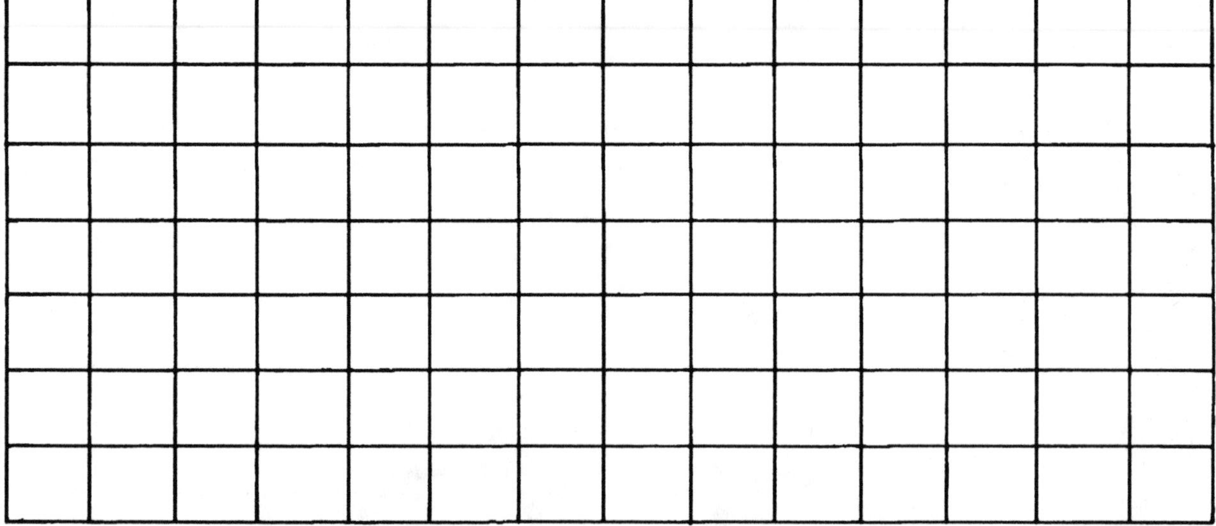

Use information from many sources to make this and other multicultural puzzles. You can find contributors from many different ethnic groups from books, encyclopedias, other activities in this book, and the Appendix.

Name ______________________________ Date ______________________________

NATIVE AMERICANS HELP NEWCOMERS

Native Americans were so friendly and understanding to explorers and other new immigrants, that they might have been responsible for helping to increase the population of the new world.

YOU'RE AN EXPLORER OF THE NEW WORLD

There are many jobs for which workers are needed. Your wish is to get as many of your countrymen as possible to come to the new world. But, since they have heard that the land is harsh and the Indians are violent, you have to convince them that it is safe in America. You know that the Indians are very helpful, friendly, and understanding.

Design a poster and write a letter to the newspapers to persuade your countrymen that it is safe and profitable to come to America.

Name ______________________________ Date ______________________________

ORIGIN OF NATIONAL AND INTERNATIONAL SPORTS

Write the name of the ethnic group that founded these sports on the correct line. Color each picture below:

ETHNIC GROUP OR COUNTRY

1. American, 1891
2. England, 1600s
3. Eastern U.S., 1800s
4. Canada, 1855
5. Indian, 400s (B.C.)
   Japan, 1600s
6. Canadian Indian, 1800s
7. China, 400 (B.C.) and Rome, 200 A.D.
8. French, 1100-1200
9. Scotland, 1100
10. England, 1880s

Note: North American Indians played with rubber balls before the year 1400. Please check your answers on the Answer Key.

Appendix

FOREIGN LANGUAGE LISTS

These are just a few of the many languages spoken by America's multiethnic population. Have fun with these words as you work on unit activities. Feel free to expand the list according to the specific languages spoken in your environment. Use the English words to locate the foreign language equivalents.

NUMBER WORDS

ENGLISH	FRENCH	SPANISH	TAGALOG	BIKOL	JAPANESE
one	un	uno	isá	saró	hitotsu
two	deux	dos	dalawá	duwá	futatsu
three	trois	tres	tatló	tuló	mittsu
four	quatre	cuatro	apát	apát	yottsu
five	cinq	cinco	limá	limá	itsutsu

COLOR WORDS

ENGLISH	GUJARATI	SPANISH	CHINESE	BIKOL	ARABIC
red	lai	rojo	hong	pulá	ahman
yellow	pado	amarillo	huang	diláw	astar
blue	bhuro	azul	lan	asúl	aezrak
green	lelo	vérde	lu	bérde	akhdarr
brown	maroon	pardo	kafe	kamagong	bonni

LEARN SWAHILI

Swahili is the major language in three African countries: Kenya, Tanzania, and Uganda. Many neighboring countries also have people who speak the Swahili language. Here are some words for familiar things in Swahili. See how many words you can pronounce. Try to memorize them and teach them to a friend or family member.

NUMBER WORDS IN SWAHILI

English Words	Swahili Words
one	moja
two	mbili
three	tatu
four	ine
five	tano

COLOR WORDS IN SWAHILI

red	rangi nyekundu
yellow	rangi manjano
blue	rangi ya bu luu
green	rangi kijani
black	rangi nyeusi

FOODS IN SWAHILI

butter	siagi
eggs	mayai
milk	magiwa
ice cream	aiskrimu
bread	mkate
rice	wali
salad	saladi

DAYS OF THE WEEK IN SWAHILI

Sunday	Jumapili
Monday	Jumatatu
Tuesday	Jumanne
Wednesday	Jumatano
Thursday	Alhamisi
Friday	Ijumaa
Saturday	Jumamosi

FOREIGN LANGUAGE WORDS* FOR EVERYDAY THINGS

(Word Search)

ENGLISH	SPANISH	FRENCH	**BIKOL	**TAGALOG
book	libro	livre	libró	liverów
clock	reloj	horloge	reló	orasan
desk	pupitre	bureau	lamesá	la mesá
balloon	globo	ballon	lobo	labop
flower	flor	fleur	burak	bulaklak
water	agua	eau	túbig	túbig
eye	ojo	yeux	matá	matá
box	caja	boîte	kahón	cahón
truck	carro	camion	auto	kotse
flag	bandera	drapeau	bandera	bandili
pencil sharpener	sacapuntas	taille crayon	pahimnan lapis	pantasa lapis
chalkboard	pizarra	tableau	tabla	sulafan
hand	mano	main	kamót	kamay
feet	pie	pied	bitis	paá
boy	niño	garçon	laláki	laláki
girl	niña	fille	babayi	babae
mother	madre	mere	ina	ina
father	padre	pere	amá	amú

ENGLISH	SPANISH	FRENCH	**BIKOL	**TAGALOG
sister	hermana	soeur	tapatid	ata
brother	hermano	frere	twya	kuya
house	casa	maison	harong	bahay
bread	pan	pain	pandibomba	padisal
computer	Computadora	ordinateur	computer	computer
school	escuela	école	eskuéla	paaralan
bird	pájaro	oiseau	gámgám	mayan
Monday	Lunes	Lundi	Lúnes	Lúnes
Tuesday	martes	Mardi	Mártes	Mártes
Wednesday	miercoles	Mercredi	Miérkoles	Miércoles
Thursday	jueves	Jeudi	Huébes	Júeves
Friday	viernes	Vendredi	Biernes	Viernes
Saturday	sabado	Samedi	Sabádo	Sábado
Sunday	domingo	Dimanche	Domínggo	Domíngo
January	enero	Janvier	Enéro	Enéro
February	febrero	Fevrier	Pebréro	Febréro
March	marzo	Mars	Márso	Márzo
April	abril	Avril	Abríl	Abríl
May	mayo	Mai	Máyo	Máyo
June	junio	Juin	Húnio	Júnio
July	julio	Juiliet	Húlio	Júlio
August	agosto	Aout	Augósto	Augósto
September	septiembre	Septembre	Septiembre	Septiémbre
October	octubre	Octóbre	Októbre	Oktúbre
November	noviembre	Novembre	Nobeímbre	Noviémbre
December	diciembre	Decembre	Disiémbre	Diciémbre

**NOTE:* Use English and foreign language dictionaries to locate more words in these or other languages.

**Bikol and Tagalog are two of the seven major languages of the Philippines. Both these languages are closely related to Spanish and within them there are various dialects. Variations in specific words and spellings can be attributed to dialects in different regions.

PLEASE NOTE: F in Spanish is P in Bikol.
V in Spanish is B in Bikol.
C is written as A in Bikol.

THINK ABOUT IT!

Why are some words in different languages alike?

MULTICULTURAL CONTRIBUTIONS

This list is expandable to facilitate the inclusion of contributors from as many cultures as possible. Other multicultural contributors to SCIENCE, LITERATURE, MUSIC, SPORTS, ART, BUSINESS, and EDUCATION can be added at any time. Selections for individual, small-group, and whole class reading and research can be made to augment the ongoing curriculum. Use the Multicultural Contributions Form for oral and/or written reports.

SCIENTISTS AND OTHER CONTRIBUTORS

NAME(S)	COUNTRY/ ETHNIC ORIGIN	INVENTION AND/OR CONTRIBUTION	DATE(S)	NEED
1. Deborah Agular-Velez	Puerto Rican American	Chemical Engineer, Computer Consultant	1983	Science/ Technology
2. James Baird	Scottish American	Television	1926	Home Entertainment
3. Benjamin Banneker	African American	First U.S. Clock	1753	Time
4. Alexander Bell	Scottish American	Telephone	1876	Communication
5. Charles Birdseye	European American	Quick-Freezing	1929	Preserve Food
6. Roberta Bondar	Canadian	Astronaut	1983	Payload Specialist
7. Edward Cartwright	English	Steam-Powered Loom	1780	Weave Cloth
8. James Cheney	African American	Volunteer Civil Rights	1965	Racial Equality
9. Dr.(s) Marie and Pierre Curie	Polish French	Discovery of Radium	1898	Treatment of Cancer
10. J. Mauchly & J. Eckert	European American	Electronic Computer	1964	Process Information

NAME(S)	COUNTRY/ ETHNIC ORIGIN	INVENTION AND/OR CONTRIBUTION	DATE(S)	NEED
11. Thomas Edison	European American	Phonograph	1877	Record Messages
12. Anna Fisher	European American	Astronaut	1984	Retrieval
13. Andrew Goodman	European American	Volunteer Civil Rights	1965	Racial Equality
14. Charles Goodyear	European American	Vulcanization of Rubber	1839	Tires
15. Johannes Gutenberg	German American	Printing Press	1440	Mass Communication
16. Leah Hing	Chinese American	Pilot	1934	Instrument Mechanic
17. Indians	Native Americans	Methods of Irrigation	—	Farming
18. Zacharias Janssen	Dutch	Compound Microscope	1590	Disease Diagnosis
19. Dr. Mae Jemison	African American	Astronaut/ Physician	1992	Space Information
20. Coretta Scott King	African American	Civil Rights Leader	1969	Racial Equality
21. Hans Lippershey	Dutch	Telescope	1608	Study of Outer Space
22. Shannon Lucid	European American	Astronaut	1985	Satellite Deployment
23. Viola Luizzo	European American	Volunteer Civil Rights	1965	Racial Equality
24. Ts' ai Lun	Chinese	Paper	105 A.D.	Recording of Information
25. Elijah McCoy	African American	Automatic Lubricator	1872	Oil for Moving Parts

NAME(S)	COUNTRY/ ETHNIC ORIGIN	INVENTION AND/OR CONTRIBUTION	DATE(S)	NEED
26. Jan Matzeliger	African American	Shoe Last	1883	Mass Production of Shoes
27. Garrett A. Morgan	African American	Traffic Signal	1923	Prevention of Accidents
28. Chiaka* Naito	Japanese	Physician/ Astronaut	1985	Heart Specialist
29. Dr. Charles Pravaz	French	Hypodermic Syringe	1853	Injection of Medicine
30. Judith Resnick	European American	Astronaut	1984	Satellite Deployment
31. Dr. Sally Ride	European American	Astronaut	1983	Flight Engineer
32. Norbert Rillieux	African American	Vacuum-Pan Evaporator	1843	Sugar Refining
33. Dr. Jonas Salk	European American	Polio Vaccine	1953	Prevention of Polio
34. Karl Von Sauerbronn	German	Bicycle	1816	Transportation
35. Svetlana Savitskaya	Russian	Astronaut	1982	Space Research
36. Michael Schwerner	European American	Volunteer Civil Rights	1965	Racial Equality
37. Dr. Richard Scott	African American	Oral Surgeon	1969	Maxillo-facial Surgery
38. Margaret Seddon	Canadian	Astronaut	1985	Satellite Deployment
39. Christopher Sholes	European American	Typewriter	1867	Recording of Information
40. Kathryn Sullivan	European American	Astronaut	1984	Satellite Deployment

*Female

NAME(S)	COUNTRY/ ETHNIC ORIGIN	INVENTION AND/OR CONTRIBUTION	DATE(S)	NEED
41. Sumarians	Egypt	System of Writing	3000 B.C.	Recording of Information
42. Valentina Tereshkova	Russian	Astronaut	1973	First Female in Space
43. Harriet Tubman	African American	Leader of the Underground Railroad	1850	Freedom for Slaves
44. Phyllis Wheatley	African American	Poet	1773	Literature
45. Granville Woods	African American	Transmitter, Telegraphy	1884 1887	Long Distance Messages from Moving Objects
46. Orville & Wilbur Wright	European American	Airplane	1903	Long Distance Travel

NOTE: Native American contributions are numerous. Many techniques and procedures were in use when immigrants from European countries came to America. The (——) above indicates that the contributions of Native Americans, as a group, were ongoing.

MULTICULTURAL MINI-BIOGRAPHIES

1. ALEXANDER GRAHAM BELL—SCOTTISH-AMERICAN

   Alexander Graham Bell was a teacher of deaf mutes. He used his skills as an elocutionist or speaker to help in his invention of the telephone. Noise and other sounds had been electronically sent through wires, but never the human voice. Bell, along with his assistant, Thomas A. Watson, worked on an instrument that would transmit words from the human voice over a wire. They succeeded. A patent for the first telephone was issued to Alexander Graham Bell on May 7, 1876.

2. MARY McLEOD BETHUNE—AFRICAN-AMERICAN

   Mary McLeod Bethune was a believer in education and spent her life providing opportunities for young blacks to pursue higher education. She founded Bethune-Cookman College and the National Council of Negro Women. Many recognized her for the work she did to contribute to the lives of others. Presidents honored her by giving her important positions in the government. She was Special Advisor on Minority Affairs and she received the Spingarn Medal. Mary McLeod Bethune was born in Mayesville, S.C. in 1875.

3. GLORIA MOLINA—HISPANIC-AMERICAN

   Gloria Molina, a politician, is a member of the Los Angeles City Council. She is known as tough, smart, and capable of overcoming obstacles to progress. A former assemblywoman, Molina's success in California politics is helping to establish a power-base for Hispanics.

4. SARAH JOSEPHA HALE—EUROPEAN-AMERICAN

   Sarah Josepha Hale was born in 1788. She was the first female journalist in early America. She convinced President Lincoln to designate the last Thursday in November as Thanksgiving. As editor of ladies' magazines, she influenced the lives of many women. One of her most famous works is the children's poem, "Mary Had a Little Lamb."

5. LEAH HING—CHINESE-AMERICAN

   Leah Hing, a pilot, was born in Portland, Oregon in 1907. She and several high school friends formed a band. For a year and a half after graduation, they toured the United States and Canada with a Vaudeville troupe, "Honorable Wu's." Leah Hing became a student pilot and earned her license in 1934. During World War II, she used her knowledge of planes as an instrument mechanic at the Portland air base.

6. QUEEN ISABELLA—SPANISH

   Queen Isabella of Spain was an important figure in the history of her country and in the discovery of the New World. During her reign, she gave Columbus permission and funds to pursue his plan to find the Indies by sailing west. Because she supported him in 1492, Spain was able to expand its empire.

7. CHIEF JOSEPH—NATIVE-AMERICAN

   The Nez Perces Indians loved their leader, Chief Joseph. He fought for their right not to be taken from their beautiful village in the Wallowa Valley in Oregon. White settlers forced them out of the only home they knew. Chief Joseph tried to protect his people by fighting for their land. Because of his military skills, he defeated the larger army many times but he would not scalp or kill wounded prisoners of war. As he and his people tried to escape to Canada, the harshness of winter and the lack of food caused Chief Joseph to have to surrender. In 1879, Joseph went to Washington, D.C. to ask the leaders to permit him and the rest of the Nez Perces to go home. He spoke of the earth as the mother of all people. He spoke of the equality of all men who were made by the same "Great Spirit Chief."

8. MARTIN LUTHER KING*—AFRICAN-AMERICAN

   Martin Luther King was a civil rights leader who used nonviolence as a means of gaining equality for Americans of African descent. He began by supporting the bus boycott in Montgomery, Alabama. King led mass demonstrations to defeat racist practices that caused black citizens to have to eat in separate restaurants, go to the back of the bus, go to separate bathrooms, go to separate schools, and drink from separate water fountains. The 1963 March on Washington was one of the highlights of his civil rights movement. There, he made his, "I Have a Dream..." speech and called the attention of the entire world to the injustices suffered in America by African-Americans. King won the Spingarn medal, a Nobel Peace Prize, and most of all, he won freedom for himself and other black Americans to live and vote and dream in America, without fear.

9. SEVERO OCHOA—SPANISH-AMERICAN

   Severo Ochoa was born in 1905 in Spain and moved to the United States when he was 35 years old. He taught at New York University where he conducted much of his research. A winner of the 1959 Nobel Prize for physiology or medicine, Severo Ochoa was a biochemist. He shared the prize with another biochemist when they discovered ways to artificially organize nucleic acids. These acids are important components of life and reproduction.

10. BETSY ROSS—EUROPEAN-AMERICAN

Betsy Ross, a seamstress, was given credit for making the first American Flag with stars and stripes. She was visited by George Washington and a committee who presented her with a rough design of the first official flag for the United States of America. Her design was adopted by Congress on June 14, 1777.

11. SACAJAWEA—NATIVE AMERICAN

Sacajawea, a Shoshoni Indian of Idaho, was the guide and interpreter for the explorers Lewis and Clark in 1804 and 1805. Enemy Indians captured and sold her as a slave to a French trader who joined the Lewis and Clark Expedition. They needed the help of Sacajawea, for she was able to get food and horses for them as they traveled to the Pacific Ocean. She has been honored by historians by having rivers, monuments and a mountain peak named after her.

12. GEORGE WASHINGTON—EUROPEAN-AMERICAN

George Washington is known as the Father of His Country. As President of the United States for two terms, he won the confidence and trust of the American people. He was an able military man, politician, and supporter of the United States Constitution. He led the country in setting up the executive, legislative, and judicial branches to help run the government. In addition, he surrounded himself with men he could trust to support him in his decisions. This was his Cabinet. Washington died on Dec. 14, 1799.

13. MINORU YAMASAKI—JAPANESE-AMERICAN

Minoru Yamasaki, a talented architect, was born in 1912. He has received numerous awards and honors for his outstanding architectural designs. His work at the Seattle World's Fair is among his most well-known. Other works include the Reynold's Metals Company Building in Detroit, Oberlin College Music Conservatory Structure, and in Minneapolis, the Northwestern Life Insurance Company building. Most of his structures are white and made of marble or quartz. He combines the classical style of Greece with some oriental influences and modern functional designs.

14. MALCOLM X EL SHABAZZ*—AFRICAN-AMERICAN

Malcolm X was a leader in the effort to gain equal rights for African-Americans. Born on May 19, 1925, he was named Malcolm Little but adopted the surname X when he became a member of the Black Muslims. Malcolm X joined this black separatist religious group while serving a prison term for burglary. He was very vocal regarding the injustices experienced by Americans of African descent. He taught that blacks and whites should live apart from each other and that the white man was "the devil." Until he made the trip to Mecca, Malcolm X believed in separating the races. On his religious pilgrimage to Mecca in India, Malcolm changed his mind. There he found people of all skin colors, races, and languages worshipping and living together. He returned to America with a new message: brotherhood among all men. He organized a group for promoting racial unity, the Organization of African-American Unity (OAAU). Malcolm X was killed on February 21, 1965.

*FOUR CIVIL RIGHTS VOLUNTEERS WHO DIED FIGHTING INJUSTICE IN MISSISSIPPI AND ALABAMA

15. JAMES CHENEY—AFRICAN-AMERICAN
16. ANDREW GOODMAN—EUROPEAN-AMERICAN
17. MICHAEL SCHWERNER—EUROPEAN-AMERICAN
18. VIOLA GREGG LUIZZO—EUROPEAN-AMERICAN

*The Civil Rights Movement was begun by African-Americans.

However, the ongoing battle was multiracial. People of various races, religions, and cultural backgrounds fought and died struggling for freedom for their fellow man.

It is important for students to grasp the multicultural aspects of this struggle for freedom. Malcolm X realized, after he went to Mecca, that people of many races and colors could get along. This is a good example to use for resolving racial, ethnic, and cultural conflicts. Students can do minimal research on these volunteers. Or they can read about many other men and women who believed in equal rights and worked in various areas of society to help obtain freedom for minorities.

There are contributors from various sectors of our society, such as educators, lawyers, teachers, students, parents, librarians, soldiers, clergy, business people, and affirmative action officers, who would be willing to come and speak to students about civil rights. Be certain to show that contributions to America and the world have always been and are still multicultural.

DISABLED CONTRIBUTORS WHO ARE NOT HANDICAPPED

1. LUDWIG VAN BEETHOVEN

Ludwig Van Beethoven was born in Germany in 1770 and died in 1827. He was one of the greatest composers of music in all of history. Beethoven made it possible for people to write and enjoy many different types of music. Before his time, music was written only for special purposes (entertainment at social functions, teaching, religion). Beethoven's music was created for its own sake and composers began to enjoy the freedom to express themselves independently. In the late 1790s Beethoven began to lose his hearing and was totally deaf at the end of his life. However, his deafness did not stop him from composing beautiful music for people all over the world to enjoy.

2. SARAH BERNHARDT

Sarah Bernhardt was born in Paris in 1844 and died in 1923. Her real name was Rosine Bernard. Making her debut as an actress in 1862, she was a big hit and went on to perform in more plays and in motion pictures. Queen Elizabeth I was one of her most famous roles. Known as one of the greatest actresses of all time, Sarah had a clear, rich voice and was admired for her grace and poetic movement on stage. In 1915, she had one of her legs amputated; however, she continued to act in plays written especially for her. During her career she performed all over the world.

3. LOUIS BRAILLE

Louis Braille was born in France in 1809 and died in 1852. At the age of three he was blinded in an accident. In 1824 when he was 15 years old, Louis developed a raised dot-dash reading system based on a communication system used to get information to soldiers at night. Dot-dash codes (messages) were punched onto cardboard. Louis got his idea from this method of communicating without words. He made an alphabet, punctuation marks, numerals, and created a method for writing music. He also invented the braille system for printing and writing. People who are blind cannot SEE words printed on a page, but they can "read" words with their fingers by using "braille." Louis Braille not only helped himself but he contributed to a better life for people all over the world.

4. ROY CAMPANELLA

Roy Campanella was one of the greatest baseball players in the National League. As a catcher with the Brooklyn Dodgers, he won three Most Valuable Player awards. In 1953 Roy had a batting average of .312, he had

142 runs batted in, and 41 home runs. His team won pennants in 1949, 1952, 1953, 1955, and in 1956, due in large part to Roy's contributions to the team. Suffering many kinds of injuries did not keep him from playing because he loved the game. On January 28, 1958 Roy was in a near fatal car accident in which he broke his neck and severed his spinal cord. Roy fought against all odds and lived. Although wheelchair-bound, Roy kept in touch with friends, ran his business and appeared on radio and television. Roy contributed much to his profession and to his fans in America and around the world.

5. MILTON FRANKLIN

The story of Milton Franklin is a wonderful account of recovery and triumph after a serious accident. Milton Franklin lost both of his legs when he was caught beneath a moving train. Determined not to let this ruin his life, for he was a runner, he decided to work to regain his former skills. He was fitted with artificial legs and had to learn to walk again. Then he began to practice his running techniques. After a lot of hard work, he was able to run again. Milton Franklin is a fine contributor for he has shown that, if a person is determined, he/she can overcome disabilities. His story appeared in a news article and proved to be an inspiration to people who might have given up had they not seen with their own eyes, how a man with artificial legs enjoys life. Milton Franklin is not handicapped.

6. IVY GUNTER

Ivy Gunter, a former fashion model, lost her right leg to cancer in the early 1980s. When she appeared on a television show, she told of her decision to live as full and as normal a life as possible. Ivy Gunter swims, dances, takes aerobics classes, and is working to become an actress. She wears different types of artificial limbs to complement her outfits and/or to aid her in various activities. Because Ivy helped to design artificial feet to wear on the prosthesis, she is able to walk in flats, medium, and high heel shoes. Her outlook on life is positive. Ivy Gunter is planning to write a book about her life in order to encourage others who have disabilities.

7. BARBARA JORDAN

Barbara Jordan was born in Houston, Texas in 1936. She graduated from Texas Southern University and earned a degree in law from Boston University. Barbara Jordan was the first black woman from the South to be elected to the United States Congress. She served from 1973 to 1979. During this time, in 1976, she became the first black keynote speaker at the national convention of the Democratic Party. She became a professor at the University of Texas in 1979 and served in the Texas Senate from 1966 to 1972. Ms. Jordan also supported laws for banning discrimination and dealing with environmental problems. In recent years Ms. Jordan developed multiple sclerosis and is unable to get around without her wheelchair. Barbara Jordan still works in her profession and makes speeches to promote her beliefs. She continues to make contributions to her fellow American citizens, her country and the world.

8. FRANKLIN DELANO ROOSEVELT

Franklin Delano Roosevelt was president of the United States for more than 12 years. He took office 11 years after he was stricken with polio at age 39 and served from 1933 to 1945. Although he was crippled by this disease, it did not stop him from leading his country and trying to help the average American citizen. He worked to help make America prosperous under a program he called The New Deal. He thought that the presidency was a way to provide the greatest public service. Franklin D. Roosevelt led his country through domestic economic crises, foreign relations, and war and is remembered as one of the greatest of all U.S. presidents.

MULTICULTURAL COSTUMES

People all over the world wear clothing which reflects their culture, lifestyles, and available materials. Listed below are a few of the types of costumes worn by different ethnic groups.

1. Haik—a long piece of white cotton or wool worn in public by the women of Algeria
2. Gandoura—a graceful robe in black, brown or dark blue worn by African women of the Sudan
3. Cheongsam or "Shangai dress"—worn by the women of China
4. Sari—cloth of silk or cotton in six-yard lengths worn by the women of India
5. Caftan—a striped silk robe worn by Russian men
6. Aba—a coat worn by a shiek of Palestine
7. Parka—cloth or fur coat worn by an Eskimo
8. Sombrero—a tall, wide-brimmed hat worn by a Mexican man
9. Kilt—a short pleated skirt worn by the men of the Scottish Highlands
10. Rebozo—a large shawl used for carrying babies on their mothers' backs

Please ask the librarian for help. An excellent source is a book by R. Turner Wilcox: *Folk & Festival Costume of the World*. B.T. Bradsford Ltd., London, © 1989.

MULTICULTURAL CONTRIBUTIONS FORM

Read as much information about a contributor as you can. Then fill out the form below and share your knowledge with someone in school, at home, or in your neighborhood.

1. Name of the contributor ______________________________

2. Date of birth ______________________________

3. Country or national origin ______________________________

4. Contribution (invention, discovery, achievement, etc.)

   ____

   ____

   ____

5. How has this contribution helped America and its people?

   ____

   ____

   ____

6. Would you honor this person with a T–shirt, stamp, monument, song, statue, etc.? Why or why not?

   ____

   ____

7. What is the name of the source from which you got your information? Identify the author, publisher, city and copyright date of your source.

   ____

   ____

8. With whom will you share this knowledge and when?

   I will tell ______________________ about this contributor.

   I will tell ______________________ on the following date

   ______________________.

HOW ALEX HALEY FOUND HIS ROOTS: A SYNOPSIS

Alex Haley's grandmother, aunts, and cousin told him of his ancestors and how they came to America. The name that stands out in his memory is that of Kunta Kinte (Koon-tah Kin-tay) who was snatched from the shores of the Gambia River in West Africa. They also told him of men called GRIOTS: men who were living records of oral history. These GRIOTS told centuries-old histories of villages, clans, families, and great heroes. Oral records had been handed down since the time of the ancient forefathers. Some of these GRIOTS could recite these stories for as long as three days without repeating themselves. The human memories, mouths and ears were the ways that human beings shared, recorded, and stored information.

The Kinte (Kin-tay) clan was well-known in the country known as The Gambia. Alex Haley went to West Africa to look for his ancestors' homeland. He traveled along the Gambian River to a village called Juffure. There he met a GRIOT who spoke in the Mandinka language. Beginning with the slave ships which took many natives of West Africa to exile in America and other places, the old man sat facing Alex Haley and began reciting the ancestral narrative of the Kinte clan. The interpreter translated as the GRIOT verbally reached across many generations. He told of marriages, children, important events, religion, occupations (the women were potters and weavers, and the men were blacksmiths), and journeys from Old Mali to Mauretamia. He spoke of how different family members traveled from The Gambia to a village called Pakali N'Ding to Jiffarong and finally to Juffure. Then the GRIOT told of the marriage of Karraba Kunta and the birth of four sons. The youngest son stayed in Juffure and married a Mandinka maiden, Binta Kabba, and they had four sons. The oldest was Kunta. The GRIOT continued to speak through the interpreter.

"About the time the king's soldiers came"—another of the GRIOT'S time-fixing references—"the eldest of these four sons, Kunta, went away from his village to chop wood...and he was never seen again..."

Alex Haley describes how he "sat as if I were carved of stone. This man whose lifetime had been in this back-country had no way to know that he had just echoed what I had heard all through my boyhood years on my grandma's front porch in Henning, Tennessee...of an African who always insisted that his name was 'Kin-tay';...who called a river in the state of Virginia, 'kamby Bolongo'; and who had been kidnapped into slavery while not far from his village, chopping wood, to make himself a drum.

"Seventy-odd people formed a circle around me, chanting softly, '...we are you, and you are us.' The men took me into their mosque and prayed around me in Arabic, 'Praise be to Allah for one long lost from us whom Allah has returned.' "

Adapted from: *Roots* by Alex Haley, Doubleday, © 1976.

FAMILY NAME ORIGINS

The need for identification is common among human beings of all races, cultures, languages, and nationalities. That there is cross-cultural sharing of personal and family names is evident in modern America. There are boys named "John" who are African-American, Asian-American, European-American, and Hispanic-American. There are girls named "Elizabeth" in these same groups. Variations in spelling and pronunciation are apparent, because of language differences. For example, the English name "Charles" is "Carlos" in Spanish and Portuguese. The Latin name "Mary" is "Maria" in Spanish, Italian, Portuguese, German, Dutch, Scandinavian, Polish, and Czech. Students can not only investigate how their English names can be translated into other languages, but they can research the origin and meanings, as well. Above all, they should discern that there is a kinship among human beings of diverse racial, cultural, and ethnic backgrounds that can be verified through the names that parents proudly choose as a heritage for themselves and their children.

Human beings of all cultures seek meaningful and beautiful names for their children. Even though there might not be equivalent English names for every ethnic group, people of various races and cultures often share the same personal names. Some examples are:

Joseph, Margaret, Donnie, Ruth, Arthur, Helen, Christopher, Lillie, Robert, Emma, David, Nicole, Richard, Mona, Herbert, James, Corinne, Steven, Yvonne, Daniel, Denise, Michael, Halima, Rael, Nathaniel, Sharie, Tiffany, Omar, Kwisa, Arlene, Monika, Matthew, Lisa, Mark, Lydia, Kevin, Carolyn, Jamal, Meredith, George, Geraldine, Mildred, Allen, Elaine, Bernard, Michelle, Jason, Sarah, Anthony, Thomas, Diana, Lawrence, Malaika, Alexander, Rachel, Sean, Risa, Harold, Leslie, Charles, Judy, Moses, Rose, Keisha, William, Ann, Theodore, and so on.

NOTE: Children will enjoy looking up the meanings of these and other names. Plan a bulletin board or showcase display depicting SHARED NAMES OF VARIOUS CULTURES. Be sure to include the names of all children in the class in the display. Add meanings and origins as a special feature. Invite parents and the community to participate. Note that many children have very creative and unusual names. Some might be combinations of two or more names. Others might be imaginative creations resulting in unique, first names such as: Taleeka, Tawana, Shaquille, Dashaun, etc. Conduct research on names which are versions of names from other cultures. All children's self-esteem will grow as their names are recognized and honored.

Expect an increase in mutual respect as children from African, Asian, Hispanic, and European backgrounds acknowledge that there are commonalities in the names their parents have chosen for them. For example, they can readily see if their personal or family names are the same. They can also compare notes regarding the reasons for their names. Research into origin and meanings of names will reveal similarities that can serve to promote ethnic/racial harmony in the school and the community.

****

WHY DO PEOPLE RECEIVE CERTAIN NAMES?

The reasons for giving certain names to babies cuts across cultural lines. People of various cultural and racial origins want their family names to live on in future generations, or they want to honor a particular person or remember a significant event. The practices of naming newborns for these reasons occur in every culture.

Human beings share last names, as well as first names. The origin of many English surnames can be traced to various cultures and countries. Furthermore, the values, heritage, customs, and culture of any society can be revealed in the names of its people. This point can be made more meaningful to children if they are given opportunities to choose a "new" name from another culture. Note the practices of different cultures regarding the naming of children:

AFRICA

(GHANA)

African-American slaves were forced to give up their real names and take the names of their owners. In recent years, many African-Americans have dropped surnames inherited from slave masters and adopted African, Arabic, and/or Islamic names. Malcolm made the choice to drop the surname "Little" for this reason and adopt X as his surname. As with many other cultures, people in various African countries are given names which reflect family heritage, nature, religious beliefs, social issues, days of the week, position in the family, and social position.

In the various areas of southern Ghana, all of the people are Akan. Among the Akans are the Ashanti and Akwapim tribes. Several different languages are spoken in these areas of Ghana such as Twi, Fanti, and Awkwapim. This results in variations in the spellings and pronunciation of names, days of the week, etc. The Awkwapim people speak Twi. The children of the Akan are given names according to the day of the week on which they are born. There are variations according to gender.

MALES

Kwalio or Kojo-Monday Kwabena or Kwabina-Tuesday Kwaku-Wednesday
Yaw-Thursday Kofi-Friday Kwame-Saturday Kwasi or Akwasi-Sunday

FEMALES

Sunday...Akosua Monday...Adwoa Tuesday...Abenaa Wednesday...Akua
Thursday...Yaa Friday...Afia Saturday...Ama

Names for Position in the Family

Baako...1st born (male or female m/f) Manu...2nd born (m/f)
Mensa...3rd born (m/f) Mansa...4th born (m/f) Anum...5th

Names for Social Issues, Nature, or Religious Beliefs

Amazu	No one knows everything (m)
Maduezue	We are complete (for a male child is in the family)
Iggwebulke	In multitude there is strength (m)
Osji and Osuagwu	In honor of the God of Yam (m)
Adanma	Daughter of beauty (for a very beautiful girl)
Nneka	Mother is supreme (f)
Obloma	Kindness; kindhearted (f)
Ngozi	Blessing (f)
Esinam	God has heard me (f)
Sosoe	Equality (f)
Afram	River
Sono	Elephant
Odom	Oak
Nmadi	My father still lives
Safoa	Brave warrior

Recent immigrants from various countries in Africa proudly continue the practice of giving their children personal names which reflect their heritage. African-American children whose parents feel a kinship to the homeland often receive African names or creative adaptations of them.

ARABIC

Arabic personal names usually originate from vocabulary words. In some cases names of deities are given to children. Note the following examples:

Aisha...alive and well Ali...elevated, to rise, ascend
Hasan...generous Iman...faith, belief Jamal...handsome

Khalil...bosom friend Muhammad...praiseworthy
Mustafa...chosen, selected Safiyya...bosom friend

ASIA

While there are differences in the naming practices of Asians, a variety of people from these countries share common traditions regarding personal and family names. Interestingly, Asian names also originate in much the same way as those in other cultures. Children's names reflect events in nature, family status, hopes and aspirations of the family, and social issues. Peculiar to Asian cultures, however, is the practice of placing family names or surnames first. Historically, countries such as China, Japan, Korea, and Viet Nam follow this tradition.

Viet Nam

Here are examples of some common family names in Viet Nam:

Ky, Le, Lee, Nguyen, Pham, Tran, Triny, Truong, Vu.

In Viet Nam these names would be followed by the first and middle names.

China

There is no gender assignment of names in the Chinese culture.

Here are examples of some Chinese surnames and first names:

Ge Shan Yen Yuen She-le Tang Ning
Li Khai Fai Kong Tai Heong Chen Chong

Japan

Here are examples of some Japanese personal names. Traditionally, boys are assigned numbers for names, words which denote virtues, or parents' hopes and aspirations for their son or daughter.

Boys might be given the following personal names:

Kiyoshi...quiet Tomi...rich Man...ten thousand
Masa...good Yu...brave Toku...virtuous

Girls might be given the following personal names:

Haru...spring Fuyu...winter Umeko...plum blossom
Sumi...refinement Setsu...fidelity

In order to avoid confusion, many Asian families relinquish their traditions of placing last names first and reverse the order when they come to America. This is especially prevalent among the people of Japan. Also, as with other cultures, Asians often adopt American personal names after immigrating to the United States.

EAST INDIA

In East India, children are believed to be their ancestors reborn and are often named after them, especially grandparents. Extended families are important in the culture; therefore, giving a child a name which is similar to his/her father, mother, brother, or sister is thought to strengthen the family unit. The main source of personal names is the religion, Hindu. Other origins of children's names are: plants, animals, positive names of deities, and vocabulary words depicting good qualities. Some examples are:

Asha...wish, desire, hope
Khalil (Khaleel) from the Arabic...bosom friend
Kishori...filly or young girl Kishore...colt or young boy
Priya...beloved, dear Rajendra...ruler, mighty king

ENGLISH-LANGUAGE (Historical)

The English language resulted from the conquering of Britain by seamen and warriors of Rome, Norway, Sweden, Denmark, Germany, and France. The Celtics, Roman (Latin), Anglo-Saxon, Scandinavian, and French speech patterns were intermingled. Celtic languages prevailed in Ireland, Manx, Wales, and Scotland. The English-speaking Pilgrims brought their language to the New World and the influences of these many cultures can be seen in the surnames of those who came to America on the Mayflower. Names listed on the Mayflower roster reflected occupations, a parent's name, an address, or indicated a person's nickname. Note these examples:

ALDEN...old friend (nickname) BROWN...dark skin (nickname)
COOKE...food preparer CARTER...drove a cart (occupations)
HOPKINS...son of Hob/Robert THOMPSON...son of Thomas (parents)
LANGEMOORE...(addresses) lived near a long moor
WILDER...lived in a forest

PARTIAL LIST OF NAMES AND ORIGINS

LATIN (ROMAN), CELTIC (IRISH), ANGLO-SAXON, SCANDINAVIAN, FRENCH

Chester—from the Latin word "caster" meaning "place of a walled encampment"
McDonald—Irish based on the Celtic word "domhall" which means "dark-haired stranger"
Friouwulf—Anglo-Saxon word meaning "peace-wolf"
Osborne—from the Scandinavian word "asbiorn" meaning "god-bear"

NATIVE AMERICANS (Historical)

Native Americans historically followed the custom of giving newborns occasion names. For example, a boy born during a storm might be named "Big Cloud." Another practice was that of using significant events later in life to bestow titles on individuals. Some examples are:

Sitting Bull (Sioux)— at birth he was given the name "Jumping Badger." His father renamed him because he was brave in battle.

Geronimo (Apache)— at birth he was given the name "Goyothley." To belittle him, his enemies renamed him "Little Jerome or Geronimo." They came to fear him.

Jim Thorpe (Sac)— he was known as "Bright Path" by his people. He was a great athlete.

Pocohantas (Powhatan)— her real name was "Matoake."

Other examples of Native American names are:

Sacajawea (Shoshoni)— Her name means, Bird Woman

Crazy Horse

María Montoya Martinez

SPANISH NAMES

The origins of Hispanic names are also based on family heritage, social issues, nature, the hopes and dreams of the people, and most especially, they reflect the Spanish devotion to the Blessed Virgin and other religious beliefs. Some examples are:

Angosto—a place where the Virgin Mary was supposed to have appeared
Dolores—sorrows Mercedes—mercy Primo—first

Some examples of Spanish surnames are as follows:

Álvarez—the son of Alvaro, "the prudent one"
Chávez—descendant of Jaime, or James
Cruz—dweller near a cross
Diaz—descendant of Diego, or Jacob
Gonzáles—descendant of Gonzalo, "battle" name of a saint
Hernández—descendant of Hernando the adventurer
Martínez—descendant of Martin
Ortiz—descendant of Ordono, "fortunate one"
Ramírez—descendant of Ramon, "wise protector"

Santiago—family from Santiago, St. James in Spain
Torres—dweller near a tower
Vásquez—a Basque family or descendant of a shepherd

In all cultures names are important because they indicate the significance of family heritage and give individuals identity. Cross-cultural sharing of names attests to the kinship of all humankind. This commonality of names and reasons for them should serve to promote tolerance and respect among various racial and ethnic groups. Moreover, it is fun for children to find these commonalities and to playfully adopt a new name from another culture.

Family names or surnames are everywhere as we read newspapers, watch television, and listen to the radio. People of all races and cultures are proud of their names. Family names are often honored when they are used to identify colleges, schools, cities, ships, streets, businesses, and so on. Elicit from children ways in which they can honor all of their family and personal names and, simultaneously, discover reasons for mutual respect.

Glossary

Ancestor—forefather, forebearer, one who comes before
Apache—a member of a tribe of Native Americans living in southwestern United States
Bikol—one of the languages of the Philippines
Braille—a system of writing and printing for blind people. The letters in Braille are represented by different arrangements of raised points and are read by touching them
Cheyenne—a member of an Algonkian tribe of American Indians, now living in Montana and Oklahoma
Chippewa—Ojibwa (Indians) are a member of a large tribe of Native Americans of Algonkian stock formerly living in the region of Lake Superior
Coat of Arms—a representation of the armoral insignia depicted on coats and worn over armor
Chado—The-Way-of-Tea, a formal Japanese tea ceremony celebrating Founder's Day
Dominican Republic—country in the east part of Hispaniola
Egypt—an African country; land of pyramids and the Sphinx
Eritrea—an African country, formerly an Italian colony and an Ethiopian province; recently won its independence from Ethiopia
Ethnic—of or related to national or racial origin
Ghana—an African country; one of the ancient dynasties of West Africa
Griot—the historian described in Alex Haley's *Roots*; a person who has knowledge of the ancestral experiences of families and recites them from memory
Gujarati—the Indic language of Gujarat and adjoining parts of western India
Hanukkah—the yearly Jewish celebration of the rededication of the temple of Jerusalem, after the victory over the Syrians; Feast of Lights; candles are lighted on each of eight days
Hieroglyphics—the ancient Egyptian writing system using pictures, characters and symbols to convey words, ideas, and/or sounds
Kwanzaa—an African-American cultural festival celebrated during a seven-day period from Dec. 26 to Jan. 1 (Swahili KWANZA, infinitive of ANZA "to begin")
Mali—one of the wealthy kingdoms of ancient West Africa
Mecca—Moslem pilgrimage center, birthplace of Mohammed

Melanin—a brownish black pigment found in skin and hair

Multicultural—the skills, arts, and the way of life of many different types of people

Navajo—a member of a large tribe of American Indians of Athapascan stock living in New Mexico, Utah, and Arizona

Palaver—a conference between European traders and people of other cultures requiring an exchange of compliments, gifts and other ritual before bringing up business matters; to talk fluently, profusely, or persuasively

Seminole—a member of a tribe of North American Indians that left the Creek Confederacy and settled in Florida. Most now live in Oklahoma.

Somalia—a country of East Africa; it is bordered by both Kenya and Ethiopia

Songhay—one of the wealthy kingdoms of ancient West Africa; extending from what is now central Nigeria to the Atlantic coast

Sudan—one of the wealthy kingdoms of ancient West Africa; located south of Egypt

Swahili—an Arabic-based language of several African countries

Tagalog—the Indonesian language on which the official language of the Philippines is based

Tigrinya—a Semitic language spoken in the north of Ethiopia; the language of Eritrea

Timbuktu—one of the wealthy cities of the ancient West African empires. Control of this great trading and center of learning changed from Ghana to Mali, Songhay and to other powerful people and nations (also spelled Timbuctu)

Bibliography

Auerbach, Susan, *Vietnamese Americans: American Voices,* Rourke Corporation, Vero Beach, Florida © 1991

Barnet, Jeanie M., *Places and Peoples of the World: Ghana,* Chelsea House Publishers, New York © 1988

Briggs, Carole S., *Women in Space: Reaching the Last Frontier,* Lerner Publications Co., Minneapolis © 1988. Photographs

Childcraft: The How and Why Library, Volumes 3, 6, 8, 9, 11, etc. Worldbook - Childcraft International, Inc., A Subsidiary of The Scott Fetzer Co., Chicago © 1982

Green, Laura and Eva Barash Dicker, *Sign Language,* Franklin Watts, New York © 1981

McCunn, Ruthanne Lum, *Chinese American Portraits: Personal Histories 1828-1988,* Chronicle Books, San Francisco, California © 1988

Madubulke, Ihechukwu, *A Handbook of African Names,* Three Continents Press, Washington, D.C. © 1976

Mintz, Malcolm W., *Bikol Text,* University of Hawaii Press, Honolulu © 1971

Murphy, E. Jefferson, *Understanding Africa,* Louise Jefferson illus., Thomas Y. Crowell, New York © 1978

Perrott, Daisy Valerie, *Teach Yourself Swahili,* The Universities Press Ltd., London © 1957

Pusch, Margaret D., Editor, *Multicultural Education, A Cross-Cultural Training Approach,* Intercultural Press, Inc., Yarmouth, Maine © 1979

Ramos, Teresita V. and Videa de Guzman, *Tagalog for Beginners,* University of Hawaii Press, Honolulu © 1971

Robinson, Wilhelmena S., *Historical Negro Biographies: The International Library of Negro Life and History,* The Study of Negro Life and History Publishers, New York © 1969

Smead, Howard, *The Peoples of North America: The Afro-Americans,* Chelsea House Publishers, New York © 1989

Stein, Lou, *Clues to Our Family Names,* Heritage Books, Bowie, Maryland © 1986

The World Book Encyclopedia, Volumes 2, 10, 12, 17, etc., World Book, Inc., A Scott Fetzer Co., Chicago © 1983

Index

This Index facilitates the location of multicultural topics that are an integral part of more than one activity sheet found in this resource. Broad categories, such as art, health, and foreign language, are not listed here since they are easily located by using the Multicultural Integration Chart (page ix). While the Multicultural Integration Chart is a valuable planning tool, the Index further helps classroom teachers who often need materials that focus on a specific topic. Teacher Directions and the Appendix provide additional information for the activity sheets listed beneath each of the following topics:

CAREERS

CELEBRATIONS/COSTUMES

CLASSIFICATION SKILLS

COMMUNICATION SKILLS

COMMUNICATION SKILLS *(cont'd.)*

CRITICAL THINKING SKILLS*

DECISIONS/VALUES

*NOTE:
Depending upon the objectives of the lesson, all activities lend themselves to the development of critical thinking skills.

HUMAN NEEDS/TRAITS

INDEPENDENCE

INTERDEPENDENCE

INTERDEPENDENCE *(cont'd.)*

NATIVE AMERICANS